Thinking about Yugoslavia

The Yugoslav breakup and conflict have given rise to a considerable literature offering dramatically different interpretations of what happened. But just how do the various interpretations relate to each other? This ambitious new book by Sabrina Ramet, an eminent commentator on recent Balkan politics and history, reviews and analyses more than 130 books about the troubled region and compares their accounts, theories, and interpretations of events. Ramet surveys the major debates which divide the field, alternative accounts of the causes of Yugoslavia's violent collapse, and the scholarly debates concerning humanitarian intervention. Rival accounts are presented side by side for easy comparison. *Thinking about Yugoslavia* examines books on Slovenia, Croatia, Serbia, Bosnia-Herzegovina, Macedonia, Montenegro, and Kosovo which were published in English, German, Serbian/Croatian/Bosnian, and Italian, thus offering the English-speaking reader a unique insight into the controversies.

SABRINA P. RAMET is a Professor of Political Science at the Norwegian University of Science and Technology (NTNU), Trondheim, Norway, and a Senior Associate at the Centre for the Study of Civil War, PRIO. She is the author of nine books, including *Balkan Babel: The Disintegration of Yugoslavia from the Death of Tito to the Fall of Milošević* (4th edn, 2002).

T0384613

Thinking about Yugoslavia

*Scholarly Debates about the Yugoslav Breakup
and the Wars in Bosnia and Kosovo*

Sabrina P. Ramet

CAMBRIDGE
UNIVERSITY PRESS

CAMBRIDGE UNIVERSITY PRESS
Cambridge, New York, Melbourne, Madrid, Cape Town, Singapore, São Paulo, Delhi

Cambridge University Press
The Edinburgh Building, Cambridge CB2 8RU, UK

Published in the United States of America by Cambridge University Press, New York

www.cambridge.org
Information on this title: www.cambridge.org/9780521616904

First published 2005

A catalogue record for this publication is available from the British Library

ISBN 978-0-521-85151-0 hardback
ISBN 978-0-521-61690-4 paperback

Transferred to digital printing 2009

To Danica Fink-Hafner
and
Mitja Hafner-Fink

Contents

Preface

I have been struck, over the years, by the persistence of certain debates – one could even say fault lines – within the scholarly community. These debates cover a wide range of subjects, riveting on the best methodology to study East-Central Europe, the nature of the collapse of the communist organizational monopoly (a collapse completely denied by one 'imaginative' scholar), the nature of the Bosnian War and the appropriate Western response, the nature of the war in Kosovo and the appropriate Western response, and the legitimacy of humanitarian intervention. But, while these debates might appear, at first sight, to be unrelated, it turns out, on closer inspection, that there are some threads running through these debates, and that in many one can identify traces of the rivalry between idealism (the belief that moral beliefs matter, that shifts in moral consensus can have political consequences, and that one can speak sensibly about universal moral norms and universal rights, with the corollary too that there are some duties incumbent upon the international community under certain conditions) and realism (the belief that what matter in the first place are stability and security, that these can be assured by means which are not necessarily moral in any sense, and that decisions taken by office-holders should be and, in fact, generally are taken on the basis of considerations of national interest, to be understood in terms of security, stability, wealth, power, and influence), or again between historical determinism which looks back over centuries to account for present developments and theoretical approaches which find the most relevant factors to be located in the more proximate past. It is, rather obviously, possible to forge one or another synthesis across these cleavages, but in practice these theoretical divides tend to define rival patterns of thought, steering analysts and policy-makers alike in alternative directions.

Other factors enter into any particular equation, of course, and not all differences in the field are determined by these fault lines. But much is, and it is these threads which run through the essays included in this volume. The chapters included herein were written as review essays of the literature, and this volume, thus, represents a series of reflections upon the literature relating to the Yugoslav breakup and subsequent conflicts. More than 130 books in four languages (English, German, Italian, and Serbian/Croatian/Bosnian) are discussed in some detail herein, and analysed in terms of their philosophical or methodological frameworks. Additional literature is discussed in passing. Taken in sum, these essays constitute a serious effort to come to terms with the growing literature on the subject and to take stock of the principal debates and controversies. It is my hope that this book will be useful not only to specialists but also to students interested in making sense of a potentially confusing avalanche of work.

The material published herein draws from the following previous publications of mine: 'Tracing the Roots of the Collapse of Yugoslavia', in *Modern Greek Studies Yearbook*, Vol. 9 (1993), pp. 429–87 (hereafter, A); 'The Transition in Eastern Europe: Prophets, Chroniclers, and Revisionists', in *Modern Greek Studies Yearbook*, Vol. 10/11 (1994/5), pp. 913–27 (B); 'Revisiting the Horrors of Bosnia: New Books about the War', in *East European Politics and Societies*, Vol. 14, No. 2 (Spring 2000), pp. 475–86 (C); 'The Sources of Discord, the Making of Harmony: Books about Yugoslav Violence – A Review Article', in *Europe–Asia Studies*, Vol. 53, No. 2 (2001), pp. 351–6 (D); 'Views from Inside: Memoirs concerning the Yugoslav Breakup and War', in *Slavic Review*, Vol. 61, No. 3 (Fall 2002), pp. 558–80 (E); 'Can a Society Be Sick? The Case of Serbia', in *Journal of Human Rights*, Vol. 1, No. 4 (December 2000), pp. 615–20 (F); 'Debates about Intervention: Recent German Books about Bosnia and Kosovo' – Part 1 in *Internationale Politik – Transatlantic Edition*, Vol. 4, No. 2 (Summer 2003), pp. 91–100 and Part 2 in the same journal, Vol. 4, No. 3 (Fall 2003), pp. 101–6 (G); 'Kuga nacionalizma in zapuščina vojne', in *Teorija in praksa*, Vol. 40, No. 4 (July–August 2003), pp. 759–70 (H); 'Milošević and Kosovo through Western Eyes: A Review Essay' (co-authored with Angelo Georgakis, currently Assistant Professor of History at Westmont College, Santa Barbara) in *Modern Greek Studies Yearbook*, Vol. 16/17 (2000/1), pp. 591–602 (I); and 'In Search of the "real" Milošević: New Books about the Rise and Fall of Serbia's Champion', in *Journal of Human Rights*, Vol. 2, No. 3 (September 2003), pp. 455–66 (J). The website for Taylor & Francis, which publishes *Europe–Asia Studies* and *Journal of Human Rights*, is **www.tandf.co.uk/journal**. I am grateful to the editors of the respective journals, etc., for permission to reuse this material.

The material is not, however, simply reprinted here. On the contrary, I have moved sections of one essay into another essay, removed some books discussed, and have added a large number of books to what I discuss. Chapter 1 is based on C, with the discussion of two books moved elsewhere and with a discussion of books by Norbert Both, Norman Cigar, and Michael Sells added. Chapter 2 is based on B. Chapter 3 is based on A, with a discussion of two books deleted and with the addition of discussion of books by John B. Allcock, Neven Andjelic, Branimir Anzulović, Christopher Bennett, Lenard J. Cohen, Vjekoslav Perica, Andrew Baruch Wachtel, and Susan L. Woodward. Chapter 4 is essentially new, but incorporates the discussion of the book by Takis Michas originally published in H. Chapter 5 is based on E, but incorporates the discussion of books by Boutros Boutros-Ghali and John Major originally published in C, with the addition of discussions of the memoirs of Veljko Kadijević, Stipe Mesić, and Javier Pérez de Cuéllar. Chapter 6 is based on D, with a discussion of Tim Judah's *Kosovo* moved elsewhere and with the addition of a discussion of books by Ivan Čolović and Jasna Dragović-Soso taken from H, and new discussions of books by Keith Doubt and Stjepan G. Meštrović; an earlier discussion of Rusmir Mahmutćehajić's *Bosnia the Good*, originally published in D, is not included in chapter 6. Chapter 7 is based on J, but incorporates the discussion of Slavoljub Djukić's book originally published in F, as well as new discussions of recent books by Dušan Pavlović, Vidosav Stevanović, and Massimo Nava. Chapter 8 is essentially new, but incorporates the discussion of books by Sumantra Bose and Elizabeth Cousens/Charles Cater originally published in H. Chapter 9 is based on I, with the deletion of discussions of books by Branislav Anzulović and Greg Campbell, and with the addition of a discussion of Tim Judah's *Kosovo*, originally published in D, and with the addition of a discussion of Alex Bellamy's *Kosovo and International Society*. Chapter 10 is an extended version of an article originally published in G. Chapter 11 is essentially new, but incorporates a discussion of Norman Cigar's *Vojislav Koštunica* originally published in F. Chapter 12 and the conclusion were written expressly for this volume. Translations are my own unless otherwise noted.

I am grateful to the three anonymous readers for comments on an earlier draft of the manuscript as a whole, and to Denis Bašić, Norman Cigar, Cathie Carmichael, Marko Hoare, Diane Koenker, Branka Magaš, Martha Merritt, and Marius Søberg for comments on portions of this manuscript. I wish to thank Karen Anderson Howes, copy-editor for this book, for her great care with my text. I am also grateful to John Haslam, the commissioning editor at Cambridge University Press, for his lively interest in this project and encouragement to develop it.

Books discussed

(Numeral in parentheses indicates the chapter in which the book is discussed; the conclusion makes only brief references to various books, and does not offer full reviews.)

Memoirs

Bildt, Carl, *Peace Journey: The Struggle for Peace in Bosnia* (8).

Boutros-Ghali, Boutros, *Unvanquished: A US–UN Saga* (5).

Dizdarević, Raif, *Od smrti Tita do smrti Jugoslavije: Svjedočenja* (5, Conclusion).

Drnovšek, Janez, *Der Jugoslawien-Krieg: Meine Wahrheit* (5).

Halilović, Sefer, *Lukava strategija*, 3rd expanded edn (5).

Izetbegović, Alija, *Sjećanja: Autobiografski zapis* (5).

Janša, Janez, *The Making of the Slovenian State 1988–1992: The Collapse of Yugoslavia* (5).

Kadijević, Veljko, *Moje vidjenje raspada: Vojska bez države* (5).

Major, John, *The Autobiography* (5).

Mamula, Branko, *Slučaj Jugoslavija* (5).

Mesić, Stipe, *The Demise of Yugoslavia: A Political Memoir* (5).

Owen, David, *Balkan Odyssey* (4).

Pérez De Cuéllar, Javier, *Pilgrimage for Peace: A Secretary-General's Memoir* (5).

Petritsch, Wolfgang, *Bosnien und Herzegowina fünf Jahre nach Dayton. Hat der Friede eine Chance?* (8).

Rose, General Sir Michael, *Fighting for Peace: Lessons from Bosnia* (4).

Rudolf, Davorin, *Rat koji nismo htjeli: Hrvatska 1991* (5).

Šarinić, Hrvoje, *Svi moji tajni pregovori sa Slobodanom Miloševićem 1993–1995, 1998* (5).

Špegelj, Martin, *Sjećanja vojnika* (5).

Tomac, Zdravko, *The Struggle for the Croatian State . . . Through Hell to Democracy* (5).

Zimmermann, Warren, *Origins of a Catastrophe: Yugoslavia and Its Destroyers*, revised edn (4).

Academic books about and popular treatments of Yugoslavia

Abrahams, Fred, *A Threat to 'Stability': Human Rights Violations in Macedonia* (12).

Allcock, John B., *Explaining Yugoslavia* (3).

Andjelic, Neven, *Bosnia-Herzegovina: The End of a Legacy* (3).

Anzulović, Branimir, *Heavenly Serbia: From Myth to Genocide* (3).

Banac, Ivo, *The National Question in Yugoslavia: Origins, History, Politics* (Conclusion).

Banac, Ivo, *With Stalin, against Tito: Cominformist Splits in Yugoslav Communism* (Conclusion).

Bartlett, William, *Croatia: Between Europe and the Balkans* (11).

Becker, Jens and Achim Engelberg, *Montenegro im Umbruch: Reportagen und Essays* (12).

Bellamy, Alex J., *Kosovo and International Society* (9).

Benderly, Jill and Evan Kraft (eds.), *Independent Slovenia: Origins, Movements, Prospects* (11, Conclusion).

Bennett, Christopher, *Yugoslavia's Bloody Collapse: Causes, Course and Consequences* (3).

Bieber, Florian (ed.), *Montenegro in Transition: Problems of Identity and Statehood* (12, Conclusion).

Bose, Sumantra, *Bosnia after Dayton: Nationalist Partition and International Intervention* (8).

Both, Norbert, *From Indifference to Entrapment: The Netherlands and the Yugoslav Crisis 1990–1995* (1).

Buckley, Mary and Sally N. Cummings (eds.), *Kosovo: Perceptions of War and Its Aftermath* (9).

Burg, Steven L. and Paul S. Shoup, *The War in Bosnia-Herzegovina: Ethnic Conflict and International Intervention* (1).

Calic, Marie-Janine, *Krieg und Frieden in Bosnien-Hercegovina*, revised and expanded edn. (10, Conclusion).

Central Intelligence Agency, *Balkan Battlegrounds: A Military History of the Yugoslav Conflict, 1990–1995*, 2 vols. (Conclusion).

Chandler, David, *Bosnia: Faking Democracy after Dayton*, 2nd edn (8).

Cigar, Norman, *Genocide in Bosnia: The Policy of 'Ethnic Cleansing'* (1, Conclusion).

Cigar, Norman, *Vojislav Koštunica and Serbia's Future* (11).

Cohen, Lenard J., *Broken Bonds: Yugoslavia's Disintegration and Balkan Politics in Transition*, 2nd edn (3).

Nava, Massimo, *Milošević: La tragedia di un popolo* (7).
Oschlies, Wolf, *Makedonien 2001–2004: Kriegestagebuch aus einem friedlichen Land* (12).
Pavlović, Dušan, *Akteri i modeli: Ogledi o politici u Srbiji pod Miloševićem* (7).
Perica, Vjekoslav, *Balkan Idols: Religion and Nationalism in Yugoslav States* (3).
Pettifer, James, *The New Macedonian Question* (12).
Pleština, Dijana, *Regional Development in Communist Yugoslavia: Success, Failure, and Consequences* (3).
Popov, Nebojša (ed.), *The Road to War in Serbia: Trauma and Catharsis* (6, Conclusion).
Poulton, Hugh, *Who Are the Macedonians?* (12, Conclusion).
Ramet, Sabrina P, *Balkan Babel: The Disintegration of Yugoslavia from the Death of Tito to the Fall of Milošević*, 4th edn (Conclusion).
Ramet, Sabrina P., *The Three Yugoslavias: The Dual Challenge of State-building and Legitimation among the Yugoslavs* (Conclusion).
Reuter, Jens and Konrad Clewing (eds.), *Der Kosovo Konflikt: Ursachen, Verlauf, Perspektiven* (9).
Roberts, Walter, *Tito, Mihailović, and the Allies* (Conclusion).
Rumiz, Paolo, *Masken für ein Massaker. Der manipulierte Krieg: Spurensuche auf dem Balkan*, expanded German edn (10).
Rusinow, Dennison I., *The Yugoslav Experiment, 1948–1974* (Conclusion).
Sadkovich, James J., *The US Media and Yugoslavia, 1991–1995* (1, Conclusion).
Schmid, Thomas (ed.), *Krieg im Kosovo* (9).
Sell, Louis, *Slobodan Milošević and the Destruction of Yugoslavia* (7, Conclusion).
Sells, Michael A., *The Bridge Betrayed: Religion and Genocide in Bosnia* (1).
Seroka, Jim and Vukašin Pavlović (eds.), *The Tragedy of Yugoslavia: The Failure of Democratic Transformation* (3).
Shrader, Charles R., *The Muslim–Croat Civil War in Central Bosnia: A Military History, 1992–1994* (4).
Silber, Laura and Allan Little, *The Death of Yugoslavia* (1, Conclusion).
Simms, Brendan, *Unfinest Hour: Britain and the Destruction of Bosnia* (4).
Snyder, Jack, *From Voting to Violence: Democratization and Nationalist Conflict* (7).
Steindorff, Ludwig, *Kroatien: Vom Mittelalter bis zur Gegenwart* (11).
Stevanović, Vidosav, *Milošević, jedan epitaf* (7).
Tanner, Marcus, *Croatia: A Nation Forged in War* (11).
Tenbergen, Rasmus, *Der Kosovo-Krieg: Eine gerechte Intervention?* (10, Conclusion).

Thomas, Robert, *Serbia under Milošević: Politics in the 1990s* (11, Conclusion).

Thompson, Mark, *Forging War: The Media in Serbia, Croatia, Bosnia and Herzegovina*, completely rev. and expanded edn (Conclusion).

Tomaševich, Jožo, *War and Revolution in Yugoslavia, 1941–1945: Occupation and Collaboration* (Conclusion).

Troebst, Stefan, *Conflict in Kosovo: Failure of Prevention? An Analytical Documentation, 1992–1998* (9).

Udovički, Jasminka and James Ridgeway (eds.), *Burn This House: The Making and Unmaking of Yugoslavia*, rev. and expanded edn (1).

Velikonja, Mitja, *Religious Separation and Political Intolerance in Bosnia-Herzegovina* (11).

Vickers, Miranda, *Between Serb and Albanian: A History of Kosovo* (9).

Volle, Angelika and Werner Weidenfeld (eds.), *Der Balkan: Zwischen Krise und Stabilität* (10).

Wachtel, Andrew Baruch, *Making a Nation, Breaking a Nation: Literature and Cultural Politics in Yugoslavia* (3).

Weymouth, Tony and Stanley Henig (eds.), *The Kosovo Crisis: The Last American War in Europe?* (9).

Woodward, Susan L, *Balkan Tragedy: Chaos and Dissolution after the Cold War* (4).

Woodward, Susan L, *Socialist Unemployment: The Political Economy of Yugoslavia, 1945–1990* (3).

Academic books about Eastern Europe

Aslund, Ånders, *Post-Communist Economic Revolutions: How Big a Bang?* (2).

Hockenos, Paul, *Free to Hate: The Rise of the Right in Post-Communist Eastern Europe* (2).

Horvath, Agnes and Arpad Szakolczai, *The Dissolution of Communist Power: The Case of Hungary* (2).

Philipsen, Dirk, *We Were the People: Voices from East Germany's Revolutionary Autumn of 1989* (2).

Poznański, Kazimierz Z. (ed.), *Constructing Capitalism: The Reemergence of Civil Society and Liberal Economy in the Post-Communist World* (2).

Poznański, Kazimierz Z. (ed.), *The Evolutionary Transition to Capitalism* (2).

Tismaneanu, Vladimir (ed.), *In Search of Civil Society: Independent Peace Movements in the Soviet Bloc* (2).

Tismaneanu, Vladimir, *Reinventing Politics: Eastern Europe from Stalin to Havel* (2).

Glossary

Consequentialism: the belief that the morality of a given law or practice or action may be best assessed by determining what its consequences are.

Conventionalism: the belief that there is no external standard by which one may assess the morality or immorality of the laws or practices of a given government and that it is meaningless to speak of universally valid moral precepts, except arguably in a nominal sense as established by written international agreements.

Universalism: the belief that one can speak sensibly of a universally valid moral standard by which one may criticize the laws or practices of a given government for being wrong (immoral) and that one can establish some universally valid moral precepts by the exercise of unaided reason.

ORIENTATIONS ABOUT THE RELATIONSHIP BETWEEN
SOVEREIGNTY AND HUMAN RIGHTS

Idealism: the belief that sovereignty is relative to morality and that governments should be held to a universal moral standard.

Realism: the belief that human rights are relative to sovereignty and that governments should enjoy a wide latitude in their domestic policies on the principle of noninterference in the internal affairs of another state.

Relativism: any orientation which relativizes morality or which treats the rights of one (group of) people as less important that the rights of some other (group of) people.

1   Debates about the war

I

The field of Yugoslav studies has long been divided. In the Tito era, much of the literature was, very roughly, divided between those who viewed Tito as 'one of ours' ('Has Tito gone bourgeois?', a 1966 article asked) and those who took a more critical view of the Yugoslav leader. Early in the post-Tito years, the field was divided – again, roughly speaking – between those who believed that Yugoslavia had achieved a degree of stability sufficient to warrant, for example, the optimistic sentiment that, 'while the problems confronting the post-Tito leadership are serious, they do appear to be subject to solution within the existing framework',[1] and those who believed that the Yugoslav socialist system 'as it exists has begun to undergo a process of decay' to the extent that the outlook for the survival of Yugoslavia could only be judged to be 'rather bleak'.[2]

More recently, the field of 'Yugoslav' (or, perhaps, post-Yugoslav) studies has again been divided largely between two camps (though not all works fall into one of these two camps, of course). On the one side are those who have taken a moral universalist perspective, holding that there are universal norms in international politics, that these norms are founded in Universal Reason and expressed in international covenants such as the Universal Declaration of Human Rights, and that, in recounting the horrors of the recent War of Yugoslav Succession of 1991–5, the analyst *must* account for the disintegration of socialist Yugoslavia and the outbreak of hostilities, identifying culpable parties. Among the works which best exemplify this school are James Gow's *Triumph of the Lack of Will* (1997, discussed in chapter 4), Thomas Cushman and Stjepan G. Meštrović's *This Time We Knew* (1996), and, among those works presently under review, Norman Cigar's *Genocide in Bosnia* (1995) and James Sadkovich's *The US Media and Yugoslavia* (1998). Authors in this school tend to believe that claims regarding state sovereignty cannot be absolute, insofar as system legitimacy is measured in terms of a system's

1

observance of basic human rights.[3] Drawing their inspiration, in at least some cases, from Immanuel Kant, these authors also find a natural affinity with Jürgen Habermas, whose writings take their point of departure as 'the universality of basic rights' and the notion that legal systems should 'enshrin[e] universal moral principles'.[4] My own affinities lie with this school.[5]

On the other side are authors who reject the universalist framework, with its emphasis on universal norms and universal human rights and who, in their accounts, embrace one or another version of moral relativism. Most of these authors embrace state sovereignty as their supreme principle, rejecting any appeal to higher values which might justify external intervention – thereby adopting a position which brings them into coalition with the moral conventionalism of Thrasymachus (Plato's *Republic*, Book I). Emblematic of this approach are Lenard Cohen's *Broken Bonds* (2nd edn, 1995, discussed in chapter 3), Susan Woodward's *Balkan Tragedy* (1995, discussed in chapter 4), Robert M. Hayden's *Blueprints for a House Divided* (1999, discussed in chapter 6), and, among the works presently under review, Burg and Shoup's *War in Bosnia-Herzegovina* (1999). Hence, for example, while Woodward 'dismisses Albanian claims to self-determination [in Kosovo] on the [conventionalist] grounds that their constitutional classification . . . as a nationality rather than as a constituent nation made them ineligible for such rights'[6] – recall Thrasymachus' assertion that justice is what the rulers say it is – Burg and Shoup subscribe to the notion of the primacy of sovereignty, supporting 'the rights of states to defend their sovereignty and territorial integrity and to conduct their internal affairs free from external interference',[7] failing to specify any qualifications or curtailment of this principle regardless of tyranny or violations of human rights (both of which are taken to qualify or set limits to sovereignty in Locke's *Second Treatise of Government* and also in the US Declaration of Independence). Authors in this second school tended to be more sympathetic, in the 1990s, to the arguments made by Milošević, Karadžić, and their collaborators and to be critical of Germany (and, in the case of Hayden, also of Slovenia). Drawing their inspiration from realist suppositions which may be traced back to Thomas Hobbes,[8] these writers tended to treat Milošević (who took power in Serbia in 1987) and Tudjman (elected president of Croatia in 1990) as equally responsible for the exacerbation of the crisis which had already engulfed the country.

Ironically, however, it was neither a work inspired by universalism nor one inspired by relativism which had the greatest impact on the general reading public but, rather, a sand castle known as 'the myth of ancient hatreds', promulgated by Robert Kaplan in his best-selling book, *Balkan Ghosts*. Lacking any sturdy foundations, Kaplan's explanation crumbled at the first touch but, in spite of that, it had its baneful influence, infecting the rhetoric of British prime minister John Major and, by their own admission, influencing the thinking of US president Bill Clinton and EU mediator David Lord Owen, not to mention the many ordinary citizens who read the book and concluded from it that, for reasons not made clear, Kaplan considered the peoples of the Balkans unusually wild and predisposed to violence. But the concept did not spring fully developed out of Kaplan's head. Nearly two decades earlier, in his widely read book, *Wartime*, which dealt with the Second World War, Milovan Djilas wrote that 'the hatred between the Orthodox and the Moslems in these parts is primeval', and referred to 'ancient tribal conflicts'.[9] For that matter, a CIA report dating from 1957 had come dangerously close to advocating an 'ancient hatreds' explanation by writing that 'the Serbs and Croats, conditioned by separate histories and cultures, have developed deep-seated mutual animosity'.[10] It is certainly true that Serbs and Croats had opposite responses to the Austrian occupation of Bosnia-Herzegovina in 1878, and that the history of Serb–Croat inter-actions between 1921 and 1945 was one afflicted by conflict and mutual misunderstanding, but to refer to 'separate histories and cultures' is to paint on a much larger historical canvas. There are three major problems with the thesis of 'ancient hatreds': first, it is simply not true that relations among the peoples of the Yugoslav area were marked by any special hostilities which distinguished their relations from, let us say, the relations between Germans and French; second, it is false, as demonstrated by the fact that those referring present problems to 'ancient' hatreds, are typically unable to cite any ancient problems (indeed, the Serbs and Croats did not even live in the Balkans in 'ancient' times, if one accepts the conventional definition of 'ancient' as referring to the roughly three millennia which end with the fall of Rome in 476 CE); and, third, it distracts the reader from examining relevant evidence which might lead one to more useful conclusions.

II

The literature on the Yugoslav war of 1991–5 has produced a dizzying array of competing interpretations and understandings. Among the most contentious issues have been the following questions:

- Who started the war and whose fault was it? Were the Slovenes in any way blameworthy?
- What was the nature of the Tudjman regime and were the Croatian Serbs *entitled* to launch an insurrection?
- Did Germany violate any written or unwritten rules of diplomatic behaviour in 1991 and was Germany to blame for the escalation of violence in Croatia and Bosnia-Herzegovina?
- Was the principle of 'one man, one vote' appropriate for Bosnia-Herzegovina in 1991/2; i.e., was there any basis on which to introduce democratic institutions, or would a version of consociational authoritarianism have been preferable?
- Was the Vance–Owen Peace Plan, actively under discussion in early 1993, a positive step or a plan to reward 'ethnic cleansing'?
- What were the war aims of the Bosnian Serbs and were they primarily offensive or defensive?
- What was the nature of Izetbegović's platform and programme – fundamentalist Islamic or secular-liberal?
- Did the war have a genocidal character?

The controversies typically emerged first in local polemics and in news-paper reports, but were carried over into scholarly works for a variety of reasons which need not detain us.

Whose fault? Not everyone has been concerned to assess responsi-bility; for some writers, the roots of the problem lie elsewhere – whether in the political system or in the economy or in history or in a combin-ation of these. Lenard Cohen, for instance, as will be shown in chapter 7, argues that Serbs as a nation have historically determined tendencies to think of themselves as victims and to prefer strong-arm rule, appeal-ing to historical experiences and shared folklore to account for these alleged tendencies. Cohen's framework is, thus, similar to (though not identical with) that found in Branimir Anzulović's *Heavenly Serbia*, which sought to identify a Serbian tradition of violence fostered by ecclesiastical elites and cultural artifacts. The two key differences are (1) that Anzulović provided specific arguments and artifacts as evidence, and (2) that, while Cohen makes no mention of the possibility of an 'escape' from historically determined patterns, Anzulović assures us that it is possible for nations to change their behaviour. Anzulović's argument is explored more fully in chapter 3.

Still, among those noting human agency, most have identified vari-ously 'Belgrade' or 'the Serbian side' or 'Milošević and his henchmen' as bearing primary responsibility for the war. Typical of this orientation is Christopher Bennett, who accordingly sees Milošević's coup within the Serbian party organization (in 1987) as marking the turning point, setting Yugoslavia on a course towards war and noting that Serbian 'military action in Bosnia-Hercegovina had been prepared many months in advance . . . [and] coordinated with the JNA [Yugoslav People's Army]'.[11] He reports that the first violence in Sarajevo involved a Serbian wedding guest being shot dead 'by an unidentified assassin'.[12]

Nataša Mrvić-Petrović, in an introductory chapter for an edited collection, says that it was 'Moslem irregulars' who fired at the Serbs' wedding party, and reports, as the first offensive action in Bosnia, a Muslim attack on a JNA column retreating from Sarajevo on 2 May 1992. Moreover, while Bennett asserts that the UN arms embargo imposed on all the post-Yugoslav republics in September 1991 at Belgrade's request crippled the Muslims' capacity to defend themselves, Mrvić-Petrović writes that 'Especially in 1992 and 1993, [Bosnia's] Moslems were generously assisted by the Organization of Islamic Conference . . . This help included weapons.'[13]

Viktor Meier, in his carefully researched treatment of Yugoslavia's collapse, clearly identifies 'the Serbian side' and in the first place Milošević as the driving force behind the war, and reports that the man killed at the wedding party had been shot by 'a criminal of Muslim nationality'.[14] Meier also notes that the Serbian offensive in Bosnia began in April – a point overlooked by Mrvić-Petrović. I have reported the differing accounts of the shooting at the wedding in order to illustrate a point, which is that there are often differences not only of interpretation but also concerning rather unimportant details.

Warren Zimmermann and Robert Hayden offer alternative accounts, however, blaming the Slovenes for contributing to the crisis. Zimmermann, the former US ambassador to Yugoslavia, identifies Milošević personally as the 'villain' in the plot, but criticizes the Slovenes for being self-centred, arguing that they should have stayed in Yugoslavia longer in order to try to help the federation to reach a solution satisfactory to all parties.[15] Hayden, by contrast, seems to want to make the Slovenian leadership co-responsible with Milošević for the breakup of the country, dwelling at length on Slovenia's constitutional amendments adopted in September 1989, which, in his view, 'made the outbreak of internal war inevitable'.[16] Moreover, while every other book with which I am familiar refers to the Slovenian–Croatian joint proposal (1990) to transform Yugoslavia into a *confederation*, Hayden prefers to use the denotatively identical but connotatively distinct term *confederacy*, and resuscitates American president Abraham Lincoln, in support of his own 'anti-Confederate' banner.[17]

But Hayden is an exception. For most analysts, including Norman Cigar,[18] Thomas Cushman and Stjepan G. Meštrović,[19] Reneo Lukić and Allen Lynch,[20] James Sadkovich,[21] Michael Sells,[22] and Laura

Silber and Allan Little,[23] there is no doubt concerning the incendiary role played by Milošević and his associates. Moreover, as a result of the publication of various memoirs and of the testimonies given in the trial of Slobodan Milošević, Belgrade's culpability in the war has been extensively documented.

III

Tudjman and his policies. Franjo Tudjman's ill-considered remark, during his electoral campaign in 1990, that he was gratified that his wife was neither a Serb nor a Jew, continues to haunt him, even after his death in December 1999. With only a few exceptions, English-language treatments of Tudjman tend to be negative. Bennett's comment that 'temperamentally Tudjman was without a doubt the least at home in a democracy'[24] is marked by its reserve. Hayden, by contrast, paints Tudjman in darker colours and invites the reader to see Tudjman as a 'milder' version of Adolf Hitler.[25] Moreover, as Cushman and Meštrović note, Serbian intellectuals produced a string of polemical works during the war years, painting Tudjman as a reincarnation of Croatian fascist Ante Pavelić, who ruled over the Nazi-sponsored Croatian puppet state during the Second World War.[26]

Sells provides a damning summary of Tudjman's 1990 book, *Wastelands of Historical Reality*, in which, says Sells,

Tudjman revealed an anti-Semitic tendency. He suggested that Jews are genocidal by nature and that Jews were the major executioners in the Ustashe death camp of Jasenovac . . . The problems of the Jews are of their own making, Tudjman implies; Jews could have avoided them had they heeded what he calls, vaguely, 'the traffic signs'.[27]

Tudjman's decisions, soon after taking office, to introduce the kuna (the currency used in medieval Croatia and in fascist Croatia alike) and to fire Serbs working in the Croatian police force were certainly unwise and, in the latter instance, showed a deep insensitivity to the welfare of ordinary Serbs living in Croatia. But Serbs also complained about the use of the *šahovnica*, the red-and-white checkerboard emblem, in the new Croatian coat-of-arms, alleging – falsely – that it was a throwback to the days of Pavelić and his Ustaša movement. But, in fact, the *šahovnica* had been featured in the Croatian coat-of-arms since the end of the thirteenth century and had also been used during the socialist era, as the Serbs must have known. Croatian Serbs must also have known, as Croats certainly did, that whereas the first square in the upper-left corner of the fascist-era coat-of-arms had been *white*, the corresponding corner in the Croatian coat-of-arms in the interwar period, the socialist era, and in Tudjman's Croatia alike was *red*.[28] Silber and Little, in their otherwise brilliantly researched and balanced account, apparently became confused, representing the *šahovnica* as something contraband in socialist Yugoslavia[29] and claiming that 'Tudjman's insistence on the *šahovnica* as the symbol of a sovereign Croatia, and his insensitivity towards legitimate Serb anxieties, were grist to the mill of Babić's Party.' But they are quite right in noting that, under Belgrade's influence, the Serbian Democratic Party in Croatia 'consciously revived memories of the 1940s' among Serbs in order to kindle hatred of Croatia.[30]

Meier, by contrast, offers a spirited defence of Tudjman's use of traditional Croatian symbols. 'The number of national symbols which a nation has at its disposal is limited', writes Meier:

The *Ustaše* had adopted a lot of the old Croatian tradition or folklore; it would have been unusual if these symbols had not been endorsed also by today's Croatian state. Even in Germany, today's national anthem and the name of the currency were used by the Nazis, but no one has ever suggested that this signified that the Federal Republic was associating itself with Nazi tradition.[31]

More controversial than his use of symbols, however, were Tudjman's speeches, writings, and policies. In this domain, Michael Sells writes that 'Tudjman refused to acknowledge the full extent of Ustashe persecution of Serbs during World War II', adding that 'nationalists associated with Tudjman' consciously stoked hatreds in order to ignite a war[32] – a point argued in detail by Silber and Little.[33]

But Tudjman has had defenders as well as detractors. One of those who has tried to present Tudjman in a favourable light is James J. Sadkovich, who, at this writing, is completing the composition of the first biography in English of the Croatian leader. Admitting that Tudjman proved to be controversial as president, Sadkovich reproves Western academics and journalists who ignored the Croatian leader's 'respect for formal, procedural democracy' and notes that Tudjman was among those who, in early 1993, 'had pressed for the creation of an international court to try war crimes'.[34] For Sadkovich, the widespread portrait of Tudjman as a provincial authoritarian is superficial and inaccurate, as is the notion that he was a 'fascist' or a 'radical nationalist'. Rather, says Sadkovich, the Croatian leader should be seen as a somewhat 'archaic intellectual' who, if 'long-winded and old-fashioned', was nonetheless a 'Croatian patriot' attracted to humanism.[35] Sadkovich also documents a pervasive tendency of Western reportage to be distinctly unsympathetic to Croats, who were sometimes blamed even when it was Croat villages which were being overrun by the Yugoslav Army and Serb paramilitary forces.

Germany's role. The huge clamour over Germany's allegedly damaging role is largely due to a combination of four factors: a relentless anti-German line taken by Serbian propaganda in the Milošević era, the desire by Lord Carrington to find a scapegoat for the failure of his efforts at mediation in the latter part of 1991, persistent anti-German sentiments carried over from the Nazi era in general and from the Second World War and the Holocaust specifically, and an influential article by Beverly Crawford, published in 1996. For Crawford, Germany's diplomatic recognition of Croatia in December 1991 was seen by its European Community partners as 'a crucial breach of consensual norms in international law' and figures, thus, as 'a case of defection from international cooperation'.[36] Burg and Shoup agree with the basic outlines of Crawford's argument, adding that the EC decision to recognize Slovenia and Croatia, taken under pressure from Germany, 'seemed to intensify the Serbian threat to Bosnia'.[37] They further mention the declaration by the Serbian Autonomous Region of Bosanska Krajina, on 18 December 1991, that it was a constituent part of 'Yugoslavia' – a country which both juridically and in point of fact had ceased to exist – rather than of Bosnia. Burg and Shoup interpret both this act and the declaration of the Serb Republic of Bosnia-Herzegovina three days later as direct responses to the EC decision to recognize Slovenia and Croatia.[38]

Not so Lukić and Lynch. Like Daniele Conversi,[39] they believe that criticism of Germany's championing of Slovenia and Croatia on the grounds that it was 'premature' or 'unilateral' or that it contributed to the escalation of violence in Bosnia is misplaced. On the contrary, they argue, encouragement to the well-armed Serbs came not from Germany but from France and Great Britain, who 'were in effect prepared to see Croatia (and later Bosnia and Herzegovina) be defeated by Serbia'.[40] Moreover, Lukić and Lynch argue, the EC had agreed in July to extend recognition to Croatia and Slovenia in October (at the end of the three-month moratorium on independence imposed on the separating republics), so that it was Britain and France that, through their opposition to recognition 'defected' – to use Crawford's term – from the EC consensus, not Germany.[41] The German view, Lukić and Lynch explain, was that 'To criticize the policy of non-recognition was tantamount to acquiescence in the continuing use of military coercion by the Serbs.'[42]

John Major, in his aforementioned autobiography, provides some backing for this viewpoint, urging that 'subsequent events do not suggest that withholding recognition would have prevented the evil that followed'.[43] Sarah Kent, finally, records a position midway between

Burg/Shoup and Crawford on the one side and Lukić/Lynch and Conversi on the other, questioning the 'wisdom' of following Germany's
advice regarding recognition but adding that 'to call that recognition
"premature" is to invoke the patronizing rhetoric of colonialism'.[44]

Norbert Both makes a nuanced contribution to the continuing debate
about Germany's role in the context of his study of Dutch foreign policy
during the Yugoslav War. He points out that, as early as November
1990, in the context of a meeting of European Community ministers,
Germany argued forcefully that human rights had to take priority over
the maintenance of Yugoslav unity – a position which, interestingly
enough, was brushed aside by most of the EC ministers present.[45] The
German Foreign Ministry voiced concerns four months later, when
Serbian security forces backed by tanks suppressed the anti-war pro-
testers who had taken to the streets of Belgrade; Germany wanted to
issue a tough warning to Belgrade, but other EC members felt that
Germany 'was racing ahead of developments'.[46] In May 1991, developments in Yugoslavia turned ugly, with violence at Borovo Selo.
According to Both, Germany circulated a draft resolution among EC
ministers calling on Belgrade to respect human rights, work for democracy, and honour the right to national self-determination; as before, most
of the other EC member states (though not all) continued to feel that
Yugoslavia's territorial integrity and unity should remain the highest
priority for the EC, ahead of those values which the German government
was championing.

What Both adds to our understanding of the EC debate over recognition of Slovenia and Croatia in 1991 is the following. The Netherlands
was, in fact, the most forceful advocate (as of July 1991) of a tough
line against Serbia and of accepting the inevitability of Slovenian and
Croatian independence.[47] But when Hans Van den Broek, foreign
minister of the Netherlands and president of the EC from summer
1991, put forward a tough resolution, Germany, on whose support the
Dutch had counted, declined to back them and, instead, joined the
French in proposing a weaker resolution. According to Both, an important reason why the Germans declined to back the Dutch proposal was
sour relations between the top politicians in the Netherlands and
Germany, which had developed at the time of German reunification,
which the Dutch had opposed.[48] But by mid-September, German foreign
minister Genscher joined Italian foreign minister Gianni de Michelis in
declaring that Germany and Italy would be prepared to recognize the
independence of Slovenia and Croatia if negotiations broke down. Even
so, it was Van den Broek who proved to be 'instrumental in opening the
way to a decision in favour of recognition' when, on 8 and 9 October, he

spent hours on the telephone with various European and American polit-
icians arguing the case for recognition.[49] Then came the fall of Vukovar to
Serb forces on 18 November, which, for the Dutch, transformed the
Yugoslav crisis from a diplomatic and political crisis to a moral one.

Both also offers an account of a meeting of Christian Democratic
government leaders and party chairmen on 26 November, which played
a pivotal role in the move towards recognition of Slovenia and Croatia.
Meeting at Stuyvenberg castle near Brussels, Christian Democratic
leaders from Germany, Italy, Belgium, Luxembourg, the Netherlands,
and Greece agreed that Slovenia and Croatia should be recognized by
Christmas at the latest.[50] In other words, what has been described in
much of the literature as a German initiative could be better described as
a Christian Democratic initiative involving leading figures from six
states. The Dutch subsequently had second thoughts, chiefly because
they feared that recognition might have negative effects on the unstable
situation in Bosnia,[51] but by then the die had been cast. Kohl and
Genscher may have been the loudest advocates of this communally
reached policy but, according to Both, it was ultimately a multilateral,
Christian Democratic initiative, rather than a German one – Croatian
gratitude to Kohl and Genscher notwithstanding.

IV

Democracy in Bosnia. Considerable controversy has also surrounded
the referendum conducted by the government of Alija Izetbegović on
28 February–1 March 1991 concerning Bosnian independence. Organized at the behest of the EC's Badinter Commission, which held that
a referendum was a prerequisite for international recognition of independence, the vote produced a clear majority in favour of independence – 99 per cent of those voting, and 63 per cent of those eligible to
vote. The problem was that, as a result of a decision taken by Radovan
Karadžić's Serbian Democratic Party (of Bosnia), the overwhelming
majority of Serbs boycotted the referendum (or were kept from the
polls by Karadžić's people, according to some reports). Indeed, as Silber
and Little point out, Izetbegović was, by then, championing the principle 'one man, one vote' (as opposed to a system whereby a majority
within any one of the national groups could veto a decision taken by
the majority of Bosnian citizens) not only within the context of the
referendum itself but also as the basis for the future organization of
the Bosnian state.[52] This was, in fact, the very principle which Milošević
had championed previously in the context of socialist Yugoslavia, when
he had tried to reduce the autonomy of the constituent republics.

Burg and Shoup argue, however, that 'simple electoral democracy was not the answer',[53] and explain much later that 'the referendum . . . was from the Serb point of view a step towards war'.[54] Yet they also claim that 'Serbia did not attempt to broaden the conflict to Bosnia'[55] – thereby implicitly denying that Belgrade had been involved in any preparations for bringing the war to Bosnia. Moreover, as they tell it, 'the first engagement of Serbian forces from outside Bosnia occurred in Bijeljina on April 2 and 3 [1992], when an armed confrontation between the Muslim Patriotic League and local Serb territorial units took place';[56] in other words, the eruption of hostilities in Bijeljina should be seen as an unplanned action in which neither side bore any special culpability.

Hayden goes further, describing 'protection of the rights of minorities' but not majority rule as 'an essential element of democracy'[57] and mentioning 'the refusal of Bosnian Serbs to accept the superior right of Croats and Muslims to proclaim a Bosnia that would include them against their wishes'.[58] Since Hayden does not use the same words when it comes to the preferences of Croats and Muslims living in Serb-controlled areas, let alone for the Albanians of Kosovo, it would seem apparent that the 'superior right' he is rejecting is *majority rule*. If I am reading Hayden's text correctly, this means that he believes that national groups in Bosnia should have enjoyed a veto over all important political decisions – an arrangement associated variously with consociational democracy or with the framework of a state organized on the basis of constitutional nationalism (to use Hayden's term), but not liberal democracy.[59]

Cigar joins Silber and Little in highlighting the hypocrisy of the Bosnian Serbs' position on the referendum, noting that they had conducted their own 'Serb-only' referendum three months earlier, voting to remain in union with Belgrade, regardless of what Bosnia's Croats and Muslims might wish for themselves.[60] Hayden does not (or did not, at the time he finished his book) consider that this Serb-run referendum involved any implicit claim to a 'superior right', however.

For Lukić and Lynch, efforts to portray the Serb offensive against non-Serbs in Bosnia as a natural or understandable response to the referendum are misguided. They note that the existence of a Serbian plan to annex portions of Bosnia-Herzegovina (the 'Ram' or 'Framework' plan) had been public knowledge since September 1991, when the independent Belgrade weekly magazine *Vreme* published details.[61] In their view, 'international recognition of Bosnia and Herzegovina was essentially a pretext exploited by Serbia to justify its act of aggression against [Bosnia]'.[62]

The Vance–Owen Peace Plan. The ill-fated Vance–Owen peace plan of 1993 has had its share of advocates and detractors and, even now, more than a decade later, it remains the subject of dissension. There have been three distinct controversies concerning the plan: first, whether it rewarded Serbian aggression or should be seen rather as a practical solution; second, whose fault it was that the plan was not accepted; and, third, whether it would have been smart for the United States and other Western states to intervene militarily to compel the three sides to accept the plan. Among the plan's harshest critics at the time were the Dutch, who opposed it because 'it was considered unjust and it was thought that a better alternative could be had'.[63] Whatever the plan's moral demerits, many writers have acknowledged its expediency. Marie-Janine Calic, for instance, writes that 'it was not entirely incorrect to describe [the plan] as "a last chance for peace"'.[64]

Brendan Simms, who protests that the plan was unjust, blames the plan's failure squarely on the Bosnian Serbs, who in fact rejected it.[65] Lord Owen blames the Americans and, in this, is seconded by James Gow, who argues that the United States could have used force to implement the plan.[66] Gow argues further that the Vance–Owen Peace Plan was a better plan than what was finally accepted at Dayton more than two years later. Carole Rogel, for her part, divides the blame for the plan's failure between the Bosnian Serbs and the Clinton administration, noting that the former thought that they were not being allocated as much land as they wanted while the latter thought that the Serbs were being allocated too much of Bosnia's territory.[67] Norbert Both, however, thinks that the Dutch government must be added to the equation, and blames 'the Bosnian-Dutch-American axis' for the plan's ultimate demise, Bosnian Serb rejectionism being also an element.[68]

But Gow's notion that the plan could have been implemented by force, over the objections of the Bosnian Serbs, admits of some refinement. Norbert Both, for example, notes that, even as the plan was under discussion during spring 1993, Bosnian Serb forces continued to make advances, in the process undermining the prospects for even an enforced implementation of the plan.[69] Both also offers a revisionist account of US objections to the plan. According to his version, the Clinton administration objected to the plan not because it was immoral or insufficiently ambitious, but, on the contrary, because it was, in the administration's view, 'overly ambitious'.[70] Moreover, it was not the Bosnian Serbs or the United States unilaterally who sounded the death knell for the Vance–Owen Peace Plan. This came, rather, when the United States joined Russia, Britain, France, and Spain – with

Germany pointedly excluded, over German protests! – in signing a resolution in support of a new plan, the so-called Joint Action Program, on 22 May 1993.

Finally, there is a pessimistic note from Tim Judah who, in his 1997 review of Serbian history, claims that 'it is a mistake to believe that had the Bosnian Serb parliament sitting in the Paradise Valley Hotel in the mountains above Sarajevo accepted it, it would ever have been implemented. Milošević urged the Bosnian Serbs to accept the plan on the premise that they had won the war and the Vance–Owen plan was the best guarantee that they could keep most of the land they now controlled. There was no intention of actually fulfilling its terms, just as the Serbian leadership had never intended to fulfill the terms of the Vance plan for Croatia.'[71]

War aims. The question of Serbian war aims is closely connected with the issues of culpability and pre-planning, and thus, here too, there are differences of opinion. For example, Francine Friedman, in a review of Cigar's *Genocide in Bosnia*, claims that Cigar gives 'short shrift to Serbian fears of marginalization in Croatia and Bosnia and Herzegovina',[72] thereby suggesting that the Serbian recourse to arms was, at least in part, defensive in nature. Bennett, however, dismisses such claims, highlighting Milošević's irredentist project and pointing to the Serbian leader's decision to move the indigenous Serbian population of western Slavonia to eastern Slavonia, from which local Croats and Hungarians had been expelled, in order to consolidate his territorial conquests.[73]

Burg and Shoup give a more Lydian interpretation of Belgrade's intentions, alleging that, by 1 November 1991, Belgrade had abandoned 'the pursuit of a greater Serbia' in favour of 'a more nuanced strategy',[74] though they do not explain why such a strategy involved the commitment of Serbian/FRY (Federal Republic of Yugoslavia) military and economic resources to the campaign in Bosnia which began only five months later. They also tread onto unabashedly normative terrain in making the following surprising statement:

Our account makes clear that one side – the Muslims – was the aggrieved party, fighting for its survival as a political community, if not for its very existence. But, at the same time, the evidence we present here makes it clear that all three parties – including the Muslims – were behaving in ways that undermined any claim to moral superiority.[75]

What is curious here, of course, is that Burg and Shoup simultaneously concede the Muslims the status of *victims*, while treating them as morally equivalent with the Serbian side, the *aggressors*. The notion that victims and aggressors should be considered morally equivalent has generally not withstood scrutiny.

Cigar, Lukić and Lynch, Sells, and Silber and Little view Serbian war aims as embracing the creation of a Greater Serbian state, to which portions of Croatia and Bosnia-Herzegovina would be attached, and from which most non-Serbs would be expelled and their religious and cultural objects destroyed. For Cigar, thus, 'ethnic cleansing', as the Serb policy of mayhem, slaughter, and forced expulsion came to be called, 'was not simply the unintentional and unfortunate by-product of combat or civil war. Rather, it was a rational policy, the direct and planned consequence of conscious policy decisions taken by the Serbian establishment in Serbia and Bosnia-Herzegovina.'[76] Francis Boyle, in *The Bosnian People Charge Genocide*, cites UN special rapporteur Tadeusz Mazowiecki's conclusion that 'ethnic cleansing does not appear to be [merely] the consequence of the war, but rather its goal'.[77] Nor was material profit irrelevant, as Silber and Little point out; on the contrary, Muslims and Croats were typically forced to sign documents surrendering their property rights to Serbs, before being allowed to flee for their lives.[78]

Sells, in a striking passage, shows how 'ethnic cleansing' worked: in the period from April through July 1992, Serb militias killed or expelled all of Zvornik's Muslims and destroyed all of the town's mosques as well as all evidence of half a millennium of interconfessional coexistence. At the end of the operation, the new Serbian mayor of Zvornik, which had hitherto had a Muslim majority, announced, 'There never were any mosques in Zvornik.'[79] In this way, 'ethnic cleansing' also entails the rewriting of history.

V

The nature of Izetbegović's programme. Throughout the war years, Serb propagandists never tired of accusing Bosnian president Izetbegović of seeking to establish an Islamic fundamentalist state, while apologists and propagandists for the Izetbegović government responded by portraying that government as a paragon of liberal tolerance, secular democracy, and advocacy of interethnic and interconfessional harmony. Parties to the dispute typically offered contrasting interpretations of Izetbegović's youthful work, *The Islamic Declaration*, which outlined certain Islamic principles of government. Ineluctably, analysts also represented the Izetbegović government in diverse ways. Aleksa Djilas, the internationally regarded Serbian writer, claimed, for example, that 'most Muslim leaders believed only a Muslim should be allowed full citizenship', though he added that 'only Muslim extremists . . . thought non-Muslims should be expelled from Bosnia'.[80]

Along the same lines, Burg and Shoup say (in the context of a discussion of 1990) that Izetbegović 'carefully avoided specifically advocating the establishment of an "Islamic state" in Bosnia', phrasing which makes sense only if one supposes that the elder Bosnian actually wanted to establish such a state in Bosnia. They also refer to the 'overtly Islamic and Muslim nationalist orientation of the SDA [Party of Democratic Action] leadership around Izetbegović', while noting that Adil Zulfikarpašić's rival Muslim Bosniak Organization 'held little appeal outside of liberal Muslim circles'.[81]

For Cushman and Meštrović, efforts to construe Alija Izetbegović as an Islamic fundamentalist were 'taken directly from Serbian propaganda' and have no basis in fact. On the contrary, they argue, in his book, *Islam between East and West*, 'Izetbegović's admiration for the West is so great as to be pathetic, given how the West has rejected him.'[82] Yet, as they note, 'The construction of Izetbegović as an Islamic fundamentalist [had] important ramifications for Western policy.'[83]

Silber and Little, as ever offering rich detail, cite a speech Izetbegović gave in 1990, in which he resolutely rejected anything smacking of fundamentalism or Muslim hegemony. 'We are not on the road to a national state', Izetbegović said on that occasion:

Our only way out is towards a free civic union. This is the future. Some people may want that [to make Bosnia a Muslim state] but this is not a realistic wish. Even though the Muslims are the most numerous nation in the republic, there are not enough of them [to justify such a political aspiration].[84]

Genocide. Of all the issues discussed here, perhaps none has such poignancy as the question of genocide: did Serbian actions in Croatia and/or Bosnia-Herzegovina constitute genocide or not? What is striking is the correlation between methodology and conclusions. Hayden and Burg/Shoup look to scholarly definitions of *genocide* and conclude that the case for genocide has not (or had not, at the time of their writing, at least) been made; Boyle, Cigar, and Cushman/Meštrović rely on the legal definition of genocide as per the United Nations Convention on the Prevention and Punishment of the Crime of Genocide (1948) and conclude that genocide *did* take place in Bosnia and that the Serbian side was the perpetrator. Bennett, for his part, relies on a commonsensical understanding of genocide to argue that 'ethnic cleansing is but a euphemism for genocide', pointing out, however, that the advantage of using the former term is that it does not place the great powers under any obligation to make an effective response.[85]

At the outset of their work, Steven Burg and Paul Shoup commendably point out that they were unable to reach agreement on the question of genocide. 'For one of us [Burg?], it is a central issue', they write, while 'for the other [Shoup?], [it is] a charge that is highly politicized and must therefore be made cautiously, if at all.'[86] In spite of this, it is the latter viewpoint which, as far as I can see, dominates in the discussion which follows, giving rise to a certain scepticism. But even allowing for some scepticism, it is hard to know what to make of Burg and Shoup's allegation that, in Operation Storm, in which, according to Human Rights Watch (final figures), a total of 526 Serbs and 253 Croats lost their lives,[87] 'the Serb population of [the] Krajina was cleansed, and its remnants subjected to systematic abuse and murder on a scale that might raise the question of genocide',[88] even while, in considering the more numerous Muslim and Croat casualties, they had questioned 'whether, in fact, genocide was taking place'.[89]

Some writers deny that the Bosnian Muslims suffered genocide, based on the argument that they were not eradicated. Sells, by contrast, returns to Rafael Lemkin, who coined the term, and notes that Lemkin never intended for the term to require the destruction of an *entire* community. Lemkin defined genocide, rather, as 'a coordinated plan of different actions aiming at the destruction of essential foundations of the life of national groups'.[90] Guided by this understanding of the term, Sells concludes that the Serbian 'effort [in the years 1992–5] to destroy both Bosnian Muslim culture and Bosnian multireligious culture and to destroy the Bosnian Muslims as a people' was indeed tantamount to *genocide*, and that only their reluctance to become involved induced NATO powers to refuse to acknowledge that genocide was in fact taking place.[91]

The first serious effort to assess the background to the genocide in Bosnia and to come to grips with its social context is, without question, Norman Cigar's insightful and brilliantly executed book. Cigar shows how political, cultural, and ecclesiastical elites in Serbia prepared the ground over a period of years, mentioning, for example, Olga Luković-Pejanović's book, *The Serbs: The Oldest Nation*, which 'revealed' that the Garden of Eden had been situated in an area presently in Serbia, that the Serbs invented writing, that the Greek poet Ovid wrote his works in Serbian, and so forth.[92] He also quotes an unnamed minister in the Serbian government who, in 1994, apparently declared:

Today, many around the world dream about being Serbs: the individual on Fifth Avenue eating a hamburger, the Eskimo breaking the ice and fishing, the Frenchman strolling along the Champs d'Elysées . . . Be happy that you are Serbs . . . Be happy that you belong to this people . . . You are eternal.[93]

Having argued for a connection between the collective mental states induced by such propaganda and the willingness to perpetrate violence against others – which is the central point in a book by Ivan Čolović to be discussed in chapter 6 – Cigar turns his attention to the policies executed and voices of protest. What he found, among other things, was that there were significantly more voices of moderation among both Croats and Bosniaks (Muslims) than among Serbs. He notes, for example, that the independent but erratic Zagreb weekly, *Globus*, showed that documents adduced by Mate Boban's Croatian Defence Council (HVO), the military arm of the Bosnian Croats, purported to prove that the Bosnian government had formulated plans to slaughter local Croats, were forgeries.[94] He also argues forcefully that air power could have been effective in disrupting the Bosnian Serbs' ability to move troops and supplies into and around Bosnia-Herzegovina.[95]

VI

The Udovički/Ridgeway volume is, in some ways, more ambitious than the aforementioned books, offering a comprehensive overview of the troubled history of the South Slavs. Although an edited collection, the chapters hold together remarkably well, generally offering a Serbian oppositionist, which is to say liberal-cosmopolitan, viewpoint, but with an insider's understanding of Serb perceptions, and Serbian developments and modalities. Tracing the course of Yugoslav history from 395 to 1999, but with emphasis on the final twelve years of this period, the volume includes, among other things, separate chapters on the Tito era, the first decade after Tito's death (i.e., 1980–90), the role of the media in stoking interethnic hatreds, the army, the resistance in Serbia, the resistance in Croatia, international aspects of the Yugoslav conflicts, and – new to the second edition – a chapter by Jasminka Udovički on Kosovo. Udovički sets the stage in her introduction by tracing the collapse of Yugoslavia to what she calls 'political ethno-kitsch' washing over Serbia in the years after 1987. The entire popular culture, including folk concerts, popular fiction, sporting events, mass rallies, and of course the media, became obsessed with the idea that the Serbs had been wronged by the other peoples of Yugoslavia, that they were, in fact, 'the Jews of the Balkans'.[96] Serbian and Yugoslav society might have been able to resist this propaganda, she implies, had the country possessed 'a resilient web of democratic institutions'. But unfortunately, she relates, the emergence of civil society and of civic consciousness alike had been stifled in both the interwar kingdom and Tito's communist Yugoslavia, with the result that the country lacked any such protective network.[97] What is more, the Yugoslav public was not able to recognize the nationalist avalanche, 'for what it was: a pernicious assault on the most basic norms of democratic life and a populist subterfuge engineered from above as a prelude to war. The public instead identified nationalism with patriotism.'[98] These lines make clear Udovički's affinity for the idealist approach to politics.

Of particular interest in this volume is the chapter on the media ('The Media Wars: 1987–1997') by Milan Milošević. In this study, the author focuses on the media in Serbia, showing how it manipulated images to stoke hatred and resentment. One example comes from 1989 when, in response to the publication of Franjo Tudjman's controversial book, *Bespuća* (Wastelands), in which the retired general had revised the conventional figures about the number of people who had died at the Jasenovac concentration camp in the Second World War and during the war as a whole, Serbian authorities undertook to have mass graves opened and their contents displayed in front of television cameras, supposedly so that people would understand just how bad the war had been.[99] This television campaign gave Tudjman a standing which he might otherwise not have attained and, ironically (since that was not the intent of the Serbian authorities), helped to propel Tudjman into the office of president of Croatia when Croats, fed up with the propaganda barrage coming out of Belgrade, looked to Belgrade's apparent nemesis to be their leader. Later, after the war had got underway, Serbian television continued its manipulations, as Milan Milošević shows: Serbian viewers, sitting glued to their television sets, watched as the corpses of Bosnian Muslims killed by Serbs were shown, but they were told that these were the bodies of Serbs killed by Muslims![100] But Croatian television was no more reliable, according to the author. What is even more striking is that, in spite of extravagant distortion and politicization of images and reportage, surveys conducted by the Institute for Political Studies in Belgrade in mid-1992 found that more than 60 per cent of Serbian television viewers did not doubt the truth of what they heard on television.[101]

The second edition of the Udovički/Ridgeway volume also includes, as already mentioned, a new chapter on Kosovo, written primarily to provide an account of the crisis of 1998–9, culminating in NATO's air campaign against the FRY. Udovički combines an astute sensitivity to historical factors with a realistic assessment of the forces which inflamed the crisis, never allowing herself to slide into historical determinism. She points out that Serb and Albanian nationalisms mirrored each other, without nationalists on either side ever being aware of the similarity of their positions.[102] She takes note of both Albanian and Serb resentments during the communist era. And she recounts how more than 20,000 Serbs left Kosovo during the years 1981–7, fuelling the general resentment which brought Milošević to power and provided the backdrop for the abolition, by Serbia, of the province's autonomy in March 1989. She sensibly describes the Dayton Peace Accords as a turning point for most Albanians of Kosovo. It is arguable that, until then, ordinary Albanians might well have considered some form of autonomy, for example as a constituent republic coequal with Serbia and Montenegro within the rump Yugoslav federation, and not have insisted on full independence. But when the Albanians saw that their concerns were not being addressed at Dayton, they lost hope of a negotiated settlement and, as Udovički puts it, after that, the Albanians treated the Belgrade authorities as 'an occupying force' pure and simple.[103] Her account of the rise of the Kosovo Liberation Army (KLA) is rich in detail. She notes, for example, that KLA fighters may have obtained training in Albania, Iran, and Pakistan, and cites Western sources to the effect that the KLA received assistance from German intelligence sources in the mid-1990s. She also writes that the KLA developed connections with the Kosovar Albanian mafia in Germany, Switzerland, and Italy.[104]

As the KLA began its violent activity against Serbian targets inside Kosovo in 1997, pressure built up on the Belgrade regime to respond. Udovički asserts:

The Serbian regime would have acted within its constitutional prerogatives had it aimed its activities against the mafia-linked, foreign-supported assassins of Serbian police, civilians, and state employees, including ethnic Albanian ones. Instead, Belgrade struck back not just at the criminal elements but at civilians as well.[105]

Yet the Belgrade regime could scarcely have done otherwise, since it was not a *Rechtstaat*, but an autocratic regime with stunted democratic institutions, whose ruling party owed its position to its promotion of intolerant nationalism. In a review of an earlier incarnation of *Burn This House,* Marko Attila Hoare criticized the contributors for failing to 'express [even] the slightest sympathy or understanding for the national rights of non-Serb peoples. In their view these are not an issue . . . Rather, "the crucial issue for Yugoslavia" was "the rights of minority ethnic groups in the republics and provinces." This turns out to mean only the Serbs in Croatia, Bosnia and Kosova, since the grievances of other minorities are given no space and their rights are not defended.'[106] The chief non-Serbian minority (using the term in a mathematical sense) within the Republic of Serbia has been the Albanians, and this

new chapter corrects any imbalance of which the first edition may have
been guilty, at least to some extent. At the same time, the volume makes
a point of emphasizing that there were not only nationalist Serbs, but
also anti-nationalist Serbs such as the 'many Serbs in Croatia [who] were
against the war and refused to be turned against their Croatian neighbors',[107] and the 'progressive activists [in Belgrade] who tried to reach
not just moderate Albanians but also their own old-time Albanian
friends'.[108] A chapter by Sven Balas (a pseudonym) argues the same
point on behalf of Croats, noting the presence of anti-nationalist and
anti-Tudjman Croats, including among intellectuals.[109] Again, where
the Muslims/Bosniaks are concerned, the chapter written jointly by
Udovički and Štitkovac records how, in March 1992, tens of thousands
of Bosnians (involving not just Muslims, for whom the term Bosniaks
is generally used) 'took to the streets of Bosnia's towns shouting, "We
want to live together."'[110] Yet, rather obviously, the voices of the anti-
nationalist opposition were drowned out in Serbia, Croatia, and Bosnia-
Herzegovina, and Serbs and Croats proved unable to dislodge their
respective governments from their disastrous courses (at least, in the
case of Croatia, until the Washington Agreement).

VII

I have already discussed some of the ideas presented in the volumes by
Sadkovich and Burg/Shoup, but return to them briefly in conjunction
with a discussion of the Magaš/Žanić volume, insofar as they offer a
study in contrasts. Both volumes provide nutshell summaries of the
Yugoslav theatre in the Second World War, both criticize American
media coverage of the war in Bosnia (Sadkovich judges it to have
been pro-Serb, while Burg and Shoup argue that it was anti-Serb), and
both offer clear interpretations of the Bosnian war, albeit from opposite
vantage points. The Sadkovich volume draws on an extensive list of
English-, Serbo-Croat-, and Italian-language works, including analyses
of the media, as well as a wide array of American media sources, more
than sufficient to give his argument weight. The Burg/Shoup volume
reflects a familiarity with English-, Serbo-Croat-, and German-language
materials, including UN documents and American newspapers such as
the *New York Times*, the *Washington Post*, and the *Boston Globe*, as well as
such local newspapers as *Borba*, *Politika*, and *Oslobodjenje*. The British
newspaper, the *Guardian*, is also cited extensively by Burg and Shoup.

Sadkovich's concern is to show how American journalists misled the
American public, whether consciously or through ignorance. He notes,
for example, that some journalists who covered the Balkans during

1991–5 had had no previous familiarity with the area and uncritically accepted the distorted view of history given in Serbian propaganda, namely, that one could draw a direct line from the Second World War (which the journalists misunderstood in some important details) to the War of Yugoslav Succession of 1991–5.[111] Overall, he criticizes the US media for having displayed a persistently pro-Serb, anti-Croat, and anti-Muslim bias, providing extensive documentation. CNN comes in for special criticism, for alleged oversimplification, shallowness, and trivialization,[112] while Sadkovich indicts the American media more generally for contributing to a dulling of the moral sense and a paralysis of the will.[113]

Sadkovich also has harsh words for the conventionalist school, aiming his toughest criticism at Woodward's *Balkan Tragedy* and Cohen's *Broken Bonds*, and associating Gale Stokes (in particular, the Yugoslav sections of *The Walls Came Tumbling Down* (1993)) with them. Woodward is criticized for reducing history to abstract forces and processes, thereby failing to identify the human agents responsible for certain policies,[114] for construing 'the Serbs as victims of an international conspiracy' involving 'Germany[,]. . . Austria, Hungary, Italy, the Vatican, Denmark, . . . and the US Congress',[115] and for repeating as if a fact Karadžić's inaccurate[116] claim that the Serbs had '"owned" 64 percent of Bosnia' prior to the outbreak of hostilities,[117] among other things. Cohen is criticized for referring to the conflict as 'a pattern of ethno-religious violence and atrocities against innocent civilians that was all too familiar in the region',[118] for anti-Croat prejudices,[119] and for accepting the notion that the hostility displayed by Croatian Serbs towards the Tudjman government was the result of spontaneously recalled memories of the Second World War rather than of the propaganda campaign which had been waged by the Belgrade media since soon after Milošević's accession to power.[120]

It is unlikely that Sadkovich would have had favourable things to say about the Burg/Shoup volume, had it appeared early enough for him to have considered it, since it is closer in spirit to the works he criticizes than to the universalist position which he articulates.[121] The Burg/Shoup volume is, in fact, a classic statement of the realist position, as I have defined it. Having already rejected any criticism of illiberal nationalism on the basis of liberal principles,[122] Burg and Shoup seek to marginalize moral arguments, asserting that 'the moral argument for intervention, however well-intentioned, did not fully address the moral dilemma of whether the lives of Western soldiers were worth less than the lives of the Bosnians the West would be trying to save'.[123] Elsewhere in the book they declare that only a threat to international peace can justify military intervention in the affairs of another state[124] – a curious claim insofar as the UN Charter codifies *two* cases in which the use of force is justified: these are the right to individual or collective defence against armed attack, and the certification that there is a serious threat to collective security.[125] More to the point, many scholars of international law argue that norms of international behaviour have evolved in the past half-century and that there is, in fact, a plausible case that massive violations of human rights not only legitimate international intervention, but actually require it.[126]

Strangely, in attempting to give an account of the major approaches to conflict management in situations of ethnic conflict, Burg and Shoup assert that (American) academia is, in their view, 'dominated' by two approaches: the 'pluralist or integrationist' approach, which, in fact, does not favour integration at all but 'calls for the isolation of groups from one another at the mass level through entirely separate networks of social and political organizations' with each group being granted a veto 'when its "vital interests" are at stake', and the 'power-sharing' approach, which is based on 'collectivist definitions of rights' and the presumption of the legitimacy of 'group claims to state-constituting status'.[127] What is striking is that neither of these approaches could be called 'liberal', which is to say that Burg and Shoup do not believe that faith in classical liberalism is a dominant view in American academic circles!

Equally controversially but consistently, Burg and Shoup criticize James Gow's allegation that the West lacked the will to take the action necessary to end the Bosnian war in 1993, countering that 'To argue that intervention could be based on "will" *alone*' – not Gow's argument[128] – 'ignores the responsibility of democratic leaders to consider the costs of intervention to their citizens in terms of "blood and treasure" . . . [On the contrary,] the refusal to intervene appears to [have] reflect[ed] responsible democratic leadership, rather than a lack of will.'[129] More than 200,000 people died in Bosnia during the war of 1992–5, while the White House hesitated. When the United States finally acted in August 1995, Bosnian Serb defences against American military might proved to be nonexistent.

The Burg/Shoup volume contains a number of strange statements, among them:

- the allegation that, concerning Bosnia's future, there were, as of 1990–2, 'two alternative views, both Serb'[130] – phrasing which suggests (whether deliberately or as a result of inattention to their own words) that the Croats and Muslims had no coherent views;

- the allegation that 'even those who advocated the use of US air power feared that fighting would intensify as a result'[131] – a representation which does not seem appropriate whether one talks of George Shulz or Margaret Thatcher or Zbigniew Brzezinski or myself, let alone Alexander Haig or the increasingly frustrated US Congress;
- their reduction of attempts to establish a liberal 'civic state' (*građanska država*) to 'efforts of one or two groups to impose their will on the third', as if there were no compelling arguments for liberal majoritarian democracy.[132]

The Burg/Shoup volume is not without its uses. The authors have compiled a lot of information, detailing sundry military, political, and diplomatic actions over the course of a decade. But their story is told from a pro-Serbian,[133] anti-Muslim,[134] relativistic[135] perspective. It is odd that they allude, in the context of their discussion of events between October 1991 and March 1992, to the JNA's 'transfer of arms' to Bosnia's Serbs, when this Serbian arms transfusion had begun, not after October 1991, but already in 1990 (so that, by mid-March 1991, the JNA had illegally transferred nearly 52,000 firearms to Serb militias in Bosnia);[136] instead, by placement, they associate this with accounts of what were in fact *later* efforts by local Croats and Muslims to arm themselves, writing that the 'Bosnian Muslim Green Berets were organized in fall 1991'[137] (which is to say, after the hostilities in Croatia had begun and at least two months after Bosnian Serbs had begun arming themselves).

The Magaš/Žanić book not only provides a useful corrective to the Burg/Shoup volume, but has quickly established itself as a classic in the field. In its original Croatian edition,[138] the collaborative volume shot to the best-seller list in Zagreb and Sarajevo and remained there for several weeks. The book is the first major study of the military aspects of the war,[139] but also sheds light on political and legal aspects of the conflict. The major chapters are written by: General Martin Špegelj, former Croatian defence minister; General Anton Tus, former chief-of-staff of the Croatian Army (HV); Ozren Žunec, professor of history at the University of Zagreb; General Jovan Divjak, former deputy chief-of-staff of the Army of Bosnia-Herzegovina; Marko Attila Hoare, a lecturer at Cambridge University; and Norman Cigar, a professor of strategic studies at the US Marine Corps Command and Staff College at Quantico Virginia. Other contributors are Dušan Bilandžić, Rusmir Mahmutćehajić, Paul Williams, Warren H. Switzer, Ofelja Backović, Miloš Vasić, and Aleksandra Vasović.

The revelations by Špegelj and Tus are particularly striking. Špegelj, for example, reports that in December 1990, when presented with a draft defence plan for Croatia, Tudjman rejected it, saying that he did not want to have *any* defence plan; indeed, Tudjman turned down two more defence plans between then and the end of July 1991.[140] Špegelj also reveals that, as early as March 1991, the Croatian Ministry of Defence had learned of a JNA plan to take control of Serb-inhabited areas of Croatia[141] – a point which makes clear that the JNA was already acting in collaboration with Milošević by that time. But Špegelj also presses a point he develops at greater length in his memoirs (discussed in chapter 5), namely, that in strategic terms, the best time for Croatia to seize JNA weaponry would have been during the period when the JNA was preoccupied with Slovenia (25 June–10 July 1991), arguing that Croatian authorities could thereby have brought the war to a speedy close.[142] Špegelj blames Tudjman for the delay in moving against JNA barracks and depots, and also for issuing an inexplicable (in Špegelj's mind) order on 26 December 1991 to halt a Croatian counteroffensive which, in the space of twenty-five days, had retaken much of western Slavonia.[143]

General Tus echoes Špegelj's criticism of Tudjman, both for his decision not to occupy all the JNA installations in Croatia[144] and for strategic errors on the battlefield. Specifically, if the Croatian Army had occupied the Petrova Gora barracks before Vukovar was surrounded, the town could have been saved, according to Tus, since Petrova Gora was crucial to the JNA siege. The HV began its thrust towards Vukovar during the night of 12/13 October, with diversionary actions in which some enemy targets were destroyed; by noon, Croatian forces had taken control of half of Marinci, a nearby village. But already at 9 a.m. on 13 October, President Tudjman had called General Tus to ask him to stop the operation so that Doctors Without Borders/Médecins Sans Frontières could get to Vukovar and evacuate the wounded. At the time, Tus told Tudjman that it was not possible to call off a successful breakthrough. But after the HV was already inside Marinci, Tudjman telephoned Tus for a second time, ordering Tus to suspend the operation at once. The HV now suspended the campaign to allow the humanitarian convoy to pass, but the JNA manoeuvred the convoy around the area for *two days* while they laid mines in the area and brought in reinforcements, cutting the road to Vukovar.[145] By the time the convoy had evacuated the wounded and left the combat area, the military situation around Vukovar had changed; the window of opportunity for a Croatian rescue operation had closed, setting the stage for the eventual collapse of the resistance in Vukovar.

Ozren Žunec, in a chapter devoted to the successful Croatian military operations of 1995 (Operation Flash in western Slavonia and Operation Storm in the Krajina), notes his fundamental agreement with Špegelj, declaring that, as of the end of 1991, Croatia 'had broken the back of the whole JNA offensive' and, according to Žunec, could easily have retaken its territory; Tudjman did not do so, says Žunec, because of his territorial pretensions in Bosnia-Herzegovina.[146] But whereas many observers had depicted the HV's reconquest of western Slavonia and the Dalmatian hinterland in 1995 as primarily *military* accomplishments, Žunec emphasizes that the Krajina Serbs had failed *politically* as well, lacking a clear strategy or even a functioning state apparatus.[147]

Jovan Divjak's chapter on Bosnia, 1992–3, is one of the most important pieces ever written about the fighting in Bosnia. He provides concrete examples of the illegal behaviour of Bosnian Serb leaders Karadžić and Krajišnik, as well as of Serb deputies to the Bosnian Assembly, and offers details of JNA/Bosnian Serb preparations for war. And where Burg and Shoup *congratulate* the international community for its long inaction in Bosnia ('responsible democratic leadership', as they call it), Divjak charges that 'The international community is responsible for failing to prevent the genocide and reducing its involvement to merely providing humanitarian aid and localizing the conflict so that it would not spread to the rest of the Balkans.'[148]

And finally, Marko Attila Hoare, in a chapter devoted to civil–military relations in wartime Bosnia, argues that, in the course of the war, the rump state and the Bosnian Army evolved into the private instruments of Izetbegović and his Party of Democratic Action (SDA).[149] He blames the general staff of the Bosnian Army for having made no effort to come to Srebrenica's assistance in summer 1995,[150] and portrays the United States, Britain, and France as cynically looking for ways to partition Bosnia, *rather* than save it.[151]

Taken as a whole, *The War in Croatia and Bosnia-Herzegovina* prompts a reassessment of the 'conventional' view of the war as fostered in segments of the Western press. Prepared well in advance, the war *cannot* be viewed as merely the desperate 'last recourse' of threatened Serbs; nor can Tudjman be exonerated *even where the defence of Croatia is concerned*; and nor, finally, is it possible to proceed as if it was clearly the earnest wish, on the part of the United States, Britain, and France to find a just solution to the conflict. On the contrary, such doubts, *inter alia*, have been raised in this book.

As for the volume assembled and edited by Quintin Hoare and Noel Malcolm, I found this to be an invaluable collection of short reviews of works relating, in whole or in part, to Bosnia, published in West

European languages (chiefly English, German, and French) since 1990, with sharp, often witty, and occasionally brief summaries of the literature. The editors' judgements impress me as generally reliable, and the book will surely remain indispensable for those desiring a summary guide to a voluminous literature on Bosnia.

The editors divide their coverage into two parts. Part One contains three sections: *essential readings* (listing twenty-one books and one monograph, three of which appear on my own list of personal favourites at the end of this volume, pp. 305–18); *other recommended readings* (listing sixty-four books and monographs, one of which appears on my list of personal favourites); and *other readings* (listing 253 books and monographs, six of which appear on my list of personal favourites). In Part Two, the editors reprint longer reviews of nineteen books. Coverage includes works in English, German, French, Italian, Spanish, Norwegian, Swedish, and Dutch.

The editors cannot be accused of indulgence towards authors for whose work they feel contempt, dismissing one work for 'half-baked populism', 'sloppy mistakes', and 'ludicrous' statements,[152] another for 'misleading if not downright mystificatory over-simplifications',[153] still another as 'touching but very insubstantial',[154] and yet another for being 'intolerably sentimental and inaccurate'.[155] Commenting on Nathaniel Harris's *The War in Former Yugoslavia* (1997), they write, 'Pity the "young people" subjected to this kind of dumbing down, where everything is relativized, facts are few and far between, explanation is perfunctory, and Western politicians like international bodies are above criticism.'[156] Some of the characterizations are so pejorative as to provoke the occasional morbid chuckle. Edgar O'Ballance's *Civil War in Bosnia* (1995) is 'dismally unintelligent, . . . [and] lacks even the slightest documentary value'.[157] Gabriel Plisson's *Mourir pour Sarajevo* (1994) is a 'rag-bag of a book', containing 'snippets of useful information, but also some errors'.[158] Mary Pat Kelly's *'Good to Go': The Rescue of Scott O'Grady from Bosnia* (1997) is an 'excessively detailed account of a minor incident' filled with 'long extracts' from interviews conducted with everyone involved.[159] Perhaps the most damning review in the Hoare/Malcolm volume is that accorded to Yossef Bodansky, whose *Offensive in the Balkans* (1995), an 'unusually shrill piece of pro-Pale [i.e., pro-Bosnian Serb] polemics', offers a warning that a military intervention in Bosnia might well ignite a Third World War. Hoare and Malcolm comment: 'Curiously, the text was produced in November 1995: anyone can get predictions wrong in advance of the event, but it requires a special talent to make false predictions about events that have already happened.'[160] But perhaps my 'favourite' review in this collection – if I may put it that way – is the editors' characterization of Edward Ricciuti's *War in Yugoslavia* (1993) as a 'picture-book, apparently produced for schoolchildren or dim students, . . . [which] manages to discuss the origins of the war without blaming anyone or anything (except "1,500 years of history". . .)'.[161]

But I would be remiss if I did not acknowledge that Hoare and Malcolm are also generous with praise when they feel that one or another book merits praise – and many books receive accolades from the polyglot reviewers.

Back in 1991, as the war in Slovenia was drawing to a close, a high-ranking Serbian official remarked that the coming conflict in Croatia would make what had happened in Slovenia look like Disneyland. Of course, picking up the Disneyland motif, one might note that the Krajina could, properly enough, be translated as Frontierland, while Kosovo has perhaps earned the sobriquet Adventureland, recalling that most 'adventures' have a desperate character to them. Macedonia might be Never-neverland, at least in the eyes of Greek nationalists who wanted nothing less than to expunge its name and history altogether. I think of Bosnia as Tomorrowland, indicating a sense of foreboding for the future and offering a warning of a possible 'future' to be avoided. Serbia under Milošević figured – dare I say *clearly*? – as a kind of Fantasyland, where fantasies of national salvation raised Serbian spirits to dizzying heights, only to see their spirits dashed in the course of eight years of war and privation. And dominating Fantasyland is, of course, Sleeping Beauty's Castle, where the slumbering beauty lies in repose until a princely kiss will awaken her. Serbia's Sleeping Beauty's Castle is the so-called House of Flowers, where Tito lies buried. But Yugoslavia's sleeping beauty, unlike Disney's, will sleep forever. The only fairy tales still circulating in this Fantasyland are the dangerous ones.

NOTES

1 Steven L. Burg, *Conflict and Cohesion in Socialist Yugoslavia: Political Decision-Making since 1966* (Princeton, NJ: Princeton University Press, 1983), p. 339.
2 George Schöpflin, 'Political Decay in One-Party Systems in Eastern Europe', in Pedro Ramet (ed.), *Yugoslavia in the 1980s* (Boulder, CO: West-view Press, 1985), pp. 312, 321.
3 See the contributions by Christine von Kohl and Julie Mertus to the round table on Kosovo in *Human Rights Review*, 1, 2 (January–March 2000).
4 Ciaran Cronin and Pablo De Greiff, 'Editors' Introduction' to Jürgen Habermas, *The Inclusion of the Other: Studies in Political Theory*, trans. from German by Ciaran Cronin et al. (Cambridge: Polity Press, 1998), pp. xxvii, xxxi.

5 See, in particular, my *Whose Democracy? Nationalism, Religion, and the Doctrine of Collective Rights in Post-1989 Eastern Europe* (Lanham, MD: Rowman & Littlefield, 1997), esp. introduction, chap. 3, conclusion; 'Evil and the Obsolescence of State Sovereignty', *Human Rights Review*, 1, 2 (January–March 2000), pp. 127–35; 'The Classical Liberal Tradition: Versions, Subversions, Aversions, Traversions, Reversions', in Oto Luthar, Keith A. McLeod, and Mitja Žagar (eds.), *Liberal Democracy, Citizenship and Education* (Niagara Falls, NY: Mosaic Press, 2001), pp. 46–67; and *Balkan Babel: The Disintegration of Yugoslavia from the Death of Tito to the Fall of Milošević*, 4th edn (Boulder, CO: Westview Press, 2002).

6 Review of Susan L. Woodward's *Balkan Tragedy: Chaos and Dissolution after the Cold War* (Washington, DC: Brookings Institution Press, 1995) by Attila Hoare, in *Bosnia Report*, 15 (April–June 1996), reprinted in Quintin Hoare and Noel Malcolm (eds.), *Books on Bosnia* (London: Bosnian Institute, nd [1999]), pp. 175–6.

7 Steven L. Burg and Paul S. Shoup, *The War in Bosnia-Herzegovina: Ethnic Conflict and International Intervention* (Armonk, NY: M. E. Sharpe, 1999), p. 10.

8 As I have noted in my 'Classical Liberal Tradition', pp. 50–1, 53–5.

9 Milovan Djilas, *Wartime*, trans. from Serbian by Michael B. Petrovich (New York: Harcourt Brace Jovanovich, 1977), pp. 40, 120.

10 CIA, 'Yugoslavia – Political', *National Intelligence Survey* (1 October 1957), classified secret, declassified 22 November 2000 under the Freedom of Information Act by the authority of NND 011144, by SDT/SL, Vol. 9, Section 50, Chap. V, NIS #21, on deposit at the National Archives II, RG-273, Box 92.

11 Christopher Bennett, *Yugoslavia's Bloody Collapse: Causes, Course and Consequences* (Washington Square, NY: New York University Press, 1995), p. 187. See also p. 94.

12 *Ibid.*, p. 186.

13 Nataša Mrvić-Petrović, 'A Brief History of the State of Bosnia-Herzegovina (from its Origins to the 1995 Dayton Peace Accords)', in Vesna Nikolić-Ristanović (ed.), *Women, Violence and War: Wartime Victimization of Refugees in the Balkans* (Budapest: Central European University Press, 2000), p. 13. See also p. 12; and Bennett, *Yugoslavia's Bloody Collapse*, p. 238.

14 Viktor Meier, *Yugoslavia: A History of Its Demise*, trans. from German by Sabrina Ramet (London and New York: Routledge, 1999), p. 211.

15 Warren Zimmermann, *Origins of a Catastrophe: Yugoslavia and Its Destroyers*, revised edn (New York: Times Books, 1999).

16 Robert M. Hayden, *Blueprints for a House Divided: The Constitutional Logic of the Yugoslav Conflicts* (Ann Arbor, MI: University of Michigan Press, 1999) p. 29.

17 *Ibid.*, pp. 64–5.

18 Norman Cigar, *Genocide in Bosnia: The Policy of 'Ethnic Cleansing'* (College Station, TX: Texas A&M University Press, 1995).

19 Thomas Cushman and Stjepan G. Meštrovic (eds.), *This Time We Knew: Western Responses to Genocide in Bosnia* (New York and London: New York University Press, 1996).

20 Reneo Lukić and Allen Lynch, *Europe from the Balkans to the Urals: The Disintegration of Yugoslavia and the Soviet Union* (Oxford: Oxford University Press, 1996).

21 James J. Sadkovich, *The US Media and Yugoslavia, 1991–1995* (Westport, CT: Praeger, 1998).

22 Michael Sells, *The Bridge Betrayed: Religion and Genocide in Bosnia* (Berkeley and Los Angeles: University of California Press, 1996).

23 Laura Silber and Allan Little, *The Death of Yugoslavia* (London: Penguin Books and BBC Books, 1995).

24 Bennett, *Yugoslavia's Bloody Collapse*, p. 135.

25 Hayden, *Blueprints*, p. 81.

26 Thomas Cushman and Stjepan G. Meštrovic, 'Introduction', in Cushman and Meštrovic, *This Time We Knew*, p. 18.

27 Sells, *Bridge Betrayed*, p. 95.

28 Slavko Granić, 'The Croatian Coat of Arms: Historical Emblem or Controversial Symbol?', *Journal of Croatian Studies*, 34–5 (1993–4), pp. 5–28.

29 Silber and Little, *Death of Yugoslavia*, p. 87.

30 *Ibid.*, p. 105.

31 Meier, *Yugoslavia*, p. 134.

32 Sells, *Bridge Betrayed*, p. 8.

33 See the case of Gojko Šušak and Josip Reihl-Kir, described in Silber and Little, *Death of Yugoslavia*, pp. 153–4, 157.

34 James J. Sadkovich, *Franjo Tuđman: A Political and Intellectual Biography* (manuscript, work in progress), chap. 1, pp. 3, 7. I am grateful to the author for permission to quote from his work-in-progress.

35 *Ibid.*, chap. 1, pp. 13–14, and chap. 5, p. 1.

36 Beverly Crawford, 'Explaining Defection from International Cooperation: Germany's Unilateral Recognition of Croatia', *World Politics*, 48, 4 (July 1996), p. 483.

37 Burg and Shoup, *War in Bosnia-Herzegovina*, p. 98.

38 *Ibid.*, p. 97.

39 For a convincing refutation of the usual anti-German 'arguments' raised in connection with the War of Yugoslav Succession, see Daniele Conversi, *German-Bashing and the Breakup of Yugoslavia*, Donald W. Treadgold Papers in Russian, East European, and Central Asian Studies, no. 16 (Seattle: Henry M. Jackson School of International Studies of the University of Washington, 1998).

40 Lukić and Lynch, *Europe from the Balkans to the Urals*, p. 271.

41 *Ibid.*, p. 272.

42 *Ibid.*, p. 273.

43 John Major, *The Autobiography* (New York: HarperCollins, 1999), p. 534.

44 Sarah A. Kent, 'Writing the Yugoslav Wars: English-Language Books on Bosnia (1992–1996) and the Challenges of Analyzing Contemporary History', *American Historical Review*, 102, 4 (October 1997), p. 109. The account given by Silber and Little in *Death of Yugoslavia* (pp. 220–1) is close in spirit to Kent's analysis, criticizing Germany's advocacy of recognition but declining to blame the subsequent flare-up of hostilities in Bosnia on that recognition.

45 Norbert Both, *From Indifference to Entrapment: The Netherlands and the Yugoslav Crisis 1990–1995* (Amsterdam: Amsterdam University Press, 2000), p. 90.

46 *Ibid.*, p. 91.

47 *Ibid.*, p. 105.

48 *Ibid.*, pp. 114–18.

49 *Ibid.*, p. 123.

50 *Ibid.*, p. 131.

51 *Ibid.*, pp. 133–4.

52 Silber and Little, *Death of Yugoslavia*, p. 231.

53 Burg and Shoup, *War in Bosnia-Herzegovina*, p. 69.

54 *Ibid.*, p. 117.

55 *Ibid.*, p. 98.

56 *Ibid.*, p. 119.

57 Hayden, *Blueprints*, p. 68.

58 *Ibid.*, p. 114.

59 Robert M. Hayden, 'Constitutional Nationalism in the Formerly Yugoslav Republics', *Slavic Review*, 51, 4 (Winter 1992), pp. 654–73.

60 Cigar, *Genocide in Bosnia*, p. 122.

61 Lukić and Lynch, *Europe from the Balkans to the Urals*, p. 204.

62 *Ibid.*, p. 205.

63 Both, *From Indifference to Entrapment*, p. 153.

64 Marie-Janine Calic, *Krieg und Frieden in Bosnien-Hercegovina*, revised and expanded edn (Frankfurt-am-Main: Suhrkamp, 1996), p. 192.

65 Brendan Simms, *Unfinest Hour: Britain and the Destruction of Bosnia* (London: Penguin, 2002 edn).

66 James Gow, *Triumph of the Lack of Will: International Diplomacy and the Yugoslav War* (London: C. Hurst & Co.), 1997, pp. 175–6, 235–49.

67 Carole Rogel, *The Breakup of Yugoslavia and the War in Bosnia* (Westport, CT: Greenwood Press, 1998), p. 63.

68 See Both, *From Indifference to Entrapment*, p. 229.

69 *Ibid.*, p. 157.

70 *Ibid.*

71 Tim Judah, *The Serbs: History, Myth, and the Destruction of Yugoslavia* (New Haven, CT: Yale University Press, 1997), p. 299.

72 Francine Friedman, review of Norman Cigar's *Genocide in Bosnia*, in *Slavic Review*, 55, 2 (Summer 1996), p. 462.

73 Bennett, *Yugoslavia's Bloody Collapse*, p. 171.

74 Burg and Shoup, *War in Bosnia-Herzegovina*, p. 89.

75 *Ibid.*, p. 181.

76 Cigar, *Genocide in Bosnia*, p. 4.

77 Quoted in Francis A. Boyle, *The Bosnian People Charge Genocide: Proceedings at the International Court of Justice Concerning Bosnia v. Serbia on the Prevention and Punishment of the Crime of Genocide* (Amherst, MA: Aletheia Press, 1996), p. 95.

78 Silber and Little, *Death of Yugoslavia*, p. 271.

79 Quoted in Sells, *Bridge Betrayed*, p. 3.

80 Aleksa Djilas, 'The Nation That Wasn't', in Nader Mousavizadeh (ed.), *The Black Book of Bosnia: The Consequences of Appeasement* (New York: New Republic Book/Basic Books, 1996), p. 25.

81 Burg and Shoup, *War in Bosnia-Herzegovina*, pp. 46, 47.

82 Cushman and Meštrović, 'Introduction', p. 28.

83 *Ibid.*

84 Silber and Little, *Death of Yugoslavia*, p. 230; first bracketed phrase inserted by Silber and Little; second bracketed phrase inserted by SPR.

85 Bennett, *Yugoslavia's Bloody Collapse*, p. 238.

86 Burg and Shoup, *War in Bosnia-Herzegovina*, p. 14.

87 'Croatia: Impunity for Abuses Committed During "Operation Storm" and the Denial of the Right of Refugees to the Krajina', *Human Rights Watch/ Helsinki*, vol. 8. No. 13 (August 1996), p. 7.

88 Burg and Shoup, *War in Bosnia-Herzegovina*, p. 414.

89 *Ibid.*, p. 402. On p. 183, in explaining why Bosnian Serb policies ought not to be viewed as genocide, they urge that 'the practice of expelling Muslims from Serb-controlled territories and the tendency to single out men and boys for execution – while in themselves despicable – seem contrary to an intent to destroy the Muslim people *as such*' (their emphasis).

90 Quoted in Sells, *Bridge Betrayed*, p. 24.

91 *Ibid.*, p. 25.

92 Cigar, *Genocide in Bosnia*, p. 74.

93 Quoted *ibid.*

94 *Ibid.*, p. 133.

95 *Ibid.*, p. 160.

96 Jasminka Udovički, 'Introduction', to Jasminka Udovički and James Ridgeway (eds.), *Burn This House: The Making and Unmaking of Yugoslavia*, rev. and expanded edn (Durham, NC: Duke University Press, 2000), p. 1.

97 *Ibid.*, pp. 3, 5–6.

98 *Ibid.*, p. 6.

99 Milan Milošević, 'The Media Wars: 1987–1997', in Udovički and Ridgeway, *Burn This House*, p. 112.

100 *Ibid.*, p. 114.

101 *Ibid.*, p. 124.
102 Jasminka Udovički, 'Kosovo', in Udovički and Ridgeway, *Burn This House*, p. 317.
103 *Ibid.*, p. 325.
104 *Ibid.*, pp. 326–7.
105 *Ibid.*, p. 330.
106 Attila Hoare, review of Jasminka Udovički and James Ridgeway (eds.), *Yugoslavia's Ethnic Nightmare* (1995), in Hoare and Malcolm, *Books on Bosnia*, p. 68.
107 Ejub Štitkovac, 'Croatia: The First War', in Udovički and Ridgeway, *Burn This House*, p. 164.
108 Udovički, 'Kosovo', p. 324.
109 Sven Balas, 'The Opposition in Croatia', in Udovički and Ridgeway, *Burn This House*, pp. 267–80.
110 Jasminka Udovički and Ejub Štitkovac, 'Bosnia and Hercegovina: The Second War', in Udovički and Ridgeway, *Burn This House*, p. 183.
111 Sadkovich, *US Media*, p. 37.
112 *Ibid.*, p. 67.
113 See *ibid.*, p. xvi.
114 *Ibid.*, p. 88.
115 *Ibid.*, pp. 157–8.
116 For a corrective, see Carole Hodge, *The Serb Lobby in the United Kingdom*, Donald W. Treadgold Papers in Russian, East European, and Central Asian Studies, no. 22 (Seattle: Henry M. Jackson School of International Studies of the University of Washington, September 1999), pp. 13 and 65, n. 34.
117 Sadkovich, *US Media*, p. 165.
118 Lenard J. Cohen, *Broken Bonds*, 1st edn (Boulder, CO: Westview Press, 1993), as quoted in Sadkovich, *US Media*, p. 239.
119 Sadkovich, *US Media*, pp. 132–3.
120 *Ibid.*, p. 143.
121 Sadkovich later reviewed the Burg/Shoup volume, which he thought 'appear[ed] sympathetic to the JNA and the Serbs'. He also charged that 'Burg and Shoup treat atrocities selectively, viewing Croatian expulsions of Muslims as "state-sponsored", but speculating that the Serbian "scorched-earth approach" suggests . . . either a total lack of control by Serb leaders over extremists, or an obsession with removing all signs of Muslim presence.' According to Sadkovich, Burg and Shoup also ignored important literature and slid into 'moral equivalency'. Sadkovich's review was published in *Review of International Affairs*, 1, 1 (Autumn 2001), pp. 99–102.
122 Burg and Shoup, *War in Bosnia-Herzegovina*, p. 11 (as already noted in the text of this chapter).
123 *Ibid.*, p. 402.
124 *Ibid.*, p. 10.
125 Bruno Simma, 'Die NATO, die UN und militärische Gewaltanwendung: Rechtliche Aspekte', in Reinhard Merkel (ed.), *Der Kosovo-Krieg und das Völkerrecht* (Frankfurt-am-Main: Suhrkamp, 2000), pp. 11–13.

126 See, for example, Andreas Hasenclever, *Die Macht der Moral in der internationalen Politik: Militärische Interventionen westlicher Staaten in Somalia, Ruanda und Bosnien-Herzegowina* (Frankfurt: Campus Verlag, 2000), p. 39.

127 Burg and Shoup, *War in Bosnia-Herzegovina*, pp. 6, 7.

128 Gow, *Triumph of the Lack of Will.*

129 Burg and Shoup, *War in Bosnia-Herzegovina*, p. 401.

130 *Ibid.*, p. 59.

131 *Ibid.*, p. 187.

132 *Ibid.*, p. 79.

133 See, for example, *ibid.*, pp. 109, 121–2, 176, 183, 367, 405.

134 See, for example, *ibid.*, pp. 13, 52, 168, 195, 284, 364, 375.

135 See, for example, *ibid.*, pp. 184, 401–2.

136 Jovan Divjak, 'The First Phase, 1992–1993: Struggle for Survival and Genesis of the Army of Bosnia-Herzegovina', in Branka Magaš and Ivo Žanić (eds.), *The War in Croatia and Bosnia-Herzegovina 1991–1995* (London and Portland: Frank Cass, 2001), p. 154.

137 Burg and Shoup, *War in Bosnia-Herzegovina*, p. 74. According to a CIA publication, the Council for the National Defence of the Muslim Nation was formed in June 1991. See *Balkan Battlegrounds: A Military History of the Yugoslav Conflict, 1990–1995*, 2 vols. (Washington, DC: Office of Russian and European Analysis of the Central Intelligence Agency, May 2002), vol. I, p. 130.

138 Branka Magaš and Ivo Žanić (eds.), *Rat u Hrvatskoj i Bosni i Hercegovini 1991–1995* (Zagreb/Sarajevo/London: Naklada Jesenski i Turk, Dani, and Bosnian Institute, 1999).

139 It was followed by: *Balkan Battlegrounds*, the second volume of which consists mainly of maps.

140 Martin Špegelj, "The First Phase, 1990–1992: The JNA Prepares for Aggression and Croatia for Defence", in Magaš and Žanić, *The War in Croatia and Bosnia-Herzegovina*, p. 39.

141 *Ibid.*, p. 29.

142 *Ibid.*, p. 34.

143 *Ibid.*, p. 35.

144 Anton Tus, 'The War in Slovenia and Croatia up to the Sarajevo Ceasefire', in Magaš and Žanić, *The War in Croatia and Bosnia-Herzegovina*, p. 50.

145 *Ibid.*, p. 56.

146 Ozren Žunec, 'Operations Flash and Storm', in Magaš and Žanić, *The War in Croatia and Bosnia-Herzegovina*, p. 71.

147 *Ibid.*, p. 83.

148 Divjak, 'The First Phase, 1992–1993', p. 167.

149 Marko Attila Hoare, 'Civilian–Military Relations in Bosnia-Herzegovina 1992–1995', in Magaš and Žanić, *The War in Croatia and Bosnia-Herzegovina*, pp. 178–9.

150 *Ibid.*, pp. 195–6.

151 Marko Attila Hoare, comments in 'Discussion: The International Response', in Magaš and Žanić, *The War in Croatia and Bosnia-Herzegovina*, pp. 308–9.

152 Hoare and Malcolm, *Books on Bosnia*, p. 68.
153 *Ibid.*, p. 69.
154 *Ibid.*, p. 73.
155 *Ibid.*, p. 69.
156 *Ibid.*
157 *Ibid.*, p. 53.
158 *Ibid.*, p. 54.
159 *Ibid.*, p. 63.
160 *Ibid.*, p. 57.
161 *Ibid.*, p. 70.

REFERENCES

Both, Norbert, *From Indifference to Entrapment: The Netherlands and the Yugoslav Crisis 1990–1995* (Amsterdam: Amsterdam University Press, 2000), p. 267.

Burg, Steven L. and Paul S. Shoup, *The War in Bosnia-Herzegovina: Ethnic Conflict and International Intervention* (Armonk, NY: M. E. Sharpe, 1999), p. 499.

Cigar, Norman, *Genocide in Bosnia: The Policy of 'Ethnic Cleansing'* (College Station, TX: Texas A&M University Press, 1995), p. 247.

Hoare, Quintin and Noel Malcolm (eds.), *Books on Bosnia* (London: Bosnian Institute, nd [1999]), p. 207.

Lukić, Reneo and Allen Lynch, *Europe from the Balkans to the Urals: The Disintegration of Yugoslavia and the Soviet Union* (Oxford: Oxford University Press, 1996), p. 436.

Magaš, Branka and Ivo Žanić (eds.), *The War in Croatia and Bosnia-Herzegovina 1991–1995* (London and Portland: Frank Cass, 2001), p. 383.

Sadkovich, James J., *The US Media and Yugoslavia, 1991–1995* (Westport, CT: Praeger, 1998), p. 272.

Sells, Michael A., *The Bridge Betrayed: Religion and Genocide in Bosnia* (Berkeley and Los Angeles: University of California Press, 1996), p. 244.

Silber, Laura and Allan Little, *The Death of Yugoslavia* (London: Penguin Books and BBC Books, 1995), p. 400.

Udovički, Jasminka and James Ridgeway (eds.), *Burn This House: The Making and Unmaking of Yugoslavia*, rev. and expanded edn (Durham, NC: Duke University Press, 2000), p. 386.

2 The collapse of East European communism

The collapse of communism throughout Eastern Europe and the Soviet Union was not irrelevant to the disintegration of Yugoslavia. On the contrary, the Yugoslav disintegration may be usefully viewed as connected with trends throughout the region, in the sense that Yugoslavia shared a common ideology of equality and problems of legitimation, economic degeneration, and institutional dysfunctionality with other states in the region. Moreover, insofar as 'self-managing socialism' was intended to constitute a third path between the 'state capitalism' of the Soviet bloc and the 'monopoly capitalism' of the American-led bloc, and insofar as the Yugoslavs had long profited from playing one superpower against the other, the implosion and breakup not only of the Soviet bloc but also of the Soviet Union itself could not but have a direct and significant impact on the Yugoslav federation. This is not to say that, once the Soviet bloc collapsed, Yugoslavia necessarily had to break up. But it is to say that Yugoslavia would inevitably have been affected by trends unleashed by that historic process. Chapters 3–4 take up the questions of why Yugoslavia broke apart and why it slid into sanguinary war. What this chapter contributes is a discussion of the context in which Yugoslavia's disintegration took place.

II

As long as the communists held sway in Eastern Europe, Western social scientists could be found arguing variously that there was no significant change occurring in the communist world (e.g., Bauman,[1] Korboński),[2] that change was occurring via erosion and decay moving ineluctably and inexorably in the direction of system collapse and revolution (e.g., Conquest,[3] Schöpflin,[4] Kux[5]), and that change was occurring through precisely identifiable phases but that elites could, through their policy choices, affect the evolutionary path through which their systems passed (e.g., Meyer,[6] Tucker,[7] Jowitt[8]).

In the period after 1989, Western social scientists interested in the Russian and East European world continued their earlier debate in a new guise. Social scientists may now be broken down once more into three groups. There are, first, those who believe that communism was a largely or purely evil phenomenon which was overthrown by democratic capitalism in a 'Glorious Revolution' (apologies to Charles II); here I am thinking of analysts such as Fukuyama,[9] Weigel,[10] and Tismaneanu.[11] These authors subscribe to an insurrection model of revolution, emphasizing the role of dissidents (or, if one prefers, opposition elites) in bringing down the communist system. Then there are those who view the events of 1989–90 not as an insurrection coming out of nowhere, but as an organic part of long-term processes of decay, on the understanding that all great revolutions (whether one thinks of the French Revolution, the Bolshevik Revolution, or the Chinese Revolution) occurred at the culmination of extended periods of decay. Of the authors under review here, Philipsen notes, for example, that 'far from being spontaneous [or sudden], the revolution had been building for years'.[12] And, finally, there are those who define revolution along the lines of the first group of authors, but share, with the second group, an understanding of the events of 1989 as organically related to the dynamics of change unfolding over the preceding decades. Adherents of this third school (Poznański in particular) therefore argue that no revolution took place in 1989, and that it makes more sense to emphasize the continuity of post-communist systems with their communist predecessors than to dwell on discontinuities.

I am struck by the theoretical compatibility between the pre-1989 advocates that communist systems were impervious to significant change and those who now deny that anything revolutionary occurred in 1989. Again, the pre-1989 analysts of decay have something in common with pluralist triumphalists such as Fukuyama, Tismaneanu, and Weigel. And, again, there are some broad theoretical continuities between pre-1989 analyses of phases in system change and post-1989 analyses that link revolutionary collapse to extended periods of decay.

The distinction between revolution and insurrection is crucial to an understanding of the tapestry of issues at stake here. R. L. Leslie distinguishes between revolutions, in which internal pressures reach the point where eruption is unavoidable, and insurrections, in which the insurgents, responding to a situation which they consider unacceptable, decide autonomously to have recourse to force.[13] According to this interpretation, then, revolution is seen as a cathartic stage in an evolving process, while an insurrection may occur even in conditions entirely unpropitious for disturbances or political upheaval. This distinction is crucial because those who most strenuously protest that no revolution occurred in 1989 (e.g., Poznański, as indicated above) generally conflate revolution with insurrection, and construe revolution as a disjunction having no organic connection with what preceded it. An alternative way to think of revolution is to construe it as 'a change in the principles of legitimation and order underpinning a political system'. In this latter view, 'Revolution does not have to occur in a flash. Few revolutions do . . . [In fact,] revolutions are *always* evolutionary, and yet they are revolutions all the same'.[14]

Confusion (or, for that matter, disagreement) over words often goes hand in hand with confusion (or disagreement) over methodologies and conclusions. Take, for example, Horvath and Szakolczai. These two authors maintain that 'the very fact of [the] collapse [of communism] and especially the way it happened overthrew *all* existing theoretical frameworks used in the past for the analysis of the internal structure of these states'.[15] If this were true, then presumably the only recourse would be to begin the slow process of building up entirely new theoretical frameworks, which would be free of the concerns, assumptions, and methodologies of the now-abandoned theories of past writers. No more would students of political science read Hobbes or Mill or Hegel or Kant or, for that matter, Almond or Verba or Pye or Huntington or Brinton's brilliant study of revolution, or any other producers of 'existing theoretical frameworks'. Was it the authors' intention to urge such vast despair? Perhaps not. But the mere fact that their doleful lament could find its way into print was symptomatic of the fact that some scholars had reached an intellectual dead end.

This despair is, moreover, founded on a myth. Various scholars, among whom Ernst Kux and George Schöpflin were, as far as I know, the first, pointed out throughout the 1980s that the communist systems were in decay, that a revolutionary transition had already begun – and it is not to their discredit that other scholars did not take them seriously or, in some cases, even deny that they had ever written anything prescient. A 1984 publication focusing on religious ferment in the East European region noted, for example, that this ferment 'presents the communist authorities with a challenge as trying and as complex as the multifaceted economic woes currently afflicting the region, and perhaps as dangerous [to the communist organizational monopoly] in the long run as the crisis of legitimacy brought into focus by the appearance of the independent trade union Solidarity between 1980 and 1981'[16] – thus identifying the crisis of legitimacy, economic deterioration, and religious ferment as forces for change. Three years later, the same author drew attention to the fact that 'in all of these countries [of Eastern Europe], the combination of countervailing pressures is producing a breakdown of earlier patterns of modus vivendi'; moreover, as the communist systems sank into crisis, 'system decay' and collapse loomed – the author noted – as a distinct possibility.[17] Students of popular culture were, moreover, particularly well situated to pick up on symptoms of decay, not because these processes started in the cultural sphere – they started in the political sphere – but because the cultural sphere provides a canvas on which the trends in politics may be projected[18] (and thereby reinforced). (Anyone who has ever seen Václav Havel's play, *The Temptation*, or read Ludvik Vaculik's *A Cup of Coffee with My Interrogator* can scarcely have failed to grasp this point.) Among those scholars whose works are discussed in this chapter, at least one (Vladimir Tismaneanu) seems to have been aware by 1987, if not earlier, that the political escarpment in Eastern Europe was shifting. But the myth of collective ignorance has had devout believers, evidence to the contrary notwithstanding.[19]

A deep methodological chasm separated the self-described 'realists' from those I call 'idealists'. Realists, specifically, emphasized party control of communications, security and military forces, the official media, political structures, and the economy itself, and therefore downplayed pressures for change. They tended to limit their research interviews to government people, the more prominent the better, thereby choosing tunnel vision and ignoring what was happening on the fringes. Idealists, by contrast, emphasized changes in the moral consensus, in political culture, the persistence of resistance in various forms, and the growing consensus among the public on two key points: (1) that the system was illegitimate, and (2) that it was necessary to create zones for legitimate social and political action, in effect to construct an underground parallel society. Idealists conducted interviews not only with government officials but also with human rights activists, ecclesiastical figures, feminists, journalists, and even, in some cases, rock stars. Based on this broader sampling, from which government officials were not excluded, idealists concluded, soon after 1980, that the pressures for change in East-Central Europe were significant and ultimately could not be resisted.

Writing as early as 1984, Schöpflin already understood the processes at work:

The East European political experience since the communist revolution has had one extraordinarily paradoxical and contradictory aspect . . . [T]he need for reform . . . [simultaneously] increases and looks ever less likely to be achieved, so that change requires a major upheaval . . . Orderly, incremental change weakens or disappears as an alternative from the mental map of politics.[20]

Schöpflin identified processes of political decay throughout the region and noted that pressures for democratization were increasing – pressures which he predicted would only accelerate the decay of communist systems throughout the region.

Even earlier, in March 1980, Ernst Kux was able to anticipate a deepening of economic and political crisis eventually leading to a situation in which 'upheavals could develop in a number or all of the East European countries more or less simultaneously'.[21] Writing nearly ten years before his prediction would be fulfilled, Kux was able to identify accurately the factors that would culminate in the collapse of the communist system in East-Central Europe. It is a pity that scholars seem to have forgotten about his work.

Somewhat later, a Helsinki Watch publication of 1986 spoke of Poland's 'quiet revolution', and detailed the strategy of the Polish underground, which was said to involve, above all, the construction of parallel social, educational, cultural, and even scientific institutions and structures that would slowly sap the communist system of its power.[22] What all of these forecasts had in common was that they took society seriously; they did not assume that all important information, decisions, and actions came from the government, as the 'realists' did. They did not assume that real change was precluded in advance, as Bauman's nonetheless brilliant essay of 1971 argued.

III

The literature to be discussed here is only a small sampling of the burgeoning literature on the post-communist transformation in Eastern Europe, but provides a lens through which to examine the theoretical debate brought into focus by the collapse of communism and the ensuing and still unfinished political transition. In particular, as I shall show, as important for the researcher's ultimate sensitivity to incipient changes and to gathering trends as the choice between realism and idealism was the choice of what is called 'level of analysis'.

The most widespread choice made by researchers throughout the period after the Second World War has been one variant or another of what could be called elite-centric (or 'top-down') analysis. This would include elite analysis (by which I mean analysis of the ruling elite), studies of party and governmental behaviour, and any analyses taking as their starting point the decision-maker (including the most common versions of both rational choice theory and nonrational analysis).[23] The fundamental assumption made by such analysts is that policies, decisions, ideas, changes – indeed, all 'important' political phenomena

– originate at the top of the political pyramid (or at least somewhere near the top) and flow downwards. It follows that the only people worth talking to are high government officials and, possibly, fellow scholars. The notion that opposition groups such as Charter 77 (in Czechoslovakia), Solidarity (in Poland), or the pacifist movement (in the German Democratic Republic) could have any impact was dismissed by many adherents of this approach, who were wont to chuckle to themselves when those studying these phenomena showed that they took them seriously. Political change, according to the 'elite-centric' view, came on the initiative of the elite, who were presumed to be able to select the timing, pace, form, and character of such change as might occur. Earlier macroadjustments, such as the economic reform packages adopted throughout the region in the 1960s, could be explained entirely in terms of elite decision-making, and even the Prague Spring of 1968 did not serve to confute the certainty that adherents of this school felt. There is a strong tendency for adherents of the elite-centric approach to be 'realists', but not all 'realists' are absorbed in elite analysis.

The chief alternative to the elite-centric approach is, as might be guessed, the socio-centric (or 'bottom-up') approach, which takes society and its composite actors as the point of departure. The political culture and (usually) interest group approaches fit in here, alongside studies of social movements and opposition currents, as well as politically driven studies of culture, among others. Shifting the level of analysis from government to society has tangible consequences for assumptions, methodology, even for one's choice of interview subjects. Indeed, a researcher subscribing to a 'socio-centric' approach would expect to learn more about social and political change from talking to people engaged in the cultural sector than from government ministers. Adherents of this approach emphasize the vulnerability of any government to pressures from below and appreciate that no political or economic system should ever be taken as permanent or final. At this level of analysis, change is typically given more emphasis. There is a strong tendency for adherents of the socio-centric approach to be idealists, but not all idealists engage in socio-centric analysis.

The works under review here include three single-authored monographs, two edited collections, and two compilations of interview data (the Philipsen compilation being far more integrated and more fully analysed than the Horvath/Szakolczai compilation). In terms of methodology, the books by Tismaneanu and Philipsen are the clearest examples of socio-centric analysis, while those by Poznański are the clearest examples, in this set, of elite-centric analysis.

The respective authors also subscribe to entirely different models of the transition. I have identified three models among this literature: the transition as revolution (Aslund, Hockenos, Philipsen, Tismaneanu); the transition as collapse (Horvath and Szakolczai); and the transition as evolutionary transformation (Poznański and some of his contributors). Differing assumptions underline these competing models. For Philipsen, for example, it is a given that the masses played a central role in the changes unleashed in 1989; his is a view of a mass-driven revolution. The attention which Hockenos pays to opinion poll data betrays the similarity of his interpretation of the events of 1989. Tismaneanu's work, however, reveals an alternative assumption, namely, that dissident elites played the central role in propelling events forward. Without such leadership, he argues, the revolution of 1989 would never have occurred. His model could be described as an insurgent-elite-driven revolution. The difference in leading assumptions helps us, in turn, to understand that there are (at least) two major branches of socio-centric analysis – one examining social attitudes, changes in collective behaviour, and other indices of political culture, and the other focusing on dissident elites and their relationship to society.

By contrast with socio-centric analysis, Horvath and Szakolczai assume that the central and most important fact of the transition was that the establishment elites (i.e., the communists) were no longer in sufficient control – an assumption that recalls Schöpflin's analysis nearly a decade earlier. And, finally, advocates of a model of evolutionary transformation assume that the establishment elites were in a position to control significant aspects of the direction of personal well-being. Elsewhere, Poznański has argued that the communists themselves destroyed the communist system, in order to construct *nomenklatura* capitalism and enrich themselves personally.[24] As a result, in Poznański's view,

Not only was the ultimate collapse *not* the result of a dramatic revolution, but neither should it be portrayed as the triumph of an abused society – workers and/ or intellectuals – over a privileged party/state intent on defending the status quo. Instead of a heroic process in which society struggled and the party/state resisted, here is a case where the elite often acted to destroy the system by itself – and largely for itself.[25]

But while most analysts write as if one or another of these models will explain processes throughout the entire region, there are grounds for suggesting that the revolutionary model best fits the East German, Polish, and Czechoslovak cases, that the collapse model best fits the cases of Slovenia, Croatia, Bulgaria, and Albania, and that a version of the evolutionary model would best fit the cases of Macedonia, Serbia, and Romania (without suggesting any equivalence among the politics of the latter three countries). Bosnia-Herzegovina's descent into war and division into three sectors marks it as a special case, while Hungary is a very mixed case, with elements of all three models: starting as a case of evolutionary change, then gathering impetus and displaying rapid decay (as per the collapse model), and finally involving mass demonstrations which gave at least the appearance, if not having some of the substance, of revolutionary transformation.

IV

In the following pages, I shall focus my discussion on the respective authors' interpretations of the transformation effected or begun in 1989, their evaluation of the roots of this transformation, and their assessments of the legacies of communism. Most of the authors discussed here would accept the definition of revolution penned by Sigmund Neumann, as 'a sweeping, fundamental change in political organization, social structure, economic property control and the predominant myth of social order, thus indicating a major break in the continuity of development'.[26] But while Philipsen emphasizes the human factor, and most especially underlines the deepening disaffection of the population as a significant element in the spiral towards revolutionary transformation, he also dwells on the speed with which the indigenous domestic opposition, in eastern Germany, disappeared before it was able to put together an effective political organization that might have offered an alternative to annexation by the Federal Republic.

For Philipsen, economic decay lay behind the country's drift towards system collapse. As he put it,

In terms of modern industrial production, the economy was in shambles. Supplies were disorganized, much of the infrastructure oversized and badly outmoded, the environment increasingly threatened by industrial pollution, and inefficiency so institutionalized that work itself proceeded at a desultory pace. As the growth of the East German economy came to a grinding halt in the midseventies, the inefficiency, waste, corruption, and lies that were an organic part of this peculiar Leninist mode of production tangibly began to undermine the system's legitimacy.[27]

Yet, for all that, the opposition, as Philipsen shows, aspired not to create a revolution, but only to reform the system. (This is in sharp contrast to Poland, where leading figures in the political underground spoke explicitly of effecting a gradual and incremental revolution from below.)

Philipsen also presents interview data that demonstrate that the communist elite had likewise become convinced by the mid-1980s that fundamental political change had become imperative.[28] The East German communist elite thought, of course, in terms of a system reform which would leave them at the helm of power, while the political opposition in the GDR believed that the system had reached a dead end and had to be replaced by some form of pluralism. Hence, while both the ruling socialist unity party (SED) and the East German opposition realized that fundamental change was ineluctable, their assessments as to what direction that change should take were themselves fundamentally different.

The thin but illuminating volume by Ånders Aslund largely confirms Philipsen's assessment of the contribution of economic decay to political decay. Aslund highlights problems of shortages, rising inefficiency, technological backwardness, poor incentives, and lack of environmental protection as endemic in the socialist systems, and argues that growth rates across Eastern Europe fell steadily in the 1970s and 1980s. He specifically notes that Poland, the USSR, Bulgaria, Romania, and Albania had reached the point of complete stagnation by 1989.[29] It was, thus, in his view, the economic insolvency of the socialist system which, more than anything else, sowed the seeds of the system's disappearance.

Aslund argued that the advantages of a fast transition (shock therapy) heavily outweighed such advantages as might be attached to more cautious strategies of privatization. Among the reasons he cited are the willingness of people to tighten their belts if they see the possibility of eventual relief, the need to minimize internal inconsistencies within the system, the prevalence of corruption during processes of transition, and his belief that 'a quick systemic change transforms the intellectual climate'.[30] He finally arrives at what he considers the ideal sequencing of transition: first, democratization and political demonopolization; second, the passage of new laws, to provide a legislative framework for subsequent economic transformation; third, passage of a combined package of macroeconomic stabilization and liberalization; fourth, the holding of parliamentary elections; fifth, privatization and the build-up of a strong private sector; and sixth, economic restructuring.[31] What is striking about this sequence is that, with the partial exception of the third factor, it is the precise reverse of the sequence of events in Spain from the end of the civil war in 1939 to the instauration of Prince Juan Carlos as king and the restoration of democracy after Franco's death – a sequencing which, further, has been held up for emulation by Juan Linz and Alfred Stepan.[32] But given that Eastern Europe was in deep economic crisis by the end of the 1980s, as well as the pervasive demands for democratization, the Spanish model was surely irrelevant to Eastern Europe.

Poznański rejects the approach taken by Philipsen and Aslund and pointedly qualifies the role played by economics. Where Aslund writes of stagnation and decline, Poznański argues that 'no economic calamity preceded the recent collapse of the political order, and . . . indeed some countries actually did rather well economically [under communism] (for example Czechoslovakia)'.[33] By contrast with Philipsen and Tismaneanu, Poznański denies that social or popular pressures constituted the primary force for change. On the contrary, Poznański credits the communist parties themselves with having chosen the path of self-destruction – a choice he attributes to a combination of ideological erosion within the party and (paradoxically, given his own mixed picture of the socialist economies) growing party disillusionment with the economic performance attainable under socialism.[34]

Poznański denies that it makes sense to talk of nonviolent revolution, quiet revolution, or gradual revolution. He concludes that the changes surrounding 1989 had a *purely* evolutionary character and criticizes what he calls an erroneous tendency to 'call the disintegration of the communist regimes of Eastern Europe revolutions'.[35] They cannot be revolutions, in his view, because 'the party itself [w]as an equal or more essential force in the collapse'.[36]

Writing no earlier than December 1991,[37] Poznański argued that some form of reformed communism remained a possible scenario for Poland and other states in the region,[38] and predicted that the dominant form of ownership reform even after 1991 would involve various corrupt forms of privatization and the forcing of new private entrepreneurs into patron-client relationship(s) with the political leadership, thus, with reformed communists.[39] Poznański's predictions have proven to be the most accurate where Serbia, Montenegro, Macedonia, Bosnia-Herzegovina, and Albania are concerned. Whereas Aslund called for rapid divesting and privatization, Poznański argued for a gradual withering away of the public sector, asserting that spontaneous privatization may be preferable to rapid privatization orchestrated from above.[40]

Among Poznański's contributors to his 1992 collection, at least one – Valerie Bunce – places a greater emphasis on economic deterioration than does her editor. She also seems to place greater emphasis on the importance of political culture and society in general. In a particularly insightful passage, she notes:

Stalinism cannot be understood simply as an obstacle to capitalism and democracy. Paradoxically . . . Stalinism made some contributions to at least the democratic side of the equation . . . What Stalinism did, in particular, was to create . . . a resourceful and autonomous society – a necessary, but by no means sufficient, condition for liberal democracy.[41]

Other contributors to the 1992 Poznański volume pay some attention to the psychological (Leszek Kolakówski) and economic (Mira Marody) legacies of more than four decades of communist rule. The chief strength of this volume is its attention to economics (especially in chapters by Josef Brada, Janos Kornai, and Jozef van Brabant).

Poznański's 1995 collection was conceived as a sequel to the earlier volume, but differs in having a more explicitly normative thrust. In his introduction, for example, Poznański highlights that 'the minimal state is the goal, while a strong state is the method'.[42] This forthright statement sets the tone for the book, which is prescriptive in the first place, and analytical insofar as analysis backs up policy prescription. Poznański and his 1995 collaborators are, with one exception, concerned to advocate gradualism in economic transformation. This gradualism is given the label 'evolutionary model', which Poznański, alone among the contributors, wants to associate also with an insistence that nothing revolutionary took place in East-Central Europe in 1989–90. In practice, these are, indeed, separable positions; i.e., there is no reason why someone who believes that a gradualist policy in post-communist East-Central Europe is best should necessarily deny the comprehensive nature of the system collapse of 1989–90.

The exception in this collection is Josef Brada, who charges that gradualists are unable to account for some salient economic developments in the Russian–East European area and argues that only a rapid transition has some assurance of realizing the twin goals of economic free enterprise and political pluralism.[43] It is to Poznański's credit that he included both sides of the debate in his book.

V

Vladimir Tismaneanu's two volumes are, without question, among the most useful and most insightful books dealing with the transformation in Eastern Europe which, although having roots earlier, entered a new phase at the end of the 1980s. These two volumes also present an alternative both to Philipsen's analysis, which emphasizes the weakness and difficulty of co-ordination within the opposition and credits spontaneous social upheaval with having effected the collapse of communism in the GDR, and to Poznański's approach, which downplays the importance of either opposition or society and stresses the convictions, decisions, and choices of the ruling elite for providing the propulsive force for change. On the contrary, for Tismaneanu, it is precisely organized opposition which most warrants study in authoritarian systems and which constitutes the most reliable barometer of impending political change.

Although published only in 1990, *In Search of Civil Society* must have been launched early in 1987 at the very latest, given the dates when the composite chapters were completed. As such, the volume's focus on independent peace movements betrayed a prescient understanding of the potential, and ultimately demonstrated, political importance of these movements. Whereas Poznański dismisses grass-roots organizations as virtually meaningless, Tismaneanu attributes to them the capacity to undermine established political systems.[44] And, in contrast to sundry writers who have construed 'revolution' as a brief, sudden, and violent mass action producing the immediate overthrow of political elites, Tismaneanu and his collaborators show deeper understanding of the incremental nature of revolution, realizing that in Eastern Europe the revolution unfolded over a period of a decade (from the appearance of the Polish trade union Solidarity in 1980 to the end of communist domination in the region in 1989–90). In his opening chapter, for example, Tismaneanu notes that Polish independent activist Adam Michnik had formulated a strategy of evolutionism, calling for patience and commitment to a long struggle. 'The democratic opposition must be constantly and incessantly visible in public life', Tismaneanu quotes Michnik as saying, 'must create political facts by organizing mass actions, must formulate alternative programs. Everything else is an illusion.'[45]

For Tismaneanu and his contributors, the independent peace movements that arose in communist Eastern Europe were much more than mere pacifist organizations. They were movements fighting for human dignity, embryos of the civil society that would eventually be restored. They were, in the view of these writers, inherently principled and democratic.

The chapters in this book were written in early 1988 and updated between January and February 1989 – months before the collapse of communism in the closing months of 1989, and well before the infamous East German elections of May 1989. Given that circumstance, the understanding shown by Tismaneanu and his contributors of the transformative potential of independent peace movements[46] is all the more refreshing, and provides a healthy corrective to the self-serving cynicism of certain sceptics who, even more than a decade later, still indulge in the self-gratifying illusion that no one had a clue as to what was going on in the region. Tismaneanu and his contributors not only anticipated the inevitable collapse of communism,[47] but also grasped the significance of the contributions of grass-roots organizations to the process of collapse.

But it is in Tismaneanu's other book, *Reinventing Politics*, that his analysis of the sources of political change emerges most clearly. In his view, political change is the work of brave individuals such as Václav Havel, Lech Wałęsa, Mihai Botez, and Adam Michnik, as well as of organizations such as the Hungarian FIDESZ. Akin to what is often called the great-man theory of history, Tismaneanu's analysis emphasizes dissidents and dissident ideas. For Tismaneanu, history is no more and no less than the history of competing *ideas*. In a characteristic passage, he quotes Michnik: 'Social changes follow from a confrontation of different moralities and visions of social order. Before the violence of rulers clashes with the violence of their subjects, values and systems of ethics clash inside human minds.'[48]

VI

In contrast with the foregoing books, the collaborative effort of Agnes Horvath and Arpad Szakolczai – *The Dissolution of Communist Power* – is a strangely incomplete work. Based on largely undigested interview material and interspersed with lengthy and largely unapplied summaries of some of the more transparently obvious ideas of Michel Foucault, the book brings together the results of questionnaires and follow-up interviews with Communist Party members and apparatchiks in Budapest in February–March 1988 and September–October 1988. What is truly surprising is that, while the interviewees clearly believed that the communist system was in a state of advanced decay, the authors themselves express surprise that the system did in fact collapse.

But the book is important in that it provides an alternative point of emphasis. Rather than attributing political change to a shift in elite strategy (as in Poznański) or to pressure of an articulate opposition (as in Tismaneanu) or even to a groundswell of popular discontent (as in Philipsen), these authors focus on the decay of party structures themselves. The party, as Horvath and Szakolczai show, took upon itself far more assignments than it could reasonably handle and experienced difficulty in ridding itself of discredited practices, even after the upper echelons of the party had called for reform.[49] One of the problems that the party experienced was an inherent inefficiency built into the very nature of authoritarianism. As they explain, the greatest danger to such a system is free thought – and most especially (in their view) on the part of office-holders. In order to squelch free thought and stifle innovative work, the party concocted the practice of holding regular, time-consuming meetings, which filled the time, compelling participants to act out rituals of conformity, and accustomed people to hierarchical control and supervision. Inevitably, these meetings also hindered efficient work methods.[50]

Ultimately, Horvath and Szakolczai argue, communism collapsed because it was a historical anomaly, a political absurdity. Its absurdity, they claim, consisted in the communists' offering outdated solutions to new problems, even while representing themselves as the vanguard of the future. They compare the practice of communism with driving a Model T in today's London.[51] They paint communism in such decadent shades that the need for the opposition disappears altogether. For Horvath and Szakolczai, it would seem, independent activism may have produced a lot of courageous writing and dramatic headlines. They might even concede that it provided a field for autonomous moral action. But, for them, independent activism was largely, if not entirely, irrelevant to the eventual collapse of communism. Communism, in their view, collapsed of its own weight.

Finally, Paul Hockenos, in his 1993 book, *Free to Hate*, paints a portrait of a revolution that runs the risk of running awry. Moreover, in his analysis, it was not just a question of the efflorescence of extreme right-wing groups that accompanied the collapse of communism; it was also a question of monopolist and nationalist tendencies on the part of the new post-communist governments themselves. In Hungary, for example – as Hockenos notes – the first post-communist government lost no time in taking steps to bring the media under control, even while mounting a full-scale assault on the modest gains that women had registered under communist rule.[52] In Poland, the heavy-handed efforts of the Catholic Church to translate Catholic ethics into national law seriously complicated Poland's transition to democracy. Moreover, much more than the other authors discussed here, Hockenos is painfully aware that socialism was not all negative and that the transition has involved an abandonment of both some of the negative and some of the positive facets of the socialist system. On this point, he quotes Pastor Almuth Berger, a former dissident: 'The GDR's collapse and outright rejection of all that it stood for and presided over also discredited any of its positive aspects. Many people, who expressed real solidarity with third world countries before, today will have nothing to do with it. It's impossible even to use the word "solidarity" today, so negative are its connotations.'[53]

Against this background, Hockenos outlines the newly emergent far-right currents in Eastern Europe, showing, at the same time, their connections – whether organic or via mythological connections – with interwar trends. Hockenos emphasizes that racial prejudice was always latent in Eastern Europe, and that its new strength has little to do with the presence of non-native people (whose numbers, at least until recently, were not especially great), but with the uncertainties created by the transition itself. As a result, as he notes in his conclusion, 'although independent society exists, nationalism and chauvinism have stymied the development of a progressive democratic political culture'.[54]

Hockenos is a paradigmatic socio-centric researcher, and many of his conversations with skinheads and other people took place in bars and discos. What emerges is a concept of political change which is unmistakably fashioned at the grass-roots. In this respect, Hockenos is closer to Philipsen than to any of the other authors under review here.

Absent from this gallery of political landscapes is a depiction of the Soviet Union as pivotal to the processes of change unleashed in Eastern Europe. Karen Dawisha's *Eastern Europe, Gorbachev and Reform*[55] probably comes closest to this model, although Charles Gati's 1987 discussion[56] was also sensitive to the Soviet factor in the gathering momentum in Eastern Europe in the late 1980s. Of the works discussed in this chapter, Tismaneanu's edited collection probably shows the most sensitivity to the importance of Gorbachev's changes in encouraging discontents in Eastern Europe.[57] But, that said, it is worth recalling that the pressures for change in Eastern Europe were building up quite autonomously (above all in the GDR, Poland, Hungary, and Czechoslovakia[58] – and, in its own way, Yugoslavia), and that what Gorbachev's reforms accomplished was not to initiate pressures for change in Eastern Europe, but to allow them to build more quickly than they might have otherwise.

VII

While the foregoing volumes speak in general terms, one may note that there were some variations in patterns of transition in the region. In Poland and Hungary, pressures in 1988 induced communist power-holders to enter into negotiations with the opposition, yielding power peacefully in the course of 1989. In East Germany and Czechoslovakia, mass demonstrations and, in the case of the GDR, mass exodus within the space of a matter of weeks were necessary to bring the communists to the negotiating table. In Romania, popular rebellion was sparked by the efforts by the secret police to take a wayward clergyman into custody and Romanian dictator Nicolae Ceaușescu, having failed to escape the country, was put on trial and executed rather hurriedly. In Albania and Bulgaria, the communists tried to manage the transition but succeeded only in postponing their loss of power briefly.

But it was in Yugoslavia that the path out of communism took a tragic detour. The Yugoslav pattern was, of course, different all along. Even during the Second World War, the Yugoslav communists were going their own way – for example, by beginning to organize Partisan resistance even before the Soviet Union was attacked. There are several reasons for Yugoslav specificity, but, when it comes to decommunization, the chief reason must be located in the federal system, which had the results (1) that decommunization and repluralization unfolded at different rates and took different forms in the different republics, (2) that local republic elites appealed to the ethnic constituencies associated with their respective republics, thereby rendering it virtually impossible that a Yugoslav consensus might be found, and (3) that the local republic elites enjoyed power bases 'at the periphery'. It is with an eye to the dangers inherent in such a formula that Jack Snyder warned, in a 2000 publication, that 'ethnically based federalism and regional autonomy should be avoided, since they create political organizations and media markets that are centered on ethnic differences'.[59] How the transition played out in Yugoslavia and how these and other factors shaped that country's path are examined in the following chapter.

NOTES

1 Zygmunt Bauman, 'Social Dissent in the East European Political System', *Archives Européennes de Sociologie*, 12, 1 (1971).
2 Andrzej Korboński, 'The Prospects for Change in Eastern Europe' and 'Reply', *Slavic Review*, 33, 2 (June 1974), pp. 219–39 and 253–8.
3 Robert Conquest, 'Who Was Right, Who Was Wrong, and Why', *Encounter* (London), July–August 1990, pp. 3–18.
4 George Schöpflin, 'Political Decay in One-Party Systems in Eastern Europe: Yugoslav Patterns', in Pedro Ramet (ed.), *Yugoslavia in the 1980s* (Boulder, CO: Westview Press, 1985), pp. 307–24.
5 Ernst Kux, 'Growing Tensions in Eastern Europe', *Problems of Communism*, 29, 2 (March–April 1980), p. 37.
6 Alfred G. Meyer, *Communism*, 4th edn (New York: Random House, 1984).
7 Robert C. Tucker, *The Soviet Political Mind: Studies in Stalinism and Post-Stalin Change* (New York: Praeger, 1963).
8 Kenneth Jowitt, 'Inclusion and Mobilization in European Leninist Systems', in Jan F. Triska and Paul M. Cocks (eds.), *Political Development in Eastern Europe* (New York: Praeger, 1977), pp. 93–118.
9 Francis Fukuyama, 'The End of History?', *The National Interest*, 16 (Summer 1989).
10 George Weigel, *The Final Revolution: The Resistance Church and the Collapse of Communism* (New York and Oxford: Oxford University Press, 1992), for example on p. 16.

11 Vladimir Tismaneanu, *Reinventing Politics: Eastern Europe from Stalin to Havel* (New York: Free Press, 1992).
12 Dirk Philipsen, *We Were the People: Voices from East Germany's Revolutionary Autumn of 1989* (Durham, NC: Duke University Press, 1993), p. 197.
13 R. F. Leslie, *Reform and Insurrection in Russian Poland, 1856–1865* (University of London: Athlone Press, 1963), p. x.
14 Sabrina P. Ramet, *Whose Democracy? Nationalism, Religion, and the Doctrine of Collective Rights in Post-1989 Eastern Europe* (Lanham, MD: Rowman & Littlefield, 1997), p. 169.
15 Agnes Horvath and Arpad Szakolczai, *The Dissolution of Communist Power: The Case of Hungary* (London and New York: Routledge, 1992), p. xi.
16 Pedro Ramet, 'Religious Ferment in Eastern Europe', *Survey*, 28, 4 (Winter 1984), p. 87.
17 Pedro Ramet, *Cross and Commissar: The Politics of Religion in Eastern Europe and the USSR* (Bloomington, IN: Indiana University Press, 1987), pp. 173, 44.
18 As I wrote in 1985, 'there has not been – to the best of my knowledge – a single serious claim, in any academic or scientific journal . . . , that rock music is a "cause" of any of these phenomena [alienation, disaffection, social nonconformity, political deviance]. Rock music can, however, provide a setting in which drug use is "comfortable" and can offer a more exciting alternative to youth organization work. But the social impact of rock does not end there. On the contrary, the political messages – more tolerable for the more secure regimes of Hungary and Yugoslavia [before Milošević], less tolerable for the less secure regimes of Poland and Czechoslovakia – constitute a kind of "counter-socialization". Rock music is, at the very least, problematic for these regimes' (Pedro Ramet [Sabrina P. Ramet], 'Rock Counterculture in Eastern Europe and the Soviet Union', *Survey*, 29, 2 (Summer 1985), p. 170).
19 For a rendering of full credit to some of the scholars who foresaw the collapse of communism in Eastern Europe, see Sabrina Petra Ramet, *Social Currents in Eastern Europe: The Sources and Consequences of the Great Transformation*, 2nd edn (Durham, NC: Duke University Press, 1995), pp. 10–11. Inadvertently omitted from the list there were Ivo Banac and Trond Gilberg (of whose predictions I was unaware at the time) who accurately predicted the outbreak of the Yugoslav war and the fall of Ceauşescu, respectively.
20 Schöpflin, 'Political Decay', pp. 307–8.
21 Kux, 'Growing Tensions in Eastern Europe', p. 37.
22 *Reinventing Civil Society: Poland's Quiet Revolution, 1981–1986* (New York: Helsinki Watch, 1986), p. 7.
23 See, for example, Janice Gross Stein, 'Can Decision-Makers be Rational and Should They be? Evaluating the Quality of Decisions', *Jerusalem Journal of International Relations*, 3, 2–3 (Winter–Spring 1978), pp. 316–39; and Miriam Steiner, 'The Search for Order in a Disorderly World: Worldviews and Prescriptive Decision Paradigms', *International Organization*, 37, 3 (Summer 1983), pp. 373–413.
24 Kazimierz Poznański, 'An Interpretation of Communist Decay: The Role of Evolutionary Mechanisms', in *Communist and Post-Communist Studies*, Vol. 26, 1 (March 1993), pp. 21–3.

25 *Ibid.*, p. 3, emphasis in the original.
26 Quoted in Michael McFaul, *Post-Communist Politics: Democratic Prospects in Russia and Eastern Europe* (Washington, DC: Center for Strategic and International Studies, 1993), p. xiii.
27 Philipsen, *We Were the People*, p. 32.
28 *Ibid.*, p. 96.
29 Ånders Aslund, *Post-Communist Economic Revolutions: How Big a Bang?* (Washington, DC: Center for Strategic and International Studies, 1992), p. 3.
30 *Ibid.*, p. 33.
31 *Ibid.*, pp. 38–9.
32 Juan J. Linz and Alfred Stepan, 'Political Identities and Electoral Sequences: Spain, the Soviet Union, and Yugoslavia', *Daedalus*, 121, 2 (Spring 1992), pp. 123–39.
33 Kazimierz Poznański, 'Introduction', in Kazimierz Poznański (ed.), *Constructing Capitalism: The Reemergence of Civil Society and Liberal Economy in the Post-Communist World* (Boulder, CO: Westview Press, 1992), p. 1.
34 Kazimierz Poznański, 'Epilogue: Markets and States in the Transformation of Post-Communist Europe', in Poznański, *Constructing Capitalism*, pp. 204–5.
35 *Ibid.*, p. 202.
36 *Ibid.*, p. 204.
37 See his reference to the "former Soviet regime" in his chapter, 'Property Rights Perspective on Evolution of Communist-Type Economics', in Poznański, *Constructing Capitalism*, p. 80.
38 *Ibid.*
39 *Ibid.*, pp. 76–7.
40 Poznański, 'Epilogue', p. 210.
41 See Valerie Bunce, 'Two-Tiered Stalinism: A Case of Self-Destruction', in Poznański, *Constructing Capitalism*, pp. 37–8.
42 Kazimierz Poznański, Introduction, in Kazimierz Z. Poznański (ed.), *The Evolutionary Transition to Capitalism* (Boulder, CO: Westview Press, 1995), p. xxiii.
43 Josef C. Brada, 'A Critique of the Evolutionary Approach to the Economic Transition from Communism to Capitalism', in Poznański, *Evolutionary Transition*, esp. pp. 193, 203.
44 Vladimir Tismaneanu, 'Preface', in V. Tismaneanu (ed.), *In Search of Civil Society: Independent Peace Movements in the Soviet Bloc* (New York and London: Routledge, 1990), p. vii.
45 Michnik, as quoted in Vladimir Tismaneanu, 'Unofficial Peace Activism in the Soviet Union and East-Central Europe', in Tismaneanu, *In Search of Civil Society*, p. 2.
46 See, for example, Tismaneanu, 'Unofficial Peace Activism', p. 47.
47 See, for example, Miklós Haraszti, 'The Beginnings of Civil Society: The Independent Peace Movement and the Danube Movement in Hungary', in Tismaneanu, *In Search of Civil Society*, p. 86.
48 Tismaneanu, *Reinventing Politics*, p. 155.
49 Horvath and Szakolczai, *Dissolution of Communist Power*, p. 58.
50 *Ibid.*, pp. 106–7.

51 *Ibid.*, p. 210.
52 Paul Hockenos, *Free to Hate: The Rise of the Right in Post-Communist Eastern Europe* (London and New York: Routledge, 1994), pp. 120–2.
53 *Ibid.*, p. 38.
54 *Ibid.*, p. 303.
55 Karen Dawisha, *Eastern Europe, Gorbachev and Reform: The Great Challenge*, 2nd edn (Cambridge: Cambridge University Press, 1990).
56 Charles Gati, 'Gorbachev and Eastern Europe', *Foreign Affairs*, 65, 5 (Summer 1987), pp. 958–75.
57 See especially the chapter by Eduard Kuznetsov in Tismaneanu's collection.
58 See Ramet, *Social Currents in Eastern Europe*, 2nd edn, esp. chapters 1–4.
59 Jack Snyder, *From Voting to Violence: Democratization and Nationalist Conflict* (New York: W. W. Norton, 2000), p. 40.

REFERENCES

Aslund, Ånders, *Post-Communist Economic Revolutions: How Big a Bang?* (Washington, DC: Center for Strategic and International Studies, 1992), p. 106.
Hockenos, Paul, *Free to Hate: The Rise of the Right in Post-Communist Eastern Europe* (New York and London: Routledge, 1994), p. 330.
Horvath, Agnes and Arpad Szakolczai, *The Dissolution of Communist Power: The Case of Hungary* (London and New York: Routledge, 1992), p. 254.
Philipsen, Dirk, *We Were the People: Voices from East Germany's Revolutionary Autumn of 1989* (Durham, NC: Duke University Press, 1993), p. 417.
Poznański, Kazimierz Z. (ed.), *Constructing Capitalism: The Reemergence of Civil Society and Liberal Economy in the Post-Communist World* (Boulder, CO: Westview Press, 1992), p. 230.
    The Evolutionary Transition to Capitalism (Boulder, CO: Westview Press, 1995), p. 240.
Tismaneanu, Vladimir (ed.), *In Search of Civil Society: Independent Peace Movements in the Soviet Bloc* (New York and London: Routledge, 1990), p. 191.
Tismaneanu, Vladimir, *Reinventing Politics: Eastern Europe from Stalin to Havel* (New York: Free Press, 1992), p. 312.

3   The roots of the Yugoslav collapse

I

The split between idealists and realists is, of course, not the only debate to have divided the field of Yugoslav studies. For as long as I have been observing Yugoslavia, I have been struck by the ongoing (and unending) debate between scholars who have wanted to have faith in any formula or arrangement that might be presented as potentially stabilizing and favourable, and scholars who have lived in expectation that catastrophe was around the corner. This temperamental difference between optimists and pessimists was reflected in differing views of self-management, the 1974 constitution, post-Titoist policy in Kosovo, the prospects for communism in Eastern Europe as a whole, the dangers (or, for optimists, 'alleged dangers') of civil war in Yugoslavia, the prospects for the establishment of the rule of law in post-communist Eastern Europe, and the prospects for a negotiated peace in ex-Yugoslavia. In the early 1990s, one of the manifestations of this debate was that optimists took to blaming the Yugoslav civil war on Western manipulation (which was, in fact, the Serbian propaganda line), on the assumption that, left to themselves, the Yugoslavs would never have gone to war, while pessimists found sufficient roots of the conflict internally.

To some extent, the difference between optimists and pessimists was sustained by differences in their very research methodologies. Optimists – who were sometimes 'cynical optimists', optimistic about system survival and institutional stability, but disinterested in human rights struggles locally – tended to focus their attention on official publications and to devote their interview energy to talking with officials. By contrast, pessimists – who were often committed to the advance of human rights, but pessimistic, say, about the capacity of communist Yugoslavia to embrace a liberal programme of human rights in a peaceful and evolutionary fashion – cast their research nets wider, taking into account religious, social, even countercultural elements, alongside the official viewpoint. Needless to say, cynical optimists never tired of dismissing East European dissidents as 'marginal types' of no real or potential importance, while pessimists were equally tireless in insisting on the power and force of dissent.

Inevitably, it was exclusively the pessimists who provided early warnings of the approaching collapse of socialist Yugoslavia and outbreak of intercommunal war (and, for that matter, of the decay and impending collapse of communism in Eastern Europe generally). Now that these events have come to pass, it is possible to look at subsequent analyses of the roots of the breakup and war, and contrast these with the analyses offered at the time, and also to look for new transformations of the unending debate between optimists and pessimists.

Undoubtedly the roots of the Yugoslav wars (in Slovenia, Croatia, and Bosnia-Herzegovina, 1991–5, and in Kosovo and Macedonia, 1998–2001) are diverse, and there is no need to engage in Procrustean efforts to reduce the complexity of socialist Yugoslav development to some supposed pre-eminent factor. On the contrary, economics, demographics, programmatic choices, institutional structures, religious cultures, elite dynamics, and deficiencies in system legitimacy all played a role in pushing the country towards violent breakup. Be that as it may, scholars have often favoured one or another element as the leading explanatory factor.

II

One approach to the Yugoslav crisis is to trace the collapse of socialist Yugoslavia to economic factors. Among such writers to emphasize the economic sources of eventual disarray is Dijana Pleština (in her *Regional Development in Communist Yugoslavia*, 1992). Outlining communist economic policy from 1945 to 1990, she highlights the political sensitivity of regional economic disparities in multiethnic Yugoslavia and describes communist efforts to ameliorate these disparities. But in spite of their efforts, Slovenia, Croatia, and the Belgrade region in northern Serbia consistently outpaced the rest of the country in terms of investment and most other economic indices as well, while Bosnia, Macedonia, Montenegro, and, above all, Kosovo continued to lag behind with high rates of unemployment. Given the nominal commitment of the communist leaders to eliminating regional economic inequalities, their failure to do so inevitably gave rise to recriminations and complaints. The less developed republics complained that the federation was not doing enough for them and noted that payments from the more developed republics were frequently late, sometimes by as much as a year and a half. The more developed republics in turn claimed that their own growth was being slowed by the necessity of providing support to the less developed republics, and complained that these funds were often ill-spent. By the early 1980s, there was deepening resentment on both sides of this debate, and everyone felt 'exploited' by the system.

But in the late 1970s, the earlier economic boom (which had benefited the developed republics and especially the Dalmatian coast more than the rest of the country) ground to a halt, and economic troubles started to pile up. What Pleština shows so well is how economists from the different republics now offered solutions which they presented as 'best' for the federation as a whole, but which turned out to be prejudicial to the needs of their own respective republics. The conclusion is inevitable: economics could not be divorced from nationality policy in multiethnic Yugoslavia. On the contrary, economic problems fuelled interethnic resentments and frictions.

The final act in the drama of the Socialist Federated Republic of Yugoslavia (SFRY) was signalled by the appearance of Serbian banker-turned-politician Slobodan Milošević on the political stage. Politically prominent since 1984, Milošević was elected secretary of the League of Communists of Serbia in 1986 and pushed his erstwhile mentor, Ivan Stambolić, who had become president of Serbia at the time Milošević assumed the secretaryship, into an early retirement at the end of 1987. Upon assuming power in Serbia, Milošević immediately transformed the language of politics, and opened a space for the convening of Serb nationalist rallies (the famous *mitinzi*) at which participants were encouraged to make demands based on the supposition of 'ethnic rights'. Ostensibly spontaneous, these meetings were carefully organized by Milošević's collaborators, and were financed by the apparatus which Milošević controlled.[1] The Serbian public was more than receptive to Milošević's chauvinistic message. Pleština's answer to the question *why?* highlights the pauperization of much of the Yugoslav labour force, with many Yugoslavs being forced to take out bank loans just to cover daily expenses. 'In that climate of uncertainty', Pleština notes, 'the chauvinist rhetoric of the man who could "right" any variety of "wrongs" – a sort of latter-day Don Quixote of the masses – propelled Milošević to the position of undisputed leader in Serbia, and in most Serb areas of Yugoslavia.'[2] And with Milošević's rise to power began the countdown to intercommunal war.

A more extreme version of the economic approach is that taken by Susan Woodward in her prize-winning *Socialist Unemployment*. What she wants is to endeavour to offer a unicausal explanation, but she does not quite manage this. Her argument is that the driving force for political

change in socialist Yugoslavia was unemployment.[3] Unemployment, she
says, affected the political elite's 'capacity to enforce policy goals',
undermined 'the delicate balance in constitutional jurisdictions of the
federal system because of the intensified competition among property
owners to protect their capital assets from declining further', negatively
affected 'the system's capacity to adapt politically to the requirements of
new economic and social conditions', and impaired 'the country's ability
to continue to manage unemployment itself'.[4] If unemployment is the
heart of the problem, then nationalism, Woodward tells us, is 'only a
negative manifestation', or perhaps, better said, an epiphenomenon, of
discontent generated by unemployment.[5] The argument is provocative,
especially insofar as it seems to be erecting the scaffolding for a unicausal
argument. But Woodward ultimately qualifies any such argument. Unemployment was, in fact, not enough to push the country over the brink.
Rather, she tells us, 'The pressure for change in Yugoslav economic
policy and for political reform in the 1980s came as it had in the past –
not from domestic political forces [or from discontent over unemploy-
ment] but from the international system.'[6] International creditors
demanded changes, reforms were carried out to accommodate those
demands, political leaders in Slovenia above all but also in Croatia reacted
to these reforms by demanding more comprehensive systemic change,
and, as a result of Slovene–Croatian pressure, the country moved steadily
in the direction of ever more encompassing decentralization, culminating
logically in the disintegration of the country, according to Woodward.[7]
Unless the international creditors were demanding changes to correct
problems created by the country's unemployment, it would appear that
that factor may have slipped out of the equation. But this does not appear
to have been the case, since she tells us that the IMF's focus was on
demanding policies to fight inflation and that this emphasis entailed
restrictions on credit and imports which, in turn, required cutbacks in
production and labour, thereby fuelling unemployment.[8]

Woodward is openly revisionist, challenging the conventional notion that the Tito–Stalin split of 1948 marked a watershed in postwar
Yugoslav history, suggesting that developments in 1946, 1947, and 1949
all make better candidates for watersheds.[9] Given her scheme for understanding the evolution of economic policy in postwar Yugoslavia, the
reform of 1965, the crushing of the liberals in 1971–2, and the passage of
the fourth postwar constitution in 1974 also cannot qualify as 'defining
moments' (her term).The year 1961 qualifies as such a moment because
it marked the peak in postwar employment, as does 1971, not because of
the crushing of the Croatian liberals (the liberals in Slovenia and Serbia
did not feel Tito's axe until the following year), but because it marked

the point in time when the rising rate of unemployment began to esca-
late dramatically. This, in turn, leads her to offer the following periodization scheme for postwar economic policy: 1950–7, transitional
period with continued problems of unemployment; 1958–67, reduction
in the labour force accompanied by the worsening of regional inequalities; 1968–78, high rate of capital formation; and 1979–89, system
breakdown.[10] The 1963 constitution and the fall of Ranković are both
folded into the second phase. It should be emphasized, however, that
Woodward does not suggest that this periodization scheme defines
phases in, let us say, federal relations or policies in noneconomic
spheres. Woodward's book excited at least some scholars when it was
published a decade ago. But its revisionism has not had any lasting effect
on the field of Yugoslav studies, and her endeavour to trace the breakup
of socialist Yugoslavia to international factors remains a minority view.
Indeed, she herself adopts a different approach in her *Balkan Tragedy*
(discussed in the next chapter), published the same year as *Socialist
Unemployment*.

Branka Magaš (*The Destruction of Yugoslavia*, 1992) takes a rather
different approach, focusing on the more purely political aspects of
Yugoslavia's evolution, 1980–91, with special stress on the deterioration
of Serb–Albanian relations in the province of Kosovo and the uses made
by Belgrade of that deterioration. Her book opens with a challenge,
declaring that the April 1981 Albanian riots in Kosovo were nothing
less than a 'watershed' for Yugoslavia as a whole.[11]

Yet, at the same time, she is bitterly aware of the menacing way in
which the past has always haunted the present in Yugoslavia – the
resentment by non-Serbs of the way the interwar monarchy 'rested
essentially upon a single nationality (albeit the largest), the Serbs, and
. . . trampled on the national rights of the remaining Yugoslav peoples',[12]
the diffuse anger associated with memories of the mutual slaughter of the
Second World War, and the different memories each of Yugoslavia's
constituent peoples has had of developments after 1945. But she avoids
the trap of historical determinism, and, rather than simply blaming the
increasing chauvinism of the Serbs after 1986 on 'the legacy of the past',
she highlights the role played by Belgrade intellectuals in stoking and
legitimating hatred of non-Serbs. She sees this as perhaps the single most
important factor contributing to the change in the political atmosphere
in Serbia after 1988, a change which, she says, 'can best be described as
tragic for the country as a whole'.[13] But institutional disarray at the
centre also played a role in allowing Yugoslavia to drift towards chaos,
as Magaš notes. The 1974 constitution, in particular, failed to lay the

foundation for the effective functioning of federal institutions,[14] thus fuelling the gradual disintegration of the centre.

Vjekoslav Perica (*Balkan Idols: Religion and Nationalism in Yugoslav States*, 2002) provides documentation of the contribution of Yugoslavia's religious organizations to the erosion of the communist system. He cites a 1980 police report which claimed that 'many clerics, particularly Serb Orthodox and Catholic, were jubilant' at the prospect of Tito's demise, hoping that it would bring about the collapse of communism in the country.[15] In the years following Tito's death, frictions flared in relations between Church and state in Croatia and Bosnia, and in 1985, as Perica reports, an influential newspaper columnist warned:

If we let the clergy continue their apology for clerical fascists like [Zagreb Archbishop] Stepinac and processions and marches across Yugoslavia, we must fear the repetition of the horrors of the Second World War . . . We communists began to believe that the crimes of the Second World War would never be repeated, especially not in Europe at the end of the 20th century. But I am afraid that we have been wrong.[16]

To cope with the challenge they saw coming from the religious sector, the authorities combined a policy of repression of more radical clergy with appeasement of clergy more receptive to co-operation with the regime. Differences among the clergy were reflected even at the highest levels, with, for example, Franjo Kuharić, then archbishop of Zagreb, actively promoting the beatification of Stepinac – a cause considered anathema by the regime – and Archbishop Frane Franić of Split expressing positive sentiments about the Partisan struggle of the Second World War and encouraging believers of his archdiocese to adopt a co-operative attitude vis-à-vis the authorities.[17]

Nor was Serbia free of problems in the religious sphere. Perica cites an internal Croatian government document from the early 1980s which reported that Serb Orthodox clergy working in the Republic of Croatia had been stirring up problems 'over land, property, or trivial conflicts between the locals and the authorities in Serb-populated areas, in order to charge discrimination against the Serbian minority and unequal status for the Serbian Orthodox Church in predominantly Catholic Croatia'.[18] For the Orthodox Church, the point of all of this was to place itself at the helm of an ethnic-confessional revival which would both draw more Serbs into the Church and inflate the Church's authority and social relevance. The Orthodox Church was playing with fire.

Although Serbs would later say that they mobilized in Croatia only in response to Croatian president Tudjman's policies, in fact, as Perica notes, 'the Serbian Church turned militant and anti-Croatian even before Tudjman's electoral triumph'.[19] The Serbian Church backed Serb nationalist parties in Croatia and Bosnia-Herzegovina and, in Serbia, tied its fortunes to the Milošević regime. The Serbian Orthodox Church also played the central role in transforming Jasenovac, site of the most fearsome concentration camp run by the Ustaše (Croatian fascists) during the Second World War, into a major pilgrimage site and symbol of the Serbian historical experience. What was not noted at the time was that, by selecting a site associated with genocide, hatred, intolerance, and ethnic strife for such emphasis, rather than a site which might be associated with ecumenism, tolerance, and ethnic and confessional dialogue, the Church was stoking potentially explosive emotions.

As Yugoslavia plummeted towards breakup and strife, the Orthodox clergy, rather than working towards reconciliation, 'held liturgies near long-forgotten [Orthodox] ruins where no religious activity had occurred for decades or, in some cases, for centuries', in order to document Serbian claims to territories lying within the Republic of Croatia.[20] Not surprisingly, when the war finally broke out, even though it had diverse roots, it quickly took on religious dimensions: specifically, the rival forces targeted each other's places of worship so that, by the end of 1995, 1,024 mosques, 182 Catholic churches, and 28 Serbian Orthodox churches and monasteries had been destroyed.[21]

Perica closes his book by noting progress, since the end of the war, in 'faith-based conflict management, reconciliation efforts, religious relief, and interfaith understanding', though even here he finds 'ambiguous outcomes', and by registering a plea for 'mutual respect [among peoples], tolerance, and observance of the laws, norms, and standards under which Western democracies operate'.[22]

III

An alternative approach, taken by Branislav Anzulović and Lenard Cohen, shifts the emphasis from situational variables to the mindset of the locals. Cohen, for example, identifies 'the [Yugoslav] population's predilection for political extremism',[23] which he says was 'identified by [Vladimir] Dvorniković' earlier. But the 'sheer terror and hatred' which flashed in the 1990s were not primarily a result of the crisis which flared in the 1980s; on the contrary, says Cohen, 'The basis for such intense feelings can be traced to the transgenerational socialization of negative stereotypes.'[24] Thus, within Bosnia, according to Cohen, although 'Nationalist political leaders of various stripes in Bosnia undoubtedly bear a major responsibility for generating an atmosphere of ethnic intolerance and hatred, . . .the historically conditioned proclivities of large segments of each ethno-religious community – particularly outside the more cosmopolitan Sarajevo area – to embrace programs of aggressive nationalism must also be taken into account.'[25] This same historical determinism re-emerges in Cohen's later volume, *Serpent in the Bosom* (2001, discussed in chapter 7) and, in *Broken Bonds,* constitutes the theoretical backdrop for a cursory overview of Yugoslav history from 1830 onwards and a rather pedestrian if detailed chronology of the war.

A kindred effort to trace present violence to socialization in the remote past is undertaken by Branislav Anzulović in his *Heavenly Serbia.* Anzulović's work differs from Cohen's in three respects, however. First, Anzulović limits his attention to the Serbs; second, he uses historical factors to explain not just violence, but also a proclivity towards genocide; and, third, unlike Cohen, who seems to believe that socialization *locks* people into fixed patterns of behaviour, Anzulović pointedly emphasizes that 'the direction in which a nation has been moving can be changed', given conscious effort and a 'reexamination of deeply entrenched ideas'.[26] Moreover, whereas Cohen is vague about the specific sources of 'transgenerational socialization', Anzulović seeks to provide a detailed accounting, tracing the destructive ethos which he finds in Serbian culture to the myth of the Battle of Kosovo, the poetry of Montenegrin Prince Petar Petrović Njegoš (1813–51), songs of Dinaric highlanders, the public role of the Serbian Orthodox Church over centuries, and even the novels of twentieth-century writers Dobrica Ćosić and Vuk Drašković. Here is an excerpt from Njegoš's celebrated poem, *Gorski vijenac* (The Mountain Wreath):

> The blasphemers of Christ's name
> we will baptize with water or with blood!
> We'll drive the plague out of the pen!
> Let the song of horror ring forth,
> a true altar on a blood-stained rock.[27]

The poem deals with the massacre of Muslims by Christian warriors, and closes with the words:

> Let Hell devour, and Satan mow down!
> Flowers will grow at the graveyard
> for some remote future generation.[28]

In Anzulović's mind, 'The rejoicing over the massacres and their depiction as a baptism in blood that leads to the nation's rebirth make the poem a hymn to genocide.'[29] But its significance, for Anzulović, lies in its alleged influence on generations of Serbs.

Anzulović locates the same problem in Drašković's popular novel, *Nož* (The Knife). Set in Second World War-era Bosnia, the novel recounts the maiming and killing of Serbs by Muslims. In one passage quoted by Anzulović, Drašković writes,

With one swing, as if he were cutting a leg of lamb, he cut off her left breast, she screamed, the blood splattered onto his forehead and cheeks. He cut off her nose, pulled the tongue out of the mouth, and cut it off. He stuck the tip of the knife into her eye, circled it a few times, and pushed the steel under the bloody ball that was moving under his fingers. After pulling the eye out he threw it on the copper tray in front of Father Nikifor. Then he slaughtered Ljubica![30]

Anzulović makes his argument that *The Knife* worked on people's minds by quoting from a commander in the Serbian Guard who reported that the novel put him into a state of constant rage, inducing him to beat up Muslims, even when he was on vacation in Cavtat.[31]

Anzulović's book has been more controversial precisely because it is more specific, more concrete – its claims can be subjected more easily to review. Cohen's book has been less controversial precisely because it is effusively vague on points which, I believe, demand to be flushed out. Few books have been as misunderstood as those written by Lenard Cohen; to associate them with the historical determinism of Anzulović is to take the first step towards understanding the thinking which lies behind his books. For both writers, it is not enough, in seeking to account for the troubles which pushed socialist Yugoslavia over the brink, to limit one's perspective to events after 1918, let alone to post-1945 developments. Quite the contrary: for both of them, a much longer perspective is needed.

IV

The more recent volumes by Christopher Bennett, Andrew Wachtel, and John Allcock take it as a given that the problem lay in Yugoslavia itself but offer contrasting accounts of what went wrong with socialist Yugoslavia. Wachtel's focus is on literature and cultural politics, where he rightly discerns the presence in the Yugoslav political establishment of advocates of the creation of a unified Yugoslav culture. But, as Wachtel notes, when the elite gave up on political centralism and initiated programmes of administrative decentralization, any notion of realizing a unified Yugoslav culture was likewise abandoned.[32] As a result of subsequent educational reforms carried out in the 1960s, the literature being read by schoolchildren varied from republic to republic, with Croatian pupils reading mainly Croatian writers, Serbian pupils reading mainly Serbian writers, and so forth. In this way, the educational reform worked to divide rather than to unify the Yugoslav community of nations.

Wachtel believes that the decentralization of educational and cultural policy was a critical wrong turn. As he writes,

The void left by the gradual collapse of a belief in any form of Yugoslav culture was quickly filled by national-based cultural formations that tended to appear before the expressions of political nationalism . . . Indeed, in certain crucial cases, most notably Croatia in the late 1960s and Serbia in the early 1980s, it would not be an exaggeration to say that nationalist political movements rose on the back of cultural ones rather than the other way around.[33]

Wachtel details the cultural incunabula of the Serbian political backlash, offering an insightful analysis of Milorad Pavić's provocative novel, *The Dictionary of the Khazars* (1984; English trans., 1989). As Wachtel tells it, Pavić's *Dictionary*, which offers parallel Jewish, Muslim, and Christian accounts of the same events, 'implied that no agreement or mutual understanding could be reached among peoples who begin from different starting points', and when, in Pavić's novel, 'the three individuals representative of their religions [finally] succeed in coming together, . . . instead of discovering the truth they seek, all are destroyed'.[34] Wachtel argues that Pavić makes it clear that he intends the reader to infer that any attempt to aspire to truth can only end in doom. Wachtel completes the argument by presenting evidence that Pavić's novel was not just a reflection of the notions of a particular writer; rather, he tells us, Pavić's *Dictionary* 'had important effects, particularly on the thinking of Serbian elites'.[35] Moreover, the novel's 'subversive potential was recognized in Yugoslavia from the beginning'.[36]

Finally, in his concluding chapter, Wachtel makes his point as explicit as possible. Here he reiterates his central argument that

the abandonment of attempts at cultural nation building on the part of both political and cultural elites created the conditions for the collapse of the Yugoslav state. In foregrounding cultural processes, I am disagreeing with the emphasis of other accounts of Yugoslavia's failure, which have placed the blame primarily on political and economic factors. This is not to say I believe that cultural analysis alone can explain Yugoslavia's demise. Such a claim would clearly be simplistic. But Yugoslavia's political and economic malaise in the 1980s, real as it was, would not have led to the disappearance of the country had a robust vision of the Yugoslav nation been in place.[37]

John Allcock's *Explaining Yugoslavia* provides a stark contrast to Wachtel's analysis. Allcock explains contending nationalist agendas through the prism of history rather than of culture, but places the emphasis elsewhere, namely, on 'the failure of the modernisation process in Yugoslavia'.[38] The problems with socialist Yugoslavia, as Allcock sees it, were (1) that socialism figured as an 'anti-modern' force, interfering with national market processes, (2) that Yugoslav socialism in particular embraced 'elements of particular vulnerability', (3) that the system lacked the ability to legitimate itself over the long term, and (4) that its economy, and especially the flow of credit, was mismanaged.[39] In other words, Allcock emphasizes precisely the political and economic factors which Wachtel de-emphasizes.

Allcock wants to offer an alternative to accounts which imagine that Balkan history is a seamless tapestry of unending violence and likewise to accounts which overstress the elements of discontinuity which one may identify over the centuries. To accomplish this, Allcock turns to socio-logical theory, weaving what might be called sociological history and arguing that some of the more 'important dimensions of the recent conflict . . . can be regarded not as reflections of Balkan atavism, but as indices of the modernity which we ourselves share'.[40] Given this, it is not surprising that chapter 2 opens with an expostulation of the concept of modernization and with an effort to situate the Yugoslav lands in a European context. While admitting that this corner of Europe, together with the rest of the Balkans, has lagged behind much of Europe in terms of economic development, Allcock stresses that, on other dimensions, this area was affected by, if not thoroughly penetrated by, trends elsewhere in Europe.[41] On the other hand, Allcock does not want the reader to conclude from this that the problem with which the Yugoslav lands have recently been beset are completely generic; accordingly, he is sceptical about hopes that the integration of Slovenia and Croatia into EU struc-tures will be a simple matter. 'The Balkans cannot escape their condition', he warns, 'by becoming more "European", as their defining condition as "Balkan" itself derives from that "European" context. Their becoming more "European" can only be expected to make them more "Balkan".'[42]

What Allcock offers, as already mentioned, is a sociological history, in which broader processes since the thirteenth century are interpreted in the light of Immanuel Wallerstein's "world-system" theory. Applying this to the breakup of Yugoslavia, Allcock concludes that theories tracing the disintegration of the SFRY to the death of Tito (an approach which Allcock attributes to Laslo Sekelj) are muddled and asserts that it was only in the context of the disintegration of communism throughout Eastern Europe and the Soviet Union that Yugoslav politics became dysfunctional. What made the difference in this regional process, in Allcock's view, was the end of the threat of Soviet intervention, which had kept Yugoslavs on the 'straight and narrow' up to then. That in itself would not have been enough to push the country over the brink, however, as Allcock recognizes; an important contributing factor 'for the collapse of Yugoslavia was the dreadful rigidity of its internal political structure and its consequent chronic inability to adapt to both internal and external change'.[43] Accordingly, when the regional environment began to change at an accelerating pace, Yugoslav political structures simply could not cope.

Turning to the question of the recent conflict, Allcock wisely notes that traditional societies do not interpret their wars in the light of the past. (The original chroniclers of the 1389 Battle of Kosovo did not refer the meaning of the battle to events which had occurred 600 years earlier, for example.) Thus, it is a mark precisely of 'modernity' when societies respond to mythologies of nation, in which a 600-year-old battle can figure prominently.[44]

But if Allcock's version of 'modernization theory' makes space for engagement with the past, then the Balkan tradition of the blood feud should be seen, he suggests, not as a symptom of the breakdown of the social order but, rather, as a manifestation of the continuing vigour of the social order of which it has been a part. Provocatively, Allcock marshals the concept of the blood feud to explain 'ethnic cleansing', noting that 'traditional codes of morality in the past would have required that people be ready to kill their neighbors, as these were precisely the people with whom it was most likely that one might be "in blood"'.[45] Similarly, systematic mutilation of the enemy, in which the eyes, the nose, and the genitals are often targeted, has a long tradition in the Balkans.[46] The point for Allcock is *not*, however, that people are locked into past patterns of behaviour, but rather that such patterns provide templates which may be reused when the circumstances are right.

Through Allcock's prism, thus, one sees an intersection of four factors: the cultural template, the changing international context, the rigidity of the political system, and the way in which the Yugoslavs themselves responded to the challenges with which they found themselves confronted and which were, in part, the product of their own making. Allcock closes his argument by highlighting – sensibly, I would argue – the tension between programmes founded on notions of collectivity (such as nationalist programmes) and the liberal-democratic stress on individual rights,[47] and by reiterating that 'The disintegration of the Yugoslav federal state after 1990 . . . [came] about because the country found itself to be particularly exposed to a conjunction of factors and developmental processes which have characterised the European continent as a whole, and especially those parts of it which participated in the experiment of "real socialism".'[48]

Christopher Bennett disagrees with both Wachtel and Allcock, and is closer to Magaš in his analysis of the factors that caused socialist Yugoslavia to collapse and sink into fratricidal violence. Bennett begins by debunking notions of historical determinism (as per alleged historically rooted hatreds) as well as the notion that socialist Yugoslavia was 'an unmitigated failure', though he does not associate any particular analyst with the notion that Yugoslavia's failure was 'unmitigated'.[49] For Bennett, the story of Yugoslavia's sanguinary collapse is incomprehensible without reference to human agency, and, as he tells the story, Tito deserves blame for having designed an unworkable system, while Milošević played a key role by setting the Serbian media on a 'war-footing' as early as 1987. The international community – which is to say, the diplomats and political leaders representing the leading Western states – also come in for blame first for having rigidly tried to block Slovenian and Croatian secession, thereby, according to Bennett, encouraging Milošević and the JNA to go to war, and, second, by contenting themselves with damage limitation, rather than seeking a solution.[50] Where Tudjman is concerned, Bennett paints the Croatian president as an 'increasingly bitter' man, given to 'far-fetched conspiracy theories', whose 'views became more extreme' over the years and more 'tainted with anti-Semitism'.[51] But, at the same time, Bennett draws a clear distinction between Tudjman and Milošević, urging that any attempt to equate the two men would be 'absurd' since Milošević had been stirring up resentments and stoking hatreds for two and a half years before Tudjman became president of Croatia.[52] (We shall return to the discussion of Christopher Bennett's *Yugoslavia's Bloody Collapse* in chapter 4.)

For myself, I find that I have points of agreement with several of the aforementioned authors (though I am uncomfortable with the historical determinism and psychological reductionism which I find in Cohen and Anzulović). Like Magaš, I have identified the Kosovo riots of 1981 as defining a watershed in post-1945 Yugoslav history and have argued that the post-Tito Yugoslav crisis first flared in and over Kosovo, spreading from there throughout the rest of the country.[53] Like Pleština and Allcock, I have highlighted economic deterioration as having made a powerful contribution towards creating the sense of crisis in the first place,[54] and, in further agreement with Allcock, I have laid especial stress on the salience of system illegitimacy in defining the state's trajectory.[55] At the same time, the extended attention I have paid to the role of literary and other cultural figures, ecclesiastical elites, and the fragmented media[56] reflects my sympathy for the stress placed by Perica and Wachtel on culture as a prism of crisis. And, finally, in describing the roles played by the principals in the gathering crisis,[57] I have signalled my concurrence with Bennett on the ineluctable necessity of including human agency in the explanation. In other words, the theories presented by these various authors need not be incompatible; on the contrary, they may be seen as complementary parts of the whole. On this understanding, one may note that the Yugoslav crisis began no later than the mid-1970s, when the combination of oil price hikes and overborrowing started the Yugoslav economic meltdown. The underlying political illegitimacy of the system was muted as long as Tito was at the helm, but when Yugoslavia took an economic nosedive just as it entered the post-Tito era, the challenge was enormous. Nor could the federal system be ignored since, 'when an illegitimate system confronts economic crisis, its ability to make a unified response is highly dependent upon the structure that system has assumed'.[58] Indeed, the federation provided the structure in which republic elites competed not for the support of Yugoslavs, but for the support of the people of their respective republics; insofar as the republics were organized along ethnic lines, this translated into a strong temptation for republic elites to compete on the basis of nationalist agendas. Federal prime minister Ante Marković, Croatian Communist Party leader Ivica Račan, and Bosnian émigré-returnee Adil Zulfikarpašić[59] resisted the temptation and were defeated at the polls. Milošević, Tudjman, and, in his own way, Izetbegović embraced nationalism and were rewarded at the polls. Thus, although the nationalist revival 'started with the writers',[60] the decisions to abolish the autonomy of Kosovo and Vojvodina in 1989, to declare a Serbian boycott of Slovenian goods, and to set up illegal paramilitaries among the Serbs of Croatia and Bosnia (in 1990), thereby disrupting the unity of the economic market, were not automatic reflexes or facets of the crisis; they were, on the contrary, decisions taken by identifiable individuals among whom Milošević was the central figure. From my standpoint, thus, the central systemic factors in the decay of socialist Yugoslavia were (1) problems associated with system illegitimacy, (2) economic deterioration, and (3) the ethnically based federal system, while (4) human agency (Milošević especially, but not solely) played a central role in taking the country down a violent path.[61]

V

By contrast with the foregoing works, Neven Andjelic wants to investigate what went wrong in Bosnia specifically. For him, the key event which sent Bosnia-Herzegovina spiralling towards fratricidal disaster took place in Bosnia – the collapse of the Agrokomerc concern amid great scandal in 1987. The basic story is well known to 'Yugophiles'. In January 1987, a fire broke out in one of Agrokomerc's factories; when company executives proved to be rather uncooperative with the police investigation of the fire, the police became suspicious and decided to expand their investigation to take in all of Agrokomerc's business. The National Bank of Sarajevo made its own investigation, and, by April of that year, authorities had documents showing that the Velika Kladuša-based company had issued more than 17,000 promissory notes to cover its insolvent operations. Fikret Abdić, the company director, had close relations with the brother of Hamdija Pozderac, a member of the SFRY presidency, and was himself a member of the Central Committee of the League of Communists of Yugoslavia (LCY) and a deputy in the Federal Assembly. When the scandal broke, Abdić was expelled from the Central Committee and the Pozderac brothers were dismissed in disgrace. According to Andjelic, the scandal was the beginning of the end for communist rule in Bosnia, resulting in the breakdown of unity in the Bosnian political establishment and providing a powerful impetus to institutional decay.[62]

But even with the local communist elite discredited and in disarray, the system continued to function, albeit with some personnel changes at the top. Even the waxing nationalist movement in neighbouring Serbia did not affect Bosnia at first, says Andjelic. In the course of summer 1988, however, there were signs of 'the first divisions along ethnic lines within the political elite' in Bosnia. There were two conditions which accounted for this, according to Andjelic: 'economic and political turbulence in Bosnia-Herzegovina and the rise of nationalism in the neighbouring republic' of Serbia.[63] These conditions, in turn, should be understood within the context of Andjelic's central argument, which is 'that it was the crucial stream of political developments, *triggered by a series of scandals in 1987 and 1988*, which led to war'.[64] But, Gordana Knežević has argued, by placing so much emphasis on developments within Bosnia-Herzegovina in his effort to understand the roots of the fighting, Andjelic allows the reader to imagine that the political leaderships in Belgrade (and to a lesser extent in Zagreb) were less culpable than they actually were.[65]

Andjelic believes that his interpretation is virtually unique – 'virtually' because he is willing to give Christopher Bennett some credit for having understood the roots of the crisis.[66] But, for the most part, Andjelic acknowledges very little debt to the works listed in his bibliography, which are, evidently, a cacophony of error. 'Scholars', he writes, 'have hardly begun to tackle this recent war in the Balkans seriously.' Indeed, he tells us, most scholarly works 'can be divided into two groups: one paying attention to history, however distant, and examples of ethnic grievances, and the other explaining everything in terms of aggression from neighbouring countries whilst ignoring internal Bosnian developments'.[67] And he proceeds to denounce 'academic and pseudo-academic works' which offer a fare more appropriate 'for journalists and politicians or military officers'.[68] I believe that Andjelic's portrayal of the field does not do it justice, and I hope that this chapter, together with a parallel study of mine,[69] may alert readers to points of view that cannot easily be collapsed into Andjelic's two cacophonous choirs.

The last book to be discussed here is an anthology – the product of editorial collaboration between an American scholar (Jim Seroka) and a Serbian scholar (Vukašin Pavlović). *The Tragedy of Yugoslavia* (1992) brings together a distinguished group of Slovenian, Croatian, and Serbian scholars; Seroka himself is the only non-Yugoslav contributor to this eight-chapter collection. The editors deserve a lot of credit for their honesty in admitting that, when they began work on the volume in March 1990, at a time when some scholars were worrying that the country was headed for intercommunal war, they considered that 'civil war was only a remote possibility', believing that 'pluralism and democracy were on the eve of an historic triumph'.[70] The best essays in this collection, at least to my mind, are those by Mirjana Kasapović on Croatian elections and Anton Bebler on the military. Writing in January 1991, Bebler showed a keen awareness of the dangers of civil war, pointing out, for example, that in December 1989, the Yugoslav Defence Ministry failed to furnish a copy of its budget to the Federal Assembly.[71] Bebler also highlights secret JNA efforts, begun already in spring/ summer 1990, to destabilize the noncommunist governments in Slovenia and Croatia, and notes that, as of late 1990, the JNA was 'disarming the Territorial Defense [forces] and denying Slovenia and Croatia light weapons for their police forces (while providing weapons to the Serbian police and official paramilitary formations)'.[72] Kasapović, for her part, highlights Serbia's role in stoking the crisis, drawing particular attention to the 'authoritarian bases of Serbian populism' and, hence, to the linkage between Serbian nationalism and anti-liberalism.[73]

Also useful is a chapter by Ivan Šiber on nationalism, values, and ideology. Šiber highlights the high levels of authoritarianism among Croatian voters overall, especially among those on the left or right extremes of the political spectrum.[74] This, in turn, suggests that it may not be enough to democratize a *system*; it may be necessary also to democratize the *citizens* – to build, in the phrase of Gabriel Almond and Sidney Verba, a civic culture.

In a more recently published work, Dejan Jović outlines eight alternative theories concerning why Yugoslavia disintegrated and sank into open warfare:

- economic deterioration;
- so-called ancient ethnic hatreds;
- persistent problems of nationalism since at least 1921;
- cultural differences among the peoples of Yugoslavia;
- changes in the international system;
- the role of specific personalities (whether Milošević and/or Tudjman and/or Izetbegović, or others);
- the premodern character of the Yugoslav state;
- structural-institutional permutations.[75]

Jović himself expresses scepticism about the utility of unicausal theories, and suggests that one needs to take into account a cluster of factors. And, indeed, the authors discussed in this chapter tend to do so. Magaš is perhaps the best example of multifactor analysis here, tracing the problems which tore Yugoslavia apart to the way the past has haunted the present, thanks in part to the role of elites prepared to manipulate people's perceptions, and also to structural-institutional permutations. Pleština, Perica, and Bennett all factor in the role of personalities, combining this, respectively, with economic deterioration, cultural-religious differences, and structural-institutional problems. Allcock also takes into account more than one variable; from Jović's list, Allcock includes economic deterioration, the premodern character of the Yugoslav state, structural-institutional factors, and the general failure of socialism, while Wachtel highlights the independent potency of cultural artifacts and differences in education. Still, one should not make too much of Pleština's and Perica's particular foci, since it was not their purpose to explain the disintegration of Yugoslavia, but rather, in Pleština's case, to explain why the regionalization of the economy presented problems for the country, and, in Perica's case, to explain and discuss the political role of ecclesiastical figures and religious organizations in Yugoslavia over a period of decades.

Among other literature, Carole Rogel, in *The Breakup of Yugoslavia and the War in Bosnia*, associates herself with theories emphasizing the primacy of politics, by identifying the dysfunctional political system as the root of the problem;[76] and Misha Glenny, in his mammoth volume, *The Balkans* – to be discussed in chapter 6 – traces the problems of Yugoslavia back to the Vidovdan constitution of 1921.

Casting a retrospective glance back to 1983, when the first warnings about Yugoslavia's drift towards civil war were sounded,[77] we may take up our last task and contrast the danger signs highlighted by writers before 1986 and those identified by writers approaching the subject after the fact. First, it is clear that, already in the early 1980s, at least some Western scholars were well aware of some of the challenges facing the country. In a collection published in 1985, for example, Dennison Rusinow noted that 'nationalist prejudices and suspicions and the number of "nationalist excesses" are at their highest levels since 1970–1971',[78] while Wolfgang Höpken drew attention to the fact that the League of Communists of Yugoslavia was, by 1984, in an advanced state of crisis.[79] In the same publication, George Schöpflin outlined the manifestations of the political decay in Yugoslavia and other one-party systems in East-Central Europe, at a time when many area specialists were still in denial.[80] Other scholars at the time noted the importance of economic deterioration. Similarly, the role played by Serbian hegemonism (noted most especially by Magaš and Pleština) in provoking tensions was understood already in the early 1980s, when it existed in a much milder strain than it would later.

On the other hand, even after the role played by Croatian intellectuals in the 'Croatian Spring' of 1967–71, Western analysts could not anticipate the role to be played by Serbian intellectuals in 1986, in drawing up the famous nationalist memorandum.[81] Nor, as far as I am aware, were any outside observers able to anticipate the abrupt reversal of policy and programme executed by Milošević within Serbia beginning in late 1987; many observers had noted the self-pitying, aggressive character of the memorandum, of course, but most, if not all, were as surprised when Milošević carried out an internal party coup against his best friend, Stambolić, as was Stambolić himself. Moreover, as far as I am aware, even the most pessimistic writers in the West tended to view the 1974 constitutional system as having merits as well as debilities, while out-and-out optimists saw in it no less than 'the legitimation of a revolution'.

Other factors cited by scholars prior to 1986 which have not been stressed in this discussion include the collapse of public confidence in the existing institutions, a trend graphically recorded in opinion polls in the early 1980s, the party's repression of autonomists in Kosovo, Croatia, and Slovenia, thereby alienating important sectors of the local publics and laying the basis for eventual separatism, and the false solution of trying to substitute regional pluralism for political pluralism, a solution which could have succeeded only if political consciousness could have been contained and limited.

NOTES

1 On this point, see Svein Mønnesland, *Før Jugoslavia og etter,* 4th edn (Oslo: Sypress Forlag, 1999), pp. 243–5.
2 Dijana Pleština, *Regional Development in Communist Yugoslavia: Success, Failure, and Consequences* (Boulder, CO: Westview Press, 1992), p. 133.
3 Susan L. Woodward, *Socialist Unemployment: The Political Economy of Yugoslavia, 1945–1990* (Princeton, NJ: Princeton University Press, 1995), pp. 339, 352–64.
4 *Ibid.,* pp. 352, 355, 359, 364.
5 *Ibid.,* p. xv.
6 *Ibid.,* p. 347.
7 This summarizes her arguments on pages 346 and 370.
8 *Ibid.,* p. 259.
9 *Ibid.,* p. 33.
10 *Ibid.,* p. 240. See also pp. 201–2, 225.
11 Branka Magaš, *The Destruction of Yugoslavia: Tracking Yugoslavia's Break-up 1980–1992* (London: Verso, 1992), p. 3.
12 *Ibid.,* p. 80.
13 *Ibid.,* p. 117.
14 *Ibid.,* p. 82.
15 Vjekoslav Perica, *Balkan Idols: Religion and Nationalism in Yugoslav States* (Oxford: Oxford University Press, 2002), p. 135.
16 Jug Grizelj, in *Slobodna Dalmacija* (Split), 27 April 1985, as quoted in Perica, *Balkan Idols,* p. 135.
17 Perica, *Balkan Idols,* pp. 136–7.
18 *Ibid.,* pp. 139–40.
19 *Ibid.,* p. 144.
20 *Ibid.,* p. 152.
21 *Ibid.,* p. 166.
22 *Ibid.,* pp. 239, 243.
23 Lenard J. Cohen, *Broken Bonds: Yugoslavia's Disintegration and Balkan Politics in Transition,* 2nd edn (Boulder, CO: Westview Press, 1995), p. 21.
24 *Ibid.,* p. 246.
25 *Ibid.*
26 Branimir Anzulović, *Heavenly Serbia: From Myth to Genocide* (London and Washington Square, NY: C. Hurst and Co. and New York University Press, 1999), p. 9.
27 Quoted *ibid.,* pp. 51–2.
28 Quoted *ibid.,* p. 52.
29 *Ibid.*
30 Quoted *ibid.,* pp. 133–4.
31 *Ibid.,* p. 139.
32 Andrew Baruch Wachtel, *Making a Nation, Breaking a Nation: Literature and Cultural Politics in Yugoslavia* (Stanford, CA: Stanford University Press, 1998), p. 174.

33 *Ibid.*, p. 184.
34 *Ibid.*, pp. 213, 214.
35 *Ibid.*, p. 217.
36 *Ibid.*, p. 218.
37 *Ibid.*, p. 229.
38 John B. Allcock, *Explaining Yugoslavia* (London and New York: C. Hurst & Co. and Columbia University Press, 2000), p. 418.
39 *Ibid.*, pp. 418–23, 428–9.
40 *Ibid.*, p. 11.
41 *Ibid.*, p. 17. For the example of the participation of Croatia and Serbia in wider European philosophical trends in the nineteenth and early twentieth centuries, see Helmut Dahm and Assen Ignatow (eds.), *Geschichte der philosophischen Traditionen Osteuropas* (Darmstadt: Wissenschaftliche Buchgesellschaft, 1996).
42 Allcock, *Explaining Yugoslavia*, p. 24.
43 *Ibid.*, p. 243.
44 *Ibid.*, p. 352.
45 *Ibid.*, p. 390.
46 *Ibid.*, pp. 395–6.
47 *Ibid.*, pp. 434–6.
48 *Ibid.*, p. 440.
49 Christopher Bennett, *Yugoslavia's Bloody Collapse: Causes, Course and Consequences* (Washington Square, NY: New York University Press, 1995), p. 7.
50 *Ibid.*, pp. 10, 13–14, 153, 236.
51 *Ibid.*, pp. 128, 129.
52 *Ibid.*, p. 242.
53 See Sabrina P. Ramet, *Social Currents in Eastern Europe: The Sources and Consequences of the Great Transformation*, 2nd edn (Durham, NC: Duke University Press, 1995), chap. 8 ('Serb–Albanian Tensions in Kosovo').
54 *Ibid.*, pp. 32–40; and Sabrina P. Ramet, *Balkan Babel: The Disintegration of Yugoslavia from the Death of Tito to the Fall of Milošević*, 4th edn (Boulder, CO: Westview Press, 2002), pp. 50–1.
55 Ramet, *Balkan Babel*, 4th edn, pp. 4, 49–50, 375–7.
56 *Ibid.*, pp. 35–41, 81–126, 153–6.
57 *Ibid.*, chaps. 1–3.
58 *Ibid.*, p. 50.
59 For Zulfikarpašić's story, see Adil Zulfikarpašić, in dialogue with Milovan Djilas and Nadežda Gaće, *The Bosniak* (London: C. Hurst & Co., 1998).
60 Ramet, *Balkan Babel*, 4th edn, p. 153.
61 This sentence also summarizes the interpretation advanced in my *Balkan Babel*.
62 Neven Andjelic, *Bosnia-Herzegovina: The End of a Legacy* (London and Portland, OR: Frank Cass, 2003), pp. 56–64.
63 *Ibid.*, p. 72.
64 *Ibid.*, pp. 21–2, my emphasis.
65 Gordana Knežević, 'Civil War and Civil Disagreement', *Bosnia Report*, new series, 39–40 (April–July 2004), p. 13.

66 Andjelic, *Bosnia-Herzegovina*, pp. 3–4.
67 *Ibid.*, p. 3.
68 *Ibid.*, pp. 3–4.
69 See my 'Explaining the Yugoslav Meltdown, 1. "For a charm of pow'rful trouble, Like a hell-broth boil and bubble"': Theories about the Roots of the Yugoslav Troubles', in a special issue of *Nationalities Papers*, edited by Thomas Emmert and Charles Ingrao, 32, 4 (December 2004), pp. 731–63, as well as my 'Explaining the Yugoslav Meltdown, 2. A Theory about the Causes of the Yugoslav Meltdown: The Serbian National Awakening as a "Revitalization Movement"', on pp. 765-79 of the same issue.
70 'Preface' to Jim Seroka and Vukašin Pavlović (eds.), *The Tragedy of Yugoslavia: The Failure of Democratic Transformation* (Armonk, NY: M. E. Sharpe, 1992), p. xi.
71 Anton Bebler, 'Political Pluralism and the Yugoslav Professional Military', in Seroka and Pavlović, *The Tragedy of Yugoslavia*, p. 124.
72 *Ibid.*, p. 138.
73 Mirjana Kasapović, 'The Structure and Dynamics of the Yugoslav Political Environment and Elections in Croatia', in Seroka and Pavlović, *The Tragedy of Yugoslavia*, p. 28.
74 Ivan Šiber, 'The Impact of Nationalism, Values, and Ideological Orientations on Multi-Party Elections in Croatia', in Seroka and Pavlović, *The Tragedy of Yugoslavia*, pp. 141–71. These findings were confirmed several years later by Ivan Grdešić. See I. Grdešić, 'The Radical Right in Croatia and Its Constituency', in Sabrina P. Ramet (ed.), *The Radical Right in Central and Eastern Europe since 1989* (University Park, PA: Pennsylvania State University Press, 1999), pp. 171–89.
75 Dejan Jović, *Jugoslavija: Država koja je odumrla – Uspon, kriza i pad Kardeljeve Jugoslavije (1974–1990)* (Zagreb: Prometej, 2003), pp. 23–102.
76 Carole Rogel, *The Breakup of Yugoslavia and the War in Bosnia* (Westport, CT: Greenwood Press, 1998), p. xiii.
77 Cited in Pedro Ramet, 'Yugoslavia and the Threat of Internal and External Discontents', *Orbis*, 28, 1 (Spring 1984), pp. 103–21.
78 Dennison Rusinow, 'Nationalities Policy and the "National Question"', in Pedro Ramet, *Yugoslavia in the 1980s* (Boulder, CO: Westview Press, 1985), p. 132.
79 Wolfgang Höpken, 'Party Monopoly and Political Change: The League of Communists Since Tito's Death', in Ramet, *Yugoslavia in the 1980s*, p. 49.
80 George Schöpflin, 'Political Decay in One-Party Systems in Eastern Europe: Yugoslav Patterns', in Ramet, *Yugoslavia in the 1980s*, pp. 307–21.
81 Concerning the memorandum, see Ivo Banac, 'The Dissolution of Yugoslav Historiography', in Sabrina Petra Ramet and Ljubiša S. Adamovich (eds.), *Beyond Yugoslavia: Politics, Economics, and Culture in a Shattered Community* (Boulder, CO: Westview Press, 1995), pp. 53, 55–6.

REFERENCES

Allcock, John B., *Explaining Yugoslavia* (London and New York: C. Hurst & Co. and Columbia University Press, 2000), p. 499.

Andjelic, Neven, *Bosnia-Herzegovina: The End of a Legacy* (London and Portland, OR: Frank Cass, 2003), p. 228.

Anzulović, Branimir, *Heavenly Serbia: From Myth to Genocide* (London and Washington square, NY: C. Hurst & Co. and New York University Press, 1999), p. 233.

Bennett, Christopher, *Yugoslavia's Bloody Collapse: Causes, Course and Consequences* (Washington Square, NY: New York University Press, 1995), p. 272.

Cohen, Lenard J., *Broken Bonds: Yugoslavia's Disintegration and Balkan Politics in Transition*, 2nd edn (Boulder, CO: Westview Press, 1995), p. 386.

Magaš, Branka., *The Destruction of Yugoslavia: Tracking Yugoslavia's Break-up 1980–1992* (London: Verso, 1992), p. 359.

Perica, Vjekoslav, *Balkan Idols: Religion and Nationalism in Yugoslav States* (Oxford: Oxford University Press, 2002), p. 332.

Pleština, Dijana, *Regional Development in Communist Yugoslavia: Success, Failure, and Consequences* (Boulder, CO: Westview Press, 1992), p. 233.

Seroka, Jim and Vukašin Pavlović (eds.), *The Tragedy of Yugoslavia: The Failure of Democratic Transformation* (Armonk, NY: M. E. Sharpe, 1992), p. 207.

Wachtel, Andrew Baruch, *Making a Nation, Breaking a Nation: Literature and Cultural Politics in Yugoslavia* (Stanford, CA: Stanford University Press, 1998), p. 302.

Woodward, Susan L., *Socialist Unemployment: The Political Economy of Yugoslavia, 1945–1990* (Princeton, NJ: Princeton University Press, 1995), p. 443.

4   Who's to blame, and for what? Rival accounts of the war

I

History – so little understood in some quarters – is a slippery art. History, even contemporary history, is not journalism, it is not akin to a steno-graphic record, it is not, by any stretch of the imagination, comprehensive. Depending on what is remembered and how it is recounted, the identity of a people, a society's mores, and even some of the society's political options at any moment may be affected, shaped, even constrained. There is no such thing as a history without an interpretation; if there were such a thing, it would resemble a scrapbook of randomly collected bits of information, without any effort having been made to assess the relative importance of one fact as opposed to another. A historian confronts a welter of different sources, some of them offering alternative accounts of the facts, and must take responsibility for doing the best job s/he can in terms of bringing together those facts which (1) are reliably confirmed and (2) are worth reporting (no one today cares what the price of nails in Zagreb was in 1926). Historians often talk of the importance of getting at the best sources, including archival sources, and there is no doubt but that this is important. However, a historian's most important virtue is integrity, for it is integrity which is the best assurance of the 'reliability' of the interpretations offered. Balance, on the other hand, is a trickier concept: is it the judicious balance in which all things are given their proper weight, and in which private interests and partisanship are not allowed to distort the evidence? In this sense, balance is even a dimension of integrity. But today, a wrong-headed species of 'balance' is often held up as the value to which we should aspire; on this latter reading, 'balance' consists in finding all sides equally guilty or equally innocent. This wrong-headed species of 'balance' is, in fact, anything but balanced. Indeed, it is the very opposite of balance in the healthy sense.

There is, thus, no necessary contradiction between identifying who is to blame for one or another result and maintaining a judicious balance in one's account. Quite the contrary, it would be the mark of unbalanced judgement, if not of an unbalanced mind, to believe that it is necessary to retell history in such a way that no one is culpable for anything at all. Can one, then, speak of villains and victims in history? David Owen, who served as British foreign secretary from February 1977 to May 1979 and then as EU representative in Bosnia during the crucial years of the war there, quickly became disillusioned with all parties to the conflict and concluded that 'we delude ourselves if . . . [we] portray the struggle [in Bosnia] as one between "good guys" and "bad guys"'.[1] But Owen has his own candidates for 'demons' – namely, US president Bill Clinton and his advisers. In Owen's words, 'what the Clinton administration seemed to want until 1994 . . . was power without responsibility',[2] and Owen does not mince words in condemning the Clinton administration's lack of enthusiasm for the plan which he had drawn up together with UN mediator Cyrus Vance – the so-called Vance–Owen Peace Plan (VOPP). Indeed, Owen personalizes his criticism by declaring his conviction that 'if President Bush had won re-election in November 1992 there would have been a settlement in Bosnia-Herzegovina in February 1993 on the basis of the VOPP, implemented predominantly by the UN, probably without US troops'[3]

Lord Owen's account is rich in detail concerning negotiations, offering some insights into behind-the-scenes manoeuvres, and suggesting, at one point, that the primary reason that Germany opposed sanctions for Croatia was Germany's fear that Zagreb might respond by closing all refugee camps in the country, thereby unleashing a flood of refugees, some of whom would flee to Germany itself, which had already taken in some 400,000 refugees from the war[4] – more than Britain, France, and Italy combined. But Owen says little about the military activities that made these negotiations necessary. Of course, a reader wanting a fuller discussion of the military side can always turn to the comprehensive CIA study, *Balkan Battlegrounds*.[5] There are occasional lapses on Owen's part – such as his suggestion that Izetbegović might have been more effective in negotiations with the Serbs 'if he had not been a devout Muslim',[6] or his belief that it was Western recognition which set off the fighting in Bosnia-Herzegovina[7] (thereby making light of the extensive military preparations undertaken by the Serbian side for launching the conflict in spring 1992), or his mistaken belief that Milošević wanted Serbia to develop a market economy.[8]

Still, for all that and for all the self-promotion and cloying criticism of his detractors throughout the book, Owen's memoirs remain an important resource for understanding what went on in the minds of the Western negotiators as they sat down to discuss war and peace with the likes of

Karadžić and Mladić, for example, whom Owen describes at one point as 'cats licking the cream'.[9] Owen rejects the idea that the problems of the region should be traced to nationalism,[10] attributing the problems rather to 'bad leaders'.[11]

The centre of gravity for Owen is the Vance–Owen Peace Plan, which he clearly believes would have produced a more just solution than was achieved at Dayton, sooner, and at a lower human and economic cost to all concerned. He therefore criticizes the US position bitterly, and describes criticism of the plan in the United States as 'ill-informed'.[12] Owen quotes widely from the US media, to the extent that one might suppose that he had no other source of information about US government deliberations than American newspapers and weekly magazines. Whatever the case may be, the American media clearly stung Owen, who cites both Serbian criticism of his efforts and British pacifist criticism, apparently in an effort to portray himself as a man of the moderate middle.[13]

Far more sophisticated than Owen's curve-ball account is James Gow's *Triumph of the Lack of Will* – truly one of the very best books dealing with the war in Bosnia and very probably the best blow-by-blow account in English of international diplomacy in that war. Gow agrees with Owen in criticizing the Clinton administration for its lack of support for the Vance–Owen plan, but also criticizes Whitehall and Paris as well. Part of the problem, as Gow sees it, is that every player interpreted the crisis not in local terms, but through its own historical lenses. The British government, thus, tended to see the Yugoslav conflict through the prism of its own experiences in Northern Ireland, and thus to consider it as a long-standing and largely 'insoluble' conflict.[14] The French saw the Yugoslav conflict as comparable to the situation in Corsica and worried that acceptance of Slovenian and Croatian independence would set a precedent for eventual Corsican independence.[15] The Germans read the Yugoslav conflict in terms of self-determination, believing that their own recent reunification was justified on the basis of a principle applicable also in the Yugoslav context. And the Americans, for their part, viewed the crisis through the lenses of their own bitter experiences in Vietnam. The application of lessons learned in the past is, of course, *potentially* healthy – but it is healthy and useful only when the lessons are applicable in the new context. In the event, the lessons that Britain, France, and the United States brought to bear led them to adopt policies which took them down a diplomatic dead end. Gow is more generous than Owen when it comes to Clinton, conceding that 'Clinton's heart was clearly in the right place', but he adds that Clinton's domestic agenda consistently took priority over foreign policy challenges.[16] Gow offers an articulate defence of the VOPP, suggesting that key people at top levels in the Clinton administration may not have familiarized themselves with the provisions of the plan. He argues that the international community could have used force to implement the VOPP, over the heads of Bosnian Serb leaders and parliamentarians, and cites Russian foreign minister Andrei Kozyrev as favouring the idea.[17] In so saying, Gow dismisses the Bosnian Serb rejection of the plan as not crucial. But if it could have been done over the heads of local leaders, why was peace not imposed in 1993, rather than waiting until the end of 1995? The answer is given in Gow's title – *lack of will*. On this point, he quotes British foreign secretary Douglas Hurd who told a Channel 4 interviewer in August 1993, 'The only thing which could have guaranteed peace with justice would have been an expeditionary force . . . And no government, no government has at any time seriously proposed that'.[18] Thus, even although Gow holds Washington primarily responsible for the collapse of the VOPP initiative, Whitehall scarcely comes off much better, being indicted by Gow for 'pusillanimous realism'.[19]

During the war years, a great deal of energy was expended in arguing as to whether the war in Croatia and Bosnia was a 'civil war' or an 'international war', with huge political conclusions being drawn from one or the other. Some observers also argued strenuously against the notion that it was an 'ethnic war', without ever defining the term; of course, if by 'ethnic war' one means that it involved the mobilization of hatreds of members of other national collectivities, then to deny that it was an 'ethnic war' would seem to entail the notion that there were no anti-Serbian, anti-Croatian, or anti-Muslim sentiments nurtured on the part of any significant number of combatants. Gow does not enter into the debate about the ethnic or nonethnic dimensions of the war, but he does insist that the war had a 'hybrid' character – in part involving residents of Croatia/Bosnia fighting each other and in part involving the complicity of Serbia in the war in Croatia, and of both Serbia and Croatia in the war in Bosnia. He also insists that the war should not be understood as the result of Slovenian and Croatian secession, but, on the contrary, their secession as well as the declaration of independence on the part of Bosnia-Herzegovina should be understood as a response to the dissolution of the Yugoslav state.[20]

The book title is ironic and suggestive, deriving its inspiration from Leni Riefenstahl's cinematic celebration of the Nazi Third Reich (*Triumph of the Will*), and drawing attention, through the device of rhetorical inversion, to the ineffectual response of the West, not only to Milošević and Karadžić and their underlings, but also, in that earlier era, to Adolf Hitler's encroachments. In this connection, Gow finds parallels between Bosnia in the 1990s and Czechoslovakia in the 1930s, comparing

Hitler's relationship with Konrad Henlein with Milošević's relationship with Karadžić, and Hitler's mobilization of German discontent with the Czechoslovak government with Milošević's mobilization of Serb discontent with the government of Bosnia-Herzegovina.[21] On this interpretation, then, British prime minister John Major comes across as the new Chamberlain. This representation of the conflict in Bosnia is, rather obviously, entirely different from Owen's more relativist account.

Gow is also more critical of the Bush Snr administration than Owen, accusing Bush's secretary of state, James Baker, and US ambassador to Belgrade Warren Zimmermann of 'a lack of sympathy for Slovenia and Croatia' throughout 1991.[22] But the tragic mistake on which Gow focuses was the US decision to let the Vance–Owen plan die, a decision he attributes to American disinclination to deploy troops in Bosnia, among other things. As for the Dayton Peace Accord, this was a success only insofar as it ended the fighting, according to Gow, but not in other regards; in his view, the VOPP was a better plan than the Dayton Peace Accord both in terms of its provision for ethnic proportionality in government and in terms of denying the Bosnian Serbs the advantage of territorial contiguity with the Republic of Serbia.

The books by Brendan Simms and General Sir Michael Rose provide interesting contrasts to Gow's classic, with Simms subjecting Her Majesty's government to more severe criticism than Gow dishes out and Rose assaying a qualified defence of the very policies which both Gow and Simms find wanting. Simms, in fact, criticizes Gow (in the 2002 edition of his book) for having allegedly 'argue[d] within one and the same book both that the arms embargo was wrong and that "Most of the UK's 'objections' over the issues surrounding the use of force (including the arms embargo) were founded on sound analysis of the circumstances."'[23] Simms has even harsher words for Lord Owen who, in Simms's account, in his surprise at the Bosnian Serb rejection of the peace plan he had drawn up with Cyrus Vance, had 'forgotten' that the Serbs were fighting not in order to obtain an equitable territorial settlement but in pursuit of a maximalist programme of territorial expansion. The VOPP, says Simms, never had a chance with the Serbs, Owen's illusions notwithstanding, while 'the territorial provisions of Dayton, lamentable though they are, were superior to the VOPP, because they were actually enforced on a militarily defeated Republika Srpska'.[24] In so saying, Simms marks out a position diametrically opposite to that of Gow. Nor does Simms agree with Gow and Owen that the reason that the Vance–Owen Peace Plan was not adopted was American unenthusiasm; on the contrary, Simms pins the blame squarely on the Bosnian Serbs, whose Assembly rejected the plan with finality in May 1993. As for the notion that the plan could have been imposed on the combatants by force, Simms insists that it would have been inconceivable that the White House and Whitehall might commit ground troops to impose 'an unjust and contested settlement' for which only one of the three warring sides (the Croats) had any enthusiasm, and expresses amazement that Lord Owen did not resign when the fruit of his labours proved to be indigestible.[25]

Simms's central argument is simple: according to him, Britain's role in the Bosnian war was 'disastrous', with British leaders 'afflicted by a particularly disabling form of conservative pessimism which disposed them not only to reject military intervention themselves, but [also] to prevent anybody else, particularly the Americans, from intervening either.'[26] What Whitehall thought it wanted, says Simms, was a strong Serbia, which is to say, a Serbian victory in Bosnia. Parliament itself, according to Simms, came under the noxious influence of 'harrumphing squires, paranoid Germanophobes and barrack-room historians.'[27] As a result, Britain did its best to obstruct any efforts to supply the Bosnian government with arms or to come to its assistance, and tried to press the Bosnian government to acquiesce in an unjust peace settlement. Nor does he paint the Americans as angels; on the contrary, he claims that US military intelligence had a strong complement of 'Serbophiles' who fed American authorities analyses that served Serbian war aims.[28] Yet, in his judgement, 'by comparison with Britain . . . US policy was a model of good sense.'[29]

Britain's errors included a general tendency to relativize the conflict, treating all parties to the conflict as morally equivalent, opposition to a French proposal to dispatch a Western European Union interposition force to Croatia in September 1991, resistance to the implementation of a 'no-fly zone' against the Bosnian Serbs, abstention from a UN General Assembly resolution comparing ethnic cleansing to genocide (in December 1992), opposition to lifting the arms embargo against Bosnia, and opposition to proposals, until late in the war, to use air strikes to change the local balance of power. And to this one may add the fact that Britain looked to Milošević to guarantee security in the Balkans, without worrying about the nature of the security which Milošević would provide.[30] The consequence of British policy, Simms concludes, was that Serb forces were given free rein for more than two years to do their worst, resulting in higher casualties than would have been the case had Whitehall faced the situation honestly. Thus, the peace-keeping operations emerge, in Simms's account, as a weak-kneed response designed to put off the moment of decision; and, while he commends General Michael Rose for 'real achievements in the field of humanitarian aid', he also criticizes the general for having spent 'a great deal of time', both while in the field and later in his memoirs, 'attacking' the Sarajevo government and defending Serbian interests.[31]

General Rose's memoirs are written with verve and communicate Rose's apparently endless frustrations, during his year as commander of the UN Protection Force (UNPROFOR) in Bosnia (January 1994–January 1995) with, as he viewed them, war-mongers in NATO, 'armchair' experts who dared to offer their own views about the situation in Bosnia, journalists apparently bent on casting Rose and UNPROFOR in the worst possible light, and the entire cast of characters including Ejup Ganić (said by Rose to have 'use[d] other people to advance his own wealth and power'),[32] Alija Izetbegović (whose 'talk of creating a multi-religious, multi-cultural state in Bosnia' struck Rose as 'a disguise for the extension of his own political power and the furtherance of Islam'),[33] Ratko Mladić (portrayed as 'either quite mad, a liar, or completely out of touch with his army'[34] and having a tendency to fly into a rage, launching into interminable tirades during which 'his eyes flashed with fury and spittle flew from his lips'[35]), and Radovan Karadžić (who by the end of 1994 'looked and spoke like a madman').[36] Rose was also 'annoyed' by UN special envoy Yasushi Akashi's allegedly 'bad manners' but 'soon discovered that, if I stared at him long enough, he would lose the thread of what he was saying and nervously fumble for words.'[37] On the other hand, Rose obviously developed an admiration for Bosnian prime minister Haris Silajdžić, whom he describes as 'the only politician I met in Bosnia who had a genuinely European attitude or offered any hope for the future of the country.'[38]

Unlike Gow and Simms, Rose is convinced that the arms embargo was a reasonable instrument of policy, that the cautious approach taken by the international community in Bosnia was the *best* response imaginable, that a policy of lifting the arms embargo and sending aircraft to strike at Bosnian Serb targets ('lift and strike', as it was popularly called) was a recipe for disaster, and that, in any event, what both the local population and sensible world leaders wanted to see was *less force*, on the part of NATO or UNPROFOR, and more focus on providing humanitarian assistance.[39] Unsurprisingly, he also devotes some space to defending UNPROFOR's role and his own achievements in Bosnia.[40] Whereas Simms had some disparaging things to say about London *Times* correspondent Misha Glenny, Rose credits Glenny's book, *The Fall of Yugoslavia*, with having 'contributed much to my understanding of the Balkans',[41] and then proceeds to outline his view of the Balkans as a region 'where national, religious, ethnic and social currents run deep and where the bloody history of the Balkans casts a perpetual shadow over *every* event and action', so that it seems to Rose 'impossible to overestimate the significance of the violent history of the region that led to the emergence of a fanatical nationalism and hatred of other races'.[42] On such an understanding, Rose is not surprised that Silajdžić is the only local politician with European values; in Rose's mind, the Yugoslav region is not entirely civilized, its people cannot escape the 'perpetual shadow' of the past, and the particulars of what happened in the past ten years, let us say, let alone in the past month, are less important for understanding the conflict than 'the bloody history of the Balkans'.

Rose treats critics of the UN's approach to the conflict in Bosnia with derision,[43] and was, apparently, especially stung by editorials contributed by the distinguished British academics Noel Malcolm and Mark Almond to British newspapers.[44] Yet, in commenting on Malcolm's exhortation to allow the Bosnian government access to arms, Rose fails to mention that, under the UN Charter, Bosnia-Herzegovina, as a member of the UN, had the legal right to obtain arms and that it was the UN Security Council which, in maintaining the arms embargo, was acting illegally. But there is a curious undercurrent running through Rose's memoirs. While he acknowledges that the Muslims were the principal victims and that the Serbs were the principal perpetrators of atrocities,[45] he repeatedly casts the principal blame for obstructing the peace process on the Bosnian government. The Bosnian government was less concerned with the alleviation of the suffering of Bosnians than with realizing its political goals, he writes early in the book.[46] Indeed, Izetbegović is said to have declared himself ready "to see 10,000 Bosnians die of starvation rather than accept a single Serb on Bosnian territory"[47] – this apparently in spite of the fact that there were Serbs loyal to Izetbegović who were fighting on the side of the government which Izetbegović headed. And, hence, the Bosnian government put 'obstacles' in Rose's way, while concealing the true nature of its policies, used the UN peace-keeping force as a shield behind which to continue the war, fired mortars from positions around a Sarajevo hospital, took actions which by themselves 'rendered the prospect of peace uncertain', repeatedly derailed peace plans by making unreasonable demands, and in general pursued policies which could only result in 'the unnecessary prolongation of the war'.[48] Since the Bosnian Serbs whose rejection of the Vance–Owen Plan, the Owen–Stoltenberg Plan, and the Contact Group plan could be thought to have prevented the combatants from reaching a negotiated solution prior to Dayton, perhaps Rose would have preferred that the Bosnian government simply accept such terms as the Bosnian Serbs and Bosnian Croats were prepared to offer Sarajevo. If that was his preference, Rose does not make this explicit. But he makes it abundantly clear that advocates of forceful responses on the part of NATO were only creating trouble for him personally, while registering his opinion that 'NATO often seemed to advocate taking disproportionate action against the Serbs, while ignoring violations on the side of the Muslims.'[49]

Rose makes an energetic case that the cautious approach taken by the international community was a reasonable one. But he seems unable to accept that that approach could also be subjected, as it was by the very critics he demonizes, to reasonable criticism. This is an important failing on his part. The chief benefit of having Rose's memoirs on hand, it seems to me, is that his account offers a kind of foil to Simms. While Simms offers what might be called a criticism from the left, Rose offers an apologia from the right. In tandem, these two mutually antagonistic accounts serve to further reinforce the credibility of Gow's more balanced approach, even if one might have reservations about Gow's enthusiasm for the Vance–Owen Peace Plan.

II

Warren Zimmermann adopts a more moralizing posture than either Owen or Simms, let alone Gow or Rose, starting his reminiscences with the words, 'This is a story with villains.'[50] He then proceeds to identify the villains as the 'nationalist leaders who coopted, intimidated, circumvented, or eliminated all opposition to their demagogic designs'.[51] Refreshingly, Zimmermann admits that he made serious mistakes – thereby earning himself a unique niche in the genre of memoirs; he even provides examples of some of his admitted mistakes. But he reserves much sharper criticism for Milošević and Karadžić, whom he blames for the deaths of tens of thousands of people in Bosnia, and for Tudjman, whom he calls a 'fanatic Croatian nationalist'.[52] Thus, for Zimmermann, the war should be traced in the first place not to systemic deficiencies, not to economic deterioration, not to Yugoslavia's diminished importance after the end of the Cold War, and most certainly not to a Western conspiracy to chop it up, but to specific personalities who took specific identifiable actions. It follows, for Zimmermann, that the situation could have been rescued had the right person come on to the political scene soon enough. His candidate for this role is Ante Marković, the Croatian communist who became prime minister of the Socialist Federated Republic of Yugoslavia (SFRY) in 1989; in Zimmermann's mind, if Marković had become prime minister immediately after Tito's death instead of nine years later, Yugoslavia might have been saved from disaster.[53] This approach reminds me of Sir Humphrey Appleby's maxim on the brilliant

British comedy series, *Yes, Prime Minister*: 'If the right people don't have power, do you know what happens? The *wrong* people get it!'[54] And, with the 'wrong people' in power, 'no imaginable political or even military intervention from outside could have arrested the nationalist-inspired drive to Yugoslavia's destruction', as Zimmermann puts it.[55] But he muses, 'Someday the normal people [the "right people"] will supplant the extremists'[56] in power, and at least some of the problems will go away. And yet, in spite of himself, Zimmermann is not oblivious to the systemic roots of the crisis, noting, early in his memoirs, the role of the 1974 constitution in creating power bases for republic elites representing national contingencies.[57]

Zimmermann's book provides behind-locked-doors glimpses into dinner conversations with interim US secretary of state Lawrence Eagleburger, into his own interactions with Milošević and others, draws upon his own cables to the State Department, and provides thumbnail sketches of the principals – sketches which are as entertaining as anything else. For Zimmermann, thus, Serbian neo-fascist Vojislav Šešelj should be understood as a 'psychopathic bully',[58] Croatian president Franjo Tudjman as a 'martinet',[59] Serbian novelist-turned-politician Vuk Drašković as 'a trickster' sporting an 'old testament beard', and future Serbian anti-Milošević dissident Momčilo Trajković as 'the Serbian Gauleiter' in Kosovo.[60] Zimmermann lives up to the charge brought against him by Gow by offering a remarkable criticism of Slovenes for what he calls ' "Garbo" nationalism – they just wanted to be left alone'.[61] Although he notes Milošević's effort to stage a massive rally in downtown Ljubljana in late 1989 in order 'to destabilize, perhaps even overthrow, the Slovenian leadership',[62] and notes Serb disinterest in Slovene offers of free airtime on Slovenian television and of free space in local Slovenian newspapers, he does not take Slovene fears of Milošević very seriously. To Zimmermann, the Slovenes seemed selfish, self-absorbed, and uncaring. Accordingly, 'They bear considerable responsibility for the bloodbath that followed their secession.'[63] Quite apart from the fact that this explanation is misguided, it is also contradicted by other portions of Zimmermann's text (including some already cited in this chapter) and, in any case, is contrary to common sense. Zimmermann was never a friend of Milošević but, in 1991, he declined to recommend to Washington that there be a military response on NATO's part to the Yugoslav People's Army (Jugoslavenska Narodna Armija, or JNA) siege of Dubrovnik – an oversight, in his own mind, for which he expresses regret in his memoirs; but, by July 1992, Ambassador Zimmermann had been converted to the notion that NATO should conduct air strikes to stop Serb aggression in Bosnia.[64]

Zimmermann has a flair for writing, and his account is lively and colourful, in the best sense. But ultimately his account is confused. Halfway through it, Zimmermann returns to the subject of the Slovenes, castigating them relentlessly. 'The Slovenes knew that their departure would bring a firestorm of violence down on the rest of Yugoslavia', he writes. 'In their self-absorption, however, the Slovenes had left the twenty-two million Yugoslav citizens they had abandoned twisting in the wind of impending war.'[65] Thus, the reader is led to believe that the Slovenes were somehow 'guilty' of the 'firestorm of violence' which hit the rest of Yugoslavia, even though they themselves were not involved in it. I am reminded of later accusations that NATO should be held responsible for Serb militias' actions against Albanian civilians during spring 1999, when the militias used the excuse of NATO bombardment to carry forward pre-existing Serb plans. And, where Zimmermann's account is concerned, having included the entire Slovene nation in a list of fantasy indictments,[66] which he imagines being brought before the international criminal court, he closes his book by musing that if Milošević's parents had committed suicide before giving birth to the future Serbian president, rather than after, Yugoslavia would not have dissolved and fallen victim to intercommunal violence.[67]

III

Susan Woodward's *Balkan Tragedy* impressed many commentators when it first appeared at the end of 1995. Strong on detail and long on explanation, it is an imposing work. Its heavy reliance on English-language sources may be excused, given the speed with which the book appeared. Indeed, its publication preceded, in the United States, that of its near-contemporary, *The Death of Yugoslavia*, written by Laura Silber and Allan Little. But the differences between the two works are at least as great as any similarities. The Silber/Little work is, in the first place, a factual narrative, telling the reader what happened, who did it, when it happened and where, and what its consequences were. Woodward's book, by contrast, routinely presents facts within the framework of explanations, so that the facts serve not to inform the reader as to what went on, but rather to support a particular explanatory theory. This difference is crucial, because it means that it is impossible to read the Woodward account as a historical narrative. It is not a historical account and, I feel confident in writing, was not intended to be such.

Woodward is critical of the notion that shared and distinct nationality entitles a group to set up its own state – a disposition I share.[68] But she takes it as a given that Slovenian (and, for that matter, Croatian) dissociation should be seen as the result of a claim to national self-determination, rather than as an act of bailing out of a failed state. She is, of course, right to assert that Britain, France, and Spain forged nations on the basis of states, while the Slovenes and Croats wanted to do the reverse.[69] But Germany and Italy took other paths, as did Norway for that matter, and, in any event, it would be difficult to mount a moral argument that there is something superior about one path rather than the other, all other things being equal. Be that as it may, Woodward believes that West European powers were confused about 'the relation between states and nations and [about] the meaning of national self-determination'[70] – a claim for which she is criticized by Gow.[71] But this theoretical groundwork serves a purpose for Woodward, that is, to criticize Germany and Austria for having allegedly advocated the 'purest notion of a nation-state'.[72] I do not know where she derived this interpretation, but I do know that it is not supported by former German foreign minister Genscher's account of German horror at JNA attacks on Croatian civilians[73] or by Viktor Meier's account of Slovene perceptions of the crisis, based on extensive interviews with Slovene political figures as well as use of Slovenian state archives.[74] Moreover, she surely goes too far in claiming that German sympathies for Slovenia and Croatia, built up over years of interaction with *Gastarbeiter* from those republics and of German tourists' developing friendships with Slovenes and Croats in the course of summer tourism there, should somehow be understood as 'an extension of the German idea of citizenship through blood alone (*jus sanguinis*) and the impossibility of ethnically heterogeneous states – ideas that had been at the core of fascist ideology'.[75] With this misrepresentation of German motivations, of course, she succeeds in characterizing not only Germany but also Slovenia, Croatia, and even Austria as somehow embodying the spirit of fascism. Even Italy gets dragged into this imbroglio, standing accused, in her account, of wanting, together with Austria, to expand its economic sphere of influence eastward.[76]

This framework permits her to equate the Slovenian dissociation from the defunct Yugoslav state with the Bosnian Serb aspiration to dissociate from Bosnia-Herzegovina, which she describes as based on 'the Slovene precedent'[77] and 'equally legitimate' with it.[78] The problem with this explanation is twofold: first, there was a basis in the 1974 constitution for the six constituent republics of the SFRY to negotiate their withdrawal from the federation, whereas there was no comparable legal basis for Bosnian Serb 'dissociation'; and, second, there had been a history of threats to Slovenes on the part of Belgrade and the JNA, while there was no comparable history of threats to Serbs living in Bosnia and she does not claim that there was. Indeed, it was the Serb nationalists who promulgated the slogan, 'All Serbs should live in one state' – a slogan strikingly akin to the allegedly 'German idea of citizenship through blood alone'. Curiously, she does not extend the same precedent to the Albanians of Kosovo, even though, within the Yugoslav constitutional system, the Albanians had had an autonomous province until it was illegally extinguished by Milošević in early 1989. Instead, she writes that their claim to 'rights to territorial self-governance on the basis of national self-determination or to national sovereignty were not at all clear' because their 'constitutional classification as a nationality rather than as a constituent nation made them ineligible for such rights'.[79] If this insistence on the relevance of the provisions of the 1974 constitution seems like conventionalism, that impression is strengthened by noting the emphasis she places on her discussion of sovereignty – the highest principle of conventionalists. The alternative, championed by universalists – human rights – does not obtain a comparable treatment in her account.

Woodward is aware of the dangerous 'Jekyll and Hyde potential of nationalism' and writes that politicians prepared to stoke fears about national survival 'had the potential to create a collective paranoia that was self-perpetuating'.[80] But, as she notes, Bosnia's multiethnic cities were resistant to nationalist propaganda, with urbanites 'ready to resist an attack on even the idea of mixed communities'.[81] This in turn explains the tactics adopted by Bosnian Serb forces of deliberately cutting telephone connections between different ethnic neighbourhoods.[82] But she does not make consistent use of this analysis, as shown in her suggestion that the establishment and arming of Serb militias in Baranja-Slavonia and in the Dalmatian hinterland, at a time when the territorial defence forces of Croatia were losing their arms to (illegal) JNA confiscations, should be understood as motivated by a desire for self-defence.[83] The same orientation is carried over in her explanation of the outbreak of open fighting in Bosnia. The Belgrade regime and the JNA had carefully laid the groundwork for an eventual assault on Bosnia beginning in 1990, when the arms flow to Serb militias began (as already noted and documented in chapter 1), and had encircled Sarajevo and other Bosnian cities with cannon and mortars. Then, in August 1991, as is well known, Milošević and Karadžić met to finalize their plans to ignite war in Bosnia the following spring (as reported in *Vreme* soon after the meeting). Under the circumstances, it is difficult to determine on what basis Woodward believes that 'the period between Kadijević's resignation [as minister of defence] in January 1992 and the EC demand of April 11, 1992, that the YPA [JNA] leave Bosnia-Herzegovina still presented opportunities for reversing the polarization and for preventing open war'. It is still more difficult to appreciate why she blames the Bosnian government's decision to call up the national guard in defence against the incipient Serbian insurrection for the war which followed.[84]

In spite of her references to the dangerous potential inherent in nationalism, Woodward traces the Yugoslav crisis not to 'villains', as per Zimmermann, but to 'the collapse of states, the problematic meaning of national self-determination in relation to human rights and borders, and the process of incorporating (or excluding) former socialist states into the West'.[85] What strikes me about this list is that people, actors, are excluded as causative agents; instead, the Yugoslav crisis is attributed to anonymous historical forces. Moreover, the collapse of the Yugoslav state itself is to be explained in terms of 'the transition of a particular constitutional order, its social and economic rights, and a society much transformed over forty years to another type of political order and its procedural and civil rights'.[86] Quite apart from the obscurantist character of this account, what is particularly striking to me is that there is no clear reference in this list to the problem of unemployment, which figured so prominently in her book on *Socialist Unemployment*, published at almost the same time as *Balkan Tragedy*.[87] She comes back to this question two pages later, however, offering that 'The real origin of the Yugoslav conflict is the disintegration of governmental authority and the breakdown of a political and civil order.'[88] But this only avoids the question as to what caused the system to break down; and, besides, not all systems break down violently. It is only seventy pages later that she returns to the question, telling us that the problems which would lead to the collapse of the system were economic deterioration and the very policies of austerity in which Zimmermann had seen some promise.[89] But there is no sign anywhere of human agency, only of blind historical forces. Here one may think of a story told by Alan Hunt and Gary Wickham about the aftermath of a talk given by philosopher C.S. Peirce early in the twentieth century. As the story goes, Peirce was approached, after his talk,

by a member of the audience. 'I enjoyed your talk,' she said, 'but it doesn't quite fit my theory of the universe.' 'Ah', replied Peirce, 'and what might that theory be?' 'That the universe stands on the back of a giant elephant.' 'Very interesting', the philosopher responded, 'but I must ask: on what does the elephant stand?' 'Easy', his interlocutor answered calmly, 'it stands on the back of a giant turtle.' Fascinated, Peirce was about to continue his line of questioning, but didn't get the chance. 'Don't bother asking', she politely suggested, 'it's turtles all the way down.'[90]

Indeed, Woodward's 'turtles' – historical forces – continue all the way to the end of her book,[91] with human agency all but obliterated. In this

respect as well as in others, Viktor Meier's brilliant expostulation provides a stark contrast, identifying the various actors whose actions took
the SFRY down the road to catastrophe.[92]

It is not that she ignores human agents. She reports, for instance, how
Milošević's brand of street politics frightened non-Serbs, asserting, however, that, as of 1988–9, Milošević did not command the loyalty of the
majority of Serbs. But when it comes to accounting for the direction in
which things moved, it is historical forces, not human agents, which are
held responsible. There are also some obscure passages in Woodward's
book. For example, she implies that Serb liberals made overtures to
fellow liberals in Slovenia and Croatia, though, regrettably, she does
not provide any details or any evidence of any such overtures.[93]

About 25 per cent of the text (chapters 6 and 9) is devoted expressly to
Western intervention in the War of Yugoslav Succession (my term, not
Woodward's). Throughout her account, there is little sign of sympathy
for the German government, which is portrayed as ignoring warnings of
disaster, rather than issuing such warnings early in the game,[94] while
Austria and the Vatican are charged with having sought, beginning in the
mid-1980s, 'to increase their sphere of economic and spiritual influence
in central and eastern Europe, respectively'.[95] But, although she notes
Austria's military alert in mid-May 1991, what is missing from her
account is any indication of German, Austrian, and US Congressional
fears, concerns, and motivations – except, that is, for her suggestion that
the US and West European governments were preoccupied with the
notion of spreading market economies throughout the formerly communist region.[96] In her account, 'German assertiveness . . . had been on
the rise since July [1991]',[97] but she does not mention that it was the
horror of the atrocities being committed by Serb forces which caused
Genscher and his associates to abandon their initial, more demure
position and demand that the international community recognize the
legitimacy of the Slovenian and Croatian declarations of independence.
She quotes John Zametica's characterization of Germany's increasingly
voluble pleading on behalf of Slovenia and Croatia as 'making a mockery
of the EC's joint approach',[98] identifying Zametica in an endnote as a
future political adviser to Radovan Karadžić.[99] She expresses doubts
concerning Genscher's belief that recognition of Slovenia and Croatia
(announced by Germany just before Christmas 1991) could result in a
ceasefire (accomplished within a week of Christmas), and attributes
German support for the Slovenes and Croats to German 'cultural arrogance – in deciding for the Yugoslavs whose rights were more valid'.[100]
The implication is that it would have been less 'arrogant' to deny
recognition to the Slovenes and Croats, in spite of their pleas, at least

until the conclusion of a comprehensive peace settlement – which, in the event, was not achieved until the end of 1995. She also ties the 'German campaign' to a 'demonization of Milošević and the Serbs'.[101] What could possibly explain German interest in Slovenia and Croatia if not a concern for the suffering of innocents? Her answer is that Germany, like Austria and the Vatican, was 'pursuing an expansionary strategy'.[102] Given that it was Serbia (not yet the Federal Republic of Yugoslavia (FRY), which was declared only in April 1992) which was using military force to try to expand its territory at Croatia's (and later also Bosnia's) expense, it is curious that Woodward is so concerned about the alleged threat posed by Germany's supposed expansionist ambitions. Moreover, in summing up her case against Germany – which case comprises the bulk of chapter 6, with all other players cast into the shadows – she characterizes German pressure on EC members to recognize Slovenia and Croatia as a 'German maneuver', complains that this 'maneuver' resulted in an 'arbitrary' application of the principle of national self-determination, and suggests that German pleading on behalf of these two republics sent a message that politicians wanting to obtain independence would do well to start a 'defensive' war[103] – phrasing which suggests that she believes that it was the underequipped Croatian forces which started the war in which some 30 per cent of Croatian territory fell into the laps of Serbian forces.

Woodward is also suspicious of Slovenian intentions, characterizing Slovenian defence minister Janez Janša's purchase abroad of weaponry as 'illegal' – it could be better characterized as a legal 'grey area' – without mentioning in that context that the purchase was necessitated, in part, by the illegal confiscation by the JNA of a portion of the armaments hitherto held by the Slovenian Territorial Defence forces.[104] She also paints the governments of Slovenia, Croatia, and Serbia with the same brush stroke, as all 'radical nationalist governments'[105] – a characterization I find incongruous in the Slovenian case.

All in all, Woodward's *Balkan Tragedy* does not pass the test of balanced scholarship. It is partisan, driven by barely disguised sympathy for the Serbian expansionist cause and by what can be politely described as a lack of sympathy for German and Austrian policies and for Slovenian and Croatian fears and motivations, as well as by an overly critical attitude towards the Vatican.

IV

Daniele Conversi's *German-Bashing and the Breakup of Yugoslavia* was written expressly in reply to such characterizations of Germany as he considered unjustified, and is directed against various writings in which he finds elements of Germanophobia, including Woodward's book.[106] He traces the wildfire of anti-German statements in the Yugoslav context to Lord Carrington, the chief negotiator at the London Peace Conference of August 1992, who, according to Conversi, opposed EC recognition of Slovenia and Croatia until he could move forward with the conference for which he was responsible, and then claimed that Germany's allegedly 'premature' recognition of Slovenian and Croatian independence had 'torpedoed' his conference, using this claim *'to cover up his own failure* to set up any meaningful peace negotiations'.[107] But, where Carrington and leading figures in the British government were concerned, there was a more sinister motivation at work, according to Conversi, namely, a desire to see the more powerful side – in the event, the Serbian side – suppress other sides as quickly as possible and restore peace and stability, and, with it, Serbian hegemony.[108] Drawing upon Timothy Garton Ash's work, Conversi notes that ordinary Germans put a lot of pressure on their government to recognize Slovenia and Croatia, and tended to equate Milošević's Serbia with Hitler's Third Reich.[109] For Conversi, German-bashing is related to anti-European sentiments, i.e., to isolationism (Fortress Albion), and to groundless fears stoked by German reunification. But, according to Conversi, there was something else at work as well, namely, the long-standing ability of politicians in Belgrade to shape the reportage of Yugoslav events in the West and, for that matter, to control the information reaching Western embassies in Belgrade. The result was that the information reaching the West had been pre-screened and modulated by Belgrade or by pro-Belgrade circles abroad.[110]

Conversi notes that some observers, including the guileless Warren Christopher, succumbed to the temptation (in Christopher's case, immediately after talks in Belgrade) to blame German advocacy of Slovenia and Croatia for the fighting in Bosnia. But Conversi considers this interpretation irrational. According to him, German recognition had 'no discernible negative impact on the crisis' and, on the contrary, dampened Serbian aggression in Croatia. As for Bosnia, to the extent that the West made errors in late 1991 and early 1992, these were not a matter of too much support for Bosnian sovereignty, but of too little.[111]

In the course of his analysis, Conversi mentions – in passing – the role of Serbian lobby groups in Britain as exercising some influence on British deliberations on the Yugoslav crisis. This is the subject of an extended monograph by Carole Hodge, *The Serb Lobby in the United Kingdom*.[112] Now in its second edition, *Serb Lobby* discusses the activities of both lobbyists and people friendly towards the Serbian side. As she shows, a key advantage enjoyed by the Serb expansionists in their efforts in Britain was precisely their better access to the media, which issued reminders of Ustaša atrocities against Serb civilians during the Second World War, for example, while forgetting that Serb Chetniks also committed atrocities against Croat and Muslim civilians during that same war. She also notes the extent to which Serb arguments against Western intervention managed to penetrate the British media in various ways, including through the agency of John Zametica.[113]

Perhaps the best-known Serb lobby group is the Serbian Unity Congress (SUC), with offices in both Britain and the United States. Crown Prince Aleksandar Karadjordjević of Serbia, a resident of Britain, was one of the founders of the SUC. During the war, the SUC, like other Serb lobby groups, tried to give the Serbian war effort the best possible interpretation and to cast a less favourable light on the Croatian and Bosniak war efforts. After the war, says Hodge, Serb lobbyists sought to denigrate and undermine the work of the UN Criminal Tribunal in The Hague, to argue against any restoration of autonomy to the Albanians of Kosovo (let alone independence), and to make the strongest possible case for international investment in Serbia/FRY and in the Republika Srpska (RS).[114] The SUC in particular criticized the US undertaking to arm and train the army of the Croat–Bosniak federation, lobbied for the transfer of the disputed city of Brčko to Serb control, and highlighted the achievements of the RS in building democratic institutions.[115] She also discusses the Lord Byron Foundation, an institution headed by Srdja Trifković, a Belgrade-born contributor to British and American media who, at one time, served as adviser to Biljana Plavšić, one of the leading figures among Bosnian Serbs.

Hodge also devotes some attention to the British media which, in her view, provided unbalanced reportage of the Yugoslav war, often offering versions of events which were inappropriately friendly to Belgrade or simply inane. She finds an example of the latter in a BBC special, 'The Mind of Milošević', aired five days into the war, in which the Serbian leader was portrayed as 'agile, adept, personally warm, defying easy definition, enjoying whiskey and conversation', with Radmila Milentijević, information minister in Belgrade, appearing in the documentary observing that Milošević is a leader 'who talks, laughs, is a good singer, and likes a drink occasionally and who, unlike President Clinton, doesn't cheat on his wife'.[116] The fact that articles by *Times* correspondent Tom Walker were copied on to Serb lobby websites seems significant to Hodge, who devotes several pages to criticizing the work of BBC correspondent John Simpson.[117]

In the second edition of her monograph, Hodge extends her analysis to the period after the fall of Milošević, showing how the Serb lobby continued to present Serbs as great victims, not only historically but also in contemporary times. She notes, in particular, that the Serbian United Congress issued a 2,300-word memorandum in 2000, blaming the Albanians for carrying out an 'ethnic cleansing' of Serbs and claimed that the US government had had an 'agenda, from the beginning of the war, to "destabilize Yugoslavia and get a foothold into the Balkans"'.[118] Throughout, she shows that Serbian lobbying efforts in Britain have been skilful and effective, and that a portion of the British establishment and the British public have been more than receptive to a view of Serbia as 'the victim'.[119] Hodge's monograph, like Conversi's, makes an important contribution to understanding perceptions of the war in Britain and other Western nations.

By contrast, Bogdan Denitch's hastily written *Ethnic Nationalism: The Tragic Death of Yugoslavia*, however well intentioned – and his good intentions are more than evident – is likely to sow confusion, rather than to provide clarity, about the war in Yugoslavia. Quite apart from the occasional factual mistakes,[120] and occasional claims offered without requisite data,[121] there is the fact that Denitch, for reasons not clear to me, subscribes to a notion of transgenerational guilt, offered at the expense of Germany and Austria,[122] though, to be fair, Denitch later realizes that this theory has its problems and wonders how long a society must repay a debt incurred by an earlier government: 'How long do these obligations last after the original crime? A century? Two centuries? Half a millennium?'[123] And if we are to think in those terms, then does anyone seriously expect Turkey to make any amends for such suffering and damage as may have been caused during the Ottoman conquest of Bosnia-Herzegovina in the fifteenth century? There are, to be sure, insights in this book – among them, Denitch's understanding that Tito must bear some responsibility for the ultimate collapse of the SFRY,[124] his suggestion that Croatia's recovery of alienated territories was a precondition for the development of a (liberal-)democratic political culture in that republic,[125] his attribution of the war to policy decisions taken by identifiable political figures combined with an instrumental use of the mass media,[126] and his clear-sighted judgement that the 'Serbian leadership bears the lion's share of the responsibility for the destruction of Yugoslavia'.[127] But his book is also a kind of curiosity shoppe, with such oddities as his claim that Yugoslav self-management was 'clearly superior to bureaucratic, top-down, managerial authority',[128] his allegation that the Catholic Church was 'more intolerant' than the Serbian Orthodox Church,[129] and a wild and entirely irrelevant pot-shot at Martin Heidegger, the self-proclaimed philosopher of Being,[130] among other things.

Denitch writes in a conversational style, so much so that I imagined myself sitting down with him over a *gusti sok od jagoda* (a thick strawberry juice) at one of the outdoor tables on Zagreb's main square, listening to him tell me about the 'cultural link between the German skinheads, French motorcyclist racists, and Yugoslav irregulars',[131] and how he feels 'very uncomfortable with all this essentialist talk about 'mentalities' and find[s] the recent revival of that fashion among intellectuals in the West alarming'.[132] Ultimately, he reaches the conclusion that Jack Snyder would reach later (discussed in chapter 7) that the communist leadership of Serbia, fearing the imminent prospect of democratization at the end of the 1980s, 'turned to mobilization of national chauvinism in order to create a new post-Communist popular base for their authoritarian rule'.[133]

Denitch's book is not a scholarly work; it has virtually no scholarly apparatus, is not the product of research, and represents largely a conversational narrative of the author's often intelligent but rarely systematic views on various subjects. It is also not a book aimed at the popular market, as revealed both in the author's disinterest in the sort of colourful characterizations that abound in the more 'popular' works by Owen and Zimmermann and in the fact that Denitch chose a university press to carry his work. In fact, the book does not really fit into any known genre.

V

One of the curiosities about the War of Yugoslav Succession of 1991–5, planned and orchestrated to a great extent by Slobodan Milošević,[134] is the way in which the Belgrade regime found allies abroad for its expansionist war. Allies included much of the Serbian diaspora, gullible sectors in some Western Churches, certain individual scholars and journalists, and some prominent politicians in Western countries, including, most prominently, the larger part of the Greek political establishment. As NATO increasingly drifted towards the conclusion that Milošević was the heart of the problem, Greece, a member of NATO, stood fast at Milošević's side. The story of this anomalous alliance – an 'unholy alliance' – is convincingly told by Takis Michas in his thin volume dealing with Greco-Serbian friendship during the Milošević years.

Painstakingly researched and carefully thought out, *Unholy Alliance* makes a convincing case that the Serbian government and the Bosnian Serbs enjoyed the enthusiastic support of the Greek Orthodox Church, the Greek Communist Party, the Greek government itself, and the bulk of the Greek public, with the result that reports of Serb atrocities were downplayed or even denied, while stories about 'Vatican conspiracies,

Muslim perfidy, Croatian cruelty, Serb bravery, Western hypocrisy, NATO warmongering, and US arrogance' were given credence.[135] Striking in this regard is the way in which Greek television actually celebrated the fall of Srebrenica in July 1995.

About 100 Greek volunteers fought with the Bosnian Serb forces, to defend Orthodox religion, as they saw it. The Greek government itself used its veto power in NATO to block military action against the Serbs, and violated the oil embargo which had been imposed by the UN. Indeed, as Michas shows, there was even support in powerful circles within the Greek government for Milošević's proposal, in December 1994, to create a confederation between Greece and Serbia, to include also the Republic of Macedonia, evidently against its will. Prime Minister Andreas Papandreou called Milošević's proposal 'pioneering and interesting',[136] while George Mangakis, who became Greek foreign minister a few months later, was 'even more enthusiastic' about Milošević's plan, according to Michas.[137] Michas also documents the role of the Greek government in leaking information about NATO air strikes against Bosnian Serb positions to General Mladić in August 1995, showing that the leak was specifically authorized by Prime Minister Papandreou.[138]

But the Greek public was not pro-Serb as such. On the contrary, as Michas notes, 'Greece's sympathies lay not so much with Serbia in general as with the Milošević regime and its henchmen in Bosnia and Kosovo.'[139] As a result, when the Serbian opposition group OTPOR ('Resistance') approached those Greek musical groups and artists who had performed in anti-NATO concerts during the wars in Bosnia and Kosovo and asked them to put on an anti-Milošević concert (in 2000), none of the major groups or artists was willing to take part, while 'the few minor music groups that did [so] were subjected to . . . threats and harassment aimed at discouraging their participation'.[140] Greek sympathy for Milošević continued even after his fall from power. Thus, on 26 June 2001, as pressure on Belgrade for the extradition of Milošević to The Hague was reaching a high pitch, seventy-nine deputies in the Greek parliament, representing all of Greece's political parties, signed a petition asking Belgrade not to extradite Milošević or any other indicted war criminal.[141]

How does one explain the lack of sympathy of ordinary Greeks for the sufferings of non-Serbs, their lack of sympathy for the democratic opposition in Serbia, the Greek Church's support for a programme of Serb expansionism, and the Greek government's general support for Serbian war aims? Part of the answer, says Michas, may be found in the behaviour of the Greek media. Although Michas believes that the 'overwhelming majority of Greece's quality journalists . . . had informed and balanced views',[142] they proved to have little influence in media coverage of the Yugoslav war. Hence, what one found in the Greek media was a steady flow of stories about atrocities said to have been committed by Muslims against Serbs, while there was almost no coverage of the more extensive atrocities committed by Serbs against Muslims.[143] Much of Greek media coverage did not rise above the level of propaganda. Hence, for example, as forces led by Mladić, Šešelj, and Ražnatović ('Arkan') massacred unarmed civilians in Bijeljina, Brčko, Zvornik, Foča, Prijedor, and elsewhere, the Greek media wrote of the 'advance of the Serb army' and compared this 'advance' to the Partisan resistance against Nazi occupation during the Second World War.[144]

A second part of the explanation for Greek attitudes in connection with Serbia and the war may be traced to the behaviour of leading figures in the Greek Orthodox Church. Certainly, the anti-Western dimension of Greek nationalist discourse received considerable encouragement from those quarters. In March 1999, for example, Archbishop Christodoulos delivered a speech in the Church of St Neapolis in Salonika, referring to the American president as 'Satan', 'Demon', 'insidious fascist', and 'Christian only in name', for having ordered aerial attacks against Serbia.[145]

But the most important factor in explaining Greek attitudes about Serbia and the war, according to Michas, may be found in the predominance of ethnic nationalism, as opposed to civic-mindedness, among Greeks. As a result, says Michas, the general indifference towards Serb crimes against Bosniaks 'could be said to reflect the inability of a people of a state based on ethnic exclusivity to consider as a crime something that they, in many respects, viewed as natural'.[146] And it is nationalism, rather than religion, which lay at the heart of the Greco-Serb alliance – and hence Michas's characterization of the alliance as 'unholy'. This alliance was also 'unholy' in another sense, insofar as Michas cites, with approval, a statement by Cornelius Castoriadis, described by the author as the most prominent social thinker in postwar Greece. 'In my eyes', Castoriadis said a few years before his death in 1997, 'the Greek politicians, the journalists, the people who work at [sic] the media, and the others who are responsible for this campaign of disinformation are moral accomplices in the cover-up of the Serb crimes in Croatia and Bosnia.'[147] Michas has produced a magnificent book, which offers important insights into both the wartime behaviour of the Milošević regime and the nature of Greek politics and foreign policy.

VI

Finally, there are Charles Shrader's study of the Muslim–Croat conflict[148] and James Gow's *Serbian Project and Its Adversaries*.[149] Shrader's purpose is to re-examine the roots and course of the fighting between Croatian forces and forces loyal to the Izetbegović government during the years 1992–4 and, in the process, to offer a revisionist account of what actually took place. The 'standard' account of that conflict, as given in the Silber/Little volume, holds that Tudjman had, from the very beginning, conspired with Milošević to carve up Bosnia, that he had found local supporters for his own expansionist programme above all among those Croats living in western Herzegovina – 'a notorious hotbed of extreme right-wing nationalism'[150] – that the Croatian side had started the conflict by proclaiming the establishment of the breakaway enclave of Herceg-Bosna already in summer 1992, and that a 'tacit alliance' between Bosnian Croat and Bosnian Serb forces had developed already by late 1992.[151] According to this account, although the conflict can be traced back to a dispute which erupted in October 1992 between rival mafiosi over petrol in the town of Prozor, it flared only the following April, when rumours circulated that tens of thousands of Muslim refugees were about to arrive in hitherto Croat pockets north and west of Sarajevo. As the story goes, Bosnian Croat militias thereupon moved into the village of Ahmići, where they 'murdered dozens of civilians, including women, children and the elderly'.[152] While some observers have claimed that the Vance–Owen plan sparked the violence between Croats and Muslims, Silber and Little note, more cautiously, that this conflict predated the publication of the plan but suggest, nonetheless, that the plan lent Bosnian Croat territorial aspirations a certain legitimacy.[153] Other accounts have held the Bosnian Croats and Croatian Army almost entirely responsible for the Muslim–Croat fighting.

Shrader disagrees with these versions of events. According to Shrader, 'the ABiH [Army of Bosnia-Herzegovina] was clearly the aggressor in the Muslim–Croat civil war in central Bosnia'.[154] According to Shrader, the HVO (the Bosnian Croat army) in central Bosnia was both outnumbered and outgunned by the Bosnian Army and the first open conflict between these sides came in January 1993, when the ABiH, reinforced by newly arriving Muslim refugees as well as by mujahideen from the Muslim world, mounted a limited military probing operation against its erstwhile ally.[155] Of course, Shrader recounts the story of growing tension between Muslims and Croats during 1992. He even reports the takeover, by HVO authorities, of the Busovača municipal government on 10 May 1992, and the Croatian demand that the Muslim-dominated territorial defence units there surrender their weapons. But he also reports that the Muslims in Busovača failed to honour their agreement on the distribution of arms seized from a captured JNA arsenal in the area.[156] He then recounts widespread Muslim–Croat clashes in central Bosnia in the course of October 1992, discussing also the aforementioned petrol dispute. But whatever one makes of the fighting during 1992, once the serious fighting began in early 1993, according to Shrader, the Croatian side adopted a purely defensive posture.[157] As for Ahmići, Shrader disputes the standard account that what happened in the village was that Croatian forces simply slaughtered innocent civilians without provocation; on the contrary, says Shrader, 'The village of Ahmići was undoubtedly a legitimate military target . . . by virtue of both its location and its probable use as an ABiH staging area.'[158] According to Shrader, it was the Croats, not the Muslims, who were the victims in what was a Muslim offensive, throughout the period November 1992–March 1994. In support of this contention, he stresses that 'the HVO, surrounded and heavily outnumbered, had neither the means nor the opportunity to engage in a planned program to attack, dispossess, and expel Muslims from the areas in which they lived. Nor did it have sufficient motive for such an improbable campaign.'[159] According to this theory, Tudjman's napkin doodles (in which he famously sketched out a fantasy map of how Bosnia-Herzegovina should be divided) have no larger historical significance, and it was the Muslims who wanted to drive out the Croats from their homes. Consistent with this approach and in partial agreement with Silber and Little, Shrader argues that it was the fall of Jajce to Bosnian Serb forces in October 1992 and not the publication of the VOPP in January 1993 which precipitated Muslim–Croat fighting.[160]

And, finally, there is James Gow's *Serbian Project and Its Adversaries,* a provocative piece of scholarship, researched in materials published in English, Serbo-Croatian, French, and Spanish. This work does not duplicate the argument of his earlier *Triumph.* His purpose here is, rather, to demonstrate that the Serbian expansionist project was the major factor contributing to the War of Yugoslav Succession and that the commission of war crimes was an essential part of the Serbian war strategy.[161] In a key passage which provides material for a possible reply to Woodward's contention that there had been a chance for peace in early 1992 but for the headstrong Izetbegović government, Gow writes:

In early 1992, throughout Bosnia, there were signs of a high state of readiness in JNA military preparation for the coming war. The JNA positioned troops and equipment in strategic areas. For example, just before the Bosnian referendum on independence, their tanks, artillery and anti-aircraft units were deployed on the Serbian side of the Drina River, across from Zvornik, to assist the forces inside Bosnia. In Foča, the JNA placed artillery in the surrounding hills in positions to shell the city, while in Brčko and Bosanski Šamac it activated, staffed and stationed reserve units, in Serbian neighborhoods and at strategic points.[162]

The book covers a decade of military operations and political manoeuvring, from the start of the war in Croatia in 1991 until the end of NATO's air campaign against the FRY in spring 1999. After chapters covering the criminal nature of Serbian war strategy, historical background, and the role and character of the JNA, Gow turns to a detailed and sophisticated analysis of the means used by the Serbian side in its struggle and the territorial and political goals pursued. Coverage includes not only the war in Croatia and Bosnia-Herzegovina, but also operations in Kosovo, where Belgrade put forces of the Ministry of Internal Affairs) on combat readiness in Kosovo by October 1997, with Yugoslav Army units deployed near the border with Kosovo, ready for use as necessary.[163] According to Gow, during operations in 1998, with the exception of a brief period during July of that year, Serb forces concentrated on civilian population centres, rather than on military targets, with ethnic cleansing as the goal of the campaign.[164] By June 1999, Serb forces had killed between 10,000 and 11,000 Albanians, according to Gow.[165]

One of the controversies to arise in connection with the NATO campaign of spring 1999 has been whether NATO did everything it could to protect Albanian civilians, whether it was somehow culpable for the actions taken by Serb forces against those civilians after 24 March 1999, and whether, perhaps, sending in ground forces might have been a more sagacious option. To Gow's mind, these worries miss the point, which is that NATO was concentrating 'on the big picture'. Accordingly, it was unrealistic to expect Belgrade to cave in immediately, since the air campaign involved a strategy of attrition which would gradually 'take the life out of the Serbian campaign'.[166]

And yet, for all of its virtues, Gow's *Serbian Project* includes some anomalies, such as his allegation that Croatia's predicament of being outgunned and under bombardment by Serbian forces was somehow part of a 'victim strategy',[167] accusing Croatia of having 'exaggerated its weakness' and of having 'craved the status of victim'.[168] Curiously, too, Gow claims that Ratko Mladić should be regarded as one of the great generals of our time. Finally, there is the suggestion at the close of the book that, 'given the relative lack of manpower available to the Serbian project, was the strategy adopted [of terrorizing Croat and Muslim civilians and driving them from their villages] justifiable, in its own terms? The strategy was precisely a way of reconciling the available means and the desired ends.'[169] It is hard to imagine that the author of *Triumph of the Lack of Will* really wants us to believe that the Serbain expansionist project took some priority over the desire of non-Serb civilians to live in peace or that the strategy of 'ethnic cleansing' was in fact 'justifiable'. In fact, Gow appears to be wrestling with a moral dilemma when he continues by citing the 'ethical' approach (I would call it 'the moral law' or perhaps 'Universal Reason') that 'questions the acceptability' of murder, rape and terror 'under any conditions'.[170] Yet, whatever one might make of these assertions, Gow's *Serbian Project* is a significant contribution to the debate about the war and will surely exert influence in the field.

VII

If the continuing outpouring of books about the Spanish Civil War and about the Second World War is any guide, then lively discussion about the War of Yugoslav Succession of 1991–5 will continue well into the future. Some controversies will, in the course of time, be laid to rest, but fresh controversies are likely to be stirred up. It is not to be excluded that future scholars will produce books proposing to rehabilitate indicted war criminals Slobodan Milošević and Radovan Karadžić and to portray Croatian president Franjo Tudjman as more than just a myopic, neo-traditional nationalist prepared to rehabilitate the Ustaša party and carve up Bosnia. Nor can it be excluded that there will be fresh efforts to blame the international community for what happened to the SFRY, or to argue the implausible thesis that the Yugoslav time of troubles should be traced ultimately, as some authors have already tried unsuccessfully to argue, to religious differences. There may even be efforts to blame the entire thing on the Muslims of Bosnia, though it is hard at the present moment to imagine what evidence might be marshalled in support of so fanciful a theory. It may even occur to someone with a taste for conspiracy theories to try to connect the breakup of the SFRY to the distribution of mineral wealth in that country and to likely beneficiaries of the break-up; indeed, such a conceptualization would not be so distant from some of the ruminations already advanced in some of the literature and, in any event, can be tied to speculative schemes already advocated on the World Socialist website.

Speaking for myself, I would welcome full-length treatments of: Germany's policy vis-à-vis the Yugoslav war, along with those of France and Russia; and Bosnian government contacts with Iran, Turkey, and other Islamic states during the conflict. A full-length study of the use and effectiveness of propaganda by the Serbian, Croatian, and Bosnian government sides could also make a major contribution to the literature, and I would love to read the memoirs of Vuk Drašković, if and when he should decide to write them. And, on this note, we turn to a review of the memoir literature concerning the Yugoslav breakup and war.

NOTES

1 David Owen, *Balkan Odyssey* (London: Victor Gollancz, 1995), p. 341.
2 *Ibid.*, p. 366.
3 *Ibid.*, p. 357.
4 *Ibid.*, p. 208.
5 *Balkan Battlegrounds: A Military History of the Yugoslav Conflict, 1990–1995,* 2 vols. (Washington, DC: Central Intelligence Agency, Office of Russian and European Analysis, May 2002), vol. II consists of maps.
6 Owen, *Balkan Odyssey,* p. 40.
7 *Ibid.*, p. 46.
8 *Ibid.*, p. 272. For a corrective, see Viktor Meier, *Yugoslavia: A History of Its Demise,* trans. from German by Sabrina P. Ramet (London and New York: Routledge, 1999).
9 Owen, *Balkan Odyssey,* p. 181.
10 *Ibid.*, p. 40.
11 See, for example, *ibid.*, p. 45.
12 *Ibid.*, p. 100.
13 For Serb criticism, see *ibid.*, p. 138; for British pacifist criticism, see *ibid.*, p. 147.
14 James Gow, *Triumph of the Lack of Will: International Diplomacy and the Yugoslav War* (New York: Columbia University Press, 1997), pp. 175–6.
15 *Ibid.*, p. 159.
16 *Ibid.*, p. 221.
17 *Ibid.*, pp. 235–49.
18 Quoted *ibid.*, p. 179.
19 *Ibid.*, p. 8.
20 *Ibid.*, pp. 31, 76.
21 *Ibid.*, p. 83.
22 *Ibid.*, p. 209.
23 Brendan Simms, *Unfinest Hour: Britain and the Destruction of Bosnia* (London: Penguin Books, 2002 edn), p. 252.
24 *Ibid.*, p. 150.
25 *Ibid.*, p. 157.
26 *Ibid.*, p. xvii.
27 *Ibid.*
28 *Ibid.*, p. 225.

29 *Ibid.*, p. 340.
30 *Ibid.*, pp. 4–5, 12, 22, 32.
31 *Ibid.*, pp. 218, 180.
32 General Sir Michael Rose, *Fighting for Peace: Lessons from Bosnia* (London: Warner Books, 1999 edn), p. 37.
33 *Ibid.*, p. 56.
34 *Ibid.*, pp. 157–8.
35 *Ibid.*, p. 244.
36 *Ibid.*, p. 200.
37 *Ibid.*, p. 203.
38 *Ibid.*, p. 38.
39 Regarding the policies he defends, see *ibid.*, pp. 121–2, 297, 299, 368; regarding what the local population and sensible world leaders wanted, see *ibid.*, pp. 109–10, 183, 354–5.
40 See, for example, *ibid.*, pp. xviii–xix, 290, 361, 362–3.
41 *Ibid.*, p. 79.
42 *Ibid.*, pp. 4, 6, my emphasis.
43 See *ibid.*, pp. 89, 289.
44 See *ibid.*, pp. 66, 224–5.
45 *Ibid.*, pp. 50, 291.
46 *Ibid.*, pp. 12–13.
47 *Ibid.*, p. 47.
48 *Ibid.*, pp. 208–9, 227, 255, 296, 347, 353.
49 *Ibid.*, p. 76.
50 Warren Zimmermann, *Origins of a Catastrophe: Yugoslavia and Its Destroyers,* revised edn (New York: Times Books, 1999), p. vii.
51 *Ibid.*
52 *Ibid.*, p. ix.
53 *Ibid.*, pp. x–xi.
54 *Yes, Prime Minister* (1987), in the episode entitled 'Power to the People'. Sir Humphrey Appleby was played by Nigel Hawthorne.
55 Zimmermann, *Origins of a Catastrophe,* p. xi.
56 *Ibid.*, p. 10.
57 *Ibid.*, p. 39.
58 *Ibid.*, p. 10.
59 *Ibid.*, p. 72.
60 *Ibid.*, p. 128.
61 *Ibid.*, p. 71.
62 *Ibid.*, p. 52.
63 *Ibid.*, p. 71.
64 Dubrovnik, *ibid.*, p. 158; July 1992, *ibid.*, p. 214.
65 *Ibid.*, p. 146.

66 *Ibid.*, p. 212.
67 *Ibid.*, p. 251.
68 See my article, 'The So-Called Right of National Self-Determination and Other Myths', *Human Rights Review*, 2, 1 (October–December 2000), pp. 84–103.
69 Susan L. Woodward, *Balkan Tragedy: Chaos and Dissolution after the Cold War* (Washington, DC: Brookings Institution Press, 1995), p. 204.
70 *Ibid.*, p. 205.
71 Gow, *Triumph of the Lack of Will*, p. 73.
72 Woodward, *Balkan Tragedy*, p. 205.
73 Hans-Dietrich Genscher, *Rebuilding a House Divided: A Memoir by the Architect of Germany's Reunification*, trans. from German by Thomas Thornton (New York: Broadway Books, 1995).
74 Meier, *Yugoslavia*.
75 Woodward, *Balkan Tragedy*, pp. 205–6.
76 *Ibid.*, p. 207.
77 *Ibid.*, p. 211.
78 *Ibid.*, p. 133.
79 *Ibid.*, p. 106; see also p. 215.
80 Jekyll and Hyde, *ibid.*, p. 224; paranoia, *ibid.*, p. 228.
81 *Ibid.*, p. 234.
82 *Ibid.*, p. 235.
83 *Ibid.*, p. 252.
84 *Ibid.*, pp. 261–2.
85 *Ibid.*, p. 13.
86 *Ibid.*
87 Both books bear a 1995 copyright date.
88 *Ibid.*, p. 15.
89 *Ibid.*, p. 85.
90 Alan Hunt and Gary Wickham, *Foucault and the Law: Towards a Sociology of Law as Governance* (London and Boulder, CO: Pluto Press, 1994), p. 136, n. 2.
91 Woodward, *Balkan Tragedy*, p. 378.
92 Meier, *Yugoslavia*.
93 Woodward, *Balkan Tragedy*, p. 97.
94 *Ibid.*, pp. 146–7.
95 *Ibid.*, pp. 148–9.
96 Military alert, *ibid.*, p. 159; market economies, *ibid.*, p. 156.
97 *Ibid.*, p. 183.
98 *Ibid.*, p. 184.
99 In n. 113, *ibid.*, p. 469.
100 *Ibid.*, p. 186.
101 *Ibid.*

102 *Ibid.*, p. 187.
103 *Ibid.*, p. 189.
104 *Ibid.*, p. 166.
105 *Ibid.*, p. 169.
106 See Daniele Conversi, *German-Bashing and the Breakup of Yugoslavia*, Donald W. Treadgold Papers in Russian, East European, and Central Asian Studies No. 16 (Seattle: Henry M. Jackson School of International Studies of the University of Washington, March 1998). Conversi cites Woodward's *Balkan Tragedy* in n. 3, on p. 59.
107 *Ibid.*, p. 15, my emphasis.
108 *Ibid.*, pp. 16–17.
109 *Ibid.*, p. 19.
110 *Ibid.*, p. 47.
111 *Ibid.*, p. 58.
112 Carole Hodge, *The Serb Lobby in the United Kingdom*, 2nd edn, Donald W. Treadgold Papers in Russian, East European, and Central Asian Studies No. 22 (Seattle: Henry M. Jackson School of International Studies of the University of Washington, July 2003).
113 *Ibid.*, pp. 16–19.
114 *Ibid.*, p. 24.
115 *Ibid.*, p. 25.
116 *Ibid.*, p. 29, quoting from Milentijević.
117 *Ibid.*, pp. 31, 39–43.
118 *Ibid.*, p. 54.
119 *Ibid.*, p. 59.
120 See, for example, Bogdan Denitch, *Ethnic Nationalism: The Tragic Death of Yugoslavia* (Minneapolis: University of Minnesota Press, 1994), pp. 43, 57, 110, 122, 140.
121 See, for example, *ibid.*, p. 58.
122 *Ibid.*, p. 53.
123 *Ibid.*, p. 83.
124 *Ibid.*, p. 58.
125 *Ibid.*, p. 49.
126 *Ibid.*, p. 62.
127 *Ibid.*, p. 123.
128 *Ibid.*, p. 65.
129 *Ibid.*, p. 62.
130 *Ibid.*, p. 128.
131 *Ibid.*, p. 75.
132 *Ibid.*, p. 136.
133 *Ibid.*, p. 185.
134 Adam LeBor, *Milošević: A Biography* (Polmont, Stirlingshire: Bloomsbury, 2002), pp. 141–3, 150, 173–7, 220.
135 Takis Michas, *Unholy Alliance: Greece and Milošević's Serbia* (College Station, TX: Texas A&M University Press, 2002), p. 6.
136 Quoted *ibid.*, p. 20.
137 *Ibid.*
138 *Ibid.*, p. 39.

139 *Ibid.*, p. 102.
140 *Ibid.*, pp 102–3.
141 *Ibid.*, p. 105.
142 *Ibid.*, p. 6.
143 *Ibid.*, p. 29.
144 *Ibid.*, p. 31.
145 *Ibid.*, p. 89.
146 *Ibid.*, p. 123.
147 *Ibid.*, p. 143.
148 Charles R. Shrader, *The Muslim–Croat Civil War in Central Bosnia: A Military History, 1992–1994* (College Station, TX: Texas A&M University Press, 2003).
149 James Gow, *The Serbian Project and Its Adversaries: A Strategy of War Crimes* (London: C. Hurst & Co., 2003).
150 Laura Silber and Allan Little, *The Death of Yugoslavia* (London: Penguin Books & BBC Books, 1995), p. 325.
151 *Ibid.*, p. 328.
152 *Ibid.*, p. 329.
153 *Ibid.*, p. 330.
154 Shrader, *The Muslim–Croat Civil War*, p. 72.
155 *Ibid.*, pp. 64–5.
156 *Ibid.*, p. 67.
157 *Ibid.*, p. 72.
158 *Ibid.*, p. 93.
159 *Ibid.*, p. 160.
160 *Ibid.*, p. 4.
161 Gow, *The Serbian Project and Its Adversaries*, p. 2.
162 *Ibid.*, p. 123.
163 *Ibid.*, p. 201.
164 *Ibid.*, pp. 202–3.
165 *Ibid.*, p. 214.
166 *Ibid.*, pp. 290, 291.
167 *Ibid.*, p. 239.
168 *Ibid.*, p. 241. I changed 'victims' to 'victim' in the interest of agreement of number.
169 *Ibid.*, p. 303.
170 *Ibid.*, p. 304.

REFERENCES

Conversi, Daniele, *German-Bashing and the Breakup of Yugoslavia*, Donald W. Treadgold Papers in Russian, East European, and Central Asian Studies No. 16 (Seattle: Henry M. Jackson School of International Studies of the University of Washington, March 1998), p. 81.
Denitch, Bogdan, *Ethnic Nationalism: The Tragic Death of Yugoslavia* (Minneapolis: University of Minnesota Press, 1994), p. 229.
Gow, James, *The Serbian Project and Its Adversaries: A Strategy of War Crimes* (London: C. Hurst & Co., 2003), p. 322.

Triumph of the Lack of Will: International Diplomacy and the Yugoslav War (New York: Columbia University Press, 1997), p. 343.

Hodge, Carole, *The Serb Lobby in the United Kingdom*, 2nd edn, Donald W. Treadgold Papers in Russian, East European, and Central Asian Studies No. 22 (Seattle: Henry M. Jackson School of International Studies of the University of Washington, July 2003), p. 99.

Michas, Takis, *Unholy Alliance: Greece and Milošević's Serbia* (College Station, TX: Texas A&M University Press, 2002), p. 176.

Owen, David, *Balkan Odyssey* (London: Victor Gollancz, 1995), p. 394.

Rose, General Sir Michael, *Fighting for Peace: Lessons from Bosnia* (London: Warner Books, 1999 edn), p. 393.

Shrader, Charles R., *The Muslim–Croat Civil War in Central Bosnia: A Military History, 1992–1994* (College Station, TX: Texas A&M University Press, 2003), p. 223.

Simms, Brendan, *Unfinest Hour: Britain and the Destruction of Bosnia* (London: Penguin, 2002 edn), p. 464.

Woodward, Susan L., *Balkan Tragedy: Chaos and Dissolution after the Cold War* (Washington, DC: Brookings Institution Press, 1995), p. 536.

Zimmermann, Warren, *Origins of a Catastrophe: Yugoslavia and Its Destroyers*, revised edn (New York: Times Books, 1999), p. 269.

5   Memoirs and autobiographies

No scholar, as far as I am aware, has ever supported, in any way, the fanciful 'ancient hatreds' thesis in any form. But the scholarly literature concerning recent Yugoslav history has not been without its serious lapses – among them, inexplicable tendencies towards occasional Germanophobia,[1] Hobbist[2] tendencies towards the elevation of state sovereignty above the moral law (flaring during discussions of possible Western duty to intervene in Bosnia during 1992–5 and in Kosovo in 1998–9), and moral relativism.[3] These tendencies have, inevitably, affected the way in which facts have been presented.

Thus, the recent flood of memoirs from principals in the Yugoslav drama is especially welcome, insofar as it affords the opportunity to see how the participants themselves would like their roles and actions to be remembered, and provides fresh accounts from inside concerning what may have happened. In the process, readers may test their own theories and interpretations concerning the breakup and war against first-hand recollections.

Among the first memoirs published were those by former president of the SFRY (Socialist Federated Republic of Yugoslavia) Presidency (May–October 1991) Stipe Mesić,[4] former SFRY defence minister (May 1988–January 1992) Veljko Kadijević,[5] former president of the SFRY Presidency (May 1990–May 1991) Borisav Jović,[6] former EU mediator David Lord Owen (discussed in chapter 4), and former US ambassador to Yugoslavia Warren Zimmermann (also discussed in chapter 4). Jović's memoirs, in particular, which took the form of a diary, provided insights into the day-to-day conversations and decision-making at the highest levels in Belgrade during the crucial final years of socialist Yugoslavia and created an enormous stir – both in Serbia and abroad.

I am grateful to Branka Magaš and Diane Koenker for helpful comments on an earlier draft of this chapter.

The volumes discussed in this chapter include four memoirs by former defence ministers (Branko Mamula of the SFRY, Veljko Kadijević of the SFRY, Janez Janša of Slovenia, and Martin Špegelj of Croatia), three memoirs by former presidents of the SFRY Presidency (Raif Dizdarević, Janez Drnovšek, and Stipe Mesić), two memoirs by former secretaries-general of the United Nations (Javier Pérez de Cuéllar and Boutros Boutros-Ghali), four memoirs by others holding high political office (Alija Izetbegović, Zdravko Tomac, Hrvoje Šarinić, and Davorin Rudolf), one by former British prime minister John Major, and one by the chief-of-staff of the Bosnian Army (Sefer Halilović). Several of these reprint the transcripts of critical sessions and include reprintings of documents and speeches. Borisav Jović's memoirs are cited or mentioned by several of these authors; indeed, the memoirs by Mamula and Rudolf have a rather hybrid character, mixing the memoirs genre with aspects of scholarly research – the inclusion of an extensive bibliography in Rudolf's volume is merely the most obvious reflection of this character. Most of the fifteen memoirs under review here are compatible with the way in which most scholars understand the events of the past decade. Two of them – those by Admiral Mamula and General Halilović – are frankly revisionist and will be enjoyed by those who have suspected, for whatever reason, that the real facts have been withheld from the public and that the 'real story' must be different from what has been generally reported.

Although I shall focus in this essay on what these sundry memoirs tell us about internal developments, several of them – those by Dizdarević, Drnovšek, Izetbegović, Šarinić, and Tomac – also offer reflections on the role and reactions (or failures to react) of the international community. Those by Halilović, Janša, Špegelj, and Tomac enter into debates about military strategy, with Špegelj and Tomac taking opposite points of view concerning Croatia's best strategy in 1991. Several of them, most particularly those by Dizdarević, Drnovšek, Janša, Mamula, and Tomac, offer some insights into deliberations at the highest levels of party or government. In this essay, I have organized the discussion more temporally, with sections on *the roots of the crisis* (where the memoirs of Dizdarević, Rudolf, Mamula, Kadijević, and Mesić are discussed), *the war in Slovenia* (with discussion of the memoirs by Drnovsek, Janša, and, in brief, Dizdarević again), *the war in Croatia* (focusing on the opposing accounts offered by Tomac and Špegelj), and *the war in Bosnia-Herzegovina* (with discussion of the memoirs by Izetbegović, Halilović, and Šarinić). These sections are followed by a section devoted to memoirs by principals from outside the Yugoslav area.

Roots of the crisis (Dizdarević, Rudolf, Mamula, Kadijević, Mesić)

In tracing the roots of the crisis, it is wise to avoid unicausal or virtually unicausal explanations, such as that economic deterioration alone or constitutional revisions almost exclusively might be responsible for the violent breakup of socialist Yugoslavia. Moreover, accounts which take their point of departure from the country's multiethnic and multi-confessional makeup cannot but end in foolishness and vapid error. Neither the Scots nor the Welsh have taken up arms against the British government in recent centuries. Nor have the Corsicans against Paris, Spanish-speakers in the United States, or the Québecois in Canada. What distinguished socialist Yugoslavia from these other cases was its lack of legitimate government, and it is this factor which should be stressed in the first place. Legitimate governments can weather economic crisis, but for illegitimate governments sustained economic crisis can be deadly. That proved to be the case in Yugoslavia. But even there, it was necessary for people to appear who were prepared to translate economic frustration into ethnic hatred and who could, operating within the framework of an illegitimate system, subvert political processes for their own purposes. In this translation, Serbian leader Slobodan Milošević and his collaborators Jović, Miroslav Šolević, and others, the Serbian press, the Serbian Academy of Sciences and Art (SANU),[7] and the Serbian Orthodox Church played the initiative role in the years 1987–90, at a time when the communist leadership in Croatia was desperately trying to put out the flames of nationalism being lit by Croatian Serbs under Belgrade's influence. The leading figures in the Serbian Orthodox Church not only contributed to stirring up Serbian anger against Croats for past wrongs, by dwelling one-sidedly – at a time when emotions in Yugoslavia were becoming increasingly raw – on the horrors of Croatian fascism during the Second World War, but allegedly also favoured the creation of a Greater Serbian state to which certain areas of Croatia where Serbs lived would be attached.[8]

It was only in April 1990, three and a half years after the Belgrade daily newspaper *Večernje novosti* startled the country by publishing extracts of the self-pitying nationalist tract known simply as 'the Memorandum', which had been drawn up by SANU, and two and a half years after Milošević had come to power in Serbia, that retired general Franjo Tudjman, who had earned a doctorate in history at the Zadar campus of the University of Zagreb and who had campaigned on a nationalist platform, was elected president of Croatia. It is plausible to argue that but for Milošević and the tidal wave of Serbian nationalism which was already moving across Yugoslavia, Tudjman might never have been elected president of Croatia. But as it was, Tudjman's election moved the SFRY one step closer to breakup. Milošević began arming Serbs in Croatia in the course of summer 1990, but, in March 1991, met with Tudjman at Karadjordjevo to discuss the partition of Bosnia between Serbia and Croatia.

Raif Dizdarević served as President of the presidency of Bosnia-Herzegovina in 1978–82, president of the federal Assembly in 1982–3, foreign minister in 1984–8, and president of the SFRY Presidency in 1988–9. His memoirs cover the decade described by these terms of office, and thus offer greater historical perspective than the other memoirs under review here. Dizdarević begins his account with descriptions of elite conversations at the time of Tito's illness and eventual death. Dizdarević says that the Yugoslav leadership feared at the time (after December 1979) that the Warsaw Pact might take advantage of Tito's incapacitation to hurl as many as fifteen to twenty divisions, including tanks and aircraft, against Yugoslavia, in an effort to snuff out Yugoslavia's 'third way', and devoted special attention to preparing the territorial defence (teritorialna obramba, TO) forces for possible defence against Soviet bloc invasion.[9] The Yugoslav leadership also obtained information at the time that anti-Tito émigré organizations were allegedly in touch with Soviet intelligence services and were planning to carry out various subversive and terrorist actions upon Tito's death.[10] Dizdarević devotes part of his account to discussing the troubles afflicting Kosovo over the decade, and identifies the anti-Belgrade demonstrations of April 1981 as marking the inception of the crisis of Yugoslav survival. Later that year, the Central Committee (CC) of the League of Communists of Serbia held a marathon session on 24–26 December, devoted to interethnic relations within the republic. This session also saw vociferous complaints that the existence of the two autonomous provinces (Kosovo and Vojvodina) damaged the constitutional unity of Serbia with some of those claiming that Serbia was not receiving treatment equal with the other constituent republics of the SFRY. Strikingly, at the same CC session, Draža Marković, one of the leading figures in Serbian politics at the time, said that Yugoslavia consisted of five peoples (*narodi*), naming the Croats, Macedonians, Montenegrins, Serbs, and Slovenes; under the formula used at the time, Marković should also have mentioned the Muslims (Bosniaks), who had been officially recognized as a narod in 1968. Dizdarević does not think that this omission was accidental, however.[11] Given the implied threats to Bosnia, Kosovo, and Vojvodina, this session inevitably sent shock waves through the country.

Dizdarević recounts the economic deterioration during the 1980s (with the purchasing power of citizens falling 30–40 per cent in 1987 alone).[12] As Dizdarević notes, the federal organs were paralysed; in his view, the accession of Slobodan Milošević to power in Serbia towards the end of the 1980s was decisive in taking Yugoslavia down the road to war. He characterizes Milošević as unscrupulous, mendacious, and shameless in his use of mobs to destabilize the legal institutions of the country. Indeed, Dizdarević says that he had evidence already at the time that Šolević's committee (which organized mass disturbances in Novi Sad, Titograd (Podgorica), and Priština in 1988–9, in order to remove independent-minded local leaderships from power) was acting on Milošević's orders.[13] But what is so striking in Dizdarević's account is the complete impotence of the SFRY Presidency in the face of Milošević's defiance. This body repeatedly met to discuss these disturbances. On 14 September 1988, for example, an expanded session of the Presidency concluded that the very survival of Yugoslavia was being threatened by the growth of organized nationalist activity (co-ordinated by Šolević and others) and by the confrontation between the Serbian leadership and the provincial leaderships in particular. This session also criticized the organization of Serb nationalist 'meetings' which the Presidency saw as highly destabilizing.[14]

One reads of Dizdarević's nervous phone calls to the embattled Nandor Major of Vojvodina, of his desperate conversations with Interior Minister Petar Gračanin and with Serbian leader Milošević, of Slovenian leader Milan Kučan's refusal to condone the proclamation of a state of emergency after Milošević's overthrow of the elected leadership in Vojvodina (evidently because he feared that the army could then use the state of emergency to clean up perceived 'troubles' in Slovenia), and of Dušan Čkrebić's brash defence of the anti-government rally in Novi Sad in October 1988, on the grounds that there had been no 'excesses'.[15] When the disturbances spread to Titograd, the capital of Montenegro, on 7/8 October 1988, the SFRY Presidency took note of the fact that the most militant demonstrators in Titograd were not locals at all, but had come from Serbia! But when the Presidium of the League of Communists of Yugoslavia called Milošević to account, since the party echelons had sufficient evidence of his implication in these events, he behaved as if nothing of consequence had transpired in Montenegro and insisted that he was in no way involved in the events in Titograd.[16] Three months later, renewed disturbances succeeded in removing the Montenegrin leadership from power. Again, Dizdarević emphasizes the 'powerlessness' of the SFRY Presidency upon finding that, after two days of protests, there was not a single organ of government or party in Montenegro capable of undertaking effective countermeasures.

In his account, Dizdarević presents himself as an honest and courageous, if largely impotent, adversary of Milošević, seeing Serbian nationalism and chauvinism as holding the greatest danger for the country. To Dizdarević's mind, Slovenian and Croatian separatism developed, in the first place, as a *reaction* to the lawlessness spreading from Belgrade, and were propelled forward by the overthrow of the Montenegrin leadership in January 1989.[17] He insists that, under the law, there was nothing more that the SFRY Presidency could have done to pull the country back from the brink, not having, for example, the authority to remove Milošević from office.[18] While Milošević emerges as the 'sorcerer' in Dizdarević's account, the author emphasizes the 'betrayal' of the army and Kadijević's personal responsibility in the final breakup of Yugoslavia; without the defection of the army, according to Dizdarević, Milošević could not have unleashed his aggression against non-Serbs.[19] Dizdarević has some sympathies for a nonfederal constitution, but insists that democratization, not a change in federal relations, was the real issue, and that only democratization could have taken Yugoslavia down a safer path.[20] Dizdarević's self-representation might be just a bit self-serving. Viktor Meier, for example, characterizes Dizdarević as opportunistic and timid,[21] notes his support for Milošević's suppression of the autonomy of the provinces,[22] and says that the 'predominantly reactionary state presidency proved, under Dizdarević's leadership, to be little more than Milošević's executive assistant'[23] – quite a different picture from that sketched by Dizdarević. What may be said in defence of Dizdarević-the-author is that belatedly he has got important parts of the story right.

If Milošević was the 'sorcerer', then, for Davorin Rudolf, who served as minister of maritime affairs of the Republic of Croatia 1990–2 and, for a few months in mid-1991, as Croatian foreign minister, Borisav Jović, the Serbian representative on the SFRY Presidency, was 'the sorcerer's apprentice' – loyal to his master, but multiplying troubles faster than he could handle himself. But ultimately, in Rudolf's view, the problems antedated Milošević's arrival on the scene. Rudolf identifies Serbia as the problem (and, hence, not just Milošević), tracing the roots of the war to the *Načertanije* of Ilija Garašanin (drafted in 1844, first revealed in 1902, it was a programme to liberate Slav areas ruled by the Ottomans and attach them to Serbia), the irredentist notions of nineteenth-century Serb writers Vuk Stefanovic Karadžić, and Vladimir Karić (the latter published a map in 1887, showing Croatia, including Slavonia, Istria, and Dalmatia, as well as Bačka, Banat, and Bosnia-Herzegovina as 'lands inhabited solely by Serbs'),[24] historian Mihailo Jović (whose 1822 *Srpska istorija* claimed that only Serbs lived in Dubrovnik), Serbian chauvinism in the interwar kingdom (1918–41), the Chetnik movement, lingering Serbian nationalist pretensions in socialist Yugoslavia, and the infamous SANU memorandum of 1986 – adding up to a consistent pattern with only a few ebbs according to Rudolf.

Because Rudolf's vantage point was from the relatively minor post as minister for maritime affairs (except for the aforementioned very brief stint as foreign minister), he was not a party to some of the key decisions. This is perhaps why his account is derived, to a considerable extent, from other memoirs and treatments. Rudolf nonetheless formed some negative views about the level of understanding of the Yugoslav crisis in European and American policy circles, and shares these with the reader.

Although Rudolf admits that there were strong differences of opinion within the Croatian political establishment after the spring 1990 elections, he insists that moderates defined the mainstream of government opinion. Indeed, one of the central themes of the book is that, alongside radicals such as Gojko Šušak (who, according to Silber and Little, actually fanned the flames of war[25]) and 'hotheads' such as General Martin Špegelj, there were also moderates in the government who wanted desperately to prevent war from breaking out – hence, the book's title ('the war which we did not want'). This theme may strike some readers as beside the point or as not worth belabouring, but it is nonetheless Rudolf's concern. Rudolf's characterization of Špegelj is, however, misleading and probably reflects Rudolf's limited role, more than anything else. Indeed, Rudolf's quasi-memoirs add essentially nothing to an understanding of the war in Croatia, his main subject – which is why I have chosen to discuss the volume in this section, rather than in the section (below) on the war in Croatia.

Branko Mamula served as chief of the General Staff from June 1979 to May 1982 and as federal minister for people's defence from May 1982 to May 1988. He begins his account in December 1979, as Tito was hospitalized, carrying it forward to the outbreak of war in 1991. Mamula reveals that, in early 1980,

the Italians expected that Yugoslavia would fall apart after Tito and that the Russians would take the largest portion [of the country's territory], and in that event they wanted to maintain their right to 'zone B'.

'Somewhere around that time [Soviet foreign minister] Gromyko made a visit to Italy, and according to the information we received, it appears that the Italians would not oppose a Russian occupation of part of Yugoslavia, on the condition that Italy's right to 'zone B' would be recognized . . . Inside Yugoslavia a special war against Italy was being planned – involving sabotage, information-warfare, and aerial and marine landing units.[26]

There were, additionally, telling troop movements into Hungary and Bulgaria at the time, as well as military exercises by Soviet bloc troops in the vicinity of Yugoslavia's borders. But, in June 1980, Soviet leaders advised Mitja Ribičič, at that time chair of the Federal Executive Council, that there would be no intervention unless socialism in Yugoslavia were to be threatened.[27] That reassurance not withstanding, developments on the ground were troubling to the authorities in Belgrade. In Hungary, for example, the four Soviet divisions already in place were reinforced during 1980 by two more (in addition to one transferred south from Slovakia), while in Bulgaria, the military exercises were on a much grander scale in 1980 than anything seen in previous years.[28]

Mamula, who was displeased that the army's warnings in December 1979 of dangers in the post-Tito era had been ignored in party echelons, felt that the JNA (Jugoslovenska Narodna Armija, or Yugoslav People's Army) had a legitimate political role to play in Yugoslavia and, upon becoming minister of defence on 15 May 1982, began to act on that conviction. Mamula claims that he was also suspicious about the territorial defence (TO) system which had been set up in 1968, under which the republics controlled TO forces and weaponry. In 1983, fully seven years before the JNA would confiscate weapons from the TOs in Slovenia, Croatia, and Bosnia-Herzegovina, the army drew up a balance sheet on lessons learned from Croatia in 1971 and Kosovo in 1981, according to Mamula, and concluded that similar situations could recur in the future; since units of the TO could be, under the legal provisions of the time, called to action by the republic governments, they could conceivably be employed against the common state. Therefore, according to Mamula, the JNA concluded that it would be best to relieve the republic leaderships of their authority within the TO system.[29] General Špegelj offers partial confirmation of Mamula's account, although Špegelj says that the 'secret mechanisms' designed to eliminate republican autonomy in defence were put in place in 1984, rather than in 1983.[30] On the other hand, the historical record does not support Mamula's claim that the implementation of this plan in 1990 was neutral. Had Mamula been primarily motivated by the concern to preserve Yugoslavia in 1988, he would have prioritized resolving the problems already being stirred up by Milošević and his flunkeys in Serbia rather than obtaining revenge against the Slovenes for the irritations he experienced in reading *Mladina*, the liberal, risk-taking

Slovenian weekly magazine published, at that time, by the League of Youth of Slovenia.

According to Mamula, the army realized in the late 1980s that socialism was breaking down, giving way to democratic pluralism and a market economy, but was worried that this could lead to interethnic fighting on the lines of what had happened in the second World War. Mamula argues that, at least in the period during which he was minister of defence, there was no consensus within the army to support a centralized Yugoslavia under Serbian hegemony.[31]

According to Mamula, the JNA was deeply disconcerted about Milošević's putsch in 1987, but did not see a way to counter it.[32] This contention strains the reader's credulity. At the same time, Mamula admits that there were also some retired generals who supported Milošević; this especially involved those who felt that they had been passed over for important appointments.[33]

It is in turning to Slovenia that Mamula's account becomes overtly revisionist. He claims, for example, that the Slovenian party and state leadership had decided already in the second half of 1984, at one of its closed sessions, to organize a campaign against the JNA, adding that Kučan and other Slovenian leaders 'prepared the game with Janša and the others over the theft of the confidential document' in order to present this as related to a purported army plot against Slovenia.[34] Given that Kučan did not become chief of the League of Communists of Slovenia until 1986 and that the theft in question occurred in 1988, it is hard to imagine that an entirely different leadership, more conservative than the Kučan leadership, had planned all of this four years in advance. Furthermore, in a version that diverges from the standard account,[35] Mamula denies that the JNA was preparing some sort of military strike against Slovenia in early 1988 or intending to arrest Slovenia's political leaders and leading dissidents; he says that, in giving this account of the army's intentions in conversation with Slovenian minister of internal affairs Tomaz Ertl, General Svetozar Višnjić, commander of the army district in Ljubljana, misunderstood the situation and misrepresented the discussions which had been held in the Military Council.[36] Finally, Mamula divides the blame for the destruction of Yugoslavia equally between Slovenia and Serbia,[37] but fails to address the Slovenian argument, developed at some length in Drnovšek's account, that all the key decisions taken by Slovenia with regard to asserting the sovereignty of the republic, proposing a confederal reorganization of the country as a whole, and, finally, preparing for independence were all undertaken *in response to the growing lawlessness displayed by Serbian authorities.*

Veljko Kadijević succeeded Mamula as SFRY minister of defence in May 1988, serving until autumn 1991. Kadijević, portrayed by Mamula as an indecisive weakling who tended to form bonds of dependency with those occupying higher posts than himself, comes across rather differently in his own account. In his recollection, he was a determined defender of Yugoslav unity, committed to the protection of the Serbian people in Croatia from attacks by Croatian 'armed formations'.[38] In his view, the Croats and Slovenes must share the blame with the United States and Germany and even unnamed neighbouring countries for the destruction of the SFRY. Stipe Mesić, Croatia's representative in the state presidency, is portrayed as 'the destroyer of Yugoslavia',[39] while it was Slovenia which, in his view, mounted an armed assault on the JNA, rather than the other way around.[40] 'The territorial pretensions of some neighbouring countries [also] played a certain role', he adds, 'in the dissolution of Yugoslavia.'[41] But, in Kadijević's view, it was above all the United States and Germany that conspired to break up socialist Yugoslavia, a state which allegedly served the interests of all of its peoples. Indeed, Germany figures as the principal demon in Kadijević's account, which traces German motivation to the desire to court popularity in the Islamic world and to 'dominate' the Balkans.[42] It was with these objectives in mind, Kadijević tells us, that Germany incited Serbs, Croats, and Muslims in Bosnia-Herzegovina to take up arms against each other.[43]

The European Community's interest in getting Mesić approved as SFRY president, after the Serbs had attempted to block his supposedly routine succession, lay in their desire, Kadijević writes, to give Mesić control over the army, so that it would be prevented from either serving Serbian interests or exercising an independent role.[44] In the general's view Mesić figured as an agent of the fascistic government of Franjo Tudjman and the Serb insurrection in western Slavonia was provoked by 'Ustaša attacks';[45] the JNA's conquest of Vukovar after a long siege in the face of desperate resistance by the townfolk emerges in his recollection as a 'liberation'. In the eyes of the West, however, the conquest of Vukovar was, among other things, 'a public relations disaster . . . , further isolating Belgrade and making it more difficult for Milošević to achieve the objectives he cared about', as the authors of a CIA-sponsored study put it.[46]

To the extent that Kadijević's account still holds interest, it is because of its description of the JNA command's strategy during the period of escalation preceding the outbreak of open hostilities as well as of JNA efforts to establish control in Bosnia, and because of the author's open admission of his efforts to dismantle the territorial defence system.[47]

Stipe Mesić served as the last president of the SFRY Presidency from
May 1991 until October of that year and was elected Croatia's president
in early 2000. His account of the period May–December 1991, which
went through two Croatian editions before being translated into English,
is among the most often cited memoirs dealing with the war. His view
of the crisis has elements in common with the views expressed by
Dizdarević and Mamula, but little or nothing in common with those of
Kadijević. In Mesić's view, the problem lay not in Slovenia or Croatia or
neighbouring countries, let alone Germany and the United States, but in
Serbia, where the leadership had decided to pursue an expansionist
programme. Asserting that Serbia had executed a coup even before he
himself arrived in Belgrade,[48] Mesić urges that Croatia's declaration of
'dissociation' in June 1991 was specifically understood by the authorities
in Zagreb as keeping open the option of reassociation with other
ex-SFRY republics on a confederal basis,[49] though it is hard to imagine
how anyone in Zagreb could have considered Serbia a prospective
partner in such a scheme.

Through extensive reconstructions of conversations in the chambers
of the SFRY collective presidency and citations of statements made by
prominent Serbian politicians, Mesić conveys the impression of growing
lawlessness in Serbia. He notes, with openly expressed scorn, Belgrade's
proposal 'that Croatia be skipped over in its right to preside over the
SFRY Presidency, instead offering the presidential position to Bogićević
of Bosnia-Herzegovina, and the vice-presidential position to Tupurkovski
in Macedonia'.[50]

Kadijević's notion that the EC backed Mesić's nomination in hopes
that he could rein in the army does not gain any credence in Mesić's
account. Rather, the EC is portrayed as being motivated by the hope
that, by compelling Belgrade to honour established legal practice and by
imposing a three-month moratorium on the operationalization of the
Slovenian and Croatian declarations of 'dissociation', it could create a
context in which the Yugoslavs could decide, in mutual consultation,
what they wished to do. As for Kadijević, he is portrayed by Mesić as
obstinate, insubordinate, and headstrong.[51]

Mesić offers some colourful descriptions of prominent Serbs, writing
that B. Kostić regularly behaved 'in a bullying manner', that 'Jović foamed
at the mouth'[52] and 'pounced on me like a wildcat',[53] and that Serb
opposition leader Vuk Drašković could be 'almost reasonable' when
removed from the influence of his wife.[54] The vocabulary is not entirely
innocent, of course; on the contrary, it reflects Mesić's outrage at what
he considered to be illegal machinations by the Serbian side, as well as
the heated atmosphere more generally. In an exchange typical of that

time, Milošević who at times – Mesić tells us – spoke 'with the force of a lucid paranoid,'[55] hypocritically assured Mesić that Serbia was not involved in the insurrection by Croatian Serbs and was 'just an observer' – to which a rather provoked Mesić replied, 'Do you really think I'm nuts?'[56]

War in Slovenia (Drnovšek, Janša, Dizdarević)

In preparing for war, Milošević, Jović, and Kadijević wanted Slovenia, Croatia, and Bosnia-Herzegovina disarmed. This is why, in spring 1990, the army was ordered to seize the arms of the TOs in those three republics and remove them to secure sites. The point was to disarm the local authorities in those republics at the same time as Serbian paramilitary groups in Croatia and later Bosnia-Herzegovina were receiving arms from JNA warehouses and training from JNA instructors. Frightened by this completely illegal move and feeling increasingly threatened by both the rhetoric in Belgrade and the various other unconstitutional and illegal moves being taken by Belgrade or with Belgrade's approval,[57] Slovenia and Croatia turned to foreign sources to replace the arms which had been confiscated and to build up armed forces capable of defending their respective republics from the expected showdown with Serbian forces. In October 1990, Slovenia and Croatia had presented a joint proposal for transforming the SFRY into a confederation, a proposal which the leaderships of both republics viewed as the last chance to save Yugoslavia in any form within its given boundaries. The proposal was drawn up out of fear of the repercussions of the transformation of politics in Serbia, but even if it had been adopted it is unlikely to have worked. After all, if illegitimate government is the problem, then the solution is to create legitimate government, and not to create autonomous spheres in which certain actors can allow themselves to think themselves 'safe' from the problems next door. On 25 June 1991, Slovenia and Croatia declared their 'disassociation' from the SFRY; a ten-day war between the JNA and the fledgling but determined armed forces of Slovenia ended when European Union (EU) mediators asked Slovenia to accept a three-month moratorium on the 'activation' of its independence. By now the federal government was well on the way to complete collapse; Milošević, the ambitious Serbian leader, had no interest in pursuing war in Slovenia, however, and by October 1991 Slovenian independence was a fact – though one not recognized by the EU until two months later. The JNA took its time to give up its barracks in Slovenia, however, with the last JNA troops leaving Slovenia only on 26 October 1991.

It is possible to read Drnovšek's and Janša's accounts as if they constituted two parts of the same puzzle, but in fact their outlooks are totally different, even, in some ways, incompatible. Janez Drnovšek, who served as president of the SFRY Presidency from May 1989 to May 1990 and who served as prime minister of Slovenia for most of the decade 1992–2002, portrays Slovenia as largely united in its political posture and represents his own actions as a member of the SFRY Presidency as astutely attuned to producing the best possible results for Slovenia; Janez Janša, who served as minister of defence of Slovenia from 1990 to 1994 and again for a few months in 2000, stresses the differences of opinion within Slovenia at the time an independent course was being charted. Janša, for example, characterizes Jozef Školc, the first president of the Slovenian Liberal Democratic Party (LDS), as an 'opponent of the formation of Slovenia's own defense system'[58] and repeatedly castigates members of the LDS (Drnovšek's party) for lack of enthusiasm for or faith in the cause of Slovenian independence. Janša also claims that the Slovenian government (which is to say, Milan Kučan, among others) consented in advance to his own arrest, together with the others put on trial in 1988, thus offering a version of events utterly divergent from Kučan's account, as related by Viktor Meier, the renowned journalist for the *Frankfurter Allgemeine*.[59] Janša gives credit to local municipalities, ultimately, for holding on to about 30 per cent of the arms allocated to the TO in May 1990, as the JNA was trying to confiscate all TO weaponry not only in Slovenia but also in Croatia and Bosnia. Later, when the JNA kidnapped Vladimir Milošević, commander of the Slovenian TO regional headquarters, Janša cut off electricity and telephone service to the key barracks until the army finally relented and released Milošević. But, as Janša recalls,

Drnovšek was a master in political appearances and . . . he knew how to take advantage of his position for his own promotion excellently. His short discussion with Kadijević and his half-hour appearance on TV [were] enough to convince a large part of the public that it was he [and not Janša] who had saved the situation and achieved the release of Milošević.[60]

When Janša further criticizes Drnovšek for his endorsement of the eleventh-hour Gligorov–Izetbegović plan for a reorganized Yugoslav state – a plan supported by the European Community – on the grounds that this was incompatible with the results of the Slovenian referendum on independence,[61] one comes to appreciate that there were (and are still) fundamental political differences between the two men.

Drnovšek's account is, of course, completely different. To begin with, there is not a hint in it of the possibility that anyone in the Slovenian government was implicated in the arrest of Janša and the others; on the contrary, it leads one to believe that the arrests and trial in 1988 had the character of a duel between the JNA and the Republic of Slovenia. Moreover, where Janša found a number of mugwumps, who doubted the capacity of the small Slovenian armed force to repel the JNA and who therefore preferred to straddle the fence on the issue of independence, in Drnovšek's account the choice for independence is presented as the overwhelming preference of Slovenes by the end of 1990[62] and as the natural response to the growing lawlessness in Serbia and threats to the political order in Slovenia.

Drnovšek presents himself unabashedly as a hero in his own time, as a kind of 'Lone Ranger' plucked from nowhere ('It was as if someone had sent me to Mars', Drnovšek says about his own personal reaction)[63] to run for the presidency, not beholden to the party or to anyone else, and as a relentless fighter for human rights, whether in Kosovo or elsewhere, and resolute defender of Slovenia's interests at the level of the federation.[64]

Raif Dizdarević's *Od smrti Tita* has some things to say about events in Slovenia in 1988 and, interestingly, offers an account distinct from both that of Mamula and that offered by either Janša or Kučan. According to Dizdarević, General Višnjić's visit to Minister Ertl in May 1988 had been completely 'routine' and the purpose of his visit had been limited to discussing ways to strengthen the security at military installations on the territory of the Republic of Slovenia.[65] Given the various representations being made in late May by Kučan, Ertl, Kadijević, and others, the party Central Committee inevitably discussed the charges being made by Kučan. During a break in the CC session, Dizdarević talked with General Višnjić who allegedly, with tears in his eyes, denied that he had in any way exceeded his mandate in the conversation with Ertl, Kučan, and Stane Dolanc, or in any way presented anything which could have been construed as threatening to the Slovenian leadership.

War in Croatia (Tomac v. Špegelj)

Serb–Croat clashes at Pakrac and Plitvice in February 1991 and in Borovo Selo in May 1991 left no doubt of the gravity of the situation, but it was only with the occupation of Baranja on 3 July by JNA troops together with Serb volunteers and paramilitary forces that the war in Croatia began in earnest. Croatian defence minister Špegelj urged that Croatian forces place JNA barracks under siege, but this was not done until September, by which point about 30 per cent of Croatian territory was controlled by Serb paramilitary forces. At the end of the year a truce was drawn up, under the provisions of which United Nations Protection Force (UNPROFOR) troops were brought into Croatia to create a buffer zone between the Republic of Croatia and the separatist-minded Serbian frontier zones ('Krajine' in Serbian).

Zdravko Tomac, a political science professor for many years, served as deputy prime minister (SDP – Socijaldemokratska partija, or Social Democratic Party) in the Government of Democratic Unity in Zagreb from August 1991 to June 1992. His memoirs are largely confined to the period during which he served in this post. His purpose in writing this book was, apparently, to justify Croatia's policies, to underline the broad base of support which Tudjman enjoyed during the period of the Government of Democratic Unity, and to offer an only slightly qualified defence of Croatian president Tudjman. Indeed, Tudjman looms large in this book, and is given a mainly positive presentation; Tomac's harshest criticism of Tudjman is to urge that it would have been better for Croatia to have avoided conflict with the Muslims (Bosniaks) and to have formed a military alliance with the Izetbegović government against the Serbs.[66] (This was later done, as is well known, after the publication of Tomac's book.) Elsewhere, Tomac expresses his disappointment with Tudjman's alleged 'lenience and hasty consent to certain agreements, sometimes even without consultation with the Government'.[67] On the other hand, Tomac excuses certain 'concessions' made by Tudjman to the extreme right as a necessary price to pay in order to maintain unity at a time of crisis.[68] Tomac is quite concerned in this book to highlight moderate and liberal currents within the Zagreb government of the time and to paint Tudjman himself as a moderate. Thus, he reports that he and other members of the government were shocked by the accord reached between Bosnian Croat leader Mate Boban and Bosnian Serb leader Radovan Karadžić in May 1992,[69] even though Tudjman favoured the accord, and highlights his own personal engagement to chasten recruits who allowed themselves to give in to chauvinistic expressions of disdain for the Serbs.

Tomac also disparages rumours which circulated at the time (i.e., during summer 1991) to the effect that Zagreb was deliberately refusing to send ammunition or medicines to the defenders of Vukovar, allegedly in the belief that the city's fall would prove useful in marshalling international support for Croatia's cause. Tomac claims that the Croatian government had medicines and ammunition flown into Vukovar by night, authorizing several attempts by Croatian forces to break through to the besieged city[70] and that he and other ministers were always available to talk by phone with those trapped there. Tomac does not mention, however, that as of 13 October the Croatian Army stood in a

position to sweep into Vukovar and relieve the siege and that the operation was stopped by the forceful intervention by President Tudjman
personally; Tudjman, as already noted (on p. 24), said that he was being
pressured by the European Community not to mount a counterattack,
since Doctors Without Borders allegedly wanted to send a humanitarian
convoy to the besieged city.[71] In other words, in military terms, Vukovar's situation was not as hopeless as Tomac paints it.

But the most potent controversy of 1991, which divided the Croatian
political establishment down the middle, was the debate concerning the
JNA barracks. Radicals, led by Defence Minister Špegelj, wanted to lay
siege to the barracks sooner rather than later; in their view, the arms kept
at the barracks were the solution to Croatia's weapons shortage. Tomac
was one of the more vocal advocates of the more dilatory strategy which
ultimately prevailed. Tomac claims that Špegelj's preferred strategy
would have been 'dangerous and possibly catastrophic'.[72] Špegelj would
have liked to see the JNA barracks placed under siege as early as January
1991 or, at the latest, in June of that year. Špegelj pressed his argument
with such force that Tudjman, who was either not convinced by
Špegelj's logic (as Tomac argues) or intent on prolonging the war in
order to carry out the partition of Bosnia upon which he and Milošević
had agreed (as Špegelj argues),[73] dismissed the general as minister of
defence on 15 June 1991, appointing Šime Djodan as his successor.
Only at the beginning of September 1991 did Croatian authorities
initiate simultaneously a siege of all JNA barracks in the republic –
belatedly adopting Špegelj's strategy but under circumstances arguably
less favourable than when Špegelj had first urged the strategy – cutting
off their water, power, telephone, and food supplies, and blocking all
access points. Croatia's strategy was to combine old-fashioned siege
tactics with negotiation. Indeed, Tomac insists that the JNA barracks
were so well fortified and armed that in most cases it would have been
out of question to have attempted a frontal assault,[74] though this is
beside the point, since no one had seriously advocated this. But Croatian
forces did score a coup by capturing the Delnice barracks, and negotiated the departure of the JNA forces from Rijeka and Istria. Yet
according to Generals Tus and Špegelj, the JNA had been broken by
the end of 1991, and the introduction of 'peace-keeping forces' served
only to delay Croatia's eventual reconquest of its own territory.[75]

Tomac reveals some interesting details concerning the Croatian
leadership's appeal to then Soviet president Gorbachev in October
1991, and how the Soviet leader intervened with Belgrade to pressure
the Serbs to back off somewhat. Tomac also recounts how, on 5 October
1991, the Croatian government received a note from Serbian prime

minister Dragutin Zelenović alleging that *Croatian* (!) forces were destroying Dubrovnik and pledging that the Yugoslav Army would 'spare
no effort to protect this historical city'.[76] The Serbs also accused the
Croatian government of firing rockets at Tudjman's presidential palace
in order to blame it on the Serbs and 'even charged President Tudjman
[with] trying to kill himself in order to spite Serbia'.[77]

Špegelj's volume, published exactly ten years after his resignation as
minister of defence, became an overnight best-seller in Croatia, and
went into a second printing within a month. Still controversial even a
decade later, Špegelj's argument is still the same: that it would have
been better for Croatia if the barracks had been captured before or at the
onset of the escalation of hostilities. Špegelj links this argument to a
further argument that Croatian defence needs would have been best
served by fuller co-ordination with the Slovenes and by taking the
initiative in launching synchronized attacks on JNA facilities across
Slovenia and Croatia. In this way, Špegelj argues, the JNA would have
been denied the initiative and would have had to deal with two foes at
once, on terms not of its own choosing.[78] He argues further that Zagreb
could have reckoned that it would take at least two months from the
outbreak of hostilities for Belgrade to mobilize its forces, and that
therefore Zagreb would have been better served by attacking the
barracks sooner.[79] (Konrad Kolšek, the commander of the Fifth Military District, who was relieved of duty several days after hostilities broke
out in Slovenia, disputes Špegelj's account, however, arguing that
Croatia had insufficient troops and insufficient weapons and could not
afford to take on the might of the JNA at that time, but Špegelj himself
says that the JNA suffered from a shortage of available recruits and was
fundamentally weak.)[80]

Špegelj notes that, at the end of July 1991, as Croatia was sliding into
war on the JNA's terms, President Tudjman was relaxing with tennis,
and that the atmosphere around him was 'as if there had been 1,000
years of peace'.[81] He also recounts his arguments with Tudjman, showing Tudjman as ignorant of the most basic figures about Croatian
military strength, casualties, and so forth. He recalls that his first ela-
borated defence plan, presented to the Croatian government on 27
December 1990, was discussed for six hours and then put on the back
burner, allegedly on the supposition that Croatia did not need to worry
about a defence plan[82]. Špegelj was clearly convinced in early 1991 that
striking at the JNA early and hard would be Croatia's best defence, and
he presented this plan not only to Tudjman but also to Prime Minister
Manolić (in July 1991), among others.[83] According to Špegelj, 'the
conditions for a complete defeat of the aggressor had been created

and there exist very strong military arguments that this could have been accomplished by the second half of 1992 at the latest (to include not only Croatia but also the defence and complete liberation of Bosnia-Herzegovina, naturally in agreement with its legal leadership [i.e., the Izetbegović government] and in alliance with its legal defense forces'.[84] Of course, if Špegelj's analysis is correct, then the late President Tudjman is guilty at a minimum of gross negligence, perhaps of incompetence, or, if his decisions were conditioned by his March 1991 agreement with Milošević at Karadjordjevo, even of treason. It is no wonder then that the book has seen a lively discussion in Croatia and elsewhere.

War in Bosnia-Herzegovina (Izetbegović, Halilović, Šarinić)

By autumn 1990, the Serbian arms transfusion to Serb militias in Bosnia was underway.[85] In August 1991, Milošević met with Bosnian Serb leader Radovan Karadžić to discuss their strategy for Bosnia; that strategy was to use military force to annex a large portion of Bosnia to Serbia, expelling or killing non-Serbs who happened to be living in those parts coveted by the Serbian leaders. The following month, the Yugoslav Army established the Serbian Autonomous Region of Herzegovina, securing its borders; additional Serbian autonomous zones were established at this time also in Bosanska Krajina (northwest Bosnia around Banja Luka) and in Romanija (east of Sarajevo). These regions immediately requested Yugoslav Army 'assistance'.[86] Before the end of 1991, Serb authorities also undertook to have some arms production facilities in Bosnia dismantled and transferred to Serbia. By December of that year, moreover, heavy weaponry was 'being brought into position around the cities of Sarajevo, Mostar, Bihać, and Tuzla, so that these cities could be bombarded at any time'.[87] Taken together, these moves suggest that there was nothing Bosnian president Alija Izetbegović could have done, short of abject supplication before Milošević, to avert the outbreak of hostilities. A report of the Second Army District on 20 March 1992 revealed that the JNA had already distributed some 51,900 light weapons to the Serbs in Bosnia by then; in addition, Karadžić's Serbian Democratic Party had procured an additional 17,300 rifles through other channels.[88] Croatian–Bosniak collaboration might have broken the back of the JNA-backed Serbian insurrection at an early stage. But Tudjman dreamt of annexing large sections of Bosnia and authorized illegal Croatian military formations operating in Bosnia to attack the Army of the Republic of Bosnia-Herzegovina and to take control of key towns, establishing a Croatian para-state under the name 'Croatian Republic of Herceg-Bosna'.[89]

Clashes between Serbs and non-Serbs in Bosnia actually began in August 1991,[90] but it was not until the following April that the Serbian assault on Bosnia-Herzegovina began in earnest. By October 1992, if not before, the Croatian Army was engaging in collaborative behaviour with Serbian forces – for example, pulling out of Bosanski Brod in order to allow Serb forces to capture the town.[91] The war eventually became a four-sided conflict, with Bosnian Serbs, Bosnian Croats, Bosnian forces loyal to the elected government of Alija Izetbegović, and forces loyal to Fikret Abdić, self-declared head of the Autonomous Province of Western Bosnia, variously fighting each other or collaborating. By the end of the fighting, in November 1995, some 215,000 people had been killed in Bosnia-Herzegovina – among them, roughly 160,000 Bosniaks (Muslims), 30,000 Croats, and 25,000 Serbs.[92]

Of all the memoirs under review here, those by Sefer Halilović, commander of the Bosnian forces from 1992 to 1993, have perhaps stirred the most controversy. Now in its third, expanded edition, the book provoked public attacks by Stipe Mesić and Martin Špegelj already in its first edition, and brought before the public Halilović's quarrels with Bosnian president Izetbegović. Those facts on which both Halilović and Izetbegović agree are: (1) that Halilović had been experiencing some problems of insubordination in the early months of 1993 (Halilović adds that the insubordination was on the part of Rasim Delić); (2) that on 8 June 1993 Rasim Delić was entrusted by Izetbegović with effective command of the Bosnian Army, with Halilović remaining chief-of-staff but being effectively subordinated to Delić; (3) that Izetbegović was prepared to agree to some Western-brokered peace agreements which called for the partition of Bosnia; and (4) that the Zulfikarpašić–Filipović initiative of 1991, which seemed to sideline the Bosnian Croats and which Izetbegović at first supported, would have reduced Bosnia to a mere appendage of a Serb-dominated Yugoslavia. Beyond that, however, there is little agreement between the two versions.

At the heart of Halilović's account is his conviction that Izetbegović, together with Fikret Muslimović, the one-time chief of KOS (the JNA's counterintelligence service) for Bosnia, Alija Delimustafić, the Bosnian minister of the interior in 1991, and, as it seems, also Delić were conspiring to partition Bosnia-Herzegovina because they favoured the creation of a rump Muslim state. Halilović also points out that Muslimović was chief of KOS in Bosnia-Herzegovina at the time that KOS was distributing arms to the Serbs in that republic, thus suggesting a certain support, on Muslimović's part, for Serb territorial aspirations in

Bosnia.[93] Halilović also sees KOS as having been behind his removal from operational command of the army and claims that Muslimović was originally supposed to be given command of the army, before the choice fell to Delić.[94]

Yet, in Halilović's mind, Izetbegović was not only committed to the destruction of the Bosnian state 'with its 1,000-year tradition'[95] but also naïve about Serbian intentions, as reflected in the Bosnian president's refusal, on two occasions, to approve plans to lay siege to JNA barracks in Bosnia (along the lines of what Špegelj proposed in Croatia). Halilović claims that, of the nine JNA barracks in Sarajevo in 1992, eight were in exposed locations where the Bosnian government could, if it had found the will, have dictated terms. But Izetbegović had signed an agreement with the JNA and, according to Halilović, insisted on sticking to it.[96]

In July 1993, Halilović's flat was struck by an artillery shell; his wife and son died in the explosion. Halilović, who had written a letter to the presidential council of the republic the previous month, in which he had challenged the constitutionality of the decisions taken by Izetbegović the previous day (restructuring the army), is convinced that Bakir Alispahić, Bosnian minister of police, and Fikret Muslimović, by then one of the five highest-ranking generals in the Bosnian Army, were implicated in this attempt on his life.[97] In fact, on 5 October 1998, Halilović filed a criminal complaint against Muslimović, Alispahić, and five others, alleging that they had conspired to kill him.

As for Delimustafić, Halilović does not accuse him of involvement in the assassination plot, but claims that the Bosnian minister collaborated with Yugoslav interior minister Petar Gračanin in the second half of 1991, bringing into Bosnia about 100 federal inspectors, whose task was to paralyse defence preparations, carry out espionage, and engage in various acts of subversion.[98] According to Halilović, Delimustafić also sent about 12,000 rifles, about the same time, to western Herzegovina, where these weapons ended up in the hands of the Croatian Defence Council (Hrvatsko Vijeće Obrane, or HVO), to be used later in combat against the Bosnian Army; as if that was not enough, Izetbegović supposedly knew about this arms transfer at the time, but did nothing.[99] This story obtains indirect confirmation from British scholar Marko Attila Hoare, who notes that both Delimustafić and Abdić were working as agents for KOS.[100] Alispahić also collaborated with KOS, according to Munir Alibabić-Munja, a former agent of the State Security Service and of the Ministry of Internal Affairs for the Republic of Bosnia-Herzegovina.[101]

Halilović further argues: that the peace movement in Bosnia was an invention of KOS,[102] that KOS was actively encouraging Bosniaks to view their collective identity through the religious prism,[103] that most of the army's budget after 25 June 1993 (i.e., after he was effectively out of the picture) was wasted on such purchases as luxury cars and electronic gadgets, with only a small portion actually going towards the purchase of armaments and combat-relevant equipment,[104] that some of Delić's military mistakes in 1993 were not mistakes at all,[105] that the Croatian Army and the HVO were on the brink of total defeat by early 1994 until Izetbegović rescued them and the prospects for partition by signing the Washington Agreement,[106] and that Izetbegović unnecessarily signed the Dayton Peace Accords at a time when the Bosnian Army was on the verge of capturing a large swathe of territory in western Bosnia, including the key town of Banja Luka.[107] The third edition of this book includes eighty-six pages of appendices designed to support his claims.

Although Izetbegović makes no allusion to Halilović's memoirs in his recently published autobiography, parts of it read as if they were directed towards replying to criticisms voiced by the general. The Bosnian president devotes very little attention to Halilović himself, however, characterizing him, rather briefly, as 'a capable officer but a man without sufficient personal courage', and claiming, in the context of reports that the army was maltreating its Serb recruits, that Halilović 'did not have sufficient authority among the troops to be able to deal with the situation'.[108] Rasim Delić is described by Izetbegović, by contrast, as 'a serious man and a very educated officer'.[109]

Izetbegović is not, however, concerned with addressing the specific charges registered in Halilović's memoirs. Rather, Izetbegović is determined, in the first place, to establish his reputation as an advocate of a tolerant, secular, multicultural society committed to liberal democracy, equality, and fair play. Quite a number of the speeches reprinted in the book show Izetbegović articulating these principles. In addition, the volume contains full or partial texts of various newspaper interviews and diplomatic exchanges, including exchanges between himself and Croatian president Tudjman.

According to Hrvoje Šarinić, who served as chief of the Office of the President of the Republic and as chief counsellor to President Tudjman during the war, what Izetbegović wanted was neither a rump Islamic state (as Halilović claims) nor a united, multiconfessional Bosnia (as Izetbegović himself claims), but rather a united but Islamic Bosnia.[110] Šarinić says further that the Sarajevo government of Izetbegović favoured the strengthening of Islamic principles in such a way as to tend towards fundamentalism, while inexplicably characterizing Izetbegović's electoral rival in 1990, Fikret Abdić, as a champion of a liberal citizens'

state, linked with the West.[111] The record of Šarinić's conversations
with Milošević and other high-ranking political figures shows that the
Croatian side was deeply concerned about the Serbs and the Muslims
forming an alliance at Croatian expense.[112]

Šarinić is convinced that Milošević did not actually have any territorial
pretensions vis-à-vis Croatian territory and that the Serbian leader's
expansionist programme was limited to Bosnia-Herzegovina.[113] Šarinić's impressions derive from conversations he held with Milošević
during the years 1993–5, by which time the military balance on the
Croatian front had already turned decisively against the Serbs; these
impressions, therefore, have nothing to do with Milošević's ambitions
at the start of the war.[114]

Šarinić's memoirs are full of thumbnail sketches of principals. Milošević is 'self-confident' and 'arrogant'.[115] Tudjman showed 'vision',
especially in rejecting Ambassador Galbraith's 'monstrous' Z-4 plan
and in pressing forward with the liberation of western Slavonia in May
1995 and the Krajina in August 1995.[116] Lord Owen is described as
'completely lucid' and 'perfidious', and as 'ill-disposed towards
Croats'.[117] Šarinić has positive things to say about British ambassador
Gavin Hewitt,[118] but characterizes US ambassador Peter Galbraith as
'unprofessional',[119] adding that the American ambassador's 'vanity, his
multitude of complexes, and his ambition constantly led him to new
attempts to become an important factor'.[120]

International involvement (Pérez de Cuéllar, Major, Boutros-Ghali)

The international community was reluctant to become involved in the
Yugoslav crisis, and first looked to Ante Marković, the powerless
federal prime minister, and then – at least where the governments of
John Major (in Britain), François Mitterrand (in France), and the elder
Bush (United States) are concerned – expected Slovenia and Croatia to
reach an agreement with Milošević. The memoirs by Pérez de Cuéllar,
Major, and Boutros-Ghali offer some insights into the diplomatic manoeuvres behind the scenes and express clear points of view on what
happened on the ground. To be sure, none of these three volumes is
devoted to discussing Yugoslav/Bosnian issues as such; indeed, in John
Major's autobiography and Pérez de Cuéllar's memoirs, the Yugoslav
imbroglio accounts for only one chapter each. Pérez de Cuéllar served
as UN secretary-general from 1982 to December 1991, serving, thus,
during the Falklands War, the Gulf War, the hostage crisis in Lebanon,
and the heating up of the crisis in Yugoslavia. His discussion of the

Yugoslav crisis is confined to the period running from June to December 1991. Notably, he points out that Tudjman was completely frank about his desire to annex portions of Bosnia-Herzegovina, at a time when Milošević coyly conveyed the impression that he was 'primarily interested in getting satisfaction on the human rights of Serbs in Croatia'.[121] He notes that, when, in autumn 1991, the European Community identified Belgrade as being primarily responsible for the crisis, Lord Carrington, the EC-appointed chair of the Conference on Yugoslavia, publicly criticized the EC; indeed, after a meeting with Milošević, Tudjman, and General Veljko Kadijević in The Hague on 4 October, Carrington thought he had achieved a 'breakthrough', concluding that the just-negotiated eighth ceasefire might actually hold.[122] Pérez de Cuéllar was sceptical about introducing peace-keepers where there was no peace, and resisted the notion, but after he appointed Sadako Ogata, the UN high commissioner for refugees, to assume responsibility for co-ordinating humanitarian assistance in the Yugoslav region, the UN was gradually sucked into the crisis.[123] Pérez de Cuéllar also mentions that Bosnian president Izetbegović contacted UN offices in December 1991 in the hope that the UN would dispatch peace-keeping forces to his republic before it was too late, but, as he freely admits, he did not believe that the conditions for introducing peace-keepers anywhere in the Yugoslav area existed.[124] He also recounts his steadfast opposition to any diplomatic recognition of either Slovenia or Croatia before a comprehensive peace settlement had been reached, and argues that international recognition of these republics (agreed by the EC in mid-December 1991) contributed directly to the outbreak of fighting in Bosnia-Herzegovina the following spring.[125]

Boutros-Ghali, who succeeded Pérez de Cuéllar as UN secretary-general in December 1991, and former prime minister John Major served in office during the entire period of the Bosnian war and, accordingly, offer more extensive comments on the fighting there. But whereas Major wants to spread the blame for the outbreak of hostilities fairly equally, even casting some blame on the Slovenes for their alleged contribution to the breakup and escalation of tensions,[126] Boutros-Ghali quotes from his own speech to the UN Security Council on 12 May 1992, in which he held the Bosnian Serbs, together with the Yugoslav people's Army, responsible for the war.[127] Again, while Major, rejecting Pérez de Cuéllar's scepticism,[128] defends the UN mission, conceding, however, that with the end of the Cold War and the dissolution of the Soviet Union 'NATO, the EC and America were all unsure of their international roles', and accepting some of the responsibility for the miscarriage in terms of the international community's response,[129] Boutros-Ghali reminds his readers of his own opposition to the very peace-keeping mission which John Major had championed,[130] but reserves his sharpest barbs for the Clinton administration, alleging at one point that 'peace-keepers had been deployed precisely because the United States and NATO were not willing to go to war'.[131] Criticizing the Europeans for allegedly having expected him to devote a disproportionate amount of his time and energy to the war in Bosnia,[132] he ultimately casts the blame for the catastrophe, rather obviously, on 'the war criminals of the former Yugoslavia' and, less obviously, on the United States for being 'so deeply involved politically and so deeply determined not to be involved militarily'.[133]

Conclusion

On the whole, however interesting these memoirs might be, there are few spectacular revelations. Still, one might mention Drnovšek's revelation that, in the Tito era, the JNA had tried for a long time to develop nuclear weapons,[134] details provided by Šarinić concerning inter-Serb rivalries (e.g., between Karadžić and Momcilo Krajišnik, one of the Bosnian Serb leaders),[135] Tomac's revelation of intelligence indicating that at the beginning of October 1991 Belgrade had been preparing for an all-out assault on Croatia, to include 'attacks on industrial facilities, with the aim of causing an ecological catastrophe',[136] Mamula's disclosure that leading figures in the Ministry of Defence and in the JNA had contacted the leaderships of Slovenia, Croatia, and Bosnia-Herzegovina in late 1987 to see if they could come to a consensus as to what Milošević's putsch in Serbia meant for the country and perhaps undertake some remedial action,[137] and that Stane Dolanc, one of the highest-ranking Slovenian politicians in the late Tito era and early post-Tito era, had suggested to Nikola Ljubičić, who had been elected to represent Serbia on the SFRY Presidency in 1984, that the party presidium should discuss Milošević's putsch,[138] and details revealed by Rudolf concerning Zagreb's debate in late June and early July 1991 about the most sensible response to the JNA's use of force against the Slovenes.[139] I will confess to a certain satisfaction in reading Šarinić's speculation that there was nothing political about the application of pressure on Zagreb, in 1995, not to launch military campaigns against Serb-held areas of Croatia; in Šarinić's view, the explanation is quite personal – the high-ranking representatives and mediators were being paid very high salaries to carry on negotiations and, if the crisis were to be resolved, their mandates would end and their handsome salaries would come to an end.[140]

The outright self-promotion which one can find in some memoirs should not deter anyone from diving into the memoir literature. Indeed, the insights one can gain into what happened behind the scenes, into what some of the principals were thinking at the time, and into how the principals regarded each other are not only valuable but arguably vital if one is going to capture the spirit of an age.

NOTES

1 For an effective rebuttal of Germanophobic accounts of the Yugoslav war, see Daniele Conversi, *German-Bashing and the Breakup of Yugoslavia*, Donald W. Treadgold Papers in Russian, East European, and Central Asian Studies No. 16 (Seattle: Henry M. Jackson School of International Studies of the University of Washington, March 1998).

2 The term 'Hobbist' is reserved for notions which are inspired by the writings of Thomas Hobbes but which offer oversimplified understandings of Hobbes's notions. The usual term for describing notions more or less true to Hobbes's inspiration is 'Hobb'sian' (or 'Hobbesian').

3 For a concise and lucid explanation of 'cynicism' and an effective rebuttal, see Thomas Cushman, *Critical Theory and the War in Croatia and Bosnia*, Donald W. Treadgold Papers in Russian, East European, and Central Asian Studies No. 13 (Seattle: Henry M. Jackson School of International Studies of the University of Washington, July 1997).

4 Stipe Mesić, *Kako smo rušili Jugoslaviju* (Zagreb: Mislav, 1992): 2nd edn published in 1994 under the revised title, *Kako je srušena Jugoslavija*.

5 Veljko Kadijević, *Moje vidjenje raspada: Vojska bez države* (Belgrade: Politika, 1993).

6 Borisav Jović, *Poslednji dani SFRJ: Izvodi iz dnevnika* (Belgrade: Politika, 1995).

7 Srpska Akademija Nauka i Umetnosti.

8 Milorad Tomanić, *Srpska crkva u ratu i ratovi u njoj* (Belgrade: Medijska knjižara Krug, 2001), pp. 37–43, 73.

9 Raif Dizdarević, *Od smrti Tita do smrti Jugoslavije: Svjedočenja* (Sarajevo: Svjedok, 1999), p. 49.

10 *Ibid.*, p. 54.

11 *Ibid.*, p. 90.

12 *Ibid.*, p. 187.

13 *Ibid.*, p. 202.

14 *Ibid.*, pp. 210–12.

15 See *ibid.*, p. 217.

16 *Ibid.*, p. 223.

17 *Ibid.*, p. 297.

18 *Ibid.*, pp. 436–7.

19 *Ibid.*, p. 420.

20 *Ibid.*, p. 437.
21 Viktor Meier, *Yugoslavia: A History of Its Demise,* trans. from German by Sabrina P. Ramet (London: Routledge, 1999), p. 68.
22 *Ibid.*, p. 90.
23 *Ibid.*, p. 107.
24 Davorin Rudolf, *Rat koji nismo htjeli: Hrvatska 1991* (Zagreb: Nakladni zavod Globus, 1999), p. 41.
25 Laura Silber and Allan Little, *The Death of Yugoslavia* (London: Penguin Books and BBC Books, 1995), p. 157.
26 Branko Mamula, *Slučaj Jugoslavija* (Podgorica: CID, 2000), pp. 15–16.
27 *Ibid.*, p. 16.
28 *Ibid.*, p. 17.
29 *Ibid.*, p. 61.
30 Martin Špegelj, 'Prva faza rata 1990–1992: pripreme JNA za agresiju i hrvatski obrambeni planovi', in Branka Magaš and Ivo Žanić (eds.), *Rat u Hrvatskoj i Bosni i Hercegovini 1991–1995* (Zagreb, Sarajevo, and London: Naklada Jesenski i Turk and Dani, for the Bosnian Institute, 1999), p. 46.
31 Mamula, *Slučaj Jugoslavija,* pp. 76–7.
32 *Ibid.*, p. 115.
33 *Ibid.*, p. 117.
34 *Ibid.*, p. 128.
35 See, for example, the account offered in Meier, *Yugoslavia,* pp. 62–7, based on a conversation with Slovenian president Milan Kučan in November 1993 and on documents held in the Archives of the Republic of Slovenia.
36 Mamula, *Slučaj Jugoslavija,* p. 124.
37 *Ibid.*, p. 109.
38 Kadijević, *Moje vidjenje raspada,* pp. 127, 130, 134.
39 *Ibid.*, p. 37.
40 *Ibid.*, p. 116.
41 *Ibid.*, p. 160.
42 *Ibid.*, pp. 18, 35.
43 *Ibid.*, p. 93.
44 *Ibid.*, p. 37.
45 *Ibid.*, p. 138.
46 *Balkan Battlegrounds: A Military History of the Yugoslav Conflict, 1990–1995,* 2 vols. (Washington, DC: Office of Russian & European Analysis of the Central Intelligence Agency, May 2002), vol. I, p. 110.
47 I am indebted to Marko Hoare for bringing these points to my attention.
48 Stipe Mesić, *The Demise of Yugoslavia: A Political Memoir,* trans. from Croation by Milena Benini (Budapest and New York: Central European University Press, 2004), p. 9.
49 *Ibid.*, pp. 12–13, 264–5.
50 *Ibid.*, p. 63.

51 See *ibid.*, p. 112.
52 Both items *ibid.*, p. 231.
53 *Ibid.*, p. 286.
54 *Ibid.*, p. 176.
55 *Ibid.*, p. 373.
56 *Ibid.*, p. 317.
57 See the partial list of such unconstitutional and illegal moves in Sabrina P. Ramet, *Balkan Babel: The Disintegration of Yugoslavia from the Death of Tito to the Fall of Milošević*, 4th edn (Boulder, CO: Westview Press, 2002), pp. 71–2.
58 Janez Janša, *The Making of the Slovenian State 1988–1992: The Collapse of Yugoslavia*, trans. by AMIDAS, ed. by Aleksander Zorn (Ljubljana: Založba Mladinska knjiga, 1994), p. 250.
59 See Meier, *Yugoslavia*, pp. 65–7.
60 Janša, *The Making of the Slovenian State*, pp. 124–5.
61 *Ibid.*, p. 139.
62 Janez Drnovšek, *Der Jugoslawien-Krieg: Meine Wahrheit*, trans. from Slovenian by Doris Debeniak (Kilchberg, Switz.: Smartbooks, 1998), pp. 243–5.
63 *Ibid.*, p. 5.
64 In 1998, after the publication of the German translation of Drnovšek's memoirs, Janša was offered the opportunity to review the book for the prestigious German newspaper, the *Frankfurter Allgemeine Zeitung*. Janša lost no time in pointing out that Drnovšek was not a political outsider, as might be supposed from a reading of *Meine Wahrheit*, but a deputy in the Yugoslav Assembly and also a member of the League of Communists. According to Janša, Drnovšek had also had contacts with the Yugoslav secret police (UDBa); Janša suggests further that Drnovšek's selection to run for president was no accident. In Janša's account, Drnovšek emerges as less than resolute, raising his voice against the JNA's expropriation of Slovenian weaponry – according to Janša – only after a huge clamour from the Slovenian public. Janša further charges that there are a number of misrepresentations in the book, including about where Drnovšek spent 29–30 November 1989, and closes his review by firing a broadside against Drnovšek's title: if the book tells only '*his*' truth' ('Meine Wahrheit' means 'My truth'), then, Janša charges, it follows that Drnovšek does not believe in '*the* truth'.
    Drnovšek's reply to this attack, published in the same newspaper more than a month later, passed over several of Janša's points but Drnovšek insisted that he had reacted to the expropriations immediately. Drnovšek also claimed that he had been instrumental, in his post in the SFRY Presidency, in keeping the JNA at bay until late June 1991. See *Frankfurter Allgemeine Zeitung*, 14 October 1998, p. 10, and 25 November 1998, p. 11, on *LexisNexis*. Janša was granted the final word in this exchange. His reply to Drnovšek was published in the *Frankfurter Allgemeine Zeitung*, 9 December 1998, p. 14.
65 Dizdarević, *Od smrti Tita*, p. 243.

66 Zdravko Tomac, *The Struggle for the Croatian State . . . through Hell to Democracy*, trans. by Profikon (Zagreb: Profikon, 1993), p. 253.

67 *Ibid.*, p. 270.

68 *Ibid.*, p. 96.

69 *Ibid.*, p. 149n.

70 *Ibid.*, pp. 338–9.

71 Anton Tus, 'Rat u Sloveniji i Hrvatskoj do Sarajevskog primirja', in Magaš and Žanić, *Rat u Hrvatskoj i Bosni i Hercegovini*, pp. 81–2.

72 Tomac, *The Struggle for the Croatian State*, p. 87.

73 Martin Špegelj, *Sjećanja vojnika*, ed. by Ivo Žanić (Zagreb: Znanje, 2001), p. 302; and Drago Pilsel, 'Radoš je novi Šušak' (an interview with Martin Špegelj), *Feral Tribune* (Split), 840 (20 October 2001), p. 40.

74 Tomac, *The Struggle for the Croatian State*, pp. 287, 289–90.

75 Jože Pirjevec, *Le guerre jugoslave 1991–1999* (Turin: Giulio Einaudi editore, 2001), p. 110; Špegelj, *Sjećanja vojnika*, p. 292; and Tus, 'Rat u Sloveniji', p. 78.

76 Tomac, *The Struggle for the Croatian State*, p. 417.

77 *Ibid.*, p. 418.

78 Špegelj, *Sjećanja vojnika*, pp. 218–19.

79 *Ibid.*, pp. 219, 375.

80 Konrad Kolšek, *Spomini: Na začetek oborozenega spopada v Jugoslaviji 1991* (Maribor: Založba Obzorja, 2001); and Špegelj, 'Prva faza rata', pp. 49–50.

81 Špegelj, *Sjećanja vojnika*, p. 241.

82 *Ibid.*, p. 257.

83 *Ibid.*, p. 239.

84 *Ibid.*, p. 292.

85 See Sabrina P. Ramet, *The Three Yugoslavias: State-building and Legitimation, 1918–2005* (Bloomington, IN, and Washington, DC: Indiana University Press and Wilson Center Press, forthcoming), chap. 15.

86 Robert J. Donia and John V. A. Fine, Jnr, *Bosnia and Hercegovina: A Tradition Betrayed* (New York: Columbia University Press, 1994), p. 228.

87 Meier, *Yugoslavia*, p. 207.

88 Alija Izetbegović, *Sjećanja: Autobiografski zapis* (Sarajevo: TKD Šahinpašić, 2001), p. 94.

89 For discussion, see Goran Borković, 'Kaznjenička brojna', *Feral Tribune*, 853 (19 January 2002), pp. 59–60.

90 Saćir Filandra, *Bošnjačka politika u XX. stoljeću* (Sarajevo: Sejtarija, 1998), p. 383.

91 See Izetbegović, *Sjećanja*, p. 130.

92 As estimated by the distinguished Croatian demographer Vladimir Žerjavić, and reported in *Globus* (Zagreb), 9 January 1998, p. 24.

93 Sefer Halilović, *Lukava strategija*, 3rd expanded edn (Sarajevo: Matica, 1998), p. 92.

94 *Ibid.*, p. 96.

95 *Ibid.*, p. 21.
96 *Ibid.*, pp. 70–2.
97 *Ibid.*, pp. 61–2.
98 *Ibid.*, pp. 74, 87.
99 *Ibid.*, p. 75.
100 Marko Attila Hoare, 'Civilno–vojni odnosi u Bosni i Hercegovini 1992–1995', in Magaš and Žanić, *Rat u Hrvatskoj i Bosni i Hercegovini,* p. 210.
101 Munir Alibabić-Munja, *Bosna u kandžama KOS-a* (Sarajevo: Behar, 1996), p. 35.
102 Halilović, *Lukava strategija,* 3rd expanded edn, p. 83.
103 *Ibid.*, p. 90.
104 *Ibid.*, p. 120.
105 *Ibid.*, p. 140.
106 *Ibid.*, p. 167.
107 *Ibid.*, p. 155.
108 Izetbegović, *Sjećanja,* p. 153.
109 *Ibid.*
110 Hrvoje Šarinić, *Svi moji tajni pregovori sa Slobodanom Miloševićem 1993–1995 (1998)* (Zagreb: Globus, 1999), p. 57.
111 *Ibid.*, p. 140.
112 See *ibid.*, pp. 72, 87.
113 *Ibid.*, pp. 44–5.
114 Among the many sources to which the reader may turn for confirmation of the fact that Milošević was still committed to annexing the Serb-inhabited areas of Croatia to a 'Greater Serbia' is Slavoljub Djukić, *Milošević and Marković: A Lust for Power,* trans. from Serbian by Alex Dubinsky (Montreal: McGill-Queen's University Press, 2001), pp. 61–2.
115 Šarinić, *Svi moji tajni pregovori,* p. 255.
116 *Ibid.*, pp. 153, 148–9.
117 *Ibid.*, pp. 156, 164.
118 *Ibid.*, p. 177.
119 *Ibid.*, p. 153.
120 *Ibid.*, p. 155.
121 Javier Pérez de Cuéllar, *Pilgrimage for Peace: A Secretary-General's Memoir* (Houndmills, Basingstoke: Macmillan, 1997), pp. 483, 484.
122 *Ibid.*, pp. 481, 485.
123 *Ibid.*, pp. 487–8.
124 *Ibid.*, pp. 490–1.
125 *Ibid.*, pp. 492–4.
126 John Major, *The Autobiography* (New York: HarperCollins, 1999), p. 547.
127 Boutros Boutros-Ghali, *Unvanquished: A US–UN Saga* (New York: Random House, 1999) p. 39.
128 Pérez de Cuéllar, in *Pilgrimage of Peace* (p. 495): 'I remain today doubtful of the wisdom of using peacekeeping troops, whether UN or UN-authorized, for enforcement purposes in internal conflicts.'
129 Major, *Autobiography,* p. 549.

130 Boutros-Ghali, *Unvanquished*, pp. 40–3.
131 *Ibid.*, p. 143.
132 *Ibid.*, p. 53.
133 *Ibid.*, pp. 248, 246–7.
134 The project was scrapped in the early 1980s, after the death of President Josip Broz Tito. See Drnovšek, *Der Jugoslawien-Krieg*, p. 32.
135 Šarinić, *Svi moji tajni pregovori*, p. 108.
136 Tomac, *The Struggle for the Croatian State*, p. 155.
137 Mamula, *Slučaj Jugoslavija*, p. 115.
138 *Ibid.*, p. 118.
139 Rudolf, *Rat koji nismo htjeli*, pp. 286–7.
140 Šarinić, *Svi moji tajni pregovori*, p. 194.

REFERENCES

Boutros-Ghali, Boutros, *Unvanquished: A US–UN Saga* (New York: Random House, 1999), p. 352.
Dizdarević, Raif, *Od smrti Tita do smrti Jugoslavije: Svjedočenja* (Sarajevo: Svjedok, 1999), p. 459.
Drnovšek, Janez., *Der Jugoslawien-Krieg: Meine Wahrheit*, trans. from Slovenian by Doris Debeniak (Kilchberg, Switz.: Smartbooks, 1998), p. 359.
Halilović, Sfer, *Lukava strategija*, 3rd expanded edn (Sarajevo: Matica, 1998), p. 307.
Izetbegović, Alija, *Sjećanja. Autobiografski zapis* (Sarajevo: TKD Šahinpašić, 2001), p. 503.
Janša, Janez, *The Making of the Slovenian State 1988–1992: The Collapse of Yugoslavia*, trans. by AMIDAS, ed. by Aleksander Zorn (Ljubljana: Založba Mladinska knjiga, 1994), p. 251.
Kadijević, Veljko, *Moje vidjenje raspada: Vojska bez države* (Belgrade: Politika, 1993), p. 166.
Major, John, *The Autobiography* (New York: HarperCollins, 1999), p. 774.
Mamula, Branko, *Slučaj Jugoslavija* (Podgorica: CID, 2000), p. 339.
Mesić, Stipe, *The Demise of Yugoslavia: A Political Memoir*, trans. from Croatian by Milena Benini (Budapest and New York: Central European University Press, 2004), p. 422.
Pérez de Cuéllar, Javier, *Pilgrimage for Peace: A Secretary-General's Memoir* (Houndmills, Basingstoke: Macmillan, 1997), p. 518.
Rudolf, Davorin, *Rat koji nismo htjeli: Hrvatska 1991.* (Zagreb: Nakladni zavod Globus, 1999), p. 411.
Šarinić, Hrvoje, *Svi moji tajni pregovori sa Slobodanom Miloševićem 1993–1995 (1998)* (Zagreb: Globus, 1999), p. 343.
Špegelj, Martin, *Sjećanja vojnika*, ed. by Ivo Žanić (Zagreb: Znanje, 2001), p. 430.
Tomac, Zdravko, *The Struggle for the Croatian State . . . Through Hell to Democracy*, trans. by Profikon (Zagreb: Profikon, 1993), p. 568.

6   The scourge of nationalism and the quest for harmony

Among the questions scholars have raised, reflecting on the brutalities committed by all sides and the suffering experienced by innocents in all the republics affected (Slovenia, Croatia, Serbia including Kosovo, and Bosnia-Herzegovina), has been how it was possible for people who had lived, in some cases, literally as neighbours, to turn on each other with such brutality. In the process, scholars have endeavoured both to trace the sources of intercommunal violence and to suggest, in some cases, what might constitute important preconditions for, or ingredients in, social harmony. These concerns transcend the supposed boundary between the humanities and the social sciences and have, in other contexts over the centuries, been addressed by such diverse luminaries as Plato, St Thomas Aquinas, Thomas Hobbes, John Stuart Mill, Samuel P. Huntington, and Giuseppe Di Palma.

For most scholars, including in this instance Misha Glenny, Robert M. Hayden, Rusmir Mahmutćehajić, Stjepan G. Meštrović and his collaborators, and Nebojša Popov and his collaborators, the answer to the question *why* includes, of necessity, some reference to particular policies and programmes adopted by specific, identifiable elites, though this is not to suggest that any of these authors would consider 'bad leadership' to be a full or adequate explanation for the intercommunal violence which broke out in the Yugoslav region in the early 1990s. The question *why* may, of course, also be referred to an account of the use made of the media and of other means of propaganda in order to change the way people view one another and treat one another,[1] or to the role played by organized crime in the war. As noted in chapter 10, Paolo Rumiz and Norbert Mappes-Niediek specifically note how some of the Yugoslav criminals-turned-warriors became rich in the course of the wars.[2] But for most of the aforementioned authors, individual culpability is a central question. Thus, for example, Vesna Pešić and Dubravka Stojanović, contributors to Popov's volume, pin the blame for the outbreak of war in 1991 squarely on Milošević, in the first place,[3] while Rusmir Mahmutćehajić blames, above all, Milošević, Tudjman, and Izetbegović, and their respective elites.[4] Hayden offers his own variation, arguing, reasonably enough, that 'the assessment of individual culpability does not necessarily suffice to explain why so many people engaged in so many horrifying acts'.[5] But, in the same breath, Hayden makes his own assessment of guilt, blaming both Milošević and his coterie, on the one hand, and 'the Slovenes', on the other, and elsewhere signals his desire to offer an alternative to works which '*presume* and then focus on the guilt of "the Serbs" and especially of Slobodan Milošević'.[6] I dare say that no conscious scholar would dream of making a priori presumptions of guilt; after all, the writing of a good history consists, at least in part, in a balanced weighing of the evidence. And Meštrović, outraged by the cynicism and relativism associated with at least one wing of postmodernist thinking, offers a new concept – 'postemotionalism', by which he means that state actors and mass publics act at least in part on the basis of pre-existing or manufactured emotions, so that the 'rational actor' paradigm thrown up by advocates of *Realpolitik* is, among other things, a flight of pure fantasy.[7]

The methodologies of these works are strikingly different. The Popov book could be described as a work of contemporary political history, for example. Hayden's analysis reflects his training as a lawyer, with its emphasis on the political consequences of constitutional and legal provisions. Mahmutćehajić's book may be understood as a work of applied theology. Misha Glenny's fat volume, covering 200 years of Balkan history, seems intended to please both the serious scholar and the general public, and combines historical analysis with lengthy X-rated passages which provide graphic details about particular acts of violence, torture, and mayhem.

Of the eight books discussed in this chapter, three – Čolović's, Dragović-Soso's, and Popov's – seem to me to join those select books which those of us in the teaching profession are apt to find most useful for our students and, indeed, most useful for understanding the Yugoslav region. Only one book in this set, that by Hayden, offers arguments which I consider seriously misleading. Only Misha Glenny's book seems to me to include more examples of graphic violence than would normally be considered appropriate. Only Keith Doubt's volume engages in a metatheoretical debate.

Popov's magisterial volume brings together some twenty critical voices from Serbia. Their common purpose is to assess what went wrong in Serbia. This purpose does not necessarily imply an exoneration of the political elites in Croatia and Bosnia-Herzegovina, or even, for that matter, of Western political elites, but their concern is to examine the rise of nationalism in their own republic. The analysis begins with the early years of communism, but most of the discussion focuses on developments after 1974, the year in which Yugoslavia's communist authorities adopted their fourth constitution in less than thirty years. Vojin Dimitrijević, a distinguished jurist, for example, argues that that constitution was itself 'a factor in the collapse of Yugoslavia'.[8]

Olivera Milosavljević also makes a contribution with her chapter, 'Yugoslavia as a Mistake', which draws a fundamental distinction between human rights and ethnic rights and includes an interesting quotation from Slobodan Milošević in which the later president predicted that 'the Serb nationalists would inflict the greater harm on the Serbian people through what they offer to it today as allegedly the best solution, to practically isolate itself through the hate and suspicion of others'.[9] Insisting on ethnic rights, she argues, leads to disharmony and risks the outbreak of interethnic conflict. The message seems obvious enough today, but I can remember making a trip to Yugoslavia in 1982, when Serbian nationalism was experiencing a kind of awakening, and being told that nationalism and the defence of ethnic rights were good things. Their advocates seemed, at the time, to be completely unaware of the danger of conflict. Still, the danger should have been clear enough when, during the night of 28 February 1989, 'thousands of students, led by their professors, gathered in the centre of Belgrade, in front of the Federal Assembly, to celebrate violence and to demand arrests and weapons'.[10]

Other chapters in the Popov collection include Sreten Vujović's study of the use of stereotypes of the city in propaganda, as preparation for the ultimate destruction of many cities and towns, Marina Blagojević's analysis of migratory trends among Serbs leaving Kosovo during the 1970s and 1980s, and further chapters about the Serbian Orthodox Church, the abuse of science, the university, the Association of Writers, football, the ruling party, the opposition, the army, and the electronic media, *inter alia*. In each of these cases, the assigned author finds the germ of nationalism subverting the institution in question or deflecting it towards politics. In his chapter on 'Football, Hooligans, and War', for example, Ivan Čolović notes the escalation of nationalist-inspired violence at sporting events in the years leading up to the outbreak of hostilities, while Drinka Gojković, in her examination of the Association of Writers, accuses that body of actively subverting the Socialist Federated Republic of Yugoslavia (SFRY) with the issuance of its 'Contribution to the Public Discussion on the Constitution' in 1988. Gojković also criticizes as facile the notion that democracy and nationalism should be seen as inherently harmonious.[11] Probably all the contributors to this volume would agree with Popov, however, that 'The war was not unavoidable. A real choice existed: a democratic process of change, or the violent destruction of society and the state.'[12] The question is why society ended up travelling the road to war.

Popov's *Road to War in Serbia* endeavours to provide an answer to that question. Milosavljević's careful analysis of the Serbian Academy of Sciences and Art (SANU), for example, traces its politicization and its contribution to the rise of nationalism. Along the way, she reveals that there were deep divisions within that body already during 1991–2, and notes that, on 4 June 1992, thirty-seven academicians submitted a letter to the SANU assembly demanding Milošević's resignation.[13] Similar processes were underway in the Serbian Orthodox Church, as Radmila Radić shows. There was, of course, the famous 1982 appeal, issued by some Orthodox clergy, calling for the protection of the Serbian people of Kosovo and their holy shrines. Then, towards the end of 1983, the patriarchate's newsorgan, *Pravoslavlje*, launched a series of articles about Serb sufferings in different regions of Yugoslavia, laying particular stress on the Second World War and, in 1985, called for the Church to become more active in politics.[14] The Church, in fact, did so, as will be discussed further in chapter 7.

I would be remiss if I did not mention Dubravka Stojanović's impressive study of opposition currents in Serbia. She explores Vuk Drašković's brave protest at the fall of Vukovar and his public opposition (in April 1992) to 'chauvinistic-fascist madness',[15] but ultimately dismisses Drašković as 'a groundless liberal, an anti-war activist with a nationalistic programme'.[16] Noting likewise Zoran Djindjić's nationalist affinities (at the time), Stojanović locates one source of the tragedy which was to befall the peoples of the SFRY in the fact that, 'at the time of the breakup of Yugoslavia, the most influential opposition parties in parliament did not publicly propose an alternative national programme which would in any way differ from the words of Slobodan Milošević, "all Serbs in one state" '.[17] Implicit (or, at times, explicit) throughout the Popov volume is the nearly complete consensus that chauvinistic nationalism is inherently dangerous and that the route to social harmony must, of necessity, entail a repudiation of chauvinism and its myths, and an embrace of the rule of law.

Robert M. Hayden's *Blueprints for a House Divided* provides a stark contrast to Popov's volume. Where Milosavljević had warned against the demand for ethnic rights, which she saw as undermining human rights, Hayden defends the ethnic rights approach, referring to the February–March referendum in Bosnia in quotation marks, as if it might not have been a referendum at all, and drawing attention to the fact that it was held over the objections of local Serb nationalist leaders. Why the majority party of one of the component groups should enjoy the prerogative to veto the holding of referenda Hayden does not explain, though it may be because all three peoples were considered 'state-forming peoples' enjoying such rights under the moribund socialist constitution. But Hayden explicitly rejects majority rule for Bosnia, on the argument that the outcome of a vote sanctifies a 'superior right' for the majority over the minority.[18] Indeed it does, but that, as Norberto Bobbio has explained, is precisely what liberal democracy is all about.[19]

And yet, for all that, Hayden, while disinterested in the will of the majority, does outline a formula for stability, which fits with his prioritization of ethnic 'rights'. He writes, thus, in the context of a discussion of post-Dayton Bosnia, that 'the best way that the "sovereignty of Bosnia and Herzegovina" could be upheld in either the Republika Srpska or the Croat-controlled parts of the federation would be through the expulsion of those people who reject inclusion in that state, which would be, in either of these cases, the majority of the population'.[20] Hayden also marshals the writings of University of Maryland professor Vladimir Tismaneanu in order to mount an argument against the utility of social tolerance for democracy,[21] apparently oblivious to the fact that Tismaneanu has himself stressed the centrality of tolerance to the liberal-democratic project.[22] He even claims that Tismaneanu considers that civil society may be but a 'political myth'. But what kind of democracy can be built without tolerance? A democracy in which intolerance is viewed as an acceptable medium for communication and as an acceptable foundation for policy? If Hayden truly means what he says, then the democracy he is championing fits all too well with the notion that a sovereign state has the right to engage in ethnic cleansing.

For Hayden, there is no authority higher than the given regime, regardless of its ideological colouration or politics. This is why he writes that 'sovereigns cannot be bound by law',[23] a statement which has an eerie resonance with Hobbes's seventeenth-century claim that the sovereign (the king) must, of necessity, be above the law.[24] It is also why, in the context of a polemical postscript devoted to Kosovo, Hayden assails 'the hypocrisy of the *idea* of humanitarian intervention',[25] a bold representation which entails not only the repudiation of NATO's intervention in spring 1999 but also the further corollary that 'humanitarian intervention' is *never* justified – not because of any incompatibility with the UN Charter, or even because it might set a bad precedent which other states might abuse, but because it violates the principle that there is no authority higher than the 'sovereign'. This position is, of course, similar to the so-called traditional view, outlined (though not advocated) by Hans Kelsen, which upholds the primacy of the laws of individual states over international law,[26] but distinct from the 'internationalist' argument, upheld by Bodin, Kant, and Habermas, among others, which maintains that states can and must be held to a universal standard of morality. The debate between Hobbes's heirs (who generally style themselves 'realists' or 'conventionalists') and the heirs of Kant (who style themselves 'idealists' or 'universalists', or sometimes 'cosmopolitans') continues.

Given Hayden's ambition to explain the Yugoslav breakup, it is perhaps surprising how little he says about Serbian preparations for war. Leaving aside the short defence of the Milošević regime's 'sovereignty' in the postscript, Hayden neglects to provide any account of what had been happening in Kosovo, as if the disintegration of socialist Yugoslavia could be understood without any reference to the mobilization of the Serbs of Kosovo against the Albanians. His endeavour to make 'the Slovenes' equally culpable with the Milošević regime is also questionable and, indeed, leads the reader into a deep darkness in which, as Plato wrote, shadows are mistaken for reality and reality itself is not even perceived. It is hard to account for these and other colossal blunders – including misrepresentations of the works of James Gow, Thomas Cushman, James Sadkovich, and myself – since Hayden promises to develop a scientific, morally neutral approach to his subject. Yet he does not stop there, but dismisses the field of Yugoslav studies with a broad but vaguely aimed brushstroke,[27] while showing no familiarity, whether in the text or the notes or the bibliography itself, with any of a number of works by prominent specialists published in the years up to 1997.[28]

II

Whereas Hayden's analysis moves in multiple directions at once, seeming at times to repudiate the liberal principles of tolerance, equality, and not harming others without need and the democratic principle of majority rule, Meštrović and his collaborators explicitly dedicate themselves to Enlightenment ideals, which means that they uphold human rights as a principle superior to state sovereignty (thereby setting themselves against the view advocated by Hayden) and consider that individuals must be held responsible for their actions (e.g., in the context of war crimes trials). Meštrović explicitly declares, already in the introduction, that he and all of his contributors 'regard themselves as children of the Enlightenment and do not subscribe to the doctrine of collective guilt with regard to Serbs or any other peoples'.[29] Meštrović's book can best be understood as having three chief intellectual pillars: Enlightenment liberalism (as expostulated by Immanuel Kant, among others), psycho-analytical theory (perhaps especially the work of Sigmund Freud, who was himself a product of the Enlightenment), and 'postemotional' theory. These three strands are compatible and even mutually support-ive, though not each strand receives equal emphasis at the hands of each contributor. C. G. Schoenfeld opens his chapter, 'Psychoanalytic Dimensions of the West's Involvement in the Third Balkan War', by citing Freud's *Civilization and Its Discontents* and his *Group Psychology and the Analysis of the Ego*, by way of introducing the subjects of human aggressiveness and the mob instinct. What psychoanalytic theory teaches us, according to Schoenfeld, is the importance of irrational-ity and emotion in human activity, i.e., that human activity, even in diplomacy, cannot be accurately viewed as the rational pursuit of inter-ests. It may, of course, be seen as the *irrational* pursuit of interests, but that takes us far beyond the *Realpolitik* paradigm, let alone the 'rational actor' model. For Schoenfeld, the Serbs provide a classic case of a people with damaged self-esteem, and – he adds, crediting Heinz Kohut with this idea – there is a tendency for 'groups whose narcissism and self-esteem ha[ve] been wounded to seek charismatic and Messianic leaders'.[30]

Schoenfeld believes that crude theories which trace intercommunal violence to 'ancient hatreds', primitive barbarism, and so forth are not merely foolish but dangerous because they may even obstruct our efforts to understand human aggression. And without understanding, it is impossible to find an appropriate response. This is why the circulation of the 'ancient hatreds' theory in some Western capitals was so pernicious – because it drew those powers into making inappropriate responses to the carnage. But, for Schoenfeld, the embrace of bad theories cannot be seen to exculpate the West. On the contrary, he writes that 'the refusal of the leaders of Britain, France, Russia, and the United States to take the necessary steps to stop (and earlier to prevent) the mass murders, tortures, and rapes by the Serbians is, by any standards, immoral'.[31] And he cites Kant, Woodrow Wilson, and Daniel P. Moynihan in support of the notion that moral principles have a 'crucial role' to play in foreign policy.[32]

Other chapters in Meštrović's book support this approach. Thomas Cushman, for example, underlines the role of collective memory in generating emotionally tainted responses in which reason is set aside. The result, Cushman shows, is that different countries are held to different standards.[33] James Sadkovich shows how different forms of nostalgia, in some cases involving a distorted recollection of the past so that it is a nostalgia for a past which never existed, influenced both Western diplomacy and American media reportage during the War of Yugoslav Succession.[34] And Norman Cigar argues that, over the course of more than a century and a half, the Serbs collectively came under the spell of 'the quest for a Greater Serbia' – a spell which Milošević tapped and energized.[35] He also notes the role of emotion in making Serbs vulnerable to such mobilization, arguing that 'the withering of authoritarianism inevitably would have meant calls to redress this unequal situation and, potentially, the dissolution of Yugoslavia. This deeply concerned many Serbs who saw a potential loss of status and privilege on an individual and communal basis.'[36]

Serbian wartime propaganda too was specifically geared to stir emotions, even provoking demands which, Meštrović notes, ran 'contrary to principles derived from the Enlightenment'.[37] As for the West, the 'postemotional' paradigm shows its utility in explaining how American fixations on (distorted) memories of the Vietnam War produced responses which reflected not the facts in Croatia and Bosnia, but fears (i.e., emotions) generated in the experience in southeast Asia.

Rusmir Mahmutćehajić takes an entirely different tack from both the conventionalist Hayden and the universalist team assembled by Meštrović, looking for solutions to political problems in a rapprochement among (though not a unification of) the chief religions of the region – Catholicism, Orthodox Christianity, Islam, and Judaism. Mahmutćehajić's *The Denial of Bosnia*, in its elegant translation by Francis R. Jones and Marina Bowder, offers a systematic discussion of the views of the principals in the War of Yugoslav Succession of 1991–5. Mahmutćehajić, who served briefly as vice president of Bosnia-Herzegovina in 1991 before breaking with Izetbegović, ultimately considers Izetbegović co-responsible for at least some of the sufferings of the region. In spite of that, Milošević and Tudjman, and their respective elites, bear the brunt of Mahmutćehajić's criticism. Mahmutćehajić has no patience with those who want to open discussions as to whether what happened in Bosnia could 'really' be called 'genocide',[38] and traces the hostilities to 'a deliberate plan for the annihilation of the country known as Bosnia-Herzegovina'.[39]

In Mahmutćehajić's view, the greatest obstacle to the realization of the plans of Serbian and Croatian nationalists was the centuries-old Bosnian model of tolerance and interreligious dialogue, a model which fostered traditions of multiculturalism and interconfessional marriage. Accordingly, as Mahmutćehajić sees it, Serb and Croat nationalists actively encouraged the development of Muslim nationalism and the growth of

Muslim separatist aspirations. But, for the author, nationalism is an ethical dead end and notions of 'ethnic rights' self-contradictions insofar as rights can be founded only on moral principle. 'The ethics of nationalism', Mahmutćehajić writes, however, 'are incapable of establishing a society and state in which a community can live and act in accord with general ethical rules.'[40] As for the alleged rights of nations to create nationally homogeneous states, Mahmutćehajić has this to say: 'Humanity has one incontestable right – the right to redemption.'[41]

Finally, the book by Misha Glenny[42] offers a largely factual and chronological, if rather colourful, account. Glenny both reported from the Yugoslav region for *The Times* and has additional journalistic experience, and this background is shown to good effect in his writing style.

III

Keith Doubt's *Sociology after Bosnia and Kosovo* provides a sharp contrast to the foregoing works. He renounces the endeavour to place analysis in service to ethical commitment (Mahmutćehajić's choice) as well as Hayden's apparent repudiation of social tolerance. And unlike Popov's volume, which focuses on the *manifest* functions of the embrace of the nationalist message by various Serbian institutions, Doubt wants to consider also *latent* functions. The distinction between manifest functions (those functions which are intended and perceived) and latent functions (those functions which are not consciously intended and not consciously noted by the actors) was first made by Robert K. Merton in his classic work, *Social Theory and Social Structure* (1968). Doubt applies this theory to an examination of 'ethnic cleansing' (a practice which corresponds precisely to the Genocide Convention's definition of 'genocide'). As Doubt notes, the 'manifest function' of ethnic cleansing was to expel members of other national groups while radicalizing one's own. But, says Doubt, crediting Noel Malcolm for this insight, 'the latent function of ethnic cleansing was to bind together with a band of collective guilt the wavering adherents within the Serbian population'.[43] This is borne out by the fact that militant Serbs made a practice, for example, of killing moderate Serbs who refused to take part in atrocities against Muslims. But the Serb militants' effort to suffuse the entire Serbian community with collective guilt served, in turn, 'to disfigure the normative orientation to which Bosnian Serbs were . . . subject as members of the Bosnian community . . . The result was to detach Bosnian Serbs from the value elements that they use to make judgements not only about others *but also about themselves*.'[44] The transformation of collective normative orientation is not innocent, Doubt argues. People affected in such a way lose the ability to view members of other nations as 'people like us'; they become *things*.[45] Worse, nationalists lose the capacity to doubt their own views. The upshot is that communities which may have lived together relatively well lose that ability; what once was functional has become dysfunctional, and the prospects for restoring harmony seem to vanish.

The Bosnian war dynamic provoked a number of responses, relevant to this dynamic and recounted by Doubt. One response is to advocate what Doubt calls 'an ethic of ultimate ends', which (in chapter 1) I have called *moral universalism*. An alternative, says Doubt, is 'the ethic of responsibility', which 'anticipates the consequences of a political action and orients accordingly'.[46] This alternative may be understood as *moral consequentialism*. Doubt illustrates the former with journalist Roy Gutman and the latter with journalist Tim Judah. Gutman, thus, represents the view that certain moral principles are indeed universal and binding; for example, he writes, 'I have yet to find anyone who will argue that we should stand by and watch genocide be committed or the principles of international order be flouted.'[47] But Doubt warns that 'Believers in an ethic of ultimate ends must at some point use violence to achieve their ends, and, whenever they do, [they face] the paradox of consequences.'[48] The paradox is that the means necessary to achieve morally good results may involve unwarranted harm to individuals or other 'evil' consequences. But the ethic of responsibility entails its own paradox, namely, that, in the calculation of optimizing consequences, adherents of this ethic may, indeed, "*must* dance with devils'.[49] This brings us to a third response, which is to collapse the ethic of ultimate ends and the ethic of responsibility into a single maxim, 'Do no harm' – the maxim embraced by Noam Chomsky. But by embracing this maxim, one is likely to advocate abstention from any response to atrocities.

That brings us to a fourth response identified by Doubt – postmodernism, as exemplified by Peter Handke. Handke, the rude German writer who gained a reputation for insulting members of his audiences, is usually regarded as merely pro-Serb (a simplification which involves conflating moderate and nonpolitical Serbs with nationalist Serbs as if all Serbs were the same), but, according to Doubt, Handke's message is 'that there is never an authentic relationship between an image and its significance',[50] so that it becomes impossible to speak of some sort of objective truth about anything. And if there is no objective truth, then the whole notion of responding to atrocities seems absurd, because one can never get at the 'objective truth' about any such thing. To undertake action against aggressors is, therefore, only to add to the darkness in which we find ourselves, not actually to escape from it, to paraphrase Handke. Doubt associates Handke with Callicles, the advocate of the self-indulgent maximization of one's own pleasure and punishing of one's enemies, without regard to moral principle, the same Callicles refuted by Socrates in the Platonic dialogue, *Gorgias*.

Doubt closes his book by counselling against 'the cynicism that undergirds the sophistry of many power elites dealing with the conflict in Bosnia'. But why *Bosnia*, specifically? Doubt has an answer:

> The reason that the observing world has focused on the conflict in Bosnia more than in other areas is not because the conflict in Bosnia is more evil or more violent or more unjust than in other areas. The reason is because Bosnia became a global media screen, a theater, upon which we witnessed a gripping and horrifying moral tale.[53]

IV

The SFRY was a state permanently in crisis. It was in crisis because its system had not resolved some of the most important problems – above all the problem of legitimacy, but also problems in the economic sphere, the problem of participation and demands for democracy, and the challenge of creating a shared political culture, not to mention the state's continued abuse of human rights in Kosovo and elsewhere. Because of this permanent state of crisis, major shocks to the system were automatically magnified. So it was with the death of Tito, whose passing was not only mourned across the country but also accompanied by widespread fear. Such fears were often nebulous, even inchoate. Many were afraid, but they were not entirely sure what they should be afraid of. Tito had, of course, always warned about the dangers of nationalism, but it was not immediately obvious that the Communist Party would prove unable to contain such nationalist discontent as there was in the country (most obviously in Kosovo, though not only there). Economic problems were much more on people's minds at the time. But, above all, the fear Yugoslavs were experiencing was a fear of the unknown.

By the mid-1980s, however, it was increasingly clear that Yugoslavia was on a rollercoaster, with Serb nationalists calling for remedies utterly unacceptable to non-Serbs and liberal Serbs (such as Vesna Pešić and Sonja Licht) alike, Albanians increasingly fed up with a state which, to their minds, did not treat them as equals with others in the multinational country, many Slovenes increasingly disgusted at what they considered to be the outright exploitation of their republic by the other republics in the federation, and a stubborn segment of Croatian society (one need only think of Tudjman and Paraga, for example) only waiting for the chance to strike out alone and set up an independent Croatia. But most rollercoaster rides do not end in tragedy. Ivan Čolović explores the role of Serb mystical thinking in preparing Serb society for war while Jasna Dragović-Soso emphasizes the role of human agency in her study of Serbian intellectuals. Both Čolović and Dragović-Soso highlight the role of myth-making in nationalist mobilization.

The volumes by Ivan Čolović and Jasna Dragović-Soso explore the proliferation of Serb nationalist thinking after the death of Tito in 1980. From Čolović's point of view, what is central is the incompatibility of 'the Serbian national myth' – as he uses the term – with democracy. In this sense, the bards of Serbian nationalism led their society towards darkness, not light. Čolović, no admirer of nationalism, offers the following summary of the Serbian national myth:

the Serbian nation is the oldest nation in the world, all other nations originated from it, just as all other languages originated in the Serbian language. But it is at the same time the youngest and freshest nation . . . This is possible because this nation stands to one side of historical time . . . It lives in an eternal present, simultaneously old and young, in an eternal union of the dead, the living, and the as yet unborn . . . The Serbs are today also the guardians of the rarest and most important civilisational values, the values of the heart and [the] spirit . . . The suffering of the Serbs today and the dangers which have gathered over them, threatening their survival, may be compared only to the persecution and annihilation of the Jews in the Third Reich . . . the Serbs are a proud nation seeking to build their state on healthy, natural foundations, a state in which all will be together, on Serbian soil, where all will be one nation, one state, with one leader, where all will celebrate one Serbian faith, speak one Serbian language, write one Serbian script and think one Serbian thought.[54]

The Serbian national myth, Čolović argues, promoted a distorted national self-image among Serbs and a warped notion about right and wrong. Indeed, as Serbian society came steadily under the spell of nationalism, Serbs' understanding of history, their sense of time, their relationship to God and Church, even their sexuality all changed. The distortion of sexuality was noted, and mocked, by the brilliant writer Danilo Kiš when he wrote, 'Genitals are a national seal, a racial brand; other peoples have good fortune, tradition, erudition, history, *ratio*, but genitals are ours alone.'[55]

The myth of Kosovo Polje – of the battle fought in 1389, now recast in the myth as a titanic contest between Christian Europe and the Islamic East – played its role in providing a mythic tableau against the background of which reports of contemporary sufferings of Serbs assumed grand proportions. But in addition, the myth – with its tale about Tsar Lazar's renunciation of the earthly kingdom for a heavenly one – was simultaneously interpreted as giving the Serbs title, by unexplained logic, to the very earthly kingdom which Lazar was said to have renounced, and exploited for the purpose of sacralizing the entire Serbian national project. The Serbian nation, accordingly, was a heavenly nation, and was authorized by God to sweep away all that stood in its path. It was entirely consistent with this portrayal that, on 22 July 1995, the Bosnian Serb newspaper *Javnost* published an article characterizing the sanguinary conquest of Srebrenica, which had been marked by the cold-blooded massacre of more than 7,000 Muslim men and boys, as the 'cleansing of a blot on the map'.[56] But for nationalistic Serbs, it was the Americans (who 'have no national identity at all' and live as a society of consumers 'without soul')[57] and the West Europeans (who are 'bogged down in materialism, humanism, and cosmopolitanism' with nothing left of their past cultural glory but a 'sick, limp, rotten identity')[58] who had sunk into immorality. Dragoljub Jeknić, a commentator in the aforementioned newspaper, *Javnost*, described Americans, for example, as "a collection of adventurers, rootless individuals, barbarians, bandits, murderers from all corners of the world'.[59] The forefathers of present-day Croats, Bulgarians, Macedonians, Bosniaks, and even Romanians and Albanians had been Serbs, but had committed the original sin of abandoning their 'true' national identity to adopt foreign or artificial identities. With non-Serbs living artificial, materialistic, and immoral lives, the summons to unite all Serbs in one state came to entail, for some writers (such as Radomir Konstantinović), 'a dream of complete separation from the world'.' Matija Bečković, president of the Serbian Writers' Association at the end of the 1980s, even imagined 'Serbia as an autonomous heavenly body . . . the Serbian planet'.[60]

But within the Serbian Orthodox Church, voices were raised warning that the greatest risk to the 'heavenly kingdom' came from within Serbia itself, and took the form of infiltrations of New Age religions such as neo-paganism, drug addiction, homosexuality, pornography, AIDS, and the decline in the birth rate, among other related evils. Archpriest Ljubodrag Petrović, Elder of the Church of St Alexander Nevsky in Belgrade, has apparently been a prominent spokesperson for such fears, expressing his concern that, *inter alia*, that many murders taking place in Serbia had a 'demonic foundation', the consequence of 'devil-immanence'.[61]

Čolović's purpose in writing this book was to effect no less than a mythic exorcism, chasing away the myths which locked much of Serbian society for too long into a paranoid discourse. In an epilogue written especially for the English edition of his book, the author calls explicitly for 'liquidating political rhetoric based on images and characters which can hardly survive in democratic political discourse', lest the society miss its chance to escape from 'the vampires' house of so-called Heavenly Serbia'.[62] Čolović's work is intellectually exciting, a monumental contribution to the understanding not just of Serbian nationalism in the 1980s, but of the dynamics of nationalist paranoia as such. No one interested in Serbia should fail to read this book.

Dragović-Soso shares Čolović's concern with the spread of nationalist myths among Serbs in the 1980s, but her approach is historical, rather than anthropological, and her focus is specifically (though not narrowly) on the role played by Serbia's intellectual community in the revival of nationalism. Her book seeks, as the author puts it, 'to explain why nationalist concerns came to overshadow all other aspects of [the Serbian intellectual opposition's] political agenda, leading many former dissidents to betray the humanist principles that were initially at the core of their activism'.[63] Like Čolović, Dragović-Soso is convinced that the specific type of nationalist discourse which spread in Serbia in the course of the 1980s was incompatible with democracy because, as she notes, of its emphasis on victimization, its use of conspiracy theories to explain the alleged hostility of non-Serbs to Serbs, its attribution of genocidal intentions to certain non-Serb groups, and the double standards employed in the solutions offered by the nationalists.[64] As she notes, it was the sympathy which Serb intellectuals felt for the Kosovar Serbs, who complained of having been attacked by Kosovar Albanians, which provided the initial impetus drawing them into nationalist discourse; but she calls their belief that the development of democracy could wait until after the national question had been 'resolved' an 'illusion'.[65]

She shows that Serb intellectuals' concerns about Serbia's position in the Yugoslav federation went back to its origins during the Second World War, and in particular that the creation of an autonomous Kosovo within the Republic of Serbia left both Albanians and Serbs dissatisfied – Albanians because they felt that they were entitled to their own republic (insofar as the republics were being set up on the basis of a mixture of ethnic and historical criteria) and the Serbs because they resented the loss of control of territory which they had ruled since the Balkan Wars of 1912–13. Thus, Mihailo Djurić, a professor of law at the University of Belgrade, told a public forum in March 1971 that he gave high priority to 'the legal and political unification of the Serbian nation'[66] – a project which, the author points out, was connected in Djurić's mind with an indictment of the Croatian people collectively for genocide.

Together with many other scholars,[67] Dragović-Soso sees Tito's purge of the liberals in 1971–2 as a turning point, effectively scuttling any chances for the SFRY's evolution into a liberal social democracy. In Croatia, the purge convinced many that human rights and democracy could be achieved only in the context of Croatian secession from the SFRY, while in Serbia the purges pushed nonconformist intellectuals such as Dobrica Ćosić and members of the Praxis group into opposition. The author recounts, in rich detail, the various controversies which emerged after the death of Tito, discussing, *inter alia*, the collapse of efforts to produce a second edition of the *Encyclopedia of Yugoslavia*, Vladimir Dedijer's contributions to de-Titoization through his *Novi prilozi za biografiju Josipa Broza Tita* (published in 1981), and the opening of public discussion about the treatment of people suspected of pro-Stalin sympathies after June 1948 at such prison camps as Goli Otok. More ominously, after nearly forty years of carefully controlled, formulaic incantations about the Partisan Struggle, in which there was no possibility for a serious discussion of the sufferings experienced during the Second World War, Serbian writers led the way in the early years after Tito's death in opening this forbidden theme up for discussion, in the course of things breaking various taboos. Various writers now offered their own estimates as to how many people were killed during that war with, for example, Velimir Terzić, a former general turned historian, suggesting in a 1983 publication that more than 1 million Serbs had died at the Jasenovac camp alone.[68] (Of course, if one allows that non-Serbs died at Jasenovac as well, and that not everyone killed by the Ustaše died at Jasenovac, and that the Chetniks, Partisans, and various occupation forces were also using live ammunition, then one would have to suppose that Terzić had concluded that perhaps as many as 10 million Yugoslavs may have died in the course of the war – a completely absurd notion.) But even more dangerous than the conjuring of wildly inflated figures about war losses was the increase in tendencies towards *dysphoric rumination*, which has been defined as 'the tendency for individuals to unhappily reimagine, rethink, and relive pleasant or unpleasant events . . . [resulting in an] increase [in] negative thinking about those events'.[69] In 1988, for example, a conference devoted to Jasenovac took place, at which participants spent considerable time detailing the various tortures experienced by Serbs at the hands of the Ustaše, including hammering nails into the brains of victims and cutting off their tongues and noses; the conference proceedings were reported in *NIN* (a weekly Belgrade news magazine).[70]

The same syndrome came to the surface after Djordje Martinović, a peasant from the Kosovo town of Gnjilane, showed up at a local hospital on 1 May 1985 with serious injuries produced by the insertion of a glass bottle into his rectum. Serbs were quick to give this a 'national' interpretation, with satirist Brana Crnčević, for example, declaring Martinović's suffering to amount to 'Jasenovac for one man'. More dramatically, Serbian artist Mića Popović created a huge painting inspired by José de Ribera's seventeenth-century 'The Martyrdom of St Bartholomew', in which he depicted Martinović being hoisted on a wooden cross by skullcapped Albanians, one of whom held a glass bottle in his hand.[71] The famous SANU memorandum, leaked to the press in 1986, was thus but the culmination of a tectonic shift in the thinking of Serbian intellectuals, confirming the depth of their frustration with Serbia's situation, as they perceived it.

But how and why did the opposition intellectuals come into an alliance with Milošević, who, in April 1987, was still excoriating all species of nationalism?[72] Dragović-Soso traces this alliance to several factors, among which she places a certain stress on the liberalization of the Serbian cultural scene which took place under Milošević; the intellectuals inevitably appreciated their new freedom of expression and welcomed Milošević's 'anti-bureaucratic revolution' as heralding the advent of democracy in the country. On the other hand, not all Serbian intellectuals took the bait. Some Serbian intellectuals, such as lawyer Ivan Janković, liberal sociologist Vesna Pešić, former Partisan general Gojko Nikoliš, and neo-Hegelian Praxis philosopher Zagorka Golubović, remained firmly anti-nationalist and even spoke out against the regime's policies in Kosovo.[73]

Dragović-Soso carefully avoids any recourse to unicausal explanation of the conversion of many Serbian intellectuals to nationalism and their political 'marriage' with the Milošević regime. On the contrary, she emphasizes that 'nationalisms do not develop in isolation, but interact with each other to produce a spiral of radicalisation'.[74] Moreover, 'the rise of extreme nationalism is context-specific and relational, rather than historically immutable and isolated'.[75] Dragović-Soso has produced an important book. Indeed, it is one of the very best books covering Serbia in the 1980s to have come out and one of the most useful books for understanding how and why developments took the course they did.

Finally, there is Misha Glenny's monumental survey of aspects of Balkan history since 1804. Breathtaking in its ambition and commendable in the depth of the author's reading of secondary literature in Serbo-Croat and English, Glenny's *Balkans* is probably the most readable among English-language histories of the region. But it is not a history in the traditional sense. Glenny quite consciously narrows his vision, steering his narrative towards the themes identified in his subtitle – nationalism, war, and the Great Powers.

Where Yugoslavia is concerned, Glenny, like most historians, sees the adoption of the so-called Vidovdan constitution (in 1921) as the beginning of the troubles which have plagued the country.[76] While correctly highlighting the centrality of the Serb–Croat conflict in the interwar era, Glenny also highlights periods of Serb–Croat co-operation both before (1905–8) and during that era. Turning to the communist era, on the other hand, Glenny damns Tito and Kardelj as 'the true villains of that period', accusing them of actively stirring up Serb–Croat tensions in order to build up their own authority.[77] There is, of course, some evidence for this interpretation, but there is also countervailing evidence, though Glenny does not consider it.

Glenny has a fascination with detail. We learn, for example, that King Boris III (1918–43) of Bulgaria liked to spend Saturday evenings 'lay[ing] down the rhythm on drums accompanied by his sister, Princess Evdokia, on the piano and three aides-de-camp on violins and flugelhorn in the palace jazz combo'.[78] And then there are the endless details Glenny provides about violent actions over the course of Balkan history – details which become a literal flood in chapter 3. Although I find much to admire in Glenny's book, and even setting aside his erroneous notion that it was President Reagan, rather than President Carter, who missed Tito's funeral (could anyone forget Carter's mother showing up for the funeral in her bright red dress?), I personally find the amount of violence in this book more than a bit excessive. Indeed, so frequent are the allusions to violence in *The Balkans* that a reader might easily conclude that Glenny considers interethnic harmony completely unattainable in that part of the world.

Ultimately, of the eight books discussed in this chapter, three kindle real enthusiasm on my part – Čolović's study of Serbian myths and symbols because of the insight it provides into the way in which mainstream thinking in Serbian society was transformed and rechannelled along nationalist lines, Dragović-Soso's volume for its detailed account of the way in which Serbia's intellectuals converted to the nationalist cause and promoted it, and Popov's collaborative book for its comprehensive survey of the proliferation of nationalism across all sectors of Serbian society – though I would not want to be without Keith Doubt's analysis of Chomsky, Handke, and others. But while all of these authors have notions about how and why the peoples of Yugoslavia went to war, only one – Mahmutćehajić – actually offers a vision of a better world, in which he believes that harmony could be attained, or at least approached. And in so doing, he joins such thinkers as Henri de

Saint-Simon (1760–1825),[79] Kant, and Habermas, all of whom have spelled out visions of social harmony, even on a global scale.

NOTES

1 See, *inter alia*, my article, 'Under the Holy Lime Tree: The Inculcation of Neurotic and Psychotic Syndromes as a Serbian Wartime Strategy, 1986–1995', *Polemos* (Zagreb), 5, 1–2 (December 2002), pp. 83–97.

2 Paolo Rumiz, *Masken für ein Massaker. Der manipulierte Krieg: Spurensuche auf dem Balkan*, expanded German edn, trans. from Italian by Friederike Hausmann and Gesa Schröder (Munich: Verlag Antje Kunstmann, 2000); and Norbert Mappes-Niediek, *Balkan-Mafia: Staaten in der Hand des Verbrechens – Eine Gefahr für Europa* (Berlin: Ch. Links, 2003). These books are discussed in chapter 10.

3 Vesna Pešić, 'The War for Ethnic States', in Nebojša Popov (ed.), *The Road to War in Serbia: Trauma and Catharsis*, English version by Drinka Gojković (Budapest: Central European University Press, 2000), p. 471.

4 Rusmir Mahmutćehajić, *Bosnia the Good: Tolerance and Tradition*, trans. from Bosnian by Marina Bowder (Budapest: Central European University Press, 2000), p. 10.

5 Robert M. Hayden, *Blueprints for a House Divided: The Constitutional Logic of the Yugoslav Conflicts* (Ann Arbor, MI: University of Michigan Press, 1999), p. 20.

6 *Ibid.*, p. 19, my emphasis.

7 Stjepan G. Meštrović, 'Introduction', in Stjepan G. Meštrović (ed.), *Genocide after Emotion: The Postemotional Balkan War* (London and New York: Routledge, 1996), pp. 11–13.

8 Vojin Dimitrijević, 'The 1974 Constitution as a Factor in the Collapse of Yugoslavia, or as a Sign of Decaying Totalitarianism', in Popov, *The Road to War in Serbia*, pp. 399–424.

9 S. Milošević, *Godine raspleta* (Belgrade, 1989), p. 172, as quoted in Olivera Milosavljević, 'Yugoslavia as a Mistake', in Popov, *The Road to War in Serbia*, p. 66.

10 Nebojša Popov, 'The University in an Ideological Shell', in Popov, *The Road to War in Serbia*, p. 303.

11 Drinka Gojković, 'The Birth of Nationalism from the Spirit of Democracy: The Association of Writers of Serbia and the War', in Popov, *The Road to War in Serbia*, p. 343.

12 Nebojša Popov, 'Traumatology of the Party-State', in Popov, *The Road to War in Serbia*, p. 104.

13 Olivera Milosavljević, 'The Abuse of the Authority of Science', in Popov, *The Road to War in Serbia*, p. 295.

14 Radmila Radić, 'The Church and the "Serbian Question"', in Popov, *The Road to War in Serbia*, p. 250.

15 Drašković's words, as quoted in Dubravka Stojanović, 'The Traumatic Circle of the Serbian Opposition', in Popov, *The Road to War in Serbia*, p. 474.

16 *Ibid.*, p. 473.
17 *Ibid.*, p. 466.
18 Hayden, *Blueprints*, pp. 94, 96, 114. That Hayden's mockery of majority rule is not just a slip but reflects a firm conclusion on his part appears to be evident insofar as he had voiced precisely the same viewpoint five years earlier in his article, 'The Constitution of the Federation of Bosnia and Herzegovina: An Imaginary Constitution for an Illusory "Federation"', *Balkan Forum*, 2, 3 (September 1994), p. 79.
19 Norberto Bobbio, *The Future of Democracy*, trans. from Italian by Roger Griffin (Cambridge: Polity Press, 1987), p. 63.
20 Hayden, *Blueprints*, p. 134.
21 *Ibid.*, p. 157.
22 See Vladimir Tismaneanu, 'Truth, Trust and Tolerance: Intellectuals in Post-Communist Society', *Problems of Post-Communism*, 43, 2 (March–April 1996).
23 Hayden, *Blueprints*, p. 50.
24 Thomas Hobbes, *On the Citizen*, trans. from Latin and ed. by Richard Tuck and Michael Silverthorne (Cambridge: Cambridge University Press, 1998), pp. 79–81.
25 Hayden, *Blueprints*, p. 167, my emphasis.
26 Hans Kelsen, 'Sovereignty and International Law', in W. J. Stankiewicz (ed.), *In Defense of Sovereignty* (New York: Oxford University Press, 1969), p. 119.
27 Hayden, *Blueprints*, p. 8.
28 For a detailed list, see Sabrina P. Ramet, 'The Sources of Discord, the Making of Harmony: Books about Yugoslav Violence – a Review Article', *Europe–Asia Studies*, 53, 2 (2001), pp. 351–71.
29 Meštrović, 'Introduction', p. 8.
30 C. G. Schoenfeld, 'Psychoanalytic Dimensions of the West's Involvement in the Third Balkan War', in Meštrović, *Genocide after Emotion*, p. 159.
31 *Ibid.*, p. 169.
32 *Ibid.*, p. 170.
33 Thomas Cushman, 'Collective Punishment and Forgiveness: Judgements of Post-communist National Identities by the "Civilized" West', in Meštrović, *Genocide after Emotion*, pp. 186–7.
34 James J. Sadkovich, 'The Response of the American Media to Balkan Neo-Nationalisms', in Meštrović, *Genocide after Emotion*, pp. 127, 131.
35 Norman Cigar, 'The Serbo-Croatian War, 1991', in Meštrović, *Genocide after Emotion*, p. 52.
36 *Ibid.*, p. 54.
37 Meštrović, 'Introduction', p. 21.
38 Rusmir Mahmutćehajić, *The Denial of Bosnia*, trans. from Bosnian by Francis R. Jones and Marina Bowder (University Park, PA: Pennsylvania State University Press, 2000), p. 33.
39 *Ibid.*, p. 1; see also pp. 37, 47, 50.
40 *Ibid.*, p. 100.
41 *Ibid.*, p. 19.

42 Misha Glenny, *The Balkans: Nationalism, War and the Great Powers, 1804–1999* (New York: Viking Press, 2000).
43 Keith Doubt, *Sociology after Bosnia and Kosovo: Recovering Justice* (Lanham, MD: Rowman & Littlefield, 2000), p. 18.
44 *Ibid.*, p. 21, my emphasis.
45 *Ibid.*, p. 27.
46 *Ibid.*, p. 92.
47 Quoted *ibid.*, p. 101.
48 *Ibid.*, p. 97.
49 *Ibid.*, p. 99, my emphasis.
50 *Ibid.*, p. 125.
51 Robert M. Hayden, as quoted *ibid.*, p. 138.
52 Doubt, *Sociology after Bosnia and Kosovo*, pp. 138–9. 'Rational' is Doubt's word.
53 *Ibid.*, p. 162.
54 Ivan Čolović, *The Politics of Symbol in Serbia: Essays in Political Anthropology*, trans. from Serbian by Celia Hawkesworth (London: C. Hurst & Co., 2002), pp. 7–9.
55 Quoted *ibid.*, p. 92, n. 1.
56 *Javnost* (22 July 1995) as quoted *ibid.*, p. 42.
57 *Ibid.*, p. 67.
58 *Ibid.*
59 *Javnost* (3 June 1995), as quoted *ibid.*, p. 67.
60 Konstantinović and Bečković, both quoted in Čolović, *Politics of Symbol*, p. 66.
61 Čolović, *Politics of Symbol*, p. 193.
62 *Ibid.*, p. 308.
63 Jasna Dragović-Soso, *'Saviours of the Nation': Serbia's Intellectual Opposition and the Revival of Nationalism* (London: C. Hurst & Co., 2002), p. 2.
64 *Ibid.*, p. 9.
65 *Ibid.*, p. 12.
66 Quoted *ibid.*, p. 44, author's emphasis removed.
67 Such as Adam LeBor. See his *Milošević: A Biography* (Polmont, Stirlingshire: Bloomsbury, 2002), p. 34.
68 Dragović-Soso, *'Saviours of the Nation'*, p. 111.
69 Roderick M. Kramer and David M. Messick, 'Getting by with a Little Help from Our Enemies: Collective Paranoia and Its Role in Intergroup Relations', in Constantine Sedikides, John Schopler, and Chester A. Insko (eds.), *Intergroup Cognition and Intergroup Behavior* (Mahwah, NJ: Lawrence Erlbaum, 1998), p. 246.
70 Dragović-Soso, *'Saviours of the Nation'*, p. 113.
71 *Ibid.*, p. 133.
72 *Ibid.*, p. 208.
73 *Ibid.*, p. 238.
74 *Ibid.*, p. 257.
75 *Ibid.*, p. 256.
76 Glenny, *The Balkans*, p. 405.

77 *Ibid.*, p. 593.
78 *Ibid.*, p. 439.
79 The Count Claude Henri de Rouvroy de Saint-Simon. For an account of his life and ideas, see Frank E. Manuel and Fritzie P. Manuel, *Utopian Thought in the Western World* (Cambridge, MA: Belknap Press of Harvard University Press, 1979), pp. 590–640.

REFERENCES

Čolović, Ivan, *The Politics of Symbol in Serbia: Essays in Political Anthropology*, trans. from Serbian by Celia Hawkesworth (London: C. Hurst & Co., 2002), p. 328.

Doubt, Keith, *Sociology after Bosnia and Kosovo: Recovering Justice* (Lanham, MD: Rowman & Littlefield, 2000), p. 183.

Dragović-Soso, Jasna, *'Saviours of the Nation': Serbia's Intellectual Opposition and the Revival of Nationalism* (London: C. Hurst & Co., 2002), p. 293.

Glenny, Misha, *The Balkans: Nationalism, War and the Great Powers, 1804–1999* (New York: Viking Press, 2000), p. 726.

Hayden, Robert M., *Blueprints for a House Divided: The Constitutional Logic of the Yugoslav Conflicts* (Ann Arbor, MI: University of Michigan Press, 1999), p. 208.

Mahmutćehajić, Rusmir, *The Denial of Bosnia*, trans. from Bosnian by Francis R. Jones and Marina Bowder (University Park, PA: Pennsylvania State University Press, 2000), p. 156.

Meštrović, Stjepan G. (ed.), *Genocide after Emotion: The Postemotional Balkan War* (London and New York: Routledge, 1996), p. 225.

Popov, Nebojša (ed.), *The Road to War in Serbia: Trauma and Catharsis*, English version by Drinka Gojković (Budapest: Central European University Press, 2000), p. 711.

7 Milošević's place in history

I

Milošević dominates discussions of both socialist Yugoslavia's last years and the wars of 1991–5 and 1998–9. As already noted, Milošević has typically been viewed as the prime mover in developments during these years, though local propaganda has painted him variously as saviour or demon. Milošević continues to absorb scholarly attention in a way that neither Tudjman[1] nor Izetbegović nor Karadžić[2] can rival. At least five studies of the Milošević era in Serbia, 1987–2000, have been published in English to date. The new studies by Cohen, LeBor, and Sell join earlier studies by Dusko Doder and Louise Branson,[3] and Slavoljub Djukić, in endeavouring to trace Milošević's rise and fall and to answer some basic questions about his impact on socialist Yugoslavia and on the rump Federal Republic of Yugoslavia (created in April 1992 with Serbia and Montenegro as constituent republics). Like the Doder/Branson book, the volume by Adam LeBor is unmistakably aimed, in the first place, at reaching a broader, educated public, while the volumes by Cohen and Sell are aimed at the scholarly community. Jack Snyder's monograph about the relationship between democratization and the eruption of nationalist violence discusses a wide array of cases, ranging from England to Germany to Japan to the Caucasus to the developing world. But insofar as it includes a discussion of the breakup of Yugoslavia and the war which followed, and offers its own analysis of what went wrong, Snyder's book may profitably be discussed in this context.

Since the fall of Milošević in October 2000, Serbian writers have also undertaken to analyse the Milošević years. The books by Dušan Pavlović and Vidosav Stevanović are among the first to be published. They are of different types, with Pavlović's book consisting of a series of topical discussions, some of them analytical, and Stevanović's subsequently

I am deeply grateful to Denis Bašić, Norman Cigar, Marko Hoare, and Martha Merritt for their helpful comments on an earlier draft of this chapter.

published work being more journalistic in nature, more chronological in organization than Pavlović's, and endeavouring to reflect on what Milošević was all about. Massimo Nava's political biography of Milošević was published a year before the Serbian/Yugoslav president's fall from power, and, like Stevanović's book, is written for the popular market.

There is some broad consensus about Milošević in these eight books. All of them take it as a given that Milošević's primary goal was simply to hold on to power, and all except Stevanović agree that Milošević was 'a brilliant tactician but a disastrous strategist'.[4] As Nava puts it, Milošević was no strategist but a 'capable tactician', good with improvisations and 'an imagination appropriate to that of a poker player'.[5] Whereas Snyder calls Milošević a 'nationalist demagogue'[6] and looks to systemic factors to explain Yugoslavia's slide into chaos and war, Cohen, LeBor, and Sell make use of psychological explanations, while Nava calls Milošević's policies 'psychotic' and quotes Serbian caricaturist Korax on 'the enormous quantity of stupidities' produced by the Milošević regime.[7] Cohen, for example, writes that Milošević, though not clinically paranoid himself, made use of a 'paranoid style' of politics,[8] while Sell cites American psychiatrists who have described the Serbian leader as a 'malignant, narcissistic' personality who was 'strongly self-centered, vain, and full of self-love'.[9] LeBor, for his part, notes that Milošević, like Stalin, Bill Clinton, and Saddam Hussein, had to endure prolonged deprivation of paternal love, even before his father committed suicide. He explains,

Psychologists argue that an absentee father is likely to produce feelings of low self-esteem in a young boy . . . The lack of a suitable domestic male role model also means that the child is deprived of guidance in forming relationships in the wider world. In later life this can create a powerful drive to overcompensate. Some will seek to validate their self-worth through sexual promiscuity. Others enter politics.[10]

Interestingly, Milošević is reported to have compared himself, in 1992, to Iran's Ayatollah Khomeini.[11]

Both LeBor and Cohen have occasion to refer to collective mental states. LeBor, for example, writes that 'Every crowd is composed of individuals who have subsumed their individuality to a collective desire',[12] and notes that Dr Milan Kovačević, a former hospital director who became involved in setting up the Serb-run concentration camp in Omarska, referred to the phenomenon of 'collective madness'.[13] Cohen, however, makes much more extensive use of this concept, describing Serbian society as 'an angst-ridden ethnic community',[14] referring to

'Serbia's "collective political personality",[15] arguing that the 'sensational, paranoid' manipulation of history and myth 'had a significant impact on many segments of society – the young, the elderly, the semi-skilled and less educated, the rural sector, and the uninformed – groups which together composed the bulk of Serbia's population',[16] and noting that the rewriting of history textbooks so that they were 'brimming with xenophobia, contempt and hatred for neighboring countries . . . made the war *psychologically* possible'.[17]

Pavlović does not make use of psychological explanations, but views Milošević as driven by a hunger for power and domination, agreeing that Milošević was a masterful tactician. Stevanović, by contrast with all of the other writers under review in this chapter, seems to have a low opinion of Milošević's intelligence and intellectual prowess. He tells us explicitly that Milošević is 'not too intelligent', arguing that if he were more intelligent he would not have repeatedly found himself in no-win situations.[18] He also claims, elsewhere, that Milošević 'never read anything aside from the writings of his wife and, a bit later, a book by Dobrica Ćosić'.[19]

Where Kosovo is concerned, Cohen, LeBor, and Sell all seem to put Kosovo to the side in characterizing Milošević's rule, and Pavlović pays little attention to dynamics in that troubled province. Stevanović, however, devotes some attention to developments in Kosovo 1998–9, suggesting that the ethnic cleansing in Kosovo was prepared patiently over a long period of time, making use of the experience gained in Bosnia.[20] He also provides interesting details concerning the regime's propaganda barrage during 1999, noting how Belgrade's propaganda machine characterized individual Western leaders (Clinton as Hitler, Javier Solana as a drug addict, etc.).[21] Djukić, in spite of his critical attitude towards Milošević, adopts the Serb nationalist perspective here, portraying the Albanian insurrection of 1998 not as an expression of despair on the part of Albanians, but as an orchestrated international conspiracy against Serbia.

For Djukić, Milošević appears as a man who might never have risen to power but for his ambitious wife. For Sell, 'Milošević was an odd kind of dictator . . . [H]is was generally a "soft" authoritarianism – at least until shortly before the 1999 war with NATO.'[22] For LeBor, 'The Milošević regime was never quite an all-out dictatorship.'[23] Pavlović characterizes Milošević's rule as authoritarian, with 'sultanist' tendencies,[24] while Stevanović says that the Serbian leader was an 'anti-democrat' and 'semi-dictator'.[25] And, for Cohen, Milošević's 'authoritarian regime – a "semi-dictatorship" that throughout most of its existence had functioned as what has been termed in this study as a "soft dictatorship" – . . . was also a "semi-democracy" that had conducted elections (albeit not fully democratic in every respect)'.[26] My feeling is that, while these characterizations may be useful in capturing the nature of Milošević's rule in heartland Serbia, at least until 1998, they do not (perhaps are not intended to) get at the repressive nature of the Milošević regime's treatment of the Albanians of Kosovo. One may note, for example, (1) that, in Kosovo, the Milošević years saw the unconstitutional suppression of the province's autonomy, the illegal suppression of its assembly, the illegal firing of about 130,000 judges, rectors, physicians, professors, factory directors, and other people of distinction between 1990 and 1995 alone because of their Albanian nationality, the illegal shutting down (in 1990) of all Albanian-language instruction from elementary school to university, the beating of Albanian intellectuals, and the confiscation of land from Albanians in order to turn it over to Serb settlers;[27] (2) that Serbian paramilitary formations were active in the Sandžak region of Serbia during the years 1992–4 and that about 100,000 Muslims are said to have fled the region in desperation between 1991 and 2000;[28] (3) that in the years 1991–9, 50,000–100,000 Hungarians and 45,000 Croats were driven from their homes in Vojvodina, with self-styled Chetnik leader, Vojislav Šešelj, playing a role in building pressure on local non-Serbs to leave;[29] and (4) that the regime published a new law on the media on 22 October 1998 laying down elastic criteria under which independent voices could be silenced, and subsequently undertook repressive actions against independent media in Serbia. Where Kosovo is concerned, these authors are not unaware of the repressive character of Milošević's policies, however. LeBor, for example, mentions the 'random arrests, beatings and prison sentences' meted out to Albanians already in the early 1990s and the resulting 'system of de facto apartheid',[30] and reports evidence of massacres of Albanian civilians during 1998–9.[31] Sell estimates that, by the end of 1993, Milošević's policies had induced about 400,000 Albanians to flee from Kosovo,[32] and provides an estimate of 12,000 Albanians killed by Serbian forces during 1998–9.[33] Cohen, too, notes that early in 1990, having suppressed Kosovar autonomy, 'the Milošević regime chose to step-up the harsh crackdown and long-term militarization of the Kosovo question (e.g., Belgrade's takeover of the Kosovo police, dissolution of local parliamentary and governmental institutions, abolition of local autonomy, seizure of the province's media outlets, etc.)'.[34] Cohen also notes that, in the course of 1998, 'Serbian massacres of civilians and shellings of villages drove many Albanians into the UCK [KLA] . . . [and] forced somewhere between 200,000 and 300,000 Albanians to flee their homes.'[35]

II

In spite of some commonality in characterizing the Serbian leader, however, the accounts by LeBor, Sell, and Cohen frame Milošević's story in entirely different ways, resulting in very different trajectories. LeBor's volume takes the personal stories of Milošević and his family as the starting point and, based on interviews with Milošević's wife Mira Marković, her half-sister Ljubica Marković, Milošević's brother Borislav, Draža Marković, Dušan Mitević, Nebojša Popov, Mihailo Crnobrnja (a key economic adviser to Milošević in the years 1974–89), Boško Krunić, Hrvoje Šarinić, and others, spins a story rich in detail, tracing the Serbian leader's life starting with his childhood when, as LeBor recounts, 'Friendless and fatherless, mocked for his weediness and unwillingness to join the rough and tumble of the playground, the young schoolboy instead took refuge in his studies.'[36] We learn from LeBor's account that Milošević was known, in the early 1980s, as 'little Lenin', because of his communist orthodoxy, that his Montenegrin ally, Momir Bulatović, was called 'the waiter' because he delivered what Milošević ordered, and that Milošević would typically hum loudly to himself when preparing for political battle.[37] We learn further that Mira Marković's 'favourite book for comfort' was Sophocles' *Antigone*, that Tahir Hasanović, the youngest member of the Serbian party presidium, was convinced, by 1990, 'that the only answer for Yugoslavia was a complete transformation into a modern democracy', and that Milošević disliked both listening to long speeches and giving them, and preferred to keep cabinet meetings short.[38]

But LeBor does not allow himself to become lost in such details and, in endeavouring to explain socialist Yugoslavia's decay, he identifies two fundamental problems: the failure to inculcate a sense of shared 'Yugoslavism' strong enough to transcend ethnic identities, and the constitutional 'weakness' in which Serbs sought to dominate the entire federation, resulting in resentments on all sides.[39] LeBor also faults Tito for not allowing Yugoslavs to 'come to terms with Yugoslavia's past', especially with conflicting memories about the Second World War.[40] LeBor is fully aware that, had the Stambolić/Pavlović team succeeded in defeating Milošević at the Eighth Session of the League of Communists of Serbia in September 1987, 'the course of Yugoslav history might have taken a very different turn'.[41] But he also recognizes the role of economic deterioration in facilitating Milošević's rise and consolidation of power,[42] while not overlooking the importance of 'the country's relatively underdeveloped political culture' in generating support for Milošević.[43] Milošević's legacy, LeBor concludes, is tragic; indeed, the author argues that 'the regime's destruction of the foundations of every-day life in modern European society – the value of money, of honest work, ethical behaviour, even common courtesy – had a profoundly corrosive effect on Serbian society, from which it has yet to recover'.[44]

LeBor did not aspire to write a scientific book. He aspired, rather, to produce a highly readable account of one of Europe's more disturbing personalities in the years since 1945, and to bring him to life, as it were. In this undertaking, he has succeeded admirably. And yet, though 'science' does not seem to have been an objective as such, LeBor has made good use of a considerable amount of scholarly material in English and memoir literature in Serbian/Croatian and can, no doubt, be of use to specialists as well.

By contrast, Sell set himself the goal of understanding 'how the Yugoslavia that I and many other foreign observers knew and loved could have so quickly succumbed to barbarism'.[45] In answering this question, Sell embraces a version of the 'great man' theory (which Cohen calls the 'evil leaders' theory), arguing that 'Yugoslavia did not die a natural death; it was murdered and Milošević, more than any other single leader, is responsible.'[46] Sell does assign some blame also to Tudjman and Izetbegović, however, and explains the failure of inter-national efforts to take steps to avert catastrophe in Yugoslavia or, later, to bring the Yugoslav conflict to a speedy end by suggesting, very plausibly, 'that no nation felt its vital interests were at stake in Yugo-slavia'.[47] Taking a retrospective glance back at Tito, Sell identifies Tito's 'two greatest failures' as 'his unwillingness to abandon one-party Com-munist rule' and 'his failure to deal honestly and openly with the national question'.[48] Like LeBor, Sell too notes that the leadership of socialist Yugoslavia 'failed to develop a true Yugoslav political culture'[49] and points out that the educational reforms adopted throughout the country in the 1970s resulted in greater stress on the history and culture of the people of each individual republic (e.g., in Croatian schools, on the history and culture of Croats) rather than conveying a sense of shared history and culture. For Sell, the wounds of the Second World War had not healed during Tito's presidency. As a result, 'thirty years after the end of the Second World War, the physical and psychological scars of conflict were evident in the Krajina. Deserted villages and ruined churches were scattered throughout the hills of the region. Dangerous memories lurked just below the surface.'[50]

Sell is intent on documenting Milošević's direct culpability for most of what happened in Croatia and Bosnia during the years 1991–5. He writes, thus, that there can be 'no doubt that Milošević either initiated or approved major military moves during the war in Croatia',[51] and specifically notes that 'throughout the Srebrenica crisis [in summer 1995], Milošević was in direct contact with [General] Mladić'.[52] He also quotes from a study prepared by the Boltzmann Institute for Human Rights in Vienna to the effect that 'the attack on Zvornik [in spring 1992] was planned, coordinated and directed by the former JNA [Yugoslav People's Army]'.[53]

Assessing Milošević's impact and legacy, Sell judges that 'the thirteen years of Milošević's rule were a period of almost unparalleled disaster for Serbia', cautioning, nonetheless, that 'the damage to Serbia caused by Milošević went much deeper than the cost to the economic system'.[54] Sell also notes the harm inflicted by Milošević's actions on the people of Croatia, Bosnia, and Kosovo, while reminding the reader that Milošević cannot be saddled with the exclusive blame for all the suffering of 1991–9, having 'had plenty of willing accomplices in Serbia and emulators elsewhere in the former Yugoslavia'.[55]

Sell's account draws upon his experience working for eight years in the Yugoslav region, both with the US Department of State and with non-governmental organizations. Among the offices which Sell held one may mention that he served as political deputy to the first high representative for Bosnian peace implementation 1995–6 and as Kosovo director of the International Crisis Group in 2000. In addition, Sell was able to interview a number of prominent people, among them Vuk Drašković, Ibrahim Rugova, General Wesley Clark, Richard Holbrooke, Louise Arbour, Adem Demaci, and others. Sources consulted include scholarly works in Serbian/Croatian, English, and French, plus memoirs in Serbian/Croatian and English, as well as other sources.

III

Cohen's purpose, as he emphasizes in the preface to his book, is not to produce a biography as such, 'but rather [to make] an inquiry into a specific illiberal political system, during a particular period of time'. He continues, quite reasonably, by urging that 'The analysis is premised on the notion that Serbian political development from the late 1980s to the early twenty-first century can best be explained by the interaction between various socio-cultural features of Serbian society, situational developments and the political personality and policies of Slobodan Milošević.'[56] In researching his book, Cohen made extensive use of both Serbian/Croatian materials and materials in English, including memoir literature, scholarly works, and, where appropriate, newspaper accounts.

But while his statement of purpose makes a good deal of sense, Cohen quickly embraces a version of historical determinism which I found puzzling. For Cohen, Serbia is a society 'where collectivist nationalism has historically excited the popular imagination, and is rooted in the mythic lore passed from one generation to another'.[57] Elsewhere, he refers to 'historically shaped factors' such as

a strong penchant for centralized modes of political control, and particularly 'heroic leaders' who can maintain political order and preserve the 'unity' of the nation; a disinclination to accept rules-of-the-game which would allow Serbs to accept minority status within other multinational Balkan political units dominated by other ethnic groups; a predilection for statist collective unity in the face of a perceived external danger to the Serb nation (including identification of non-conformists as traitors or enemies, and a suspicion of democratic pluralism as a potential threat); and an exaggerated emphasis on sanguinity – 'Serbian blood and origins' – territorial control, and national religious myths as defining features of collective identity. *This historical experience of the Serbs – especially under the long period of Turkish domination, and the nineteenth and twentieth century struggles with Austria-Hungary's and Germany's intervention in the Balkans – also created a deep sense of victimization in the Serbian political psyche and political culture.*[58]

This monochromatic (and unflattering) portrait of Serbs is the result of Cohen's belief that the Serbs cannot escape their past, indeed that they are locked into patterns of behaviour formed centuries ago. It is, moreover, a classic statement of the largely discredited 'national character' school of thought. It is, of course, reasonable to argue that the present is affected by the past; indeed, no sensible chronicler of political and social developments would dispute this claim. But Cohen is offering us a list of modal attitudes which supposedly guide Serbian behaviour and treating the predilections of unnamed Serbs living under Ottoman rule and, implicitly, of certain past Serbian political figures (such as King Aleksandar and Nikola Pašić or, in more recent decades, perhaps also Aleksandar Ranković) as determinative of a supposed Serbian penchant for centralized control, while ignoring contrary tendencies in Serbian history (as manifested, in the interwar period, by Stojan Protić, Jaša Prodanović, Dragoljub Jovanović, and Dragiša Cvetković, and in the communist era most notably by Marko Nikezić and Latinka Perović, but also, by the late 1980s, I would argue, by Tahir Hasanović and Dragiša Pavlović). The fact that certain leaders are able to stir up support for one or another programme which may be reminiscent of the past by no means proves that these plans are the result of fixed and unchangeable political attitudes on the part of all or even most Serbs. Cohen also believes that Serbs' historical experience with the *zadruga* (communal farming and irrigation) system continues to shape contemporary Serbian political culture and that, because of 'the collectivist nature of the patriarchal legacy' (undefined), Serbs (and possibly, in his view, also other Balkan peoples) understand democracy differently from the way other peoples do.[59] Lest his effort to connect contemporary political culture with the remote past be misunderstood or overlooked, Cohen emphasizes that 'the illiberal facets in the Serbian political legacy were reinforced by the long period of Ottoman rule'.[60]

I have already noted that Cohen makes use of the notion of collective mental states, referring to Serbia as an 'angst-ridden community' having a 'collective political personality'. There is, in fact, a large literature in psychology dealing with collective mental states, most, if not all, of which is premised on the assumption that one may speak of collective mental states as, broadly speaking, comparable or analogous to individual mental states. This field has been investigated, among others, by Robert Waelder,[61] Roderick Kramer and David Messick,[62] and, for that matter, Emile Durkheim.[63] Towards the end of his book, however, Cohen abruptly changes his mind about the notion of collective mental states and rejects 'psychological analogies between individuals and entire ethnic groups' as 'glib and ethnocentric',[64] thereby contradicting himself. He also rejects the notion, in this context, that Serbia could be thought *to have become, in the Milošević years*, in some sense 'locked in the past',[65] suggesting that it is 'ethnocentric' to believe that a society may develop 'obsessive behavior' even though the text which he cites made no argument that Serbia was unique in this regard. But Cohen himself nonetheless writes that 'The "cult of the past" or "cult of the ethno-nation" effectively resulted in a state-sponsored re-socialization of the Serbian population with an ostensibly "new" value system.'[66] As far as I can see, Cohen ends up arguing that the Milošević regime did, indeed, work to try to 'lock' Serbs in the past, or at least in the regime's version of the past. On the other hand, to the extent that Cohen believes that the political attitudes of Serbs may be treated monochromatically and traced to the distant past, he may be treading onto dangerous terrain. Similar arguments, applied to both Serbs and Croats, have been analysed and criticized by Dušan Kecmanović in the *Australian and New Zealand Journal of Psychiatry*. Kecmanović, a consultant psychiatrist in New South Wales, looked at, *inter alia*, M. Jakovljević's claim that Serbs 'have a paranoic political culture, the main features of which are "megalomania, expansiveness, hegemony, and pathological possessiveness"',[67] and at J. Rašković's claim that Croats are introspective and 'afraid of being deceived, of being fooled by someone, and of being subjected to some unpleasant treatment that will endanger his/her dignity'.[68] Kecmanović rejects such approaches, however, arguing that 'the existence of national character itself is very dubious' and that the model characteristics of communities may change over time.[69]

Yet, insofar as we may take Cohen's historical determinism literally, it comes as no surprise that he disparages what he calls the 'evil leaders' theory of politics,[70] since that approach (which is, more or less, part of the apparatus assumed by Sell) emphasizes the role played by human agency and the sense that things could have been different (a point also stressed by LeBor). Cohen repeats (commendably) in several places how important 'cultural factors' are in endeavouring to understand Serbian politics (and presumably the politics of any other country). But I found precious little about 'turbo-folk' and was unable to find any discussion of Dobrica Ćosić's *Vreme smrti* or of Danko Popović's *Knjiga o Milutinu* – two novels which exercised considerable influence in Serbia in the 1980s.

Consistent with his undertaking that *Serpent in the Bosom* is not to be understood as a biography, Cohen does not provide a summing up of the legacy of the Milošević regime at the end of his book. Rather, he criticizes tendencies to overestimate the role played by political leaders in stoking up 'aggressive nationalism'. He cautions that 'Treating every concern advanced by nationalist leaders as inappropriate or unacceptable in diplomatic negotiations ignores the fact that while leaders are exploiting nationalism for their own ends, they may also be reflecting deeply held and genuine attitudes in their society.'[71] That the Western leaders, with their various partition plans, should be thought to have treated 'every concern advanced by nationalist leaders as inappropriate or unacceptable' comes as a surprise to me, since the partition plans look, on the face of it, like alternative strategies to try to accommodate all players in the field. But the subtext, that specific nationalist demands (e.g., for the annexation of 70 per cent of Bosnia-Herzegovina to an expanded Greater Serbian state) should be seen as 'reflecting deeply held and genuine attitudes' is disquieting. Finally, in the last few pages of the book, Cohen tells us that 'the structure of Serbian civil society had gradually burgeoned in the 1990s'[72] – an interpretation explicitly refuted by Eric Gordy's brilliant study of Serbian society[73] – and asks us to believe that 'the basis and disposition for democratic participation had also flourished within the confines of his repressive rule'[74] – an interpretation which flies in the face of massive documentation about the corruption of the electoral process, the manipulation of the legislature, the diversion of capital to Milošević's cronies, the entire strategy of controlling the most influential media and either marginalizing or shutting down opposition media, not to mention the murder of journalist Slavko Ćuruvija (for which some analysts hold the Milošević regime responsible), the disappearance of Stambolić in summer 2000, and the beating of Vuk Drašković and his wife in June 1993.[75] Then, after having

advised us earlier of his conviction that Serbs were still strongly influenced by their alleged 'strong penchant for centralized modes of political
control, and particularly "heroic leaders"', and so forth, Cohen closes
his book by asserting that, after the fall of Milošević, 'The Serbian people
remained immensely proud of their cherished traditions.'[76] Since the
book does not deal with Serbian traditions, this flourish does not have
any *logical* connection with the rest of the book as such.

By contrast with the foregoing books, Jack Snyder's *From Voting to
Violence* looks for explanations as to why nationalist conflicts erupt when
they do – not by looking for 'historically shaped factors' or even by
exploring the psychology of individual leaders. Snyder is convinced,
rather, that democratization can result in the outbreak of nationalist
conflict when existing elites fear that they could lose office in a fair
election and see no way to hold onto power other than to stoke up
interethnic hatreds. Casting his eye back to nineteenth-century Serbia,
Snyder notes that the Obrenović dynasty promoted ethnic nationalism, not because it was in accord with 'deeply held and genuine
attitudes', but because the Obrenovićes felt that they needed ethnic
nationalism, in spite of its uncivic character, if they were going to
mobilize public support; Snyder adds that when 'liberalism' subsequently developed in Serbia, it emerged in an ethnic nationalist form.[77]
Turning to more contemporary events, Snyder makes no effort to tie
developments in Yugoslavia or elsewhere to the remote past. Rather, he
argues that variations in the proclivity to violence among postcommunist states were a factor of differences in patterns of democratization,
emphasizing '(1) the state's degree and timing of economic development, (2) the degree to which democratization threatened elite interests,
and (3) the nature of its political institutions during the transition'.[78] But
even this is not sufficient to account for differences in the postcommunist trajectory, and Snyder adds to the list of relevant factors also the
presence of ethnic-based federal structures (warning against them), the
existence of a patronage-based administrative system, rates of illiteracy,
infant mortality, and urbanization, and the population's level of civic
skills. Snyder, thus, finds that, in comparing Yugoslavia with six other
states (Bulgaria, Czechoslovakia, Hungary, Poland, Romania, and the
USSR), for the years 1939–70, during much of which period these
countries were under communist control, Yugoslavia recorded the
highest rate of illiteracy, the highest rate of infant mortality, and, by
1970, the lowest rate of urbanization.[79] He concludes that 'democratization is likely to spark nationalist conflict in countries that have
an underdeveloped economy; a population with both poor civic skills
and underdeveloped representative and journalistic institutions; and

elites who are threatened by democratic change'.[80] In recounting the story of Yugoslavia's descent into violence, Snyder stresses, among other things, the 'hijacking' of the media by nationalists.[81]

IV

Slavoljub Djukić has made a career out of writing books about Milošević. *Milošević and Marković: A Lust for Power*, a translation of Djukić's fourth analysis of his favourite subject, is distinctly curious. Djukić is well informed and reveals many interesting details. It is well known, for example, that both of Milošević's parents committed suicide. But Djukić points out that Milošević's maternal aunt died under suspicious circumstances as well, either committing suicide or being murdered, while his maternal uncle was shot.

Djukić is critical of Milošević, but mocks Milošević's wife, Mira Marković, as 'obsessed with bodily hygiene'.[82] Djukić even quotes Marković as characterizing (with unconscious comedy) members of the opposition as 'frustrated men who never learned to bathe properly'.[83] Djukić writes as a long-time opposition critic of the Milošević regime. But his opposition is coloured by nationalism, indeed may spring from nationalism, and in this way bears witness to the proliferation of nationalism throughout Serbian society.

If one were to pick one word to sum up Djukić's nationalism, it might well be *myopia*, insofar as Djukić, while keenly aware of the sufferings, ruined lives, dashed hopes, and political perspectives of the Serbs, seems totally oblivious of the sufferings, ruined lives, dashed hopes, and political perspectives of non-Serbs. And it is precisely such myopia which keeps intolerant nationalism alive.

Particularly striking is the fact that the only specific events from the wars discussed in this book are either atrocities committed by non-Serbs against Serbs or atrocities attributed to the agency of non-Serbs. Along these lines, Djukić claims that the Croats 'had shelled Šibenik, their own city, in order to compromise the Serbs'.[84] Or again, the author complains that the shelling of Sarajevo's Markala square on 5 February 1994, in which innocent civilians died, was *blamed* on the Bosnian Serb forces, as if it were likely that the Muslims might have bombed themselves.[85] He dismisses as an exercise in hypocrisy the Slovene–Croat proposal of October 1990 to convert Yugoslavia into a confederation.[86] He suggests that estimates of the number of Muslim women raped were complete fabrications and offers his own estimate (which he attributes without documentation to an unspecified 'UN report') that only 115 women from all three nationalities were raped during the war in

Bosnia.[87] He paints a picture of Slovenes, Croats, and Albanians involved in an international conspiracy with the Vatican, the Pentagon, and Hans Dietrich Genscher to break up Yugoslavia,[88] but plays down Miloševic's crucial role in this process. And after the entry of Croatian forces into the so-called Krajina and the flight of some 150,000 Serbs, Djukić comments that 'a Serb dream ended in despair'.[89] But just what was the nature of that dream? Djukić remains silent on this point.

How would Djukić like the reader to understand the breakup of Yugoslavia? At one point, he writes, 'Yugoslavia's collapse served the interests of many nations in the West, but Germany's involvement was particularly decisive.'[90] I have argued elsewhere against conspiratorial theories concerning Germany's role in the Yugoslav crisis,[91] but what is especially surprising here is Djukić's belief that '*many* nations in the West' thought that they stood to benefit from a process which could only involve regional instability, rising levels of intolerance, waves of refugees who just might look to those same Western countries to take them in, and the need to commit Western forces and Western funds to Bosnia over a relatively long period. Which nations does he have in mind? Which nations should we believe were welcoming such a major disruption in Balkan politics and economic life? Again, he does not say; nor does he explain just how the breakup of socialist Yugoslavia might be thought to have been capable of serving the interests of *any* external actors. After all, the IMF and the West were already dictating economic conditions to socialist Yugoslavia, and Western firms were already beginning to invest in that country. Nor does Djukić explain why the West, if it was so eager to break up socialist Yugoslavia, postponed recognition of Slovenia and Croatia for six long months, and imposed an arms embargo which, at least in the short run, crippled Bosnian efforts at self-defence while complicating Croatian efforts to build up its armed forces.

Again, the only refugees discussed in the context of 1991–5 are Serb refugees, whose sufferings are individualized and described in some detail.[92] He clearly has empathy for Serb civilians driven from their homes in Croatia, but expresses no concern in this book for Croat civilians driven from their homes by Serb forces. Croatia's speedy reconquest of Knin is predictably and rather disturbingly demonized as a 'Croatian blitzkrieg',[93] even though Serb conquests in summer 1991 had also been a 'quick war' or 'blitzkrieg', if one wishes to import foreign words which may sabotage the thinking process.

Djukić devotes some space to developments in Kosovo. But true to the established pattern, he says nothing about Albanian sufferings, devoting his attention only to the sufferings of the Serbs. In recounting the Albanian insurrection of 1998, he alleges that American, British, and Germany military instructors provided assistance to the Albanians, alongside mercenaries from Germany, Slovenia, and Croatia, 'arms shipments from many nations', and all told, a mass of 'thirty thousand fanatics and mercenaries'.[94] I do not know of any other source which confirms these allegations. He enumerates Serb casualties in 1998, but does not mention even a single Albanian casualty, much less the wanton destruction of Albanian villages and the swelling number of homeless Albanians (at least 250,000)[95] by the end of summer 1998. According to Djukić, the American purpose in allegedly supporting the Albanian insurrection was 'to land troops in Kosovo'.[96] Djukić characterizes the NATO aerial campaign, in which some 500 civilians were killed by NATO bombing, as 'a military orgy unlike anything Europe had witnessed in over fifty years'.[97] Surely Djukić is aware that an estimated 215,000 people died during the war in Bosnia alone.[98] But in that event, does it really make sense to describe NATO's generally surgical bombing (even given some rather obvious errors, such as the stray bomb which destroyed a shoe shop) as dwarfing the sufferings inflicted on Bosnia in part by Karadžić's Serbian forces? In retrospect, Djukić finally admits that 'both sides were guilty of atrocities' in Kosovo – the only admission of Serb culpability for anything which I was able to find in this book. But then Djukić goes on to claim that the mass graves in Kosovo contain the remains of both Albanians and Serbs.[99] As far as I know, this is not the case.

Further examples could be adduced in support of my characterization of Djukić as myopic. So why should anyone read Djukić's book at all? Certainly, if the book were dishonest, there would be no reason to bother with it. But Djukić's omissions do not strike me as the result of deliberate obfuscation. On the contrary, Djukić is telling the story of the Milošević era *and how it affected Serbia* as he and many fellow Serbs see it. He is simply not concerned with the effects which Milošević's policies and the various conflicts may have had on non-Serbs. But this narrowing of the field of vision becomes myopic insofar as he ends up with only a part of the story, leaving out parts without which the resulting picture becomes distorted.

The book's importance, in fact, lies precisely in its myopia, because it is this which demonstrates the extent to which Serbian society, including those who were against Milošević from early on, remains infected by the nationalist virus. And insofar as mainstream nationalism in Serbia is characterized by an apparent disinterest in, or even perhaps in the case of some Serbian citizens denial of, the sufferings inflicted on other people by members of one's own nation and – at least in Koštunica's case – by an inappropriate interest in the land currently under another jurisdiction, it is fair to describe such nationalism as unhealthy, perhaps even as a species of 'collective neurosis'.

V

Djukić's book was written while the Serbian defeat in Bosnia and Kosovo was still fresh in Serbian minds and before Milošević had been driven from power. The books by Pavlović and Stevanović were written after Milošević's fall from power, and reflect a certain analytical distance. Pavlović's short study is a brilliant foray into theoretical discussions about the Milošević era. He notes that, in response to the question, 'Why was there no democracy in Serbia under the Milošević regime?', Serbian writers have alternatively looked to five different sets of explanatory variables: socio-economic factors (associated with Todor Kuljić and Vladimir Ilić), cultural factors (Zagorka Golubović and Bora Kuzmanović), the role of the Great Powers and globalization (Radmila Nakarada and Radovan Radinović), institutions and institutional dynamics (Vladimir Goati and Ognjen Pribićević), and the actors themselves, whether leaders or other figures (Vučina Vasović and Slobodan Antonić).[100]

Pavlović devotes considerable energy to rebutting the 'culturalists' (as he calls them). In his account, the culturalists place their stress on authoritarian political culture as the root of Serbia's contemporary authoritarianism. The corollary of this interpretation, as Pavlović summarizes it, is that Serbs come to be seen as 'not ready for democracy because the majority of Serbs' are more oriented to authoritarian values than to democratic values.[101] Pavlović's chief criticisms of the culturalist approach are that its advocates (and here he has Golubović in mind, above all) are fuzzy about the question or set of questions they wish to answer, and that the approach is both deterministic and simplistic.[102] In fact, Pavlović denies that Serbs are particularly authoritarian; rather, he judges that Serbs (like other peoples) tend to find conformity easier than resistance, so that – the protest actions of March 1991, June 1993, winter 1996–7, etc., notwithstanding – it was simply easier for Serbs to accept Milošević's rule for fourteen years than to fight against it.[103]

Of the five theories he outlines, Pavlović is inclined to favour the theory emphasizing the role of personalities, arguing that neither political culture nor institutional obstacles nor the interests of the Great Powers could obstruct a nation's path to democracy, given pro-democratic leaders. But personalities alone cannot explain why regimes collapse, as Pavlović realizes. On the contrary, he tells us, 'the greatest number of authoritarian regimes start to collapse because of lack of legitimacy'.[104] Guided by this theory, Pavlović provides the most straightforward explanation of the impotence of the Serbian opposition during the 1990s: the reason, says Pavlović, is that, to be effective, the opposition needed to be united around a single leader, but instead, it had two rival leaders, Vuk Drašković and Zoran Djindjić. It was a mark of Milošević's tactical perspicacity that he reached an agreement with Drašković in 1997, agreeing to give him greater access to the media in his run for the presidency of Serbia. In the absence of a parliamentary majority to back him up, the post would have brought Drašković little real power, but it would have significantly reinforced his claim to be the leader of the opposition. In the unlikely event that Djindjić would simply accept this state of affairs, Milošević would have succeeded in co-opting the head of the opposition into his regime; and, in the more likely event that Djindjić would realize the threat that this posed to himself personally, Djindjić might (as he did) call for a boycott, which would only deepen the rift between the two opposition rivals.[105]

As already mentioned, the books by Stevanović and Nava are more popular treatments; while they do offer insights into Milošević's career, they should not be mistaken for academic books. Stevanović is more fascinated by the question of how Milošević could have succeeded at all. For Stevanović, the Milošević era was an era of criminalization of the state, fascicization of society, and blundering on the part of Milošević. As an example of Milošević's blundering, he mentions the Serbian leader's rush to welcome the hardline coup against Gorbachev in August 1991, when Boris Yeltsin rallied the opposition to the coup; according to Stevanović, Yeltsin never forgot or forgave Milošević for this mistake and the episode would later poison Serbian–Russian relations.[106]

Stevanović broods about the inefficacy of intellectuals who were opposed to Milošević but who did essentially nothing to fight his regime, but shows too how Milošević captured the mood of Serbia in the late 1980s, promising Serbs not only a brighter political future, but also a brighter economic future – indeed, a world-class economy![107] He also embraced, for a while, the concept of 'partyless pluralism', the brain-child of academic Mihajlo Marković. To Stevanović's mind, the collapse of the Milošević regime was only a matter of time, because each blunder only brought it closer to collapse.

One may get a sense of Massimo Nava's book by glancing at the table of contents, in which Nava's subject is cast in various roles in the chapter titles themselves: the model boy, the communist, the nationalist, the warrior, the pacifist, the instigator, the speculator, the tyrannosaurus, the alchemist, the hangman, the victim, the traitor, the spectre, and the walking dead. His account starts with a discussion of Milošević's family, pointing to Mira Marković's disproportionate influence on her husband's policy decisions. Like many other writers, he notes that Milošević lived through the suicides of both of his parents (his father committing suicide when Milošević was twenty-one years old, and his mother a decade later). But Nava also points out that the first suicide in the family was Milošević's uncle, Milislav, a Partisan general and admirer of Stalin, who was 'very affectionate with little Slobo'.[108] The sense of abandonment which these events kindled in Milošević engendered deep depression in the future Serbian leader and scarred his personality for life, according to Nava, who also notes that Croatian president Tudjman's father also committed suicide – in his case, after killing his wife.[109] For that matter, Karadžić's father was accused of having killed his own cousin, while, as Nava records, Mladić's daughter committed suicide shortly after the massacre at Srebrenica, possibly in part 'because her father did not welcome the engagement of his daughter to a Muslim'.[110]

Nava adds some interesting details to the story of 'il Macellaio dei Balcani' (the butcher of the Balkans), noting, for example, Milošević's aversion to press conferences, Dobrica Ćosić's efforts to convince Milošević to resign from office, and Radovan Karadžić's early career not only as poet and psychiatrist but also as author of children's stories.[111] He quotes from Milošević's interview with *Corriere della sera*, given shortly after the war had broken out. In a classic expression of Belgrade's propaganda line, Milošević told the Italian newspaper,

The Serbian people have organized to defend their houses and their families. The Serbs in Croatia are not an occupation force, but people who have lived in those lands for centuries. *Nobody wants a Greater Serbia*. We have always said that Serbia has no territorial ambitions.[112]

Milošević made other claims during his political career – for example, claiming that he was not able to control Krajina president Milan Martić or General Ratko Mladić.[113] But Nava quotes what Martić himself told a Belgrade newspaper at one point: 'No one in the Krajina', said Martić, 'took [even] the smallest decision without consulting Milošević' first.[114] Even General Mladić reportedly travelled to Belgrade on a weekly basis on Tuesdays; to General Rose it seemed 'clear that Mladić at least was receiving direct orders from the military HQ there'.[115]

Nava calls Milošević many things, among them 'the alchemist'. Alchemists, as is well known, wanted to turn lead into gold, but always failed. Milošević too hoped to turn lead into gold, but, unlike the alchemists, who could scarcely tell their clients that the lead in front of their eyes was in fact gold, Milošević claimed, after Dayton, that he had achieved a great 'success' in war, in spite of the flood of Serbian refugees who had streamed out of Croatia and much of Bosnia, and would later try to persuade Serbs that he and Serbia had somehow 'won' the war against NATO in spring 1999. Milošević used words as the Sirens did in Homer's *Odyssey*, namely, to lure men to their doom. Even on the eve of the war he offered, disingenuously, 'It is in the interest of all the republics and all of their peoples that Yugoslavia continue to exist . . . We want a unity based on equality.'[116] And a final image drawn from Nava's account – Milošević singing 'Tenderly' at Dayton to the delight of the hotel staff.

VI

In picking up any book about politics, one is always aware that there is a point of view, an interpretation, even a selective filter at work. But one tends to hope that one can rely on the facts presented and even, up to a point, on there being some minimal consensus as to what the facts mean. In comparing the volumes by Cohen and Sell, however, I found this not to be the case, and I would like to present four examples. First, there is the matter of Operation Horseshoe, the plan under which the Serbian authorities were thought to have plotted to drive out most of the Albanian inhabitants of Kosovo, killing just enough of them to terrorize the rest into taking flight, and the existence of which was announced by American officials in autumn 1998. Cohen apparently doubts that there was any such plan. He refers, at one point, to 'the infamous plan, Operation Horseshoe (*Potkovica*) that supposedly had been detected by Austrian and German intelligence in the fall of 1998',[117] elsewhere arguing that 'there is no proof that a plan called Operation Horseshoe even existed'.[118] Cohen is not the only writer to make this claim, however; Jürgen Elsässer, editor of the German magazine, *Konkret* – whose book on this subject is discussed in chapter 10 – makes the same argument and cites corroborative articles in the European press. Sell, by contrast, writes that

> Before the bombing began, Austrian intelligence officials presented their US counterparts with a chilling document. Called 'Operation Horseshoe', it was described by US officials as a comprehensive and detailed operational military plan for the [ethnic] cleansing of Kosovo that laid out the movement of Serb units on a day-to-day basis.[119]

Moreover, Sell claims that the Kosovo Liberation Army (KLA) captured hundreds of incriminating documents, turning them over to NATO officials. According to Sell, these documents 'may have provided evidence linking Operation Horseshoe "to Serb army generals and police commanders all the way up to President Slobodan Miloševič". A NATO intelligence officer told Western correspondents that the documents helped [to] show that "it was organized from the top".[120]

The second example relates to the massacre at Srebrenica in July 1995, generally blamed on General Mladić and his Bosnian Serb troops (with a report that Mladić had actually been filmed giving orders for the massacre). Cohen apparently remains sceptical about accounts of the massacre and writes that 'reports of the mass killing of several thousand Muslim civilians seized at Srebrenica by Serb forces, *allegedly* at the direction of General Ratko Mladić, turned the incident into a "defining moment"'.[121] Sell's account is entirely different. Here there is no doubt as to whether Mladić was responsible and the emphasis for Sell is not on the effect of the reports on the Western public, but on the massacre itself. 'Mladić', Sell writes, 'who was on the scene part of the time, bears most of the responsibility [for the massacre] . . . A knowledgeable journalist reported that Chief of Staff Momĉilo Perišić gave Mladić explicit permission in early July to attack Srebrenica.'[122]

Then there are the rival accounts offered of the 28 August 1995 shelling, even offering alternative figures for the numbers of shells and casualties. Here is Cohen's account:

On August 28 [1995], a shell exploded in Sarajevo's main market killing 38 people and wounding 85 others. It was the worst attack on the city in more than a year, and occurred only yards from where a similar blast had killed 68 people in February 1994. *The question of who fired the shell was disputed by some observers. But in view of the extensive shelling of Sarajevo by Serbian forces since 1994, the burden of proof was quite low.*[123]

As before, Sell's version is strikingly different. Here is Sell's account:

On 28 August, five mortar shells slammed into Sarajevo's central market, near the site of the similar tragic attack in February 1994. This time, thirty-seven people were killed and ninety wounded. As with the previous incident, the Serbs immediately disclaimed responsibility – almost as though their guns had not been shelling Sarajevo for more than three years – and Serb military sources in Belgrade spread the word that it was the work of a Moslem splinter group. . .

This time, however, (there was little) question about the perpetrators. By the next day, UN forces in Sarajevo had 'concluded beyond doubt' that the mortars were fired from Serb territory . . . Analysis of the impact craters and the observations of UN soldiers showed that the five mortar rounds came from southwest of the city, while data from the British radar indicated that they were fired from a range of 1,550 to 3,500 meters. Since the distance from the impact site to the confrontation line between Bosnian and Serb forces in the direction from which the shells were fired was 1,050 meters, it was obvious that they had originated within Serb lines.[124]

Daniel Eisermann agrees with Cohen in writing that it was a single mortar grenade which struck downtown Sarajevo on 28 August, but agrees with Sell that thirty-seven people were killed (rather than thirty-eight). Eisermann further reports that within twenty-four hours the United Nations released a report holding the Serbs responsible, but does not comment on the believability of the conclusions in the report.[125]

But in spite of this mixed result, I find myself more inclined to trust Sell than to trust Cohen. Quite apart from the more diverse use of sources on Sell's part and the fact that I find myself more comfortable with an approach which situates developments within the complex of problems in contemporary time rather than within the complex of 'historical factors' from the remote past, it seems to me that Cohen sometimes writes things which it is hard to imagine he can actually know. How, for example, does he know that the burden of proof for determining who had fired the mortar in August 1995 was low? How is it that he is certain that no authentic documents exist concerning Operation Horseshoe? Why is he sceptical about Mladić's role in the massacre at Srebrenica? In regard to this last point, various testimonies given in The Hague in the context of the trial of Slobodan Milošević have confirmed Sell's account.

And, finally, the fourth example relates to Milošević's rejection of the Rambouillet draft accord. Cohen writes,

Particularly galling to Belgrade was Appendix [i.e., Annex] B of the proposed accord which provided, among other things, that NATO troops would not be under Yugoslav legal jurisdiction, international troops could go anywhere in Yugoslavia in order to perform their duties, and [they would have] had complete access to all forms of transportation and communication in Yugoslavia.[126]

Sell believes that the facts are entirely different, however, writing:

One factor that was not crucial in Milošević's rejection of Rambouillet was the existence of so-called Annex B. This document, which would have provided NATO personnel, vehicles, and aircraft with unimpeded access to all FRY territory, is sometimes cited as being tantamount to a NATO occupation and therefore a reason for Belgrade's rejection of the accord. Yet the annex was actually a Status of Forces Agreement (SOFA), which US and NATO forces generally prefer to have in areas where they operate, largely for legal reasons . . . At the time of Rambouillet, Serb negotiators did not raise Annex B as an obstacle to signing; they had much more fundamental objections to the presence of NATO troops in Kosovo at all.[127]

That Louis Sell's mature, balanced, and well-reasoned account is my favourite of the seven books about Serbia and Milošević under review here (Jack Snyder's work cannot be characterized as a book about

Serbia) will not surprise anyone at this point. Indeed, if someone were to ask me to recommend just one study of Milošević, I would pick the volume by Sell. Yet the volume by LeBor, with its rich detail, is also *very* well worth reading and specialists might well learn more from the LeBor volume than from any of its competitors. The LeBor book has more details of a private or behind-closed-doors nature, while Sell's book offers more details about developments in Kosovo.

Dušan Pavlović's well-researched volume would rank third on my listing. With its sturdy analytical framework and rich detail, the book is likely to prove useful to any scholar interested in the Milošević era. I find that I am roughly equally impressed by the works of Nava and Stevanović, which are thus tied for fourth place. Nava's book is lively, weaving serious commentary into a palatable package, while Stevanović offers the occasional curious detail, such as his report that, at the height of the war in Bosnia, there was talk of Biljana Plavšić, then vice president of the Republika Srpska, marrying Prince Tomislav Karadjordjević, the last living son of King Aleksandar.[128] I would rank Slavoljub Djukić's book sixth among this set; its primary utility lies in its effectiveness in presenting the nationalist-opposition viewpoint – critical of Milošević but sensitive only to the sufferings of Serbs, not to the sufferings of Croats, Bosniaks, and Albanians. Cohen's book is not without its uses, and the depth of his research in written materials is broadly comparable to the research of the works by Doder/Branson, LeBor, and Sell, but, as already indicated, it is flawed by a tendency towards historical determinism and by a scepticism which does not always seem to have any necessary connection with the available facts; I would therefore judge it the least useful among this set. Among them, only the books by Djukić and Cohen could, in my view, be judged as potentially misleading, albeit in different ways. And, finally, in a separate category, Jack Snyder's broadly comparative and theoretical work makes a significant contribution to an understanding of the relationship between democratization and nationalist conflict, between nationality-based federalism and the proclivity to fissiparous fracturing, and between the hasty introduction of elections and expanded political participation in a setting characterized by ethnocentrism and bigotry, on the one hand, and the likelihood of disintegration into (renewed) interethnic conflict, on the other.

NOTES

1 A number of studies of Tudjman and his years in power have been published in Croatia in recent years, among them, Nenad Ivanković's *Predsjedniće, što je*

ostalo? Psihološko-politički portret prvog hrvatskog predsjenika (Varaždin: TIVA, 2001).

2 Two books recently published in Serbia deal with Karadžić's career. These are: Marko Lopušina, *Radovan Karadžić: Najtraženija sprska glava* (Niš: Zograf, 2001); and Ljiljana Bulatović, *Radovan* (Belgrade: Evro, 2002).

3 Dusko Doder and Louise Branson, *Milosevic: Portrait of a Tyrant* (New York: Free Press, 1999).

4 Louis Sell, *Slobodan Milošević and the Destruction of Yugoslavia* (Durham, NC: Duke University Press, 2002), p. 4.

5 Massimo Nava, *Milošević: La tragedia di un popolo* (Milan: Rizzoli, 1999), pp. 22–3.

6 Jack Snyder, *From Voting to Violence: Democratization and Nationalist Conflict* (New York: W. W. Norton, 2000), p. 52.

7 Nava, *Milošević: La tragedia*, pp. 22, 18.

8 Lenard J. Cohen, *Serpent in the Bosom: The Rise and Fall of Slobodan Milošević* (Boulder, CO: Westview Press, 2001), p. 84.

9 Unnamed American psychiatrists, as quoted in Sell, *Slobodan Milošević*, p. 173.

10 Adam LeBor, *Milošević: A Biography* (Polmont, Stirlingshire: Bloomsbury, 2002), p. 25.

11 Sell, *Slobodan Milošević*, p. 169.

12 LeBor, *Milošević*, p. 80, attributing the notion to Elias Canetti's book, *Crowds and Power* (London: Phoenix Press, 2000).

13 LeBor, *Milošević*, p. 179.

14 Cohen, *Serpent*, p. 64.

15 *Ibid.*, p. 399.

16 *Ibid.*, p. 105. University students were the most significant element in the opposition to Milošević. For further discussion, see Eric D. Gordy, *The Culture of Power in Serbia: Nationalism and the Destruction of Alternatives* (University Park, PA: The Pennsylvania State University Press, 1999).

17 Cohen, *Serpent*, p. 101, quoting from Dubravka Stojanović, *The Balkans, Wars and Textbooks: The Case of Serbia* (Belgrade, 1999), my emphasis.

18 Vidosav Stefanović, *Milošević, jedan epitaf* (Belgrade: Montena, 2002), p. 166.

19 *Ibid.*, p. 9.

20 *Ibid.*, p. 226.

21 *Ibid.*, p. 228.

22 Sell, *Slobodan Milošević*, p. 193.

23 LeBor, *Milošević*, p. 304.

24 Dušan Pavlović, *Akteri i modeli: Ogledi o politici u Srbiji pod Miloševićem:* (Belgrade: Samizdat B92, 2001), pp. 224, 227.

25 Stevanović, *Milošević, jedan epitaf*, p. 17. See also pp. 161–2.

26 Cohen, *Serpent*, p. 423.

27 See, *inter alia*, Fabian Schmidt, 'Kosovo: The Time Bomb That Has Not Gone Off', *RFE/RL Research Report* (Munich), 1 October 1993, p. 28; Elez Biberaj, *Kosova: The Balkan Powder Keg*, Conflict Studies No. 258 (London: Research Institute for the Study of Conflict and Terrorism, February 1993), pp. 6–7; Julie Mertus, *Open Wounds: Human Rights Abuses in Kosovo* (New York: Human Rights Watch/Helsinki, March 1993); and Sabrina P. Ramet, *Whose Democracy? Nationalism, Religion, and the Doctrine of Collective Rights in Post-1989 Eastern Europe* (Lanham, MD: Rowman & Littlefield, 1997), pp. 146–54.

28 Miroslav Filipović, 'The Sandžak Dilemma', BCR No. 125 (17 March 2000), published by The Institute for War and Peace Reporting (1 August 2000), at www.iwpr.net.index.p15?archive/bcr/bcr_20000317_2_eng.txt; *Christian Science Monitor*, 11 April 1994, p. 2, on LexisNexis; and *Washington Post*, 29 May 1993, p. A2, on LexisNexis. See also 'Human Rights Abuses of Non-Serbs in Kosovo, Sandžak, and Vojvodina', *Human Rights Watch Helsinki*, 6, 6 (May 1994).

29 For details and documentation, see Sabrina P. Ramet, *Balkan Babel: The Disintegration of Yugoslavia from the Death of Tito to the Fall of Milošević*, 4th edn (Boulder, CO: Westview Press, 2002), p. 346.

30 LeBor, *Milošević*, p. 277.

31 *Ibid.*, pp. 316–17.

32 Sell, *Slobodan Milošević*, p. 270.

33 *Ibid.*, p. 306.

34 Cohen, *Serpent*, p. 184.

35 *Ibid.*, p. 236.

36 LeBor, *Milošević*, p. 13.

37 *Ibid.*, pp. 62, 91, 133, 195.

38 *Ibid.*, pp. 17, 154, 158.

39 *Ibid.*, p. 9.

40 *Ibid.*, p. 10.

41 *Ibid.*, p. 94.

42 *Ibid.*, pp. 129–30.

43 *Ibid.*, p. 156.

44 *Ibid.*, p. 211.

45 Sell, *Slobodan Milošević*, p. xv.

46 *Ibid.*, p. 4.

47 *Ibid.*, p. 6.

48 *Ibid.*, p. 19.

49 *Ibid.*, p. 38.

50 *Ibid.*, p. 113.

51 *Ibid.*, p. 324.

52 *Ibid.*, p. 233.

53 Quoted *ibid.*, p. 324.

54 *Ibid.*, pp. 358, 359.
55 *Ibid.*, pp. 360, 361.
56 Cohen, *Serpent*, p. xiv.
57 *Ibid.*, p. 398.
58 *Ibid.*, p. 81, my emphasis.
59 *Ibid.*, p. 82.
60 *Ibid.*
61 Samuel A. Guttman, 'Robert Waelder and the Application of Psychoanalytic Principles to Social and Political Phenomena', *Journal of the American Psychoanalytic Association*, 34, 4 (1986), pp. 835–62.
62 Roderick M. Kramer and David M. Messick, 'Getting by with a Little Help from Our Enemies: Collective Paranoia and Its Role in Intergroup Relations', in Constantine Sedikides, John Schopler, and Chester A. Insko (eds.), *Intergroup Cognition and Intergroup Behavior* (Mahwah, NJ: Lawrence Erlbaum, 1998), pp. 233–55.
63 Emile Durkheim, *The Rules of the Sociological Method* (New York: Free Press, 1964).
64 Cohen, *Serpent*, p. 395.
65 Sabrina P. Ramet, *Nationalism and Federalism in Yugoslavia, 1962–1991*, 2nd edn (Bloomington, IN: Indiana University Press, 1992), p. 254; quoted with disapproval in Cohen, *Serpent*, p. 395.
66 Cohen, *Serpent*, p. 102.
67 Dušan Kecmanović, 'Psychiatrists in Times of Ethnonationalism', *Australian and New Zealand Journal of Psychiatry*, 33, 3 (1999), p. 310.
68 Quoted *ibid.*, p. 312.
69 *Ibid.*, p. 313.
70 Cohen, *Serpent*, pp. 385, 397.
71 *Ibid.*, p. 398.
72 *Ibid.*, p. 423.
73 Gordy, *The Culture of Power in Serbia*.
74 Cohen, *Serpent*, pp. 423–4.
75 For exhaustive documentation of these and other transgressions, see Robert Thomas, *Serbia under Milošević: Politics in the 1990s* (London: C. Hurst & Co., 1999), reviewed in chapter 11.
76 Cohen, *Serpent*, p. 426.
77 Snyder, *From Voting to Violence*, pp. 169–70, 176.
78 *Ibid.*, p. 195.
79 *Ibid.*, pp. 199–201.
80 *Ibid.*, p. 305.
81 *Ibid.*, pp. 219–20.
82 Slavoljub Djukić, *Milošević and Marković: A Lust for Power*, trans. from Serbian by Alex Dubinsky (Montreal: McGill-Queen's University Press, 2001), p. 169.

83 Quoted *ibid.*
84 *Ibid.*, p. 47.
85 It has been a recurrent theme in Serb nationalist rhetoric to accuse the Croats and Muslims of having attacked themselves. The claim was even registered at one point that the Croats had themselves shelled Tudjman's presidential palace, risking the loss of their president, in order to embarrass the Serbs. But if self-destructive behaviour is so cunning and so obviously 'profitable', why are there no examples of Bosnian Serbs shelling themselves?
86 Djukić, *Milošević and Marković*, p. 42.
87 *Ibid.*, p. 46.
88 *Ibid.*, p. 47.
89 *Ibid.*, p. 80.
90 *Ibid.*, p. 50.
91 See Sabrina P. Ramet and Letty Coffin, 'German Foreign Policy Towards the Yugoslav Successor States, 1991–1999', *Problems of Post-Communism*, 48, 1 (January–February 2001), pp. 48–64.
92 Djukić, *Milošević and Marković*, pp. 74–7.
93 *Ibid.*, p. 78.
94 *Ibid.*, p. 122.
95 See Ramet, *Balkan Babel*, 4th edn, p. 320.
96 Djukić, *Milošević and Marković*, p. 122.
97 *Ibid.*, p. 130.
98 This is the figure calculated by Croatian demographer Vladimir Žerjavić, as reported in *Globus* (Zagreb), 9 January 1998, p. 24.
99 Djukić, *Milošević and Marković*, p. 132.
100 Pavlović, *Akteri i modeli*, p. 171.
101 *Ibid.*, p. 186.
102 *Ibid.*, pp. 189–90.
103 *Ibid.*, pp. 193–4.
104 *Ibid.*, p. 214.
105 *Ibid.*, pp. 114–18.
106 Stevanović, *Milošević, jedan epitaf*, pp. 101ff.
107 *Ibid.*, pp. 11, 65, 70, 144.
108 Nava, *Milošević: La tragedia*, p. 24.
109 *Ibid.*, pp. 25 6.
110 *Ibid.*, p. 129.
111 *Ibid.*, pp. 31, 67, 125.
112 Quoted *ibid.*, p. 82, my emphasis.
113 *Ibid.*, pp. 100–1.
114 Quoted *ibid.*, p. 83.
115 General Sir Michael Rose, *Fighting for Peace: Lessons from Bosnia* (London: Warner Books, 1999 edn), p. 49.
116 Quoted in Nava, *Milošević: La tragedia*, p. 81.
117 Cohen, *Serpent*, p. 269.

118 *Ibid.*, p. 274.
119 Sell, *Slobodan Milošević*, p. 304.
120 *Ibid.*, p. 320.
121 Cohen, *Serpent*, p. 149, my emphasis.
122 Sell, *Slobodan Milošević*, pp. 232–3.
123 Cohen, *Serpent*, p. 156, my emphasis.
124 Sell, *Slobodan Milošević*, pp. 246–7.
125 Daniel Eisermann, *Der lange Weg nach Dayton: Die westliche Politik und der Krieg im ehemaligen Jugoslawien 1991 bis 1995* (Baden-Baden: Nomos Verlagsgesellschaft, 2000), p. 335.
126 Cohen, *Serpent*, p. 267.
127 Sell, *Slobodan Milošević*, p. 301.
128 Stevanović, *Milošević, jedan epitaf*, p. 148.

REFERENCES

Cohen, Lenard J., *Serpent in the Bosom: The Rise and Fall of Slobodan Milošević* (Boulder, CO: Westview Press, 2001), p. 438.
Djukić, Slavoljub, *Milošević and Marković: A Lust for Power*, trans. from Serbian by Alex Dubinsky (Montreal: McGill-Queen's University Press, 2001), p. 183.
LeBor, Adam, *Milošević: A Biography* (Polmont, Stirlingshire: Bloomsbury, 2002), p. 386.
Nava, Massimo, *Milošević: La tragedia di un popolo* (Milan: Rizzoli, 1999), p. 307.
Pavlović, Dušan, *Akteri i modeli: Ogledi o politici u Srbiji pod Miloševićem* (Belgrade: Samizdat B92, 2001), p. 244.
Sell, Louis, *Slobodan Milošević and the Destruction of Yugoslavia* (Durham, NC: Duke University Press, 2002), p. 412.
Snyder, Jack, *From Voting to Violence: Democratization and Nationalist Conflict* (New York: W. W. Norton, 2000), p. 384.
Stevanović, Vidosav, *Milošević, jedan epitaf* (Belgrade: Montena, 2002), p. 320.

8   Dilemmas in post-Dayton Bosnia

I

The literature on post-Dayton Bosnia-Herzegovina is divided by three major controversies: (1) whether reunification or partition is the better strategy for achieving stability in the area; (2) whether democratization (i.e., including turning governmental authority over to locals) should be (or should have been) undertaken as soon as possible or whether it is preferable to build a civic culture in Bosnia first, before entrusting the locals with autonomous power; and (3) for how long should the international community maintain a presence in the unfortunate republic and continue to funnel in money.

The leading academic champions of partition in recent years have been Donald L. Horowitz,[1] Chaim Kaufmann,[2] and John J. Mearsheimer;[3] the leading antagonists have been Radha Kumar,[4] Joachim Hösler,[5] and Nicholas Sambanis.[6] The argument in favour of partition (Kaufmann's version) runs as follows: the nature of the causes of intercommunal warfare is beside the point – says Kaufmann – because 'solutions to ethnic wars do not depend on their causes'.[7] What counts, for Kaufmann and other advocates of partition, is that the proliferation of hatred in the course of war constitutes a problem in its own right. As a result, the successful resolution of an ethnic civil war requires that the members of the polarized groups have as little contact with each other as possible; that makes partition the answer. Kaufmann concedes that 'ethnic separation does not guarantee peace', but he emphasizes that 'it allows it. Once populations are separated, both cleansing and rescue imperatives disappear; war is no longer mandatory.'[8] He considers the possible objection that population transfers cause people to suffer, but rejects this objection, saying that planned population transfers are 'safer'; what is dangerous, he says, is population *flight* – or, as he calls this, 'spontaneous refugee movement'.[9]

Critics of the process argue that the process does not solve the problem it is designed to solve. Joachim Hösler, for example, records four waves of ethnic homogenization in the Balkans, involving population transfers, over the past hundred years: 1912/13, 1923, 1941–5, and 1984–99. The problem, as he points out, is that these waves of partition and ethnic homogenization seem not to have calmed intercommunal frictions, but, quite on the contrary, to have deepened and intensified them.[10] Kumar, reviewing the history of partitions in Cyprus, India, Palestine, and Ireland, comes to the same conclusion as Hösler and concludes that, 'rather than separating irreconcilable ethnic groups, [these partitions] fomented further violence and forced mass migration. Even where partition enabled outside powers to leave, as in India, it also led to a disastrous war.'[11]

The debate concerning the strategy of democratization revolves around the question of whether one can proceed at once – as soon as a peace treaty has been signed and international peace-keepers are on site – to hold elections, to turn over responsibility for administration to local authorities, and to pull out the peace-keepers, or whether one must take a more patient approach, deferring the transfer of authority to locals until liberal values have been successfully disseminated in the society. This debate is related to an exchange of views staged in the pages of *Foreign Affairs* a few years ago, between Fareed Zakaria and Marc F. Plattner. Zakaria's argument was that liberalism and democracy are distinct phenomena, and that there has been a rise of illiberal democracies in recent years.[12] If Zakaria is right, then moving quickly with the transfer of authority to locals could be asking for trouble. Plattner, on the other hand, takes a more sanguine view, arguing that liberalism and democracy go together, and that the practice of democracy brings liberal values in tow.[13] If Plattner is right, then Zakaria's concerns are misplaced and there is no reason to delay the transfer of administrative control to locals, once truly democratic institutions are in place. Plattner, thus, is optimistic about human nature, feeling that even the intercommunal hatreds stirred up by recent war cannot impair people's ability to choose wisely.

II

The war in Bosnia left more than half of Bosnia's 4.3 million citizens displaced, up to a quarter of a million people dead, between $15 billion and $20 billion worth of infrastructure in rubble, industrial production sliced to less than 10 per cent of prewar levels, and as much as 80 per cent of agricultural equipment destroyed.[14] To that one may add the psychological damage – with widespread incidence of post-traumatic stress, melancholia, withdrawal, and distrust of members of other ethnic groups – and the damage to religious and other cultural objects. With the

Dayton Peace Accords, an attempt has been made to rebuild Bosnia. Two of the books under review – *Towards Peace in Bosnia*, written by Elizabeth M. Cousens and Charles K. Cater, and *Bosnia after Dayton*, by Sumantra Bose, who has also written about Spain and Sri Lanka – address this theme. Five of the volumes discussed here (those by Bildt, Bose, Chandler, Kumar, and Cousens/Cater) were written without reference to materials in the local language; indeed, judging from their bibliographies, four of these works appear to have been written entirely on the basis of English-language materials, with Bildt citing also materials written in German, French, and Norwegian.

Kumar fixes her focus on the first of the three questions raised – the question about partition. She objects to partition both on normative grounds, calling the use of partition to stop intercommunal warfare a kind of *laissez faire* policy which is morally problematic,[15] and on grounds of feasibility, viewing this recourse as a formula for continued instability. Her account also lends support to the 'liberal values first' approach to the holding of elections, noting that, at least in the short run, nationalist parties won the largest shares of the vote in the speedily scheduled elections. The implementation of Dayton faced other problems too, as she notes, including lack of funds and manpower to start up the International Police Task Force (IPTF) and vote-rigging, for example when the Serbian Democratic Party (SDS) tried, contrary to the Dayton Accords, to register refugee voters; thus, of Brčko's prewar population of 87,300, about 18,000 had been Serbs, but about 51,200 Serb voters were registered to vote in 1996.[16]

Meier favours partition but supports the 'liberal values first' approach, criticizing High Representative Carl Bildt for naïveté and for a limp approach.[17] Meier identifies the effort to hold Bosnia together as the root of its dysfunctionality; according to Meier, Bosnia's difficulties would be on the way to solution if, at Dayton, the republic had simply been divided in three. But he adds that, in that event, the Serbs, representing about 31 per cent of the population, could not have been allowed to retain political jurisdiction over 49 per cent of the territory.[18] Meier admits that 'Petritsch and many others are of the opinion that the international community must simply have the patience and remain in Bosnia for "some years" still. Whether it will in fact summon this patience is an open question.'[19] But Meier is not confident that any amount of 'patience' will produce the results which the international managers want; the majority of local Serbs and a majority of local Croats want to be attached to their respective national states.

David Chandler offers an alternative to both Kumar and Meier, agreeing with Kumar on the desirability of keeping Bosnia together but rejecting the 'liberal values first' approach taken by both Kumar and Meier. For Chandler, the sooner the Bosnians are allowed to run their own political show, the better. His documentation is impressive: it is the sundry interventions by High Commissioners Carlos Westendorp and Wolfgang Petritsch which, Chandler says, have held up the process of democratization in Bosnia. Chandler draws attention to the fact that the stated aims of the Dayton Accords included 'Bosnian self-government'.[20] Chandler does admit that 'there is a link between the low level of support for civil society alternatives to the leading political parties and a lack of democracy in Bosnia', but he insists that 'the relationship between civil society and democracy is not necessarily the one suggested by the advocates of greater international support for NGO-led civil society-building strategies'.[21] He concludes that the assumption that one needs to build 'civil society' – one possible operationalization, though not the only one, of the 'liberal values first' thesis – is open to question.

'Democratisation in Bosnia', Chandler writes, 'would appear to have little to do with democracy as traditionally understood.'[22] Still, the approach he champions has more to do with the strategy of democracy-building tried in the German Weimar Republic, where institutions were put in place before liberal values had become entrenched, than with the more gradual evolution of liberal democracy in Great Britain, where some liberal ideas (religious tolerance, respect for the harm principle, rule of law) were gaining powerful supporters long before there was any hint of democracy in the country. Chandler admits that, in Bosnia, 'democracy is no longer defined as the outcome of popular decision-making but as an adherence to democratic ethics and values',[23] but, in so saying, he blurs the distinction between liberalism (as a set of values) and democracy (as a set of institutions and practices). Chandler distinguishes between 'democratization' (by which he means the promotion of liberal values) and 'democracy' (by which he means elections and institutions and self-government) and may be closer to Plattner than to Zakaria, but apparently this rapprochement is unconscious. This is reflected in, *inter alia*, the exclusion of any consideration of textbook reform and school reform from his analysis. That said, to Chandler, the record of the international community's involvement in Bosnia, at least until July 1998, is not merely one of failure to move the country forward, but actually of having *done damage* to Bosnia's future prospects. As Chandler argues, 'there is little question that, in the case of Bosnia, democratization has undermined autonomy and self-government on the assumption that external assistance is necessary for building an alternative that will more effectively bridge segmented political divisions'.[24]

III

The Cousens/Cater collaboration is on the whole successful. Unfortunately, the thoroughness of their research on their subject was not matched by similar thoroughness in reviewing the literature on the Bosnian war itself. The result is that the authors made three easily avoidable factual errors at the beginning of their volume.[25] Still, this should not be given too much stress, since, as a brief review of the 'Dayton experience' in Bosnia, the book is quite useful. The authors evaluate the record of Dayton implementation in five key areas: security, the return of displaced persons, the economy, reunification, and democratization, giving the Dayton process mixed marks. As they note, Bosnia-Herzegovina remains even today divided among three jurisdictions, with three contesting governments, three armies and their related paramilitaries, and three parallel security regimes.[26] Moreover, the three groups (Bosniaks, Croats, and Serbs) have maintained separate school curricula and resisted efforts by the Office of the High Representative (OHR) to agree on an integrated educational system.[27] On the other hand, the peace-keeping operations have contributed to preventing the outbreak of renewed fighting – which must be counted as a success.[28] Distinguishing between 'refugees' (displaced beyond Bosnia's borders) and 'internally displaced persons' (seeking to return to their prewar homes), the authors note that, of 1,200,000 refugees at war's end, only 349,650 had been repatriated to Bosnia by the end of 1999, by which time only 324,100 refugees declared themselves still in need of a solution; the other 526,250 had found more or less permanent solutions outside Bosnia in the meantime. Of a total of more than a million internally displaced persons as of December 1995, only 295,991 had succeeded in returning to their homes by the end of 1999, with some 830,000 still seeking relocation as of that latter year.[29] Ironically, they argue, one of the major obstacles to returns has been problems of coordination among international actors, and timidity on the part of the UNHCR.

Economic recovery has been slow, and, by 1998, industrial production still stood at only 30 per cent of its prewar level.[30] In terms of unemployment, the record is mixed, with unemployment reduced to 50 per cent in the Bosniak–Croat federation by 1997, but still as high as 90 per cent in the Serb-controlled Republika Srpska; unemployment had been recorded at more than 80 per cent for the republic as a whole in 1995.[31] Moreover, with the moratorium on debt repayment coming to an end, Bosnia's external debt obligations were to rise by a tangible amount precisely as donor assistance would taper off.

And, finally, where democratization is concerned, the authors implicitly call into question the wisdom of rushing with elections in September 1996, noting that problems in those elections included the
registration of more voters than possible, poor handling of absentee
balloting, the locating of several polling stations at sites of major violence, ballots being taken to counting centres by unauthorized people,
and the OSCE decision to destroy all ballots one week after the results
had been certified.[32] More ominously, the enforcement of the human
rights provisions of the Dayton Peace Accords was seriously lacking, due
in part to conflicts of interest among the Council of Europe, the OSCE,
the European Court of Human Rights, the UN High Commissioner
for Human Rights, the Human Rights Office of the IPTF, and the
OHR's Human Rights Coordination Centre, all of which claimed
jurisdiction and responsibility in the field of human rights protection.[33]
Given these problems plus the obstructionism of some nationalists
elected to office, the high representative (first Carlos Westendorp, then
Wolfgang Petritsch) started to use his powers to remove individuals from
office when they were thought to be acting contrary to the Dayton
Accords. The authors appear to feel uncomfortable about this, arguing
that 'To attempt to implement democratic reforms through what are
viewed as nondemocratic methods is inherently contradictory.'[34] They
also fear that recourse to the 'Bonn powers' is apt to prove 'self-perpetuating', thereby retarding Bosnia's path towards democracy.[35]

This slender volume presents a useful introduction to the challenges
facing post-Dayton Bosnia, blaming many of the problems on co-
ordination deficiencies and failures on the part of authorities responsible
for implementation, rather than on active resistance from intransigent
local nationalists. The authors do note, pessimistically, that the American
preoccupation with exit strategies and with setting deadlines for com-
pletion of the peace-keeping mission 'may have played well with a
relatively isolationist Congress . . . [but] also encouraged those parties
hostile to Dayton to just "wait out" what would supposedly be a short-
lived international military presence'.[36] On the negative side, most of the
figures provided do not go beyond 1999, rendering the book already a
bit dated.

By contrast with the Cousens/Cater collaboration, the volume written
by Sumantra Bose is simultaneously narrower and more ambitious. It is
narrower in the sense that Bose wishes to focus on the debate between
'integrationists', who would like to reassemble a unified Bosnia, and
advocates of partition, who feel that the present lines of division should
be allowed to become more or less permanent. It is more ambitious
because Bose wants to use this prism to assess the entire post-Dayton

experience, going far beyond the five areas highlighted by Cousens and Cater. Insofar as Bose is hostile to *both* integrationists and advocates of partition, he is under obligation to identify a third option. That third option is to advocate nothing, but to merely assist Bosnians in reaching their own solutions.[37]

Most analysts believe that, left to their own devices, local Croats and Serbs will work towards making the lines of division permanent, with the Serbs perhaps seeking to attach their statelet to the Republic of Serbia. In other words, Bose's position might put him in de facto alliance with advocates of partition. It is therefore somewhat surprising to see the vehemence with which he attacks and ridicules the ideas of Chaim Kaufmann, John Mearsheimer, and Robert Pape – all three being well-known advocates of partition. Claiming that Mearsheimer and Pape had 'airily' 'glossed over' logistical problems with their partition plan, Bose dismisses their claims on behalf of partition as 'ludicrous' and urges that 'not a single major aspect of or element of this plan is remotely "realistic"'.[38] Harsh words indeed.

But it is in turning to Kaufmann that Bose drops all inhibitions. 'Ensconced in the academic ivory tower', Bose writes, 'Chaim Kaufmann has attracted attention to himself by tenaciously promoting partition'.[39] From this phrasing, an uninured reader might conclude that Kaufmann's sole motivation in discussing the merits of partition was to call attention to himself! And if this is the point, what is Bose's evidence? But Bose does not stop here, adding that Kaufmann 'blithely conflates the root cause of the problem with its "remedy"', that 'Kaufmann has been misled by his own "security dilemma" dogmatism', that Kaufmann's discussion is 'littered with factual errors' (Bose provides three examples), that 'Kaufmann's ignorance does not stop at matters of detail', that Kaufmann's account is 'breezy and incorrect', 'crude, shallow', 'limited and static', 'inherently ahistorical, [and] teleological', 'factually questionable', and 'riddled with factual errors'.[40] The impression is thus conveyed (1) that Bose is unacquainted with customary rules of etiquette in academic debate, (2) that Bose wrote some parts of this book in a state of uncontrollable anger, and (3) that the copy-editor did not read the manuscript very carefully.

Not that Bose's ire is limited to the aforementioned advocates of partition. In a similar vein, he dismisses American commentator Thomas Friedman's ideas as 'tendentious, overdrawn . . . [and] superficial',[41] characterizes Allan Little's argument that the national divisions in Bosnia are artificial as 'absurd', though without explaining what Little meant by so saying,[42] claims that 'so many scholars and journalists' have treated life in Sarajevo as typical of Bosnia as a whole[43] (I wonder who has ever thought this), accuses Robert Hayden and David Chandler of having 'sneered' at the human rights provisions in the federation and common-state constitutions,[44] calls Bishop Ratko Perić 'deeply bigoted',[45] and suggests that Susan Woodward's interpretation of the Dayton Peace Accords as anti-Serb in inspiration 'sounds strangely similar to a conspiracy theory'.[46] And while Bose defends Hayden by suggesting that 'Hayden's "pro-Serb" leanings are evident but his argument merits critical consideration nonetheless',[47] he ignores Hayden's real contribution, which is to have offered a bold statement of the conventionalist position, in which there is no moral standard aside from the written law by which to ascertain which rights are legitimate,[48] his lack of familiarity with major books in the field, and his difficulty in summarizing the arguments of some scholars. On the other hand, in turning to India and Pakistan, which is to say that part of the world where Hayden first made a reputation, Bose accuses Hayden of an 'erroneous assertion',[49] charges that 'Hayden seriously underestimates the long-term, negative legacies of India's partition',[50] and dismisses Hayden's views on Bosnia as 'pious'.[51]

I have detailed Bose's proclivity towards name-calling because I believe that it is inappropriate in scholarly endeavours, that he has exceeded normal limits, and that this excess of ad hominem attacks detracts from the book as a whole. That said, Bose's challenge seems to be much in the spirit of John Stuart Mill's *Concerning Representative Government*, even if Bose does not actually cite the younger Mill. It was, after all, in that tract that Mill advised that people in any society would be best left to their own devices to develop democracy for themselves, and that it would not do to try to fashion democracy from above and simply hand a finished system to people on a silver platter. Thus, while I am more in sympathy with the efforts of Westendorp and Petritsch than with the protests of Mill and Bose, I recognize that their argument (that of Mill and Bose) is a respectable one. Moreover, it is an essential one. The answer is probably not going to be black-and-white. After all, the experience of building democracy in Germany, Austria, and Italy after the Second World War certainly shows that a top-down approach to democratization may work under some specified conditions. But it does not follow that it will work under all conditions. So what about in Bosnia?

One of the problems which Bose notes in connection with Mostar, but which surely will apply to much of the republic, is that its 'prospects of civic activism . . . have been seriously weakened by the continuous exodus of educated professionals and bright young people, now remaking their lives and careers in many distant lands'.[52] Moreover, one of the legacies of war is that 'many [locals] are still fundamentally unreconciled, while others are at best reluctant participants [in civic life]'.[53] Further, if one accepts the tacit assumption that reunification requires prior reconciliation, then reunification is probably at least two generations away, since both the generations that witnessed the war and the next generation, hearing the stories from their parents, are apt to remain bitter about the war and its outcome. As for Dayton itself, Bose finds that the Dayton Peace Accords created 'dubious foundations' for the Bosnian state,[54] but nonetheless concludes that Dayton, for all of its flaws, is apt to evolve into a permanent framework for the Bosnian state, no doubt with some modifications along the way. Lest anyone mistake this for optimism, Bose points out that the solution imagined by the Dayton framework is 'consociational' in nature, meaning that the three ethnic communities preserve spheres of autonomy and self-governance as well as the capacity to veto some legislation, and then quotes from now-retired political scientist Paul Brass to the effect that 'A consociational system is inherently undemocratic and violates both the rights of non-recognized groups and the rights of individuals.'[55]

IV

Carl Bildt's *Peace Journey* falls into a hybrid genre, combining elements of memoirs with elements of scholarly research. Bildt, who had served previously as prime minister of Sweden, was called to succeed David Lord Owen as European co-chairman of the International Conference on the Former Yugoslavia in June 1995 and continued as high representative in Bosnia, relinquishing that post in June 1997. Bildt confirms the difficulty in obtaining start-up funding noted above by Kumar and provides some interesting details concerning the shabby and unheated office in which he had to work during the first few weeks of January 1996.[56] Then there was the challenge of integrating Serbs, Croats, and Muslims into a multiethnic police force as prescribed by Dayton.[57] Meanwhile, Sarajevo was drowning in conspiracy theories, making reconciliation all the harder.[58] Where Viktor Meier had blamed Bildt for, *inter alia*, failing to send in the international police when Grbavica was transferred to federation control in March 1996, resulting in widespread arson,[59] Bildt claims that he and his advisers had anticipated the problem and had tried in vain to persuade IFOR (NATO's Implementation Force) to play a stronger part and to get the IPTF operational in time for the transfer.[60]

Dayton had been negotiated, for the Serbian side, by Slobodan Milošević, but Karadžić had not reconciled himself to the provisions of Dayton when, on 1 April 1996, he told the parliament of the Republika

Srpska that he continued to be committed to the unification of all Serbs in a single Greater Serbian state, using the occasion also to criticize the international representatives for having blocked Serbian political aspirations.[61] The international community confronted not only political challenges but also the imperative of economic reconstruction. By Bildt's account, about 60 per cent of all houses had been rendered uninhabitable in the course of the war, while hydro-electric power, coal mining, and the power distribution grid itself had been put out of action. People had deserted their farms, cattle had been killed, land mines made it treacherous to return to the farms, and industrial production stood, in Bildt's estimate, at about 5 per cent of prewar production levels.[62] Both governments – that of the Muslim–Croat federation and that of the Republika Srpska – were short of funds needed to cover the basic budget. But Bildt was clear that progress on both the political and the economic front depended upon moving towards the reunification of Bosnia-Herzegovina: 'our mission was to reunite Bosnia – not to divide it. I felt that we had to give priority to projects that benefited all parts of the country and which would gradually link them closer together. Reintegration was for me the key concept.'[63]

Bildt had to spend much of his time presenting his case to the donors' conferences, making briefings in the European Parliament, mobilizing support from Japan and the Islamic world, and providing a liaison on behalf of Bosnia with the World Bank. Then there was the case of Radovan Karadžić, the indicted war criminal on the run. Bildt provides an interesting tidbit about the dynamics between Karadžić and US secretary of state Madeleine Albright who allegedly

did not regard him as a war criminal, but had increasingly come to see him as a war profiteer, putting his own personal interests above everything else. Once she had supported him as the person creating the Republika Srpska, but now she was equally strong in rejecting him as the man who risked destroying the same Republika Srpska. While she was convinced that he would have to go, he was increasingly seeing everything as a huge international conspiracy to bring them all under 'Muslim rule'. Later, I asked her about this last meeting between them [on 4 June 1997]. She just shook her head. He does not understand, she said. He is becoming crazy.[64]

Bildt begins his book by calling nationalism 'the evil dragon'[65] and ends his story by warning that nationalism continued to pose a threat to the region, and that extremist nationalism could end up 'destroying what was left of Serbia and Yugoslavia'.[66] Bildt even tried to convince Milošević that his policies were leading Serbia towards disaster, but to no avail. As for Bosnia, Bildt rejects both partitionist and integrationist approaches, finding both of them unrealistic. Rather than trying to force unification quickly or simply dividing the country in three, Bildt calls for a gradualist, piecemeal approach which, he says, holds the only hope for eventual stabilization of Bosnia.[67]

Wolfgang Petritsch served as the third high representative in Bosnia, assuming office in mid-August 1999, at the expiration of Carlos Westendorp's mandate in June 1999. Petritsch served in Bosnia until May 2002, when he was succeeded by Paddy Ashdown, a veteran British diplomat and politician. *Bosnien und Herzegowina fünf Jahre nach Dayton* was published in 2001 and consists of reflections on the war and on the mandates of his two predecessors, as well as memoirs concerning the first year of his activity as high representative; the volume is rounded out with three 'essays', nine 'commentaries', the texts of various lectures he has presented, the texts of interviews he has given to the press, reprints of articles he has written for the press, and relevant documents.[68]

Where Chandler is critical of Westendorp's active role, Petritsch is full of praise, commending Westendorp for 'some spectacular actions undertaken' soon after Westendorp, a former Spanish foreign minister, had taken the reins in Bosnia.[69] The difference between Bildt and Westendorp was, in the first place, the result of the so-called Bonn Powers which dramatically expanded the powers of the high representative just about the time that Westendorp came into that office. It was, thus, Westendorp who took the decision in January 1998 leading to the introduction of the 'convertible mark' as the official currency of Bosnia-Herzegovina and again Westendorp who, in the absence of any concord among Bosniaks, Serbs, and Croats, decreed the flag which has been used, as a result, since February 1998.[70] Again, it was Westendorp who, in April 1998, removed the deputy major and police chief of Drvar from office, along with other politicians in July, August, and October.[71] Yet Petritsch also has some criticism of Westendorp, saying that the Spanish diplomat sometimes replaced uncooperative office-holders with people who were disposed to be just as uncooperative, but who entered office under the cloud of being dependent on the high representative's favour.[72] Chandler and Bose notwithstanding, Petritsch insists that 'one of my [i.e., Petritsch's] goals from the beginning was to actively promote the democratization of Bosnia and Herzegovina', and that, to this end, he wanted to bring local politicians into responsible engagement and to marginalize nationalist discourse.[73] It was, thus, Petritsch who introduced the Anglo-American concept of 'ownership' in a political sense into public debate, arguing that the concept entailed structural reforms. Petritsch explains that, by 'ownership', he means that people in the area will come to see Bosnia-Herzegovina as their own state, shifting their primary loyalty from one or the other 'entity' to the Bosnian state as such.[74] To Petritsch's mind, among the concrete tasks vital to the building of liberal democracy in Bosnia-Herzegovina are the strengthening of the central organs of state and the development of independent media operating free of the influence of one or another political party.[75] Readers of Petritsch's volume will also find details about international assistance, about economic reconstruction, about the return of refugees, and about the need to make creative and sensible adjustments to the Dayton Peace Accord which, he says, 'is not the New Testament'.[76]

V

Judging from the volumes by Bose, Chandler, and Cousens/Cater, there may be a growing consensus, from which I nonetheless abstain, that the directive approach to state-building in Bosnia is backfiring and that it would be better to let the Bosnians work things out for themselves. The advocates of *laissez faire* in Bosnia nonetheless are not oblivious to the dangers entailed in such an approach, of course, but consider that the likely benefits may outweigh the dangers. And, finally, there is a growing consensus about the role played by both systemic factors (system illegitimacy, economic problems, federalism) and contingent factors (specific leaders, specific myths, specific propaganda, and specific interactions) in stoking the flames of ethnic nationalism in the Socialist Federated Republic of Yugoslavia.

NOTES

1 Donald L. Horowitz, *Ethnic Groups in Conflict* (Berkeley and Los Angeles: University of California Press, 1985), at p. 588.
2 Chaim Kaufmann, 'Possible and Impossible Solutions to Ethnic Civil Wars', *International Security*, 20, 4 (Spring 1996), pp. 136–75; and Kaufmann, 'After Pax Americana: Benign Power, Regional Integration, and the Sources of a Stable Multipolarity', *International Security*, 23, 2 (Fall 1998), pp. 120–56.
3 John J. Mearsheimer, 'Shrink Bosnia to Save It', *New York Times*, 31 March 1993; and Mearsheimer and Stephen W. Van Evera, 'When Peace Means War', *New Republic*, 18 December 1995, pp. 16–21.
4 Radha Kumar, 'The Troubled History of Partition', *Foreign Affairs*, 76, 1 (January–February 1997), pp. 22–34.
5 Joachim Hösler, '"Balkanisierung" – "Europäisierung"? Zu Südosteuropas historischer Spezifik und den Folgen westeuropäischen "Zivilisations- und Stabilitätsexports"', in J. Hösler, Norman Paech, and Gerhard Stuby, *Der gerechte Krieg? Neue Nato-Strategie, Völkerrecht und Westeuropäisierung des Balkans* (Bremen: Donat Verlag, 2000), pp. 9–47. I discuss this book in chapter 10.

6 Nicholas Sambanis, 'Ethnic Partition as a Solution to Ethnic War: An Empirical Critique of the Theoretical Literature' (unpublished paper, 18 September 1999), nsambanis@worldbank.org.

7 Kaufmann, 'Possible and Impossible', p. 137.

8 *Ibid.*, p. 150.

9 *Ibid.*, p. 171.

10 Hösler, 'Balkanisierung', pp. 29–31.

11 Kumar, 'Troubled History', p. 24.

12 Fareed Zakaria, 'The Rise of Illiberal Democracy', *Foreign Affairs*, 76, 6 (November–December 1997), pp. 22–43.

13 Marc F. Plattner, 'Liberalism and Democracy: Can't Have One without the Other', *Foreign Affairs*, 77, 2 (March–April 1998), pp. 171–80.

14 Elizabeth M. Cousens and Charles K. Cater, *Towards Peace in Bosnia: Implementing the Dayton Accords* (Boulder, CO: Lynne Rienner, 2001), p. 25.

15 Radha Kumar, *Divide and Fall? Bosnia in the Annals of Partition* (London and New York: Verso, 1997), p. 11.

16 *Ibid.*, p. 129.

17 Viktor Meier, *Jugoslawiens Erben: Die neuen Staaten und die Politik des Westens* (Munich: Verlag C. H. Beck, 2001), pp. 65–6.

18 *Ibid.*, pp. 66, 76.

19 *Ibid.*, p. 76.

20 David Chandler, *Bosnia: Faking Democracy after Dayton*, 2nd edn (London and Sterling, VA: Pluto Press, 2000), p. 37.

21 *Ibid.*, p. 152.

22 *Ibid.*, p. 158.

23 *Ibid.*, pp. 162–3.

24 *Ibid.*, p. 194.

25 On page 14, they credit 'a centuries-old history of interethnic antagonism and bloodshed' with having 'played some role in Bosnia's postwar developments', though, of course, there is no reference in the book to anything earlier than 1974. On page 18, they allege that Croatia's HDZ (Hrratska Demokratska Zajednica, or Croatian Democratic Community) 'replaced the emblems of Yugoslavia with Croatian symbols last seen during Croatia's collaboration with Nazi Germany'; insofar as this seems to refer to the chequerboard coat-of-arms used through the socialist period as the symbol of Croatian statehood, this would be false. And, on page 22, they claim that the German government, in pressing for recognition of Slovenia and Croatia, argued that this 'would solve the problem'. Neither Kohl nor Genscher was so gullible as to believe that *all* the problems in the post-Yugoslav area would disappear the moment that recognition was conferred; their view, rather, was that diplomatic recognition of de facto states was the right thing to do, especially when the only alternative was to deliver them up to a neighbouring tyrant with an appetite for expansion.

26 Cousens and Cater, *Towards Peace in Bosnia*, pp. 64–5.

27 *Ibid.*, p. 81.

28 *Ibid.*, p. 140.

29 *Ibid.*, pp. 72–5.

30 *Ibid.*, p. 91.
31 *Ibid.*, p. 92.
32 *Ibid.*, p. 114.
33 *Ibid.*, p. 119.
34 *Ibid.*, p. 124.
35 *Ibid.*, p. 147.
36 *Ibid.*
37 Sumantra Bose, *Bosnia after Dayton: Nationalist Partition and International Intervention* (London: C. Hurst & Co., 2002), p. 274.
38 *Ibid.*, pp. 170, 173.
39 *Ibid.*, p. 174.
40 *Ibid.*, pp. 180–7.
41 *Ibid.*, pp. 44, 45.
42 *Ibid.*, p. 44.
43 *Ibid.*, p. 45.
44 *Ibid.*, p. 69.
45 *Ibid.*, p. 271.
46 *Ibid.*, p. 267.
47 *Ibid.*, p. 166.
48 Robert M. Hayden, *Blueprints for a House Divided: The Constitutional Logic of the Yugoslav Conflicts* (Ann Arbor, MI: University of Michigan Press, 1999), p. 50.
49 Bose, *Bosnia after Dayton*, p. 188.
50 *Ibid.*, p. 193.
51 *Ibid.*, p. 192.
52 *Ibid.*, p. 140.
53 *Ibid.*, p. 194.
54 *Ibid.*, p. 205.
55 *Ibid.*, p. 246.
56 Carl Bildt, *Peace Journey: The Struggle for Peace in Bosnia* (London: Weidenfeld & Nicolson, 1998), pp. 173–4.
57 *Ibid.*, p. 180.
58 *Ibid.*, p. 189.
59 Meier, *Jugoslawiens Erben*, pp. 65–6.
60 Bildt, *Peace Journey*, pp. 196–7.
61 *Ibid.*, p. 207.
62 *Ibid.*, p. 240.
63 *Ibid.*, p. 242.
64 *Ibid.*, p. 360.
65 *Ibid.*, p. xv.
66 *Ibid.*, p. 365.
67 *Ibid.*, p. 392.
68 Wolfgang Petritsch, *Bosnien und Herzegowina fünf Jahre nach Dayton: Hat der Friede eine Chance?* (Klagenfurt and Vienna: Wieser Verlag, 2001).
69 *Ibid.*, p. 92.
70 *Ibid.*, pp. 105–6.
71 Details *ibid.*, pp. 109–10.
72 *Ibid.*, p. 124.

73 *Ibid.*, p. 123.
74 *Ibid.*, p. 317.
75 *Ibid.*, pp. 127–8, 163–6.
76 'Dayton ist nicht das Neue Testament' (Wolfgang Petritsch in interview with Ivan Lovrenović), *Feral Tribune*, 22 April 2000, reprinted in Petritsch, *Bosnien und Herzegowina Fünf Jahre nach Dayton*, pp. 339–46.

REFERENCES

Bildt, Carl, *Peace Journey: The Struggle for Peace in Bosnia* (London: Weidenfeld & Nicolson, 1998), p. 423.
Bose, Sumantra, *Bosnia after Dayton: Nationalist Partition and International Intervention* (London: C. Hurst & Co., 2002), p. 295.
Chandler, David, *Bosnia: Faking Democracy after Dayton*, 2nd edn (London and Sterling, VA: Pluto Press, 2000), p. 254.
Cousens, Elizabeth M. and Charles K. Cater, *Towards Peace in Bosnia: Implementing the Dayton Accords* (Boulder, CO: Lynne Rienner, 2001), p. 189.
Kumar, Radha, *Divide and Fall? Bosnia in the Annals of Partition* (London and New York: Verso, 1997), p. 207.
Meier, Viktor, *Jugoslawiens Erben: Die neuen Staaten und die Politik des Westens* (Munich: Verlag C. H. Beck, 2001), p. 156. – chap. 5 ('Bosnien-Hercegovina: Auf dem Weg in eine unsichere Zukunft', pp. 62–78).
Petritsch, Wolfgang, *Bosnien und Herzegowina fünf Jahre nach Dayton: Hat der Friede eine Chance?* (Klagenfurt and Vienna: Wieser Verlag, 2001), p. 482.

9   Crisis in Kosovo/a (*with Angelo Georgakis*)

I

After decades of almost total neglect by Western scholars – Elez Biberaj and Peter Prifti figuring among the handful of Western scholars to write about tensions in Kosovo/a[1] during the 1970s and 1980s – Kosovo has recently become the focus of a continuing flood of books, presaged in 1982 by Jens Reuter's short monograph on the subject[2] and in 1993 by Julie Mertus and Vlatka Mihelić's research into human rights abuses for Helsinki Watch,[3] later augmented by a tome more contemporary in orientation, co-authored by Ivo Daalder and Michael O'Hanlon.[4] Of the thirteen books under review here, four – those edited by Jürgen Elsässer and Thomas Schmid, together with Stefan Troebst's succinct monograph and Joseph Marko's edited collection – focus largely on the crisis of 1997–9 and the international response. Three works under review – those by Julie Mertus, Noel Malcolm, and Miranda Vickers – discuss a longer period of history, with Mertus presenting local views of events over the past thirty years, Vickers surveying the past 400 years, and Malcolm reviewing the past millennium. But the purposes, methodologies, questions, and conclusions of these three works differ radically. Eric Gordy's book endeavours to set forth an argument that Milošević maintained his grip on power over a period of what proved to be thirteen years in all by systematically eliminating alternatives in politics, the media, and popular culture, while Judah examines Milošević's strategy for containing and suppressing Albanian insurrection in Kosovo. Also discussed in this chapter are ambitious collections assembled by Mary Buckley and Sally Cummings, Jens Reuter and Konrad Clewing, and Tony Weymouth and Stanley Henig. The Reuter/Clewing volume is the most comprehensive among this set in its coverage, while the Buckley/Cummings tome focuses on perceptions of the crisis, with the Weymouth/Stanley contribution probing international responses. Finally Alex Bellamy's monograph examines the question of the relationship of the Kosovo question to international law and international security.

The best in this set are Noel Malcolm's and Miranda Vickers's sweeping historical surveys of this long-neglected region, the collection of essays assembled by Jens Reuter and Konrad Clewing, and Julie Mertus's magisterial study of attitudes, perceptions, and myths among the Albanians and Serbs of Kosovo. Also extremely useful are the books by Bellamy, Gordy, Judah, Marko, Schmid, and Troebst, and the collections edited by Mary Buckley and Sally Cummings, and by Tony Weymouth and Stanley Henig. Jürgen Elsässer's collection contains some useful information but is flawed by twin tendencies to accept uncritically Belgrade's position on some of the issues at stake, and to dismiss out of hand the outrage felt by many in the West in connection with the plight of Kosovo's Albanians, as allegedly irrelevant to the launching of the NATO aerial campaign against the Federal Republic of Yugoslavia (FRY) on 24 March 1999.

II

Several of the works at hand seek to understand why Serbs and Albanians came to blows. For Mertus, the answer is to be sought in the differing 'truths' nurtured by the two communities. To tap into these 'truths', Mertus interviewed a large number of Kosovar Albanians and Serbs over a period of years, including Kosovar Serbs who had in the meantime moved out of Kosovo. Given that popular consciousness generally focuses on highly publicized events which assume symbolic value, Mertus structures her book accordingly, taking up issues such as the meaning of the 1981 Albanian riots in Kosovo and the 1985 'Martinović affair', in which a 56-year-old Serbian peasant named Djordje Martinović went to a local hospital with a bottle jammed into his anus, alleging that his predicament was the result of an attack by two Albanian men. Martinović subsequently withdrew that allegation, however, only to reaffirm it still later. In the meantime, the community leaders of Gnjilane had issued a statement describing Martinović's anal injuries as the 'accidental consequences of a self-induced [sexual] practice',[5] while newspapers in Belgrade hyperbolically associated the case of Martinović, as noted in chapter 6, with the Jasenovac concentration camp operated by the Ustaše during the Second World War.[6]

Especially instructive in Mertus's work are her explications of the transformative effects of the myths which sprang up around the events discussed by her interviewees and her demonstration that 'Serbs and Kosovo Albanians do not even know what each other wants'[7] – scarcely a sound basis for dialogue. In contrast to those who adhere to the baseless thesis of 'ancient hatreds', Mertus finds that Serb–Albanian tensions in Kosovo are 'the result of *recent* hatreds, fueled by *recent* propaganda campaigns'.[8]

Eric Gordy, in a work replete with citations to on-site interviews and quotations from Serbian 'turbo-folk' song texts, confutes conventional wisdom by arguing that, to the extent 'that the regime succeeded in producing . . . feelings of defeat, exhaustion, and hopelessness among its potential opponents, its continuation in power was relatively more secure'.[9] For Gordy, Milošević's underlying goal has never been a Greater Serbia but, one might say, a 'Greater Milošević'.[10] Hence, insofar as the war in Bosnia allowed the regime to portray its opponents as unpatriotic traitors, and thereby to marginalize them, to the extent that it provoked an exodus of the young, the urban, and the professional classes from the country, and to the extent that it induced a 'shift in economic power from the cities to the rural areas', the war was advantageous for Milošević and his cohorts, even if at the expense of the Serbian population more broadly.[11] Gordy completed the writing of his book before the tensions in Kosovo peaked in 1998–9, but his analysis suggests strongly that Milošević believed that he stood to gain from the escalation of tensions in the province, regardless of the eventual outcome, and most certainly regardless of any NATO undertaking on behalf of local Albanians.

Gordy captures, with considerable sophistication, the culture which Milošević sought to establish and reinforce, and shows how the culture of 'turbo-folk' buttressed the power of the Milošević family. The 1993 song, 'Mali knindža' ('Little Ninja from Knin') aptly illustrates the point:

> They can hate us
> or not love us
> but nobody
> can do anything to a Serb.
> This nation will live
> even after the Ustaše
> because God and the Serbs
> [are together;]
> the heavens are ours.
> They can hate us
> all our series of enemies
> but Serbs are the strongest,
> my grandfather told me.[12]

III

The volumes by Miranda Vickers and Noel Malcolm both appeared in 1998, and endeavour, in different ways, to offer a historical introduction to Kosovo. In *Between Serb and Albanian: A History of Kosovo*, Miranda

Vickers reconstructs the history of Kosovo from the earliest times, providing a coherent survey focusing on the period since the middle of the fourteenth century. Vickers begins her discussion with the prehistory of the region, when a group known as the Illyrians populated the rugged terrain of Kosovo. Vickers notes that Albanians claim the ancient Illyrian tribes as their ancestors, thereby establishing an Albanian presence in Kosovo predating that of the Serbs, whose ancestors first migrated into the region during the sixth century CE.[13]

Vickers provides a detailed overview of the important features of the medieval Serb empire, pointing out that, during the late twelfth century, many Albanians converted to the Orthodox faith. During the rule of Tsar Stefan Dušan (1331–55), when the medieval Serb empire reached its greatest extent, it became official state policy to promote the conversion of the Albanians to Orthodoxy. Vickers discusses the Battle of Kosovo (1389), noting that Serbs and Albanians fought side by side against the common Ottoman enemy. She argues that there was no true victor in the battle, noting that both the Ottoman leader, Sultan Murad, and the Serbian leader, Tsar Lazar, were killed. But, on the other hand, the battle signalled the beginning of the decline of the once-mighty Serbian kingdom even while the Ottomans regrouped and continued their advance in the Balkans. With the Ottoman conquest of Serbia in 1459 and during the subsequent four centuries of Ottoman rule, religion became the most important dividing line between Serbs and Albanians (according to Vickers), as many Albanians eventually converted to Islam, the official faith of the Ottoman Empire.[14] This increased their power and influence relative to that of the Serbs, most of whom remained Orthodox.

Vickers's main concern is with the years since 1610; 85 per cent of the book is devoted to the following four centuries, with separate chapters on the great migrations of the late seventeenth century, the period of Ottoman decline after 1878, the Balkan Wars, the First World War, and the Serbian colonization programme of the interwar period. We found Vickers's account of the Second World War to be particularly interesting. As she notes, during the war, the Italian occupation forces encouraged 72,000 Albanians to settle in Kosovo,[15] but, quite apart from the separatist aspirations of the Albanian nationalist Balli Kombëtar, wartime disagreements between Albanian and Yugoslav communists concerning the postwar future of Kosovo sowed the seeds of further distrust in the years after 1945. The socialist Yugoslav federation created at the end of that war tried to muffle ethnic particularisms but the substitute it offered – 'Yugoslav socialist patriotism' – never erased local ethnic attachments. Moreover, Vickers argues, by the 1960s and 1970s, other factors had coalesced to create controversies concerning Kosovo. The constitutional revision of 1974 granted autonomy to Kosovo, which at the time was more than 80 per cent Albanian in composition. Many Serb politicians never accepted the legal and constitutional changes brought about between 1968 and 1974, and, following the death of Tito in 1980, there was an increase in tensions between Serbs and Albanians living in Kosovo. Vickers extends her interpretation into the early 1990s, with three perspicacious chapters outlining the tumescence of reactive Serbian nationalism. The final chapter covers the recent history of the troubled province, in which Vickers identifies a state of apartheid imposed by the Serb authorities. Grounding itself primarily, though by no means exclusively, on secondary sources in several languages, *Between Serb and Albanian* is a valuable general history of Kosovo, rivalling that by Noel Malcolm.

Noel Malcolm's *Kosovo: A Short History* covers much of the same historical terrain as Vickers, but with different emphases (lengthy discussions of ancient and medieval times, briefer treatment of the Tito era) and with clearer sympathies than Vickers for the Albanian side. Malcolm's research is grounded primarily in archival research; as a result of his knowledge of at least twenty languages and his close attention to many original early sources, Malcolm is able to offer a more extensive account of the history of Kosovo before 1912 than Vickers does; on the other hand, Malcolm's discussion of Kosovo in the Tito era is surprisingly brief, while his discussion of the post-Tito era is not as extensive as Vickers's. On a number of important matters, Malcolm reveals that standard Serbian accounts, such as that concerning the Serb exodus of 1690, are at variance with the archival record and stand in need of correction. As for the famous battle of 1389, Malcolm likewise points to the well-known fact that Albanians and Serbs fought alongside each other against the invading Ottoman forces, and discusses daily life in the first few centuries of Ottoman rule.

Responding to controversies in Balkan scholarship, Malcolm documents that both Serbs and Albanians resisted the Ottomans during the Austro-Turkish war.[16] Malcolm emphasizes, further, migratory movements out of and into Kosovo during the eighteenth and nineteenth centuries, challenging the validity of the Arnautas thesis advocated by some Serbian scholars, which holds that the Serbs were in the majority in Kosovo throughout the nineteenth century, an argument founded, in part, on the specious supposition that a substantial portion of the Albanian-speakers living in Kosovo at the time were Albanianized Serbs, hence Serbs.

The last section of the book brings the reader up to the late 1990s. Malcolm confirms the work of other scholars who have argued that the human rights of Albanians in Kosovo were being violated beginning already in the 1920s, citing plans in the interwar kingdom to expel large numbers of Kosovar Albanians to Turkey.[17] Malcolm's account of the Tito era reflects a recognition of Tito's efforts to correct the ethnic imbalance in the power structure in Kosovo (at least after 1966). Malcolm's voluminous tome, researched in Albanian-, French-, German-, Italian-, Latin-, Serbo-Croatian-, Turkish-, and, of course, English-language sources, as well as other materials, some of these sources dating from 1500s or 1600s, represents a monumental effort and stands in a category by itself. This nearly 500-page long 'short' history will undoubtedly remain a standard in the field for the foreseeable future.

Even a cursory examination of the table of contents reveals dramatic differences in emphasis between the two books. Vickers's account runs for 313 pages of text; the mid-point in the text finds one in the midst of a discussion of 1956. Malcolm's book includes 356 pages of text, with the year 1772 as the mid-point in the text. Miranda Vickers is clearly more interested in contemporary history, and devotes just 11 pages to ancient and medieval Kosovo and some 50 pages to Ottoman Kosovo up to 1908; by contrast, she devotes 50 pages to the Tito era and 120 pages to the years 1980–97. Noel Malcolm's heart apparently lies in medieval and Ottoman Kosovo: he devotes 71 pages to ancient and medieval Kosovo and fully 146 pages to Ottoman Kosovo up to 1908; he reserves only 20 pages for discussing the Tito era, and just 23 pages for the years 1980–97. This means that, in practical terms, a reader more interested in the earlier history should turn to Malcolm's account, which dwells lovingly on these centuries, while a reader with an interest in the more contemporary era would do better to turn to Vickers's account, which provides a more extensive narrative of recent decades.

A textual analysis of these two books also reveals some interesting differences and commonalities, and helps to illustrate the respective strengths of the two books. Looking at the Battle of Kosovo (1389), for example, both authors agree that the battle assumed mythic importance, especially in the course of the nineteenth and twentieth centuries, and both agree that the Battle at the River Marica (1371) was of greater strategic importance than the battle of 1389 for the subsequent Ottoman conquest of the Balkans, including Serbia. But where Vickers says that the Battle of Kosovo involved about 30,000 troops on both sides, Malcolm says that Murat alone probably had a force of 27,000–30,000 troops, facing a force of 15,000–20,000 troops commanded by Lazar, adding up to a combined engagement of 42,000–50,000 troops.[18] They also differ concerning who killed the sultan on the day of the battle. Vickers follows conventional accounts in attributing the assassination to a Serb noble named Miloš Kobilić, whereas Noel Malcolm cites a report submitted by a group of Florentine senators in October 1389, in which they said that the sultan had been killed by a group of twelve Serbian lords. Malcolm discusses the legend about Kobilić but concludes that it is the product of literary invention.[19] The difference in their accounts of the battle is rooted in a different use of sources: Vickers relies, for her account, on secondary sources alone, albeit respectable sources, while Malcolm takes in not only secondary sources but also narratives written in earlier centuries, undertaking a systematic comparison of their accounts.

There are also differences in Vickers's and Malcolm's versions of the great migration of 1690, when a certain number of Serbs, led by Arsenije III Črnojević, left Kosovo and headed to Habsburg-ruled Hungary, settling in the area known today as Vojvodina. Vickers adheres to the traditional, but erroneous, account and claims that 37,000 Serbian families came to Hungary at that time, accepting an offer of asylum from Emperor Leopold I; Malcolm, noting that 'it has often been claimed that 37,000 families joined Arsenije on this epic march', estimates that in fact only about 30,000 *people* made the trek to Habsburg-ruled Hungary. Moreover, while some Serb historians cite a document issued by the emperor on 6 April 1690 as an 'invitation' to come to Hungary, Malcolm, referring to the original Latin text, shows that the letter urged the Serbs to rise up against the Ottomans, and specifically advised them '*not* to desert' their ancestral lands – rather the opposite of an invitation.[20]

There are also small differences between their respective accounts of the League of Prizren, which was founded on 10 June 1878 by a group of more than 300 Albanian delegates, consisting, as Vickers reports, pre-dominantly of conservative Muslim landowners, for the purpose of preventing Albanian-inhabited lands from being transferred to Serbian and Montenegrin rule. Vickers, whose primary interest lies in the more contemporary history of Kosovo, actually says rather little about the League, and nothing about any Christian participation, noting that 'Sultan Hamid hoped to use the League to instill a form of pan-Islamic ideology as a counterbalance to the growing national discontent' in his empire.[21] Malcolm, by contrast, devotes seven times as much space to discussing the League, pointing out, among other things, that there were five Christian delegates in attendance and that, in the wake of the famous meeting in June 1878, there was a serious contest, lasting for a few months, between Muslim traditionalists, who pushed through decisions which ignored social reform, education, and autonomy for Kosovo, and more reform-oriented people who put a stress on all these points.[22]

Where the interwar years and the Second World War are concerned, the two accounts are rather evenly matched. Both authors note that the incorporation of Kosovo into the Kingdom of Serbs, Croats, and Slovenes was fiercely resisted by many Albanians, some of whom joined the Kaçak movement, and both authors provide details of the regime-sponsored colonization of Kosovo by Serbs, as well as of the regime's efforts to force Albanians to emigrate to Turkey. In the discussion of the Second World War, Malcolm probably offers greater detail concerning Albanian collaboration, noting, for example, the Blackshirt battalion established in Prizren, while Vickers seems more interested in the activities and discussions among Tito's Partisans where Kosovo is concerned. Both authors discuss the Mukje and Bujan conferences.

Malcolm's chapter on Tito-era Kosovo covers the early discussion concerning the constitutional status of Kosovo, the house searches for weapons in the early 1950s together with the Prizren trial involving an alleged network of pro-Albanian spies and agents, the riots of 1968 and 1981, the provisions of the 1974 constitution, Kosovo's relative economic stagnation in the Tito era, and the question of Albanian birthrates. Malcolm notes, thus, that the 1974 constitution extended to Kosovo and Vojvodina, Serbia's two provinces, the right to issue their own constitutions, rather than being governed under statutes issued by the Serbian Assembly, and points out, in another context, that Serbs from Kosovo were not the only group among Yugoslavia's peoples engaging in internal migration in the late Tito era, and provides examples.[23] While acknowledging Kosovar Albanians' recent tendency to look back on the Tito era as a better time, Malcolm underlines that 'it was Tito's legacy of a stultified political system and a collapsing economy' which created the context in which Slobodan Milošević could make his nationalist bid for power.[24] He closes his chapter on the Tito era by pointing out that one of the reasons why the birthrate was higher in Kosovo than in inner Serbia – a point which troubled nationalist-oriented Serbs – was that, for every 100 live births in Serbia, Serbian women had 214 abortions while, among Albanian women of Kosovo, there were only 20 abortions for every 100 births.[25]

Vickers covers much the same terrain as Malcolm, where Tito-era Kosovo is concerned, but offers more detail on the impact of the Tito–Stalin rift on Kosovo, on the 1963 and 1974 constitutions, and on the 'Turkification' programme. The last mentioned involved a programme under which the regime opened schools teaching in Turkish (in 1951) and pressed Albanians to declare themselves Turks.[26] She points out further that between 36,000 and 47,000 Albanians of Kosovo fell victim to mass executions during the years 1944–6, and goes into some depth regarding the cultural and educational societies, theatres, and musical groups set up in early postwar Kosovo, even mentioning a marionette theatre offering performances in Serbo-Croatian and Albanian.[27] Vickers ends her account of the Tito era with a short account of Tito's fifth and final official visit to Kosovo in October 1979 (just seven months before his death) and by noting that by that time 'the national culture of the Albanians was flourishing in Kosovo'.[28]

As already noted, Vickers is strongest where the more recent decades are concerned and her treatment of the post-Tito years is more extensive than Malcolm's account. What she adds includes greater detail concerning the declaration of Kosovar independence in October 1991 as well as the activities in Kosovo of Ražnatović and Vojislav Šešelj. She devotes some attention to the impact of the collapse of communism in Albania and shows that, as a result of its approach to security in Kosovo, Belgrade spent an estimated $6 billion to maintain 'peace' in Kosovo between 1989 and 1992; in other words, the politics of repression was not only injurious to human rights but also financially costly. But as the situation deteriorated, as Vickers shows, there were increasing challenges to the leadership of Ibrahim Rugova, a scholar turned politician, among Kosovar Albanians, and, by 1996, there were some fifteen Albanian political parties active in Kosovo.[29]

Noel Malcolm's treatment of the post-Tito years in Kosovo is more concise. Beginning with the upheaval of spring 1981, he covers also the expulsion of Mahmud Bakalli from the communist leadership in Kosovo, controversies about the outmigration of Serbs and Montenegrins from Kosovo, controversies about alleged rapes, and the notorious 'Martinović affair' (noted above). His discussion of Milošević's drive to remove Azem Vllasi and Kaqusha Jashari from the provincial party leadership and the response of the miners of the Trepça (Trepča) mine leads directly to a vivid account of how the provincial assembly of Kosovo met, on 23 March 1989, with tanks and armoured cars parked in front of the building, to vote away its prerogatives. Malcolm mentions too that, according to some accounts, functionaries from Serbia took part in the vote, even though they were not authorized to do so.[30] A year later, as Malcolm notes, the Serbian Assembly passed a 'Programme for the Realization of Peace and Prosperity in Kosovo', which, among other things, provided for investments in Serb-majority areas and for the construction of new houses for Serbs who were willing to move (or return) to Kosovo, introduced family planning for Albanians, and annulled recent sales of property to Albanians by Serbs who had left the province.[31] The policies introduced in the wake of these measures included the administrative dismissal of Albanian employees (especially those in positions of responsibility), the expulsion of Albanians from state-provided flats, the sacking of some 6,000 school teachers, arbitrary arrest, and police violence. One of the ironies in all of this came with the eventual election of the Serbian bank-robber turned paramilitary leader, Željko Ražnatović 'Arkan', to represent a constituency in Kosovo – a development made possible by an Albanian boycott of all elections.

Malcolm ends his magnificently researched book with a warning:

According to the mythic history of the Serbs, what happened in Kosovo in 1912 was an act of liberation which rescued an oppressed people from a kind of alien, colonial rule. There is an element of truth in this, but it is very much less than the whole truth. Serbs will never understand the nature of the Kosovo question unless they recognize first that the territory conquered in 1912 already had a majority non-Serb population, and secondly that the experience of alien, colonial rule is precisely what Serbian policy inflicted on that majority population during most of the next eighty-five years.[32]

IV

Tim Judah's book nicely complements the aforementioned volumes by Malcolm, Mertus, and Vickers, offering a work more geared to the general reader and more focused on the present. Judah begins his fast-paced account by suggesting that 'much of the Kosovo conflict can be related to the fact that too many Serbs have never been willing or able to rid themselves of the idea that the Albanians, with whom they shared a state for the best part of a century, were not to be treated as equals'.[33] But the problems were never merely so nebulous or abstract, as Judah makes clear both in his discussion of Serb–Albanian relations 1918–87 and, more particularly, in his retelling of the repressive policies perpetrated by the Milošević regime. By its policies of discrimination and repression, the Milošević regime managed to destroy local traditions of coexistence, mutual acceptance, and harmony between Serbs and Albanians of Kosovo,[34] so that, by the mid-1990s, if not earlier, 'it was absolutely obvious to all outside observers and Kosovar analysts like Shkëlzen Maliqi that an explosion was inevitable; but when, nobody knew'.[35]

Judah's *Kosovo*, which reflects extensive on-site interviews and experience as well as reading in Serbo-Croat, French, and English materials, does not duplicate previous work by Noel Malcolm and Julie Mertus; on the contrary, it complements their earlier books and will have an appeal, in the first place, to those whose primary interest lies in answering the question of what led up to NATO's 1999 campaign.

Then there are the three books by German scholars dealing with the Kosovo crisis as such. The first published was that by Stefan Troebst, which documents the intensification of ethnic tensions between 1992 and 1998. Published months before the NATO bombing campaign of Yugoslavia, this work provides an excellent discussion of the international community's response to the growing crisis in Kosovo from 1992 onwards. Like other scholars, Troebst argues that the current problems in Kosovo date back to the early 1980s. During the winter of 1997/8, Kosovo became one of the most violence-prone crisis zones in Europe. Troebst seeks to discover how the crisis over Kosovo has worsened since the Dayton Accords of late 1995, which officially ended the war in Bosnia. The voice of the Kosovo Albanians was not heard at these peace talks, and the united front of Albanian political forces of Kosovo split up shortly afterwards. Until Dayton, the Albanian position was relatively unified within Kosovo, but, after the disappointment at Dayton, the consensus on nonviolence broke down. The Albanian shadow government headed by Ibrahim Rugova (who had been elected president of the 'Republic of Kosova' in 1992) no longer had exclusive rights over the articulation and defence of Kosovar Albanian national interests.

Troebst then reviews a number of alternatives which have been proposed since 1995 by the Serb and Albanian leaderships in order to achieve a lasting settlement of the issue of Kosovo. These alternatives include allowing Kosovo a kind of autonomy similar to that granted by Tito's 1974 constitution, outright independence for Kosovo, a new Yugoslav (con)federation with expanded jurisdiction for Montenegro and Kosovo, partition of Kosovo along ethnic lines, the devolution of power to local communities but under the framework of a unified, centralized system, and (in a solution favoured by the late Željko Ražnatović) the expulsion of the province's entire Albanian population. Tragically, the final scenario began to unfold in the course of 1998 and early 1999. In this connection, Troebst argues that Macedonia and Albania had been preparing for the potential influx of hundreds of thousands of Kosovar Albanian refugees for several years already.[36] Many people in the region had also begun to consider a continuation of the tense status quo as yet another alternative, especially given the repeated failure of negotiations between the Serb and Albanian sides.

Troebst also details the internationalization of the Kosovo crisis. For much of the 1990s, the United Nations, the Organization for Security and Cooperation in Europe (OSCE), NATO, and other contact groups monitored the situation in Kosovo closely. The general consensus in the international community was to push for greater autonomy for Kosovo, without changing any international borders, and to avoid another ethnic war in the Balkans. Troebst points out that, in addition to large international organizations, numerous nongovernmental organizations also became involved in the region, some of them focusing on human rights, others offering suggestions aimed at improving education, health care, and the media in the troubled region. With its exhaustive discussion of the sundry organizations to have become involved in the Kosovo crisis, Troebst's relatively brief analysis clarifies the international context in which the problems unfolded.

Whereas Troebst's volume was published on the eve of NATO's aerial campaign, the volumes edited by Elsässer and Schmid respectively were conceptualized only *after* the outbreak of hostilities, written in great haste, and rushed into print with a speed which we cannot recall having seen matched by scholarly publishers in the United States. But then the volume by Elsässer, at least, may not in fact be addressed to a scholarly audience. Even allowing for the differences of opinion expressed by the contributors to each of these volumes, we are nonetheless far more impressed by the differences between the two volumes than by such themes as they may share.

Nie wieder Krieg ohne uns (Never again war without us) is unabashedly critical of the Bonn government, NATO, the United States, and the entire Western undertaking from the Holbrooke–Milošević accord of October 1998 through the failed Rambouillet peace 'talks' of early 1999 to the aerial campaign itself. Generally 'left-isolationist' in inspiration, the volume repeats some of the standard anti-German diatribes (e.g., that the Federal Republic began to promote Slovenian and Croatian separatism already in the 1970s, that the German government of Gerhard Schröder and Joschka Fischer was positively eager to make war on Serbia in early 1999, and that alleged German chauvinism was somehow relevant to the background to NATO's intervention)[37] and repeatedly cites Belgrade's official policy line as if it might safely be taken at face value.[38]

The issue of sovereignty emerges in the course of the book and is linked by Sibylle Tönnies, in a roundtable discussion appended at the end of the book, with the notion of a just war – a notion which Tönnies considers to have been obsolete ever since the 1648 Treaty of Westphalia.[39] Most of the contributors seem to agree with Tönnies that the international community has no grounds in international law to judge any 'sovereign' state, let alone intervene in its internal affairs. Taking up this theme, the editor denigrates the notion that Milošević might usefully be considered the 'Hitler of the Balkans' and contends, instead, that, on the strength of his combination of nationalist demagoguery and alleged social democratic proclivities, Milošević might, more accurately, be seen as the 'Schröder of the Balkans', concluding that Milošević, unlike Hitler, has not conducted an aggressive war against a 'sovereign' state.[40] One is, in this connection, entitled to inquire as to the mechanisms whereby sovereignty is thought to be established. Certainly, if the existence of a legally elected government claiming independence, recognition of that claim by key members of the international community, and admission to the UN suffice to establish the sovereignty of a state,[41] then Bosnian sovereignty was established at the time of the Serbian assault, in which Yugoslav Army units took part.

There is another problem with the claim that Milošević never attacked a sovereign state. As of 1991, the socialist government of Yugoslavia was rapidly disintegrating and Izetbegović, Tudjman, Gligorov, and even, via certain legalistic argumentation, Kučan could all claim with as much 'right' as Milošević (i.e., with none at all) to be president of the 'core' republic from which the others were separating. After all, none of the aforementioned was a member of the collective presidency, none of them was the prime minister, and the Yugoslav prime minister in 1991, Ante Marković, was, for all that, a Croat, not a Serb. Therefore, to the extent that Elsässer is construing Milošević as the legitimate heir to the presidency of the Socialist Federated Republic of Yugoslavia (SFRY), he is skating in the clouds.

V

That brings us to Thomas Schmid's exceptionally fine collection of essays, assembled, amazingly, within a matter of weeks. In his commendable desire to include several alternative viewpoints, Schmid has included a rather quirky piece by Dragan Velikić, which alleges that the only reason that NATO undertook to defend the Albanians of Kosovo as opposed to the Kurds of (NATO-ally) Turkey is the Western community's alleged concern with 'capital circulation'.[42] Albanian contributor Shkëlzen Maliqi, on the other hand, argues that NATO's intervention was *legitimate* under international law,[43] while yet another contributor, Dieter Lutz, says that the NATO campaign was not justified under international law. Lutz cites a number of reasons in support of his conclusion, including (1) that such enforcement should lie under the authority of the UN, (2) that an aerial campaign is not the appropriate means to try to avoid a humanitarian catastrophe, and (3) that 'people' may not be bombed in the name of human rights.[44] Most of the chapters in Schmid's collection deal with Kosovo in the years 1996–9, although Fabian Schmidt contributes a fine overview of some of Kosovo's turbulent history (including a very useful summary of activities in the province during the Second World War), while Stefan Troebst offers some thoughts concerning neighbouring Macedonia's Albanian question.

The orientation of this book is firmly 'universalist' and stands in sharp contrast to the volume assembled by Jürgen Elsässer. Whereas Elsässer and his collaborators expressed deep suspicions of the West's motives and profound opposition to the NATO aerial campaign of spring 1999, Schmid and his collaborators tend, on the whole, to give the West the benefit of the doubt as to motives. But while contributor Richard Herzinger criticizes the West only for taking so long to realize the danger presented by Milošević's oppressive tyranny and endorses the NATO campaign as a legitimate 'humanitarian intervention' inspired by liberal universalism,[45] Cora Stephan argues that the moral incentive is dangerous and expresses concerns that interventions inspired by the desire to defend human rights could fuel war and lead to an escalation of regional hostilities.[46] Of particular interest in this volume are the chapters by editor Thomas Schmid,[47] Matthias Rüb,[48] and Andreas Zumach,[49] which collectively provide a useful and balanced overview of the escalation of Serb–Albanian tensions beginning in 1996 and the course of events in both military and diplomatic spheres during 1998–9, noting especially the lack of any response on the part of the Serbian opposition to the Milošević regime's oppression of the country's Albanian minority.

Alex Bellamy's *Kosovo and International Society* is closer to Schmid's volume than to Elsässer's. Like the contributors to Schmid's volume, Bellamy argues that NATO's military intervention against the FRY in 1999 was motivated by outrage at atrocities being perpetrated against Kosovar Albanians by Belgrade's forces and by a conviction that the instability in Kosovo threatened regional peace and security. And, like the contributors to Schmid's volume, Bellamy emphasizes that the intervention came only after extensive diplomatic efforts and after a wide-ranging debate in Western capitals. Moreover, whereas Elsässer, in another volume (see chapter 10), calls into question whether 'Operation Horseshoe', as the Serbian plan to expel Albanians from Kosovo was known, actually existed, Bellamy argues forcefully that Operation Horseshoe was real, noting, among other things, that the plan 'provides a good description of what actually happened in Kosovo during and immediately after the Paris [Rambouillet] negotiations'.[50]

Bellamy's goal in the volume is three-fold. First, he sought to overturn various myths which he believes have sprung up concerning Western

intervention in Kosovo; among these myths are the notions that 'the
Račak massacre was faked, the Kosovo Verification Mission was
designed to fail as were the Rambouillet negotiations, the Chinese Embassy in Belgrade was bombed deliberately, and the ethnic cleansing and
mass murder which were witnessed in 1999 were at least provoked, if not
caused, by NATO'.[51] A second purpose for Bellamy was to argue that it
was the growth of shared values in the international community and the
emergence 'of a mature security community in Western Europe that on
the one hand allowed NATO to justify its actions without having explicit
UN Security Council [endorsement] but on the other ruled out the
possibility of its members using force unilaterally'.[52] And, third, Bellamy
aspired to provide a detailed account of Western policy debates leading
up to the intervention and of the intervention and its aftermath. Based in
part on interviews with principals and researched in Serbian-/Croatian-,
Albanian-, French-, German-, Italian-, and English-language materials,
Bellamy's volume will prove useful to anyone wishing to understand why
NATO went to war in 1999.

Joseph Marko's recent edited volume illuminates many dimensions of
this troubled region. Marko applies the analogy of the Gordian knot to
the problems of Kosovo, producing a volume rich in political and legal
analyses of issues such as human rights violations, sovereignty, and
questions of self-determination. The introduction by Marko himself
reviews the development of a legitimate state consciousness among the
people of Kosovo since the end of the Balkan Wars in 1913, noting the
Albanians' unrelenting aspiration for self-determination, whether
through outright secession and annexation to Albania, or, in a comprom-
ised form of self-determination, through republic status within the
SFRY.

A collaborative chapter by Kumer, Polzer-Srienz, and Polzer[53] treats
various views concerning claims about the historic rights of the Serbs
and democratic rights of the Albanians, summarizing the views of the
Serbian Orthodox Church, the Serbian political opposition, and
the Albanians of Kosovo. The authors conclude that there is increasingly
a willingness on the Serbian side to consider new approaches to resolve
the crisis in Kosovo, provided that the province remains juridically part
of Serbia; this may be a case of too little, too late, however.

Sabina Dujak analyses the political and legal views of the Serb leadership of the Federal Republic of Yugoslavia, concluding that the Serbian
political elite blamed the local Albanian leaders for the problems in the
province.[54] A brief essay by Elmar Pichl[55] provides insight into how
complicated the Albanian question in Macedonia is. Further chapters by
Stefan Böckler,[56] Giovanni Poggeschi,[57] and Stephanie Risse-Lobis[58]

argue that the cases of Trentino/South Tyrol, Catalonia, and the Basque region in Spain, as well as Tatarstan in Russia could provide models for potential solutions to the problems in Kosovo. The final section of Marko's volume looks at humanitarian aspects of the crisis, closing with a reappraisal of recent developments by the editor himself. Marko notes that the reactive nature of the crisis management employed by the Western powers failed to avert a spiralling escalation of the problems in the province,[59] and closes with an indictment of Western approaches to the Kosovo problem.

The NATO intervention has also inspired the publication of a number of edited collections, among which three may be highlighted here. Jens Reuter and Konrad Clewing's *Der Kosovo Konflikt* is probably the most comprehensive collection dealing with the background to the Kosovo crisis and its unfolding.[60] Packed into its 568 pages are contributions dealing with the history and culture of Kosovo, the national ambitions of Serbs and Albanians, the responses of the neighbouring Balkan countries, and separate chapters on the responses of the United Nations, the United States, Russia, Germany, Great Britain, Italy, Romania, the EU, the OSCE, and NATO. Other topics included among the twenty-nine chapters comprising the book are the history of the Kosovo Liberation Army, the history of human rights abuses during the years 1989–9, an analysis of humanitarian intervention, and issues related to postwar reconstruction in Kosovo. Contributors include some of the leading German specialists in southeastern Europe as well as some contributors from other countries.

Tony Weymouth and Stanley Henig's *The Kosovo Crisis* combines chapters of a general nature ('Why War, Why NATO?', 'Kosovo: A Fuse for the Lighting') with chapters assessing policy debates in Germany and the United States, chapters on more general policy responses in Britain, Italy, France, Russia, the UN, and the EU, and chapters assessing the role of the media, the strategic and legal aspects of the NATO strike, and Serbian perspectives and Western 'counter-perspectives'.[61] The book was designed, as coeditor Weymouth notes in his introduction, to address the question as to just why did NATO go to war over Kosovo in 1999, with Henig arguing that, while in formal terms NATO's actions might be represented as 'illegal', the war itself contributed to an evolution of thinking about human rights under international law.[62]

And, finally, Mary Buckley and Sally N. Cummings's *Kosovo: Perceptions of War* complements the Weymouth/Henig volume nicely, by focusing on the perceptions of the leading actors.[63] The longest treatments are those dealing with American, Russian, and East-Central European perceptions. Shorter chapters deal with perceptions in Serbia, the other

Yugoslav republics, Britain, France, Germany, Italy, the Commonwealth of Independent States, China, and the Middle East, as well as
the perceptions of the Kosovar refugees. The volume also includes a
chapter on European security after the NATO intervention in Kosovo,
a chapter on geopolitics, and a discussion of the concept of humanitarian
intervention. As the editors note in their introduction, it was their
assumption, in launching the book, that 'both elite and non-elite
perceptions matter because leaders and parliaments, albeit to varying
degrees, take public opinion into account and react to it'.[64] These books
provide useful material for anyone wishing to research the history and
politics of Kosovo.

These works, which appeared within a five-year period, are a reminder
that scholarship still tends, all too often, to respond to crisis, rather than
to maintain a constant level of interest. We are reminded of the fact that,
some two decades ago, when the Soviet Union invaded Afghanistan,
there were few scholarly works dealing with that landlocked country.
Within a matter of a few years, a flood of books on Afghanistan had
appeared, but then, after the Soviets withdrew from that country, Western scholarly interest dried up once again. We suspect that the same fate
will befall Kosovo, as a subject of research. But perhaps we may be
entitled to hope that, even if work on Kosovo may, at such point as the
problems are either 'solved' or removed from the Western policy agenda,
slow to a trickle, some of the works discussed in this review essay may
continue to inform historical works on Balkan topics generally and
inspire future scholarly endeavours on Serbia and Kosovo in particular.

NOTES

1 Kosovo is the Serbian spelling, Kosova the Albanian.
2 Jens Reuter, *Die Albaner in Jugoslawien* (Munich: R. Oldenbourg Verlag,
   1982).
3 Julie Mertus and Vlatka Mihelić, *Open Wounds: Human Rights Abuses in
   Kosovo* (New York: Human Rights Watch/Helsinki, March 1993).
4 Ivo H. Daalder and Michael E. O'Hanlon, *Winning Ugly: NATO's War to
   Save Kosovo* (Washington, DC: Brookings Institution Press, 2000).
5 Quoted in Julie A. Mertus, *Kosovo: How Myths and Truths Started a War*
   (Berkeley and Los Angeles: University of California Press), p. 101.
6 *Ibid.*, p. 110.
7 *Ibid.*, p. 249.
8 *Ibid.*, p. 4, our emphases.
9 Eric D. Gordy, *The Culture of Power in Serbia: Nationalism and the Destruction
   of Alternatives* (University Park, PA: Pennsylvania State University Press,
   1999), p. 7.

10 Our expression, not Gordy's.

11 Gordy, *The Culture of Power*, p. 24. See also p. 59.

12 Quoted *ibid.*, p. 132.

13 Miranda Vickers, *Between Serb and Albanian: A History of Kosovo* (New York: Columbia University Press, 1998), pp. 4–5.

14 *Ibid.*, p. 25. Regarding the conversion of Catholic Albanians to Islam in the course of the seventeenth century, see Stavro Skendi, 'Religion in Albania during the Ottoman Rule', *Südost-Forschungen* (Munich), 15 (1956), pp. 316–17; and Georg Stadtmüller, 'Die Islamisierung bei den Albanern', *Jahrbücher für Geschichte Osteuropas*, 3, 4 (1955), p. 406. Regarding the conversion of Orthodox Albanians to Islam at the end of the eighteenth century, see Peter Bartl, *Die albanischen Muslime zur Zeit der nationalen Unabhängigkeitsbewegung (1878–1912)* (Wiesbaden: Otto Harrassowitz, 1968), p. 25.

15 Vickers, *Between Serb and Albanian*, p. 123.

16 Malcolm, *Kosovo: A Short History* (London and New York: Macmillan and New York University Press, 1998), pp. 140–1.

17 *Ibid.*, pp. 284–5.

18 Vickers, *Between Serb and Albanian*, p. 13; and Malcolm, *Kosovo: A Short History*, p. 64.

19 Vickers, *Between Serb and Albanian*, p. 15; and Malcolm, *Kosovo: A Short History*, pp. 69, 72–4.

20 Vickers, *Between Serb and Albanian*, p. 27; and Malcolm, *Kosovo: A Short History*, pp. 159, 161.

21 Vickers, *Between Serb and Albanian*, p. 44.

22 Malcolm, *Kosovo: A Short History*, pp. 221–2.

23 *Ibid.*, pp. 327, 330.

24 *Ibid.*, p. 314.

25 *Ibid.*, p. 333.

26 Vickers, *Between Serb and Albanian*, p. 149.

27 *Ibid.*, pp. 148, 153.

28 *Ibid.*, p. 193.

29 *Ibid.*, p. 300.

30 Malcolm, *Kosovo: A Short History*, p. 344.

31 *Ibid.*, p. 346.

32 *Ibid.*, p. 356.

33 Tim Judah, *Kosovo: War and Revenge* (New Haven, CT: Yale University Press, 2000), p. 16.

34 Documented in Ger Duijzings, *Religion and the Politics of Identity in Kosovo* (London: C. Hurst & Co., 2000).

35 Judah, *Kosovo*, p. 119.

36 Stefan Troebst, *Conflict in Kosovo: Failure of Prevention? An Analytical Documentation, 1992–1998*, ECMI Working Paper No. 1 (Flensburg: European Centre for Minority Issues, 1998), p. 17.

37 Jürgen Elsässer, 'Last Exit Jerusalem: Wenn Deutsche Juden Menschenrechte lehren', in Jürgen Elsässer (ed.), *Nie wieder Krieg ohne uns: Das Kosovo und die neue deutsche Geopolitik* (Hamburg: Konkret, 1999), pp. 130–5.

38 See, *in various chapters*, for example, *ibid.*, pp. 52, 58, 85, 123, 155, and 159.

39 Sibylle Tönnies, 'Wollt ihr den totalen Friedeneinsatz?', in Elsässer, *Nie wieder Krieg*, p. 159.

40 Jürgen Elsässer, 'Schafft zwei, viele Kosovo: Der Aufstand der Stämmer gegen die Nationen', in Elsässer, *Nie wieder Krieg*, p. 123.

41 On these points, see Francis A. Boyle, *The Bosnian People Charge Genocide: Proceedings at the International Court of Justice Concerning Bosnia v. Serbia on the Prevention and Punishment of the Crime of Genocide* (Amherst, MA: Aletheia Press, 1996).

42 Dragan Velikić, 'Eine Erfindung names Slobodan Milošević oder Die Archäologie einer Niederlage', in Thomas Schmid (ed.), *Krieg im Kosovo* (Reinbek bei Hamburg: Rowohlt Taschenbuch Verlag, 1999), p. 46.

43 Shkëlzen Maliqi, 'Ein Gleichgewicht der Schwachen. Nach dem Krieg: Das Kosovo braucht Schutz und Hilfe', in Schmid, *Krieg im Kosovo*, p. 172.

44 Dieter S. Lutz, 'Das Faustrecht der Nato: Politische und rechtliche Aspekte der gegenwärtigen Entwicklung der westlichen Staaten', in Schmid, *Krieg im Kosovo*, p. 236.

45 Richard Herzinger, '"Unheiliger Wahnsinn/Hocket über grimmigen Waffen": Vom Versagen des Westens zum Krieg der Werte', in Schmid, *Krieg im Kosovo*, pp. 243–5.

46 Cora Stephan, 'Der moralische Imperativ: Die Friedensbewegung und die neue deutsche Aussenpolitik', in Schmid, *Krieg im Kosovo*, pp. 276–7.

47 Thomas Schmid, 'Krieg im Kosovo', in Schmid, *Krieg im Kosovo*, pp. 15–36.

48 Matthias Rüb, '"Phönix aus der Asche". Die UÇK: Von der Terrororganisation zur Bodentruppe der Nato?', in Schmid, *Krieg im Kosovo*, pp. 47–62.

49 Andreas Zumach, '"80 Prozent unserer Vorstellungen werden durchgepeitscht": Die letzte Chance von Rambouillet und die Geheimdiplomatie um den "Annex B"', in Schmid, *Krieg im Kosovo*, pp. 63–81.

50 Alex J. Bellamy, *Kosovo and International Society* (London: Palgrave Macmillan, 2002), p. 164.

51 *Ibid.*, pp. ix–x.

52 *Ibid.*, p. 210.

53 Anton Kumer, Mirjam Polzer-Srienz, and Miroslav F. Polzer, 'Politische Ordnungsvorstellungen . . .", in Joseph Marko (ed.), *Gordischer Knoten. Kosovo/a: Durchschlagen oder entwirren? – Völkerrechtliche, rechtsvergleichende und politikwissenschaftliche Analysen und Perspektiven zum jüngsten Balkankonflikt* (Baden-Baden: Nomos, 1999), pp. 27–45.

54 Sabina Dujak, 'Politische und rechtliche Argumentationslinien der serbischen jugoslawischen Führung', in Marko, *Gordischer Knoten*, p. 52.

55 Elmar F. Pichl, 'Die "albanische Frage" in Mazedonien', in Marko, *Gordischer Knoten*, pp. 57–73.

56 Stefan Böckler, 'Das Autonomiestatut für Trentino-Südtirol: Ein Modell für die friedliche Regelung des Kosovokonfliktes?', in Marko, *Gordischer Knoten*, pp. 87–104.

57 Giovanni Poggeschi, 'Katalonien und das Baskenland: Zwei vom Kosovo "weit entfernte" Modelle', in Marko, *Gordischer Knoten*, pp. 105–14.

58 Stephanie Risse-Lobis, 'Die Republik Tatarstan und ihre Souveränität: Ein Modell für Kosovo?', in Marko, *Gordischer Knoten*, pp. 115–26.

59 Joseph Marko, 'Kosovo/a – Ein Gordischer Knoten? Zusammenfassende Analysen und Politikempfehlungen', in Marko, *Gordischer Knoten*, p. 261.
60 Jens Reuter and Konrad Clewing (eds.), *Der Kosovo Konflikt: Ursachen – Verlauf – Perspektiven* (Klagenfurt and Vienna: Wieser Verlag, 2000).
61 Tony Weymouth and Stanley Henig (eds.), *The Kosovo Crisis: The Last American War in Europe?* (London: Reuters, 2001).
62 Anthony Weymouth, 'Why War, Why NATO?', *ibid.*, pp. 1–2, 13. See also Stanley Henig, 'Conclusion: Retrospect and Prospect', *ibid.*, pp. 282, 286–7.
63 Mary Buckley and Sally N. Cummings (eds.), *Kosovo: Perceptions of War and Its Aftermath* (London: Continuum, 2001).
64 Mary Buckley and Sally N. Cummings, 'Introduction', *ibid.*, p. 3.

REFERENCES

Bellamy, Alex J., *Kosovo and International Society* (London: Palgrave Macmillan, 2002), p. 259.
Buckley, Mary and Sally N. Cummings (eds.), *Kosovo: Perceptions of War and Its Aftermath* (London: Continuum, 2001), p. 288.
Elsässer, Jürgen (ed.) *Nie wieder Krieg ohne uns: Das Kosovo und die neue deutsche Geopolitik* (Hamburg: Konkret, 1999), p. 164.
Gordy, Eric D., *The Culture of Power in Serbia: Nationalism and the Destruction of Alternatives* (University Park, PA: Pennsylvania State University Press, 1999), p. 230.
Judah, Tim, *Kosovo: War and Revenge* (New Haven, CT: Yale University Press, 2000), p. 348.
Malcolm, Noel, *Kosovo: A Short History* (London and New York: Macmillan and New York University Press, 1998), p. 492.
Marko, Joseph (ed.), *Gordischer Knoten. Kosovo/a: Durchschlagen oder entwirren? – Völkerrechtliche, rechtsvergleichende und politikwissenschaftliche Analysen und Perspektiven zum jüngsten Balkankonflikt* (Baden-Baden: Nomos, 1999), p. 280.
Mertus, Julie A., *Kosovo: How Myths and Truths Started a War* (Berkeley and Los Angeles: University of California Press, 1999), p. 378.
Reuter, Jens and Konrad Clewing (eds.), *Der Kosovo Konflikt: Ursachen, Verlauf, Perspektiven* (Klagenfurt and Vienna: Wieser Verlag, 2000), p. 568.
Schmid, Thomas (ed.), *Krieg im Kosovo* (Reinbek bei Hamburg: Rowohlt Taschenbuch Verlag, 1999), p. 283.
Troebst, Stefan, *Conflict in Kosovo: Failure of Prevention? An Analytical Documentation, 1992–1998*, ECMI Working Paper No. 1 (Flensburg: European Centre for Minority Issues, 1998), p. 107.
Vickers, Miranda, *Between Serb and Albanian: A History of Kosovo* (New York: Columbia University Press, 1998), p. 328.
Weymouth, Tony and Stanley Henig (eds.), *The Kosovo Crisis: The Last American War in Europe?* (London: Reuters, 2001), p. 316.

10   Debates about intervention

I

Since 1999, the United States and Britain have carried out three armed interventions against authoritarian regimes – in the now-defunct Federal Republic of Yugoslavia (FRY) in 1999 (over Kosovo), in Afghanistan in 2001, and in Iraq most recently. In all of these cases, the United Nations was marginalized and brought in only after the fact, for the purpose of legitimating the intervention. Already there are widely reported rumours that the George W. Bush administration has intentions to topple the regimes in North Korea, Syria, Saudi Arabia, and even Jordan, replacing them with secular-democratic governments. Inevitably, these interventions have stirred controversy, with Noam Chomsky even offering the un-Bodinian definition of sovereignty as 'the right of political entities to be free from outside interference'.[1]

Where Yugoslavia is concerned – and here I am using the term 'Yugoslavia' to refer simultaneously to the Socialist Federated Republic of Yugoslavia which expired in 1991 and to its successor states – the debate, waged both in policy-making circles and in academic publications, assumed the form of a three-sided struggle. On the one hand, there were the *realist-isolationists*, whom I have elsewhere referred to as 'relativists',[2] who tended to dwell on two principal themes: the need to weigh the interests and likely costs for the United States (and the West) before undertaking a military intervention, and the importance of respecting the sovereignty of all states, regardless of their character. Within the US Congress, for example, Congressman Moody demanded to know (in 1990), 'Can Members [of Congress] imagine how we would react if we – say, the British Parliament passed a resolution condemning the North Dakota Legislature for its treatment of the Indians? We would say that is not their competence to do that.'[3] Or again, nearly a decade later, Congressman Paul raised his voice against the NATO air campaign against Yugoslavia (in 1999): 'the bombing in Serbia must stop immediately. Serbia has never aggressed against the United States. Serbia is involved in a bloody civil war of which we should have no part.'[4] Later, after the United States became involved with peace-keeping in postwar Kosovo, Congressman Metcalf objected (in 2000), arguing that 'we have no business in Kosovo. We have no overriding national interest there.'[5]

The realist-isolationist position was also advanced in academic circles, for example, by Martti Koskenniemi, who has argued that 'Rights do not exist as such – "fact-like" – outside the structures of political deliberation . . . Rights are a product of Western culture and history and their principal propagandists have been Western organisations, activists, and academics. But this is a problem only if one thinks that rights are universally good – for it is *that* position that tends to lead into thinking that Western culture is universally good, too.'[6] Koskenniemi goes further, too, urging that 'the universality of rights is pure hegemony',[7] suggesting that he would have us believe that people should be 'free' to be unfree! While stated more radically, Koskenniemi's position reminds me of Burg and Shoup's argument that to engage in 'the condemnation of societies or states simply because they are nationalist . . . would be an arrogant presumption of the superiority of the West'.[8] Michael J. Smith, an idealist advocate of the legitimacy of humanitarian intervention, has criticized 'most realists' for 'insisting on the irrelevance or hypocrisy of ethical concerns'.[9]

The second position which emerged was that of *realist-interventionism*. Advocates of this position share the realist-isolationists' belief that national interests should guide foreign policy, but set the question of sovereign rights to the side. In this spirit, Senator Symms warned the US Senate in 1992, 'If the West ignores Kosova and other potential hot-spots, the war will spread.'[10] Or again, Senator Hatch, in advocating the 'lift-and-strike' approach, declared, 'Those who argue that we have no interests at stake in Bosnia are wrong. The war involves open – and so far unchallenged – aggression in Europe. It involves ethnic cleansing and other war crimes on an enormous scale. It has the potential for spreading into other parts of the Balkans.'[11] Or again, Senator Biden, in urging the continued commitment of US forces to peace-keeping in Bosnia and Kosovo, argued, 'Instability that spread to Western Europe would directly and adversely affect the United States of America in a major way. In other words . . . we do not have the luxury of being able to distance ourselves from the Balkans, no matter how emotionally appealing such a policy may appear at times.'[12]

By contrast with realists, idealist-interventionists believe, as Habermas has put it, 'in a universally binding practical reason'.[13] For those subscribing to this approach, 'Observance of the norms of international law, resolution of disputes through peaceful means without resort to the use of military force, and respect for human rights and for the right of self-determination for populations such as the Albanian ethnic population of Kosova are the qualifications for recognition and normal interaction among civilized states.'[14] Idealists are also apt to agree with then Senator Dole's belief, stated in 1990, that 'democracy and respect for human rights form the basis for effective and lasting solutions to the current crisis in Yugoslavia'.[15]

Smith, basing his position explicitly on Kant's categorical imperative,[16] urges further that 'a state that is oppressive and violates the autonomy and integrity of its subjects forfeits its moral claim to full sovereignty'.[17] This position also hearkens back to Jean Bodin (1529/30–96), the French jurist who, in his *Six Books of the Commonwealth* (1576), equated sovereignty with *legitimate* authority, arguing that there is no such thing as sovereignty except where the authority acts in accord with Natural Law and Divine Law, respects all covenants into which he enters, and respects the inviolability of private property.[18] W. Michael Reisman, in an article for the *American Journal of International Law*, points to the heart of the problem, as it is perceived by idealist-interventionists, which is that international law protects not the sovereignty of the people but the sovereignty of the sovereign, but, in a bold statement, urges that 'no serious scholar still supports the contention that internal human rights are "essentially within the domestic jurisdiction of any state" and hence insulated from international law'.[19] Reisman closes his article by declaring that 'Those who yearn for "the good old days" and continue to trumpet terms like "sovereignty" without relating them to the human rights conditions within the states under discussion do more than commit an anachronism. They undermine human rights.'[20]

While the foregoing represent the three principal positions on the question of humanitarian intervention, it is possible to sketch out a framework based on *idealist-isolationism*, generally the preserve of the left, which argues that nonintervention is a primary norm and that no state or group of states is entitled to 'impose' its own particular understanding of morality on any other state. Noam Chomsky is probably best associated with this current of thought, as is Robert Jackson, who, while embracing the notion of universal moral norms, nonetheless writes, 'A people has no right to be rescued from misrule. And international society has no right to come between a people and its government, even a brutal, tyrannical government.'[21] Advocates of this point of view can, quite properly, trace their heritage back to John Stuart Mill, who argued in his day that people should be allowed to find their own way to democracy or to whatever form of government they wished for themselves.

II

The debate concerning the nature of sovereignty and humanitarian intervention, as applied in the Yugoslav setting, inevitably raged in the German-speaking world as well. Of the eleven books under review here, four of them (those by Jürgen Elsässer, Rasmus Tenbergen, and Joachim Hösler and his collaborators, as well as the volume edited by Reinhard Merkel) bear directly on this dual question, a fifth (the wide-ranging analysis by Andreas Hasenclever) deals expressly with the role of morality in foreign policy, and six others, even though having other foci, take positions on this question or throw light on the argument.

Rasmus Tenbergen's short book, *Der Kosovo-Krieg: Eine gerechte Intervention?*, is surely one of the best summaries of the debate. At the outset, Tenbergen provides a definition of humanitarian intervention as 'a military interference in the internal affairs of a sovereign state for [the purpose of] the protection of human rights'.[22] This definition is useful in that it draws attention to the importance of the intervener's intentions, rather than the actual results of the intervention, in assessing whether an intervention should be characterized as 'humanitarian'. But when is an intervention *legitimate*? Tenbergen, in identifying himself with transcendental pragmatism (which is apparently his own term), declares that his objective is to defend the consequentialist position 'that humanitarian interventions are legitimate when they protect more human rights than they damage. Human rights are defined . . . as rights which one cannot dispute without self-contradiction and which, because of their consequent validity, apply to all people.'[23]

Grounding himself in extensive literature in both German and English, Tenbergen outlines three alternative theories of humanitarian intervention, which he identifies as realism, liberalism, and transcendental pragmatism. Realism has, in fact, both normative and empirical dimensions. On the normative level, realists believe that policy-makers should be guided, in the first place, by national interest. On the empirical level, as Tenbergen argues, realists tend to dismiss moral arguments as mere 'cover' for the pursuit of national interest and may even argue that giving priority to moral considerations could be dangerous. Realists, as we have already seen, do not rule out intervention a priori (as do strict pacifists) but argue (as per J. Stedman, whom Tenbergen cites) that humanitarian considerations are not sufficient to justify the expenditure of limited resources, demand that strategic interests be affected, and in any event stress the limits to resources in urging that interventionism must, of necessity, be selective.[24]

Liberals (whom I have called 'idealists') come in two varieties, according to Tenbergen: advocates of the just-war thesis ('intervention-ists' in my vocabulary) and pacifists. As an example of an advocate of the just-war thesis, Tenbergen cites Stanley Hoffmann's challenge, 'Whether it is in our "interest" to intervene to stop genocide or war crimes on a colossal scale I will let the sophists of national security argue among themselves; what I know is that it is our moral duty to act, whenever there is a chance of success.'[25] As an example of a pacifist position, Tenbergen cites H. R. Reuter, who warned, in a 1996 publica-tion, that the use of military force against one state could legitimate countervailing force.[26]

Tenbergen's own 'transcendental pragmatism' is, in fact, a variation on the interventionist approach. Criticizing realism for tending to condemn appeals to morality when they are all too appropriate, Tenbergen calls for a return to the tradition of the just-war, viewing the 1648 Treaty of West-phalia (which abandoned Bodin's morally informed notions of sovereignty and embraced the principle 'might makes right') as a 'wrong turn'; for Tenbergen, the two central theses of just-war theory – that morality has a role to play in politics and that the recourse to armed intervention can be justified – cannot be disputed without self-contradiction.[27] But here he returns to the role of intentions. 'Legitimate grounds [for intervention] and proper intentions are by no means identical criteria', he warns. 'There can be a good reason for an intervention which is carried out from an ignoble motive.'[28] Basing himself on this distinction, Tenbergen next argues that *foreseeable* results be placed at the centre of discussion and calls those humanitarian interventions legitimate where the intended and foreseeable results are seen as conducive to the promotion of human rights.[29] The Hesse Foundation for Peace and Conflict Research reached the conclusion, in 1999, that one's judgement about the legit-imacy of humanitarian intervention hinges on whether one considers interstate peace or respect for human rights the higher good;[30] and, indeed, this gets at the heart of the controversy.

Where Kosovo is concerned, Tenbergen dismisses claims made by people sympathetic to the Milošević regime that the persecution of Kosovar Albanians escalated at the end of March 1999 *only* in response to NATO's attack,[31] and points to the Albanians' 'extremely positive' reactions to the NATO operation, which he offers as an argument against the notion that NATO's intervention denied the Albanians the possibility to sort things out for themselves, noting that the expulsions of Albanians from Kosovo began even 'while the negotiations in Rambouillet were still underway'.[32] Ultimately, Tenbergen concludes that NATO's intervention was *legitimate*, in part on the assessment that (in numerical terms at least) the NATO operation protected the rights of a greater number of people than were harmed.[33]

In assessing the rectitude of humanitarian intervention in the case of Kosovo, much depends on what one thinks happened there. Was there a pattern of systematic Serbian oppression in the province? If so, was it escalating? What took place in Raçak in January 1999? Was the draft treaty prepared at Rambouillet in February–March 1999 a compromise fair to both sides or a diktat unfair to the Serbian side? And was there an Operation Horseshoe, as alleged by the German, Austrian, and American governments? Jürgen Elsässer, in his book, *Kriegsverbrechen: Die tödlichen Lügen der Bundesregierung und ihre Opfer im Kosovo-Konflikt*, takes up some, at least, of these questions, raising doubts about the 'standard' version of events and, thereby, about the legitimacy of the NATO intervention.

Elsässer makes much of the case of the Raçak massacre. The case involves the discovery of forty to forty-five bodies of Albanians, among them at least three women and one child, in January 1999. The Albanians claimed that the dead were civilian victims of a Serbian massacre. The discovery had a galvanizing effect, bringing the Western states to the conclusion that something had to be done to stop the Belgrade regime. But what actually happened in Raçak? Kosovo Liberation Army (KLA) leader Hasim Thaqi himself conceded that there had been a battle on that day, and Serbian police claimed that very afternoon (15 January) that they had killed fifteen KLA fighters. What is curious, though, is that, when the bodies found in Raçak were examined, it was found that, while all of them had died from gunshot wounds, the civilian clothes they were wearing did not, allegedly, have gunshot holes.[34] The conclusion seems to follow, as Belgrade pathologist Dušan Dunjić urged, that the dead in Raçak were KLA fighters killed in battle elsewhere, whose bodies the KLA subsequently brought to that village, undressing them and redressing them in civilian clothes. Indeed, *Die Welt*, in its edition of 8 March 1999, questioned whether there had been a 'massacre' at all, and Elsässer quite clearly thinks not.[35]

Elsässer portrays the West as having engaged in an anti-Serbian strategy over a period of years, questioning whether Vukovar (the Croatian city demolished by the Yugoslav People's Army in 1991) had perhaps given some provocation to the Serbs, disputing reports about the number of people killed at Srebrenica and charging the Muslims with having used that city as a bastion from which to make attacks on Serbian forces outside, accusing the West of having demonized Serbia, and arguing that the German and American governments insisted, at Rambouillet, on stipulations to which no responsible Serbian leader

226 Thinking about Yugoslavia

could possibly have agreed. He also argues, further, that there never was an Operation Horseshoe, and cites Defence Minister Rudolf Scharping's inability to remember the number of casualties from one day to the next as evidence, asserting further that the evidence on which the indictment of Yugoslav president Milošević for war crimes in Kosovo was based was 'not serious' and that the indictment was politically motivated, being designed to delegitimate the leadership of Serbia and Yugoslavia.[36]

Elsässer also provides a transcript of a cockpit-to-base conversation to document that NATO commanders knowingly ordered the bombing of a convoy of refugees, in spite of the protests of the pilot, who reported seeing only tractors and civilian cars, and no tanks or military vehicles.[37] Nor was the bombing of the Chinese embassy a mistake, according to Elsässer. Rather, it was bombed because the Chinese had made their radio equipment available to the Yugoslav Army after the latter's transmitter had been put out of commission. As for the evidence of systematic murders of Albanians, Elsässer cites a report in a Berlin newspaper to the effect that there were 'no indications of systematic mass killings in Kosovo'.[38] Finally, Elsässer concludes that NATO constituted at least as great a threat to the Albanian population of Kosovo as the Serbian paramilitaries(!) – an astonishing claim in light of Tim Judah's research into this question[39] – and finds that NATO's campaign 'became illegitimate not because of the so-called collateral damage, but because of the equation of Hitler and Milošević, [and] of the fate of the Jews with that of the Kosovar Albanians'.[40]

Jürgen Elsässer is the editor of the German magazine, *Konkret*, which has taken a consistently critical view of German policy in Kosovo. Elsässer's website includes a short biographical statement, in which he points out that Germany's leading weekly magazine, *Der Spiegel*, had denounced him at one time as a 'professional cynic' given to 'old-fashioned left[-wing] stereotypes'.[41] Elsässer is not, however, the only one to have disputed the existence of an Operation Horseshoe. Franz-Josef Hutsch, writing in the pages of the *Hamburger Abendblatt* (21 March 2000), has also questioned its existence, citing a book by Heinz Loquai, the leading military adviser in the German legation to the Organization for Security and Co-operation in Europe (OSCE) in Vienna, in support of his contention.[42]

Where Elsässer sees a Western conspiracy against Serbia, Rolf Paasch, in a contribution to the volume coedited by Angelika Volle and Werner Weidenfeld, sees rather 'a mixture of political naïveté, diplomatic negligence, lack of historical understanding, and insufficient readiness for an engagement for Europe.'[43] Along similar lines, Markus Spillmann, in a chapter for the same volume, accuses the international community of failing to undertake preventive measures in the unfolding Yugoslav crisis and of contenting itself with trying to contain – or, I would add, negotiate solutions with – Slobodan Milošević.[44] On the other hand, the volume edited by Hannes Hofbauer offers at least partial support for Elsässer's thesis. Hofbauer, for example, cites an article published in the French newspaper, *Le Figaro*, which called into question OSCE chief inspector William Walker's version of what had happened in Raçak, and notes that *Le Monde* and the *Guardian* cited OSCE observers who could not find any evidence that the massacre had actually taken place in the village, raising the question as to whether the KLA had brought to the village the bodies of people killed elsewhere.[45] Michel Chossudovsky, in a chapter likewise included in Hofbauer's volume, agrees with Elsässer in seeing the West as pursuing a policy directed against Belgrade, but where Elsässer stresses the demonization of Serbia, Chossudovsky stresses the West's alleged strategic and economic interests in going to war in March 1999.[46]

By contrast with the volumes by Tenbergen and Elsässer, the collaborative venture by Joachim Hösler, Norman Paech, and Gerhard Stuby adopts a conventionalist approach, stressing the stipulations of the UN Charter and other documents of international law.[47] Thus, Johannes Klotz, in his introduction to the book, writes that the essays by Hösler, Paech, and Stuby demonstrate that NATO's war in 1999 lacked any grounding in international law and that the Western democracies had neglected conflict prevention long before the outbreak of conflict in Yugoslavia.[48] Paech, for example, emphasizes that NATO proceeded to war without first obtaining a UN authorization – a recourse which set a precedent for the American–British war to remove the regime of Saddam Hussein in Iraq in 2003. As Paech shows, the war was an outcome of a strategic reorientation on NATO's part, which began with the NATO summit in London on 6 July 1990. The new orientation was formulated subsequently at a NATO conference in Rome on 7/8 November 1991, which assessed the nature of the threats to which NATO should respond. NATO ministers no longer identified the threat as emanating from Russia; instead, the threat lay in the endangerment of access to vital natural resources, the uncontrolled proliferation of 'weapons of mass destruction', and the worldwide escalation of terrorism.[49] But even so, German defence minister Volker Rühe underlined, on 4 February 1995, on the occasion of a security conference in Munich: 'The central condition for the introduction of military forces is its legitimation under international law. A UN mandate is a prerequisite.'[50] However, after Resolution 1199 of the UN Security Council (23

September 1998) declared that the worsening situation in Kosovo constituted 'a serious threat to peace and stability in the region', NATO's secretary general would later claim that this resolution already provided a legal basis for NATO's intervention.[51] Paech and his collaborators dispute this claim, however. Hösler, for his part, contends that NATO's war against the FRY, 24 March to 10 June 1999, was 'an illegal war, which had effects opposite to its proclaimed goals'.[52] Moreover, Hösler mounts a forceful argument against those (such as Paul Latawski)[53] who believe that the expulsion of ethnic minorities can be justified, insofar as ethnically more homogeneous states may be more stable. Hösler, citing research by Holm Sundhaussen which showed that in the course of four waves of homogenization in the Balkans, during the period 1912–97, some 12 to 14 million people lost their homes or their lives,[54] argues that, quite to the contrary, such policies not only did not solve interethnic problems, but may have even proven to be aggravants and destabilizing in effect.

Unlike the volumes written by Tenbergen, Elsässer, and the team of Hösler, Paech, and Stuby, the collection edited by Reinhard Merkel[55] does not offer a single point of view. In fact, between its covers one may find universalist, conventionalist, and consequentialist approaches, and both defences and denials of the legitimacy of the NATO air campaign of 1999. Four of the contributors to this magnificent collection refer expressly to Immanuel Kant (1724–1804);[56] two contributors have established reputations for expertise about Kant.[57] Thus, it is perhaps worthwhile to recall that Kant, in his short essay, *Perpetual Peace* (1795), contended that 'there can be no conflict between politics, as an applied branch of right [law], and morality, as a theoretical branch of right (i.e., between theory and practice)',[58] because, in his view, applied law is necessarily concerned with assuring what is right. Or, to put it another way, to choose an outcome that is morally wrong, even if it serves one's own material interests, is a betrayal of law properly understood, and hence of 'politics' as such. Consistently, Kant urges 'states to arrive at a lawful settlement of their differences by forming something analogous to a universal state'.[59]

Bruno Simma provides a useful introduction to the subject, in Merkel's collection, conceding that NATO's intervention in 1999 violated the letter of the UN Charter but observing that, from time to time, there may be 'hard cases' for which one finds that one has no choice but to act outside the framework of international law. But he warns, 'the more isolated such cases remain, the less will be their potential to undermine the rules of international law, in our case the UN Charter'.[60] Several chapters in the book discuss the notion that the war in Kosovo might provide a springboard, as Jürgen Habermas puts it in his chapter, to a 'cosmopolitan law of a world society'[61] – such as he proposed in his *Inclusion of the Other*[62] – but, to Merkel's mind, there is a fundamental incompatibility between what he sees as an illegal war and any notion that, as such, it could do anything to promote a universalization of basic norms. On the contrary, says Merkel, even high moral values cannot justify a nondefensive war which, thus, subverts the underpinnings for an international legal order. Moreover, to Merkel's mind, there is no such thing as a legitimate war in which innocent people are killed.[63] Rejecting Benthamite consequentialism,[64] Merkel mounts an explicitly Kantian argument against NATO's intervention, saying that there can be no moral justification in killing even a handful of innocents, even if for the purpose of saving millions of people from tyranny.[65] Furthermore, Merkel argues, even if one wanted to allow that 'humanitarian intervention' might constitute a legitimate exception to the UN Charter's ban on force, only the Security Council should be authorized to approve recourse to such action.

Dieter Senghaas strikes a different note, however, pointing out that the proscription of war is not the only binding norm in international law; proscriptions against genocide, the slave trade, race discrimination, crimes against humanity, deportation, and ethnic cleansing may also be counted as binding normative structures. As a result, humanitarian intervention may actually be *required* under international law, he argues,[66] though, as Wolfgang Kersting urges, in a contribution to the same collection, there can be a right to intervene *only* when there is a *duty* to do so.[67] Kersting warns against particularist relativists (also known as 'cultural relativists') who argue that notions of human rights are merely 'the cultural expression of western individualism',[68] as if torture might not offend some universal sense of justice. He further distinguishes between 'transcendental human rights' (which are basic) and 'programmatic human rights' (which are not basic), and says that intervention by outside powers can be justified in defence of transcendental human rights, but not in defence of programmatic human rights.[69] His argument coincides with the thinking of Jürgen Habermas, who has written that 'Violations of human *rights* must not be reduced to the scale of offences against *values*. The difference between rights, which are exempt from weighing, and goods, which can be weighed and ranked accordingly as primary or secondary, should not be blurred.'[70] Habermas, in his chapter for Merkel's collection, mounts an argument against the claims of the realist school, asserting that the claims of human rights establish a basis for limiting the principle of nonintervention, on moral grounds.[71]

But did the air campaign against the FRY establish a precedent for future humanitarian interventions and does it mark the dawn of a new era of morally driven foreign policy? The consensus, at least among this set of readings, appears to be that it does *not* constitute such a milestone. Wolfgang Ishinger, in a chapter for the volume edited by Volle and Weidenfeld, speaks for many in writing that 'the military engagement against the Milošević regime was not the expression of a general and one-sided "moralization of foreign policy" as some people want to see it',[72] i.e., it does not mark a new phase in which foreign policy will be guided by moral principles. Ulrich Beck strikes a different note, however, writing of the emergence of 'a new-style, post-national politics of *military humanism*' in which the 'hegemonic power determines what is just, what is human right. And war becomes the continuation of *morality* by other means'.[73]

III

Of course, debates about any specific recourse to 'humanitarian intervention' require an understanding of the facts on the ground. On this point, the volumes by Paolo Rumiz[74] and Norbert Mappes-Niediek[75] offer provocative perspectives that may inspire analysts to revise their thinking about what has been happening in the Balkans over the past fifteen years. Rumiz offers two insights. The first, which provides an explanation for Hösler's puzzle concerning why ethnic cleansing and ethnic homogenization do not produce greater harmony and peace, is his understanding that the real cultural divide is not usually between the members of different ethnic groups per se, but between those people whose families have lived in a region for ages (*starosedioci*, or 'old settlers') and those who have arrived more recently (*došljaci*, or 'newcomers').[76] This confirms the findings of Ger Duijzings in the context of interethnic relations in Kosovo.[77] In Rumiz's case, this analysis applied to Vukovar, where old-settler Serbs and Croats shared a common dialect and a common regional identity, and among whom – before 1991 – young people socialized together regardless of ethnicity. But after the Second World War, Hungarians and Germans who had been living in eastern Slavonia were expelled from the cities (including from Vukovar) and their houses were turned over to immigrants from the south of Yugoslavia. During 1990–1, it was the post-Second World War Serbian *došljaci* who responded to the propaganda barrage coming out of Belgrade. Among both Serbs and Croats of Vukovar, the *došljaci* 'tried to win their coethnics over to the patriotic mobilization, and when they had no success with that, they killed them, plundered their property and goods, or drove them away. The old settlers would not let themselves be stirred up against other nationalities.'[78] This consideration, in turn, leads Rumiz to the conclusion that 'ethnic polarization was not the cause, but rather the consequence of the Balkan conflict'.[79]

Rumiz's second major thesis is that the war was, in the first place, about criminality and theft. In his view, the war in Kosovo was about business, specifically about rival mafia clans competing for more favourable conditions for their illegal trade in weapons and drugs. There was not only an Albanian mafia but also a Serbian mafia, e.g., Arkan's clan, which controlled some of the drug trade in Europe. Among the Serbian drug tsars was Radovan Stojičić AKA 'Badža', who served as deputy interior minister of Serbia before being gunned down in the Mamma Mia restaurant in Belgrade. In his heyday, Stojičić had controlled the drug trade in Yugoslavia and had also been involved in illegal business in Montenegro.[80] For Rumiz, the Peace of Dayton did not usher in a *pax americana*, but a *pax mafiosa*, while, in his view, in recognizing the KLA as an acceptable partner (e.g., for negotiations at Rambouillet) and launching its air campaign against the FRY, NATO 'had decided . . . that in Kosovo too the peace would be guaranteed by the mafia'.[81]

Norbert Mappes-Niediek's research into the operations of the Balkan mafia provides support for Rumiz's second thesis. According to Mappes-Niediek, some of the national-liberation movements in the Balkans, most particularly those associated with the Albanians of Kosovo and Macedonia, are better seen as criminal organizations making use of effective propaganda, so that Western diplomats intending to mediate in interethnic conflicts end up taking the side of one or another mafia. Among those accused of corruption, smuggling, or illegal appropriation in this book are the late Croatian president Tudjman, Bakir Izetbegović (son of Bosnian president Alija Izetbegović), Menduh Thaçi (vice president of the Democratic Party of Albanians, in Macedonia), Bosnian Serb leader Radovan Karadžić, Bosnian Serb parliamentary president Momčilo Krajišnik, KLA figure Ramush Haradinaj, Montenegrin extremist Vladimir Bokan AKA 'Vanja', Ljubisav Ivanov AKA 'Zingo' (a parliamentary deputy in Macedonia), Bosnian Serb prime minister Milorad Dodik, and Croatian general Slobodan Praljak (best known for having ordered the destruction of the historic bridge in Mostar) – and let's not forget Montenegrin president Milo Djukanović, robber-baron Željko Ražnatović AKA 'Arkan', and the now-dethroned Serbian 'Godfather' himself, Slobodan Milošević. If the purpose of the various Western-imposed embargoes was to give a massive boost to organized crime in the Balkans, then they succeeded admirably. In Croatia, to take one example, the arms embargo impelled the Croatian government to make contact with two opulent Croatian gangsters – Mladen Naletilić AKA 'Tuta' and Vinko Martinović AKA 'Stela'.[82] Tuta would later be fêted as a national hero, before being packed off to The Hague to face charges for having committed war crimes.

At this point in time, according to Mappes-Niediek, Albanian criminal gangs – larger and better organized than their non-Albanian rivals – dominate the Balkan underworld. Albanians are now the largest exporters of heroin to the Scandinavian countries, and are also involved in the heroin market in Germany, Switzerland, and the United States. Indeed, half of the heroin trade in Western Europe is in Albanian hands, with groups from Kosovo dominating the heroin market in Poland and Slovakia. The Albanian mafia also maintains its visibility in the prostitution racket; indeed, Italian aid organizations estimate that there are about 30,000 Albanian prostitutes working in Western Europe, none of them thought to be doing so of their own free will.[83] And, of course, if the KLA, say, is knee-deep in criminal activity, does it make sense for NATO to have fought a war on its behalf, let alone to have allowed the KLA to be converted, after the fighting ended, into a local *police* force, of all things?

IV

The remaining three books under discussion here all deal with Bosnia, either in whole or in significant part. The volumes by Marie-Janine Calic[84] and Daniel Eisermann[85] focus on the war of 1991–5, while the volume written by Andreas Hasenclever examines the role of morality in international politics, using three case studies: Somalia, Rwanda, and Bosnia-Herzegovina.[86] Given the constraints of this essay, I shall be discussing only the theoretical portions of Hasenclever's book and the section dealing with Bosnia.

I must confess that I am enormously impressed by the scholarship and maturity of judgement found in these books, which are complementary, rather than overlapping. Calic concentrates on the years 1991–5, thus on the war itself (though not without setting the story in its historical context) and Eisermann is concerned with the Western response to the Bosnian war, while Hasenclever devotes his attention to sorting out alternative ways of understanding Western responses to the crises in Somalia, Rwanda, and Bosnia-Herzegovina.

Calic, in setting the stage for the war, notes that, during most of the post-1945 period up to the 1980s, nationality and religion were *not* the primary markers for identity; social class, educational level, and career were much more important.[87] Moreover, even at the end of 1991, a public opinion poll conducted in Bosnia-Herzegovina found that only one in every ten respondents considered nationality to be a critical criterion for friendship, while the overwhelming majority attributed no importance to a person's nationality.[88] Nationalism, she argues, was manufactured. Still, it is not without significance that, in an opinion poll conducted in November 1991, nearly 60 per cent of Muslims and 70 per cent of Croats felt that Serbs had the greatest influence in Bosnia-Herzegovina, while, among Serbs, 52 per cent thought that the Croats had the most influence in the republic, with 44 per cent of Serbs thinking that the Muslims were the most influential.[89]

Calic's analysis provides a speculative answer as to why Yugoslavia descended into violence. She highlights, for example, the fact that, as of 1990–1, 22 per cent of the adult population had only an elementary school education, while another 24 per cent had less than that.[90] If one takes it as a given that, on the whole, the less education, the greater the receptivity to manipulative propaganda, then the low educational attainment of the population of Bosnia was probably a contributing factor.

In endeavouring to understand why the war was fought with such brutality, Calic notes several factors, including (1) the argument that the very brutality served to advance the goals of the nationalist leaders, (2) the fact that one out of every five volunteers had had problems with the law previously, (3) the fact that a large portion of the paramilitary forces came either from the countryside or from a low urban caste, (4) the fact that some perpetrators of atrocities had a history of pathology, and (5) the fact that many of the atrocities were perpetrated in groups in which social pressure and status played a role.[91] She also notes, wisely, that psychologists believe that it is not so much aggression as the sheer exceptionality of circumstances which is attractive in war.[92] When Serb propagandists described the fighting in Slovenia as 'Disneyland', they may have been saying more than they realized.

In approaching the Western debate about lifting the embargo, conducting air strikes, and the appropriate response in general, she notes that at the centre of the debate was the dispute concerning whether the war in Bosnia was a civil war (the interpretation preferred by the Serbian side) or an international war of aggression (as alleged by Croats and Muslims). The interpretive model one might adopt was not without consequence: under international law, an arms embargo could only be imposed in the case of a civil war and at the request of the government of the given country (the embargo was in fact requested by Belgrade). Moreover, according to Calic, the European states (and, for that matter, the United States) did not believe at first that the war in Yugoslavia affected their interests in any meaningful way. Later, a consensus emerged that the war in Croatia and Bosnia was damaging to humanitarian, democratic, legal, and other standards recognized under international law.[93] But by the time the international community found its way to a measured response, more than 200,000 people had died in Bosnia. Calic, accordingly, judges Western policy in the Bosnian war a 'relative failure', finding that that failure 'resulted less from the choice of false instruments than from the timing and the way in which they were used. Many reactions came with a delay, had a purely symbolic character, or remained self-contradictory.'[94]

Eisermann's purpose in his *Der lange Weg nach Dayton* is more modest. He does not aspire to an explanation of why the war broke out; the closest he comes is to identify, as the central questions in the Yugoslav 'constitutional conflict' on the eve of the war, the questions as to (1) whether the individual republics could secede unilaterally, and (2) whether, in the event of the federation breaking up, interrepublican boundaries would remain valid or be open to revision.[95] What Eisermann wants to accomplish, however, is to understand why the major powers did what they did – and his answer is that they were primarily motivated to protect their own interests. The reason that it took the West that period of time to make a decisive response is that it took that period of time before the West saw its priorities on the line. There were two major events in 1995 which affected Western interests: the first was the arrest and handcuffing of 367 international peace-keepers at the end of May of that year, which was profoundly embarrassing to the Western powers; the second was the televised reports of the massacre in Srebrenica (in July of that year), which contributed to the discrediting of international security institutions and affected the Great Power interests of the United States, *inter alia*, because the prestige of NATO had been damaged.[96] If there was a third event which contributed to a change in Western perceptions of its interests in Bosnia, according to Eisermann, it was the accession of Jacques Chirac to the French presidency on 17 May 1995. Already in his first month in office, President Chirac characterized the Serbs as 'unscrupulous people, terrorists',[97] and in July 1995, on the eve of Bastille Day celebrations and against the opposition of his generals, Chirac demanded that the West undertake 'military action' against the Serbs.[98] But during the war there was a period of time during which first UN secretary-general Boutros Boutros-Ghali and later his special representative, Yasushi Akashi, exercised the authority to approve or disapprove NATO air strikes against the Serbs, making a habit of disapproving requests for such strikes. As a result of the frustration associated with this experience, Eisermann tells us, 'the notion of a direct military co-operation between the United Nations and NATO was effectively discredited. One did not have to be a prophet to foresee that the experiment of a "dual key" involving the UN and NATO would not see another day.'[99]

Finally, there is the study of the power of morality in international politics by Andreas Hasenclever. The author's purpose in this study is to outline three schools of thought – realism, rational liberalism, and the moral-sociological approach – and to make an argument on behalf of the last of these. At the outset, Hasenclever declares his intention 'to show that human rights are firmly anchored as fundamental moral principles of state behaviour both on the international and on the national level. From there I would like to suggest that it is plausible that an ethos of altruism [*Hilfsbereitschaft*] corresponds to human rights [norms] in western societies."[100] But, in developing his argument that morality does indeed play a role in foreign policy, Hasenclever consciously excludes overdetermined military interventions (i.e., interventions for which both moral reasons and material interest could seem to have been operative), appreciating that, in such cases, no definite conclusion can be reached.

Hasenclever has sharp words for the realists. 'Realists are professional pessimists', he tells us. 'For them, history is inextricably bound up with violence, greed, and envy. Wars are recurrent phenomena.'[101]Realism is not a coherent theory, however, but a school of thought following a certain research programme, with adherents proceeding from the same or similar premises and having common questions and strategies for seeking answers. Realists see states as rational, unitary, goal-oriented actors, pursuing ends which they have set for themselves and avoiding goals which are beyond their means.[102] Realists believe that states behave in accordance with strategic interests, and, Hasenclever adds, are not guided in any important matters by moral precepts. Hasenclever also distinguishes among three strains of realists – defensive realists, who want to defend the status quo, offensive realists, who want to expand the power and influence of their respective states, and post-classical realists, who believe that the defensive and offensive realists are too fixated on military security and who want to shift the emphasis to economic power. But he criticizes the realist school for not having been able to generate a coherent theory of military intervention, a deficiency which he endeavours to correct (albeit not from sympathy) by generating hypotheses compatible with the realist perspective.

Rational liberals, Hasenclever writes, shift the analytical focus to competing interests within a given state. This school would embrace, among others, interest group theory. For rational liberals, 'States intervene with force in the internal affairs of foreign lands, when this is useful for a social group and when this group is in the position to promote its interests in foreign-policy formation.'[103]

Adherents of the moral-sociological approach, by contrast, believe that moral considerations may oblige actors to behave in certain ways, but the question is *how?* Adherents of this approach, in effect, are bringing an idealist perspective to empirical analysis, and Hasenclever, at least, locates the power of morality in public outrage. Thus, he argues, when ordinary people are outraged by massive human rights violations, their governments come under pressure to react appropriately (or at least to pretend to do so). Consequently, against the realist claim that NATO's change of heart after May 1995 was prompted by anger that the Serbs had made the West look ridiculous and by a desire to prevent the erosion of NATO's prestige or even its collapse, Hasenclever argues that what occurred in summer 1995 was a tidal change in public perceptions of the Serbs in key Western states.[104] As he sees it, 'over the years, the arguments of opponents of intervention became weaker while those of advocates became stronger. This was connected essentially with a transformation in the moral structure of the problem field. Because of that public pressure on the governments in London, Paris and Washington in summer 1995 grew stronger than it had been in previous years.'[105] The strong world reaction after Srebrenica provides support for the moral-sociological interpretation, says Hasenclever, but even in May 1993, 63 per cent of a poll sampling of 1,000 Americans told pollsters that they believed that the United States had a moral obligation to stop atrocities being committed against an ethnic group in another country.[106] Opinion polls conducted in Britain and France in 1996–7 found strong support for the notion of universal human rights.[107]

But the moral-sociological approach does not limit itself to interpreting how the public understands morality and pressures the government. On the contrary, Hasenclever says, the moral-sociological approach argues that people have a *right* to assistance, and that right, in turn, places those capable of rendering assistance under the obligation to do so.[108]

All of the books reviewed in this chapter enrich our understanding of recent history in Bosnia or Kosovo, and in some cases, also of the issues surrounding humanitarian intervention. Of this set, three books stand out as especially valuable: Marie-Janine Calic's study of the war in Bosnia, which, among those books dealing with that war which I have read, is now my favourite and which I would recommend to anyone able to read German; Rasmus Tenbergen's sophisticated and wide-ranging study of humanitarian intervention, using Kosovo as a case study; and Andreas Hasenclever's smart defence of the moral-sociological approach. For those wanting an 'easy read' which nonetheless offers some insight into what was happening in the Yugoslav region in the 1990s, Paolo Rumiz's reflections are recommended. But to highlight those four is not to detract from the other books discussed here, all of which have their merits.

NOTES

1 Quoted critically in David Aaronovitch, 'Why the Left Is Wrong on Saddam', *The Observer*, 2 February 2003, at www.observer.co.uk.

2 Sabrina P. Ramet, 'Revisiting the Horrors of Bosnia: New Books about the War', *East European Politics and Societies*, 14, 2 (Spring 2000), esp. pp. 477–8.

3 'Regarding Albanian Minorities in Yugoslavia', Congressman Moody addressing the US House of Representatives (22 October 1990), *Congressional Record*, at thomas.loc.gov/cgi.

4 'The Bombing in Serbia Must Stop', Congressman Paul addressing the United States House of Representatives (15 April 1999), *Congressional Record* at thomas.loc.gov/cgi.

5 'Opposing Continued US Involvement in the Balkan Conflict', Congressman Metcalf addressing the United States House of Representatives (30 March 2000), *Congressional Record* at thomas.loc.gov.

6 Martti Koskenniemi, 'Human Rights, Politics and Love', *Mennesker & rettigheter: Nordic Journal for Human Rights*, 4 (2001), pp. 38–39, emphasis in original.

7 *Ibid.*, p. 41.

8 Steven L. Burg and Paul S. Shoup, *The War in Bosnia-Herzegovina: Ethnic Conflict and International Intervention* (Armonk, NY: M. E. Sharpe, 1999), p. 11.

9 Michael Joseph Smith, 'Ethics and Intervention', *Ethics and International Affairs*, 3 (1990), p. 7.

10 'Keeping it Safe for Serbia', Senator Symms addressing the United States Senate (8 October 1992), *Congressional Record*, at thomas.loc.gov/cgi.

11 'Tragedy in Goražde', Senator Hatch addressing the United States Senate (21 April 1994), *Congressional Record*, at thomas.loc.gov/cgi.

12 'For Continued US Engagement in the Balkans', Senator Biden addressing the United States Senate (4 May 2000), *Congressional Record*, at thomas.loc.gov/cgi.

13 Jürgen Habermas, *The Inclusion of the Other: Studies in Political Theory*, ed. by Ciaran Cronin and Pablo De Greiff (Cambridge: Polity Press, 2002), p. 83.

14 'Strong Action Is Needed to Protect Bosnia and Other Former Yugoslav Republics', Congressman Lantos addressing the United States House of Representatives (19 May 1992), *Congressional Record*, at thomas.loc.gov/cgi.

15 'It Is Time to Support Democracy in Yugoslavia', Senator Dole addressing the United States Senate (8 February 1990), *Congressional Record*, at thomas.loc.gov/cgi.

16 Smith, 'Ethics and Intervention', p. 21.

17 Michael J. Smith, 'Humanitarian Intervention: An Overview of the Ethical Issues', *Ethics and International Affairs*, 12 (1998), p. 76.

18 Jean Bodin, *Six Books of the Commonwealth*, abridged and trans. by M. J. Tooley (Oxford: Basil Blackwell, 1955), no copyright asserted, Book I, posted at www.constitution.org/bodin/bodin_1.htm. See also Max Adams Shepard, 'Sovereignty at the Crossroads: A Study of Bodin', *Political Science Quarterly*, 45, 4 (December 1930), p. 599.

19 W. Michael Reisman, 'Sovereignty and Human Rights in Contemporary International Law', *American Journal of International Law*, 84, 4 (October 1990), p. 869. It is not apparent whether Reisman is quoting from an unnamed source or placing the marked phrase in quotation marks merely to signify that this concept appears more or less in this form.

20 *Ibid.*, p. 876.

21 Robert Jackson, *The Global Covenant: Human Conduct in a World of States* (Oxford: Oxford University Press, 2000), as quoted in Jack Donnelly, 'Genocide and Humanitarian Intervention', *Journal of Human Rights*, 1, 1 (March 2002), p. 96. For further discussions of humanitarian intervention, see: Pierre Laberge, 'Humanitarian Intervention: Three Ethical Positions', *Ethics and International Affairs*, 9 (1995), pp. 15–35; Amir Pasic and Thomas G. Weiss, 'The Politics of Rescue: Yugoslavia's Wars and the Humanitarian Impulse', *Ethics and International Affairs*, 11 (1997), pp. 105–31; Richard Caplan, 'Humanitarian Intervention: Which Way Forward?', *Ethics and International Affairs*, 14 (2000), pp. 23–38; Martin L. Cook, '"Immaculate War": Constraints on Humanitarian Intervention', *Ethics and International Affairs*, 14 (2000), pp. 55–65; and Terry Nardin, 'The Moral Basis of Humanitarian Intervention', *Ethics and International Affairs*, 16 (2002), pp. 57–70.

22 Rasmus Tenbergen, *Der Kosovo-Krieg: Eine gerechte Intervention?* (ILD Verlag, 2001), p. 12.

23 *Ibid.*, p. 14.

24 *Ibid.*, p. 17.

25 Stanley Hoffmann, 'In Defense of Mother Teresa', *Foreign Affairs*, 75, 2 (March–April 1996), p. 174, as quoted in Tenbergen, *Der Kosovo-Krieg*, p. 19.

26 Tenbergen, *Der Kosovo-Krieg*, p. 20.

27 *Ibid.*, pp. 36, 40.

28 *Ibid.*, p. 60.

29 *Ibid.*, pp. 38, 61.

30 *Ibid.*, p. 83.

31 *Ibid.*, pp. 101–2.

32 *Ibid.*, p. 119; see also p. 105.

33 *Ibid.*, p. 110.

34 Jürgen Elsässer, *Kriegsverbrechen: Die tödlichen Lügen der Bundesregierung und ihre Opfer im Kosovo-Konflikt*, 4th edn (Hamburg: Konkret, 2001), pp. 51–2, 54.

35 *Ibid.*, pp. 55–7.

36 *Ibid.*, pp. 73–103.

37 *Ibid.*, pp. 120–1.
38 *Tageszeitung* (Berlin), 3 December 1999, p. 1, as quoted in Elsässer, *Kriegsverbrechen*, p. 109.
39 Tim Judah, *Kosovo: War and Revenge* (New Haven, CT: Yale University Press, 2000).
40 Elsässer, *Kriegsverbrechen*, p. 113.
41 'Biography', at Jürgen Elsässer's web site, at www.juergen-elsaesser.de/html/template_en.php.
42 'Kritische Töne: Zum Hufeisenpan', in *Friedenspolitischer Ratschlag*, at www. uni-kassel.de/fb10/frieden/aktuell/Hufeisen.html.
43 Rolf Paasch, 'Die halbherzige Intervention: Lektionen aus dem Bosnien-Krieg', in Angelika Volle and Werner Weidenfeld (eds.), *Der Balkan: Zwischen Krise und Stabilität* (Bielefeld: W. Bertelsmann Verlag, 2002), p. 10.
44 Markus Spillmann, 'Der Westen und Kosovo: Ein leidwoller Erfahrungs-prozess', in Volle and Weidenfeld , *Der Balkan*, p. 17.
45 Hannes Hofbauer, 'Neue Staaten, neue Kriege', in Hannes Hofbauer (ed.), *Balkan Krieg: Die Zerstörung Jugoslawiens* (Vienna: ProMedia, 1999), p. 136.
46 Michel Chossudovsky, 'Die ökonomische Rationalität hinter der Zerschla-gung Jugoslawiens', in Hofbauer, *Balkan Krieg*, p. 242.
47 Joachim Hösler, Norman Paech, and Gerhard Stuby, *Der gerechte Krieg? Neue Nato-Strategie, Völkerrecht und Westeuropäisierung des Balkans* (Bremen: Donat Verlag, 2000).
48 Johannes Klotz, 'Vorwort', in Hösler et al., *Der gerechte Krieg*, p. 8.
49 Norman Paech, 'Neue NATO-Strategie – neues Völkerrecht?', in Hösler et al., *Der gerechte Krieg*, pp. 53, 57–8.
50 Quoted *ibid.*, p. 61.
51 *Ibid.*, p. 63.
52 Joachim Hösler, '"Balkanisierung" – "Europäisierung"? Zu Südosteuropas historischer Spezifik und den Folgen westeuropäischen "Zivilisations- und Stabilitätsexports"', in Hösler et al., *Der gerechte Krieg*, p. 9.
53 Paul Latawski, 'What to Do about Nationalism?', in Paul Latawski (ed.), *Contemporary Nationalism in East Central Europe* (Houndmills: Macmillan, 1995), p. 180, as cited critically in György Péteri, 'Between Empire and Nation-State: Comments on the Pathology of State Formation in Eastern Europe during the "Short Twentieth Century"', *Contemporary European History*, 9, 3 (2000), p. 377. Péteri comments, quite properly, that 'in our modern world, the ethno-demography of which has been and will to an increasing extent be in a state of constant flux, there is *nothing* that can recommend policies of homogenisation/nationalisation'.
54 Hösler, 'Balkanisierung', pp. 29–32.
55 Reinhard Merkel (ed.), *Der Kosovo-Krieg und das Völkerrecht* (Frankfurt-am-Main: Suhrkamp, 2000).
56 Reinhard Merkel, Ulrich K. Preuss, Otfried Höffe, and Wolfgang Kersting.
57 Jürgen Habermas and Wolfgang Kersting.

58 Immanuel Kant, 'Perpetual Peace: A Philosophical Sketch', in I. Kant, *Political Writings*, trans. from German by H. B. Nisbet, ed. by Hans Reiss (Cambridge: Cambridge University Press, 1970; reprinted 1991), p. 116.

59 *Ibid.*, p. 123.

60 Bruno Simma, 'Die NATO, die UN und militärische Gewaltanwendung: Rechtliche Aspekte', in Merkel, *Der Kosovo-Krieg*, p. 49.

61 Jürgen Habermas, 'Bestialität und Humanität. Ein Krieg an der Grenze zwischen Recht und Moral', in Merkel, *Der Kosovo-Krieg*, p. 53.

62 Habermas, *The Inclusion of the Other*, pp. 192–3.

63 Reinhard Merkel, 'Das Elend der Beschützten: Rechtsethische Grundlagen und Grenzen der sog. humanitären Intervention und die Verwerflichkeit der NATO-Aktion', in Merkel, *Der Kosovo-Krieg*, pp. 66–7, 73.

64 Jeremy Bentham (1748–1832) was an English philosopher who developed a theory called utilitarianism, and coined the phrase, 'the greatest good for the greatest number'.

65 Merkel, 'Das Elend der Beschützten', p. 90. Merkel refers to Kant's categorical imperative in n. 19 on the same page.

66 Dieter Senghaas, 'Recht auf Nothilfe', in Merkel, *Der Kosovo-Krieg*, pp. 101–2, 109.

67 Wolfgang Kersting, 'Bewaffnete Intervention als Menschenrechtsschutz?', in Merkel, *Der Kosovo-Krieg*, p. 208.

68 *Ibid.*, p. 209.

69 *Ibid.*, pp. 218–21.

70 Jürgen Habermas, *The Future of Human Nature* (Cambridge: Polity Press, 2003), pp. 36–37, emphases in the original.

71 Habermas, 'Bestialität und Humanität', p. 59. Kersting ('Bewaffnete Intervenention', p. 207) agrees with Habermas.

72 Wolfgang Ischinger, 'Keine Sommerpause der deutschen Aussenpolitik: Zwischenbilanz nach dem Kosovo-Krieg', in Volle and Weidenfeld, *Der Balkan*, p. 23.

73 Ulrich Beck, 'Über den postnationalen Krieg', in Merkel, *Der Kosovo-Krieg*, p. 236.

74 Paolo Rumiz, *Masken für ein Massaker. Der manipulierte Krieg: Spurensuche auf dem Balkan*, expanded German edn, trans. from Italian by Friederike Hausmann and Gesa Schröder (Munich: Verlag Antje Kunstmann, 2000).

75 Norbert Mappes-Niediek, *Balkan-Mafia. Staaten in der Hand des Verbrechens – Eine Gefahr für Europa* (Berlin: Ch. Links Verlag, 2003).

76 Rumiz, *Masken für ein Massaker*, p. 102.

77 Ger Duijzings, *Religion and the Politics of Identity in Kosovo* (London: C. Hurst & Co., 2000).

78 Rumiz, *Masken für ein Massaker*, p. 103.

79 *Ibid.*, p. 129.

80 *Ibid.*, pp. 205–7.

81 *Ibid.*, p. 211.

82 Mappes-Niediek, *Balkan-Mafia*, p. 47.

83 *Ibid.*, pp. 109, 112, 114, 115.

84 Marie-Janine Calic, *Krieg und Frieden in Bosnien-Hercegovina*, revised and expanded edn (Frankfurt-am-Main: Suhrkamp, 1996).

85 Daniel Eisermann, *Der lange Weg nach Dayton: Die westliche Politik und der Krieg im ehemaligen Jugoslawien 1991 bis 1995* (Baden-Baden: Nomos Verlagsgesellschaft, 2000).

86 Andreas Hasenclever, *Die Macht der Moral in der internationalen Politik: Militärische Interventionen westlicher Staaten in Somalia, Ruanda und Bosnien-Herzegowina* (Frankfurt: Campus Verlag, 2000).

87 Calic, *Krieg und Frieden*, p. 36.

88 *Ibid.*, p. 58.

89 *Ibid.*, p. 80.

90 *Ibid.*, pp. 81–2.

91 *Ibid.*, pp. 141–6.

92 *Ibid.*, pp. 158–6.

93 *Ibid.*, p. 228.

94 *Ibid.*, p. 237.

95 Eisermann, *Der lange Weg*, p. 26.

96 *Ibid.*, p. 413.

97 Quoted *ibid.*, p. 309, from *Le Monde*, 13 June 1995.

98 *Ibid.*, p. 310.

99 *Ibid.*, p. 409.

100 Hasenclever, *Die Macht der Moral*, p. 21.

101 *Ibid.*, p. 46.

102 *Ibid.*, pp. 46, 48.

103 *Ibid.*, p. 19.

104 *Ibid.*, pp. 192, 365–74.

105 *Ibid.*, p. 391.

106 *Ibid.*, pp. 409–10, 394.

107 *Ibid.*, pp. 162–3.

108 *Ibid.*, p. 155. See also p. 128.

REFERENCES

Calic, Marie-Janine, *Krieg und Frieden in Bosnien-Hercegovina*, revised and expanded edn (Frankfurt-am-Main: Suhrkamp, 1996), p. 289.

Eisermann, Daniel, *Der lange Weg nach Dayton: Die westliche Politik und der Krieg im ehemaligen Jugoslawien 1991 bis 1995* (Baden-Baden: Nomos Verlagsgesellschaft, 2000), p. 443.

Elsässer, Jürgen, *Kriegsverbrechen: Die tödlichen Lügen der Bundesregierung und ihre Opfer im Kosovo-Konflikt*, 4th edn (Hamburg: Konkret, 2001), p. 190.

Hasenclever, Andreas, *Die Macht der Moral in der internationalen Politik: Militärische Interventionen westlicher Staaten in Somalia, Ruanda und Bosnien-Herzegowina* (Frankfurt: Campus Verlag, 2000), p. 468.

Hofbauer, Hannes (ed.), *Balkan Krieg: Die Zerstörung Jugoslawiens* (Vienna: ProMedia, 1999), p. 263.

Hösler, Joachim, Norman Paech, and Gerhard Stuby, *Der gerechte Krieg? Neue Nato-Strategie, Völkerrecht und Westeuropäisierung des Balkans* (Bremen: Donat Verlag, 2000), p. 134.

Mappes-Niedliek, Norbert, *Balkan-Mafia. Staaten in der Hand des Verbrechens – Eine Gefahr für Europa* (Berlin: Ch. Links Verlag, 2003), p. 190.

Merkel, Reinhard (ed.), *Der Kosovo-Krieg und das Völkerrecht* (Frankfurt-am-Main: Suhrkamp, 2000), p. 241.

Rumiz, Paolo, *Masken für ein Massaker. Der manipulierte Krieg: Spurensuche auf dem Balkan*, expanded German edn, trans. from Italian by Friederike Hausmann and Gesa Schröder (Munich: Verlag Antje Kunstmann, 2000), p. 219.

Tenbergen, Rasmus, *Der Kosovo-Krieg: Eine gerechte Intervention?* (ILD Verlag, 2001), p. 172.

Volle, Angelika and Werner Weidenfeld (eds.), *Der Balkan: Zwischen Krise und Stabilität* (Bielefeld: W. Bertelsmann Verlag, 2002), p. 182.

11   Lands and peoples: Bosnia, Croatia, Slovenia, Serbia

I

Bosnia

The breakup of socialist Yugoslavia clearly provided a spur to the writing of English-language histories of Bosnia. Of the three volumes being discussed here, two – those by Noel Malcolm and by the team of Robert Donia and John Fine – were published more or less simultaneously, while the volume by Mitja Velikonja was published nearly a decade later, and lists the two aforementioned works in its bibliography. The volumes by Malcolm and Velikonja include full bibliographies, while the volume by Donia and Fine includes a set of recommended readings in English.

No doubt Donia and Fine had been driven to the brink of despair by the constant repetition in the press of the inane notion that the peoples of Bosnia had been hating each other for thousands of years, i.e., even before they came to Bosnia, because they make a point, early in the book, of stating, 'despite its *ad nauseam* repetition in the international press, nowhere do we find evidence of the alleged centuries of hatred (whether religious or ethnic) among various Bosnian groups that has supposedly permeated their history'.[1] They drive home their point by asserting further that the peoples inhabiting Bosnia never went to war against each other until 1941, though they concede that there was some religious persecution in the final five years of the medieval state. But they immediately add that 'this was forced on an unwilling Bosnian king by an intolerant papacy which made persecution of a local denomination a condition for Western aid against the Ottomans'.[2] It follows, for Donia and Fine, that 'religious rivalry and violence were . . . not part of Bosnia's heritage'.[3] This interpretation is, however, disputed by both Malcolm and Velikonja, as will be seen shortly.

Donia and Fine note that the Slavs came to Bosnia only in the late sixth and early seventh centuries and underline that all three groups –

243

Bosniaks, Croats, and Serbs – came from the same Slavic stock, though they also say that ancestors of today's Croats and Serbs probably came from Persia. On the subject of the controversial Bosnian Church, Donia and Fine dispute the conventional notion that it had 'neo-Manichean'/ Bogomil associations and insist that it maintained Catholic doctrines even though it broke with Rome.[4] Noel Malcolm offers a more complex account of the Bosnian Church, noting that the Bogomil theory of that Church was the work of Franjo Rački, a nineteenth-century Croatian historian, and suggesting that the Bosnian Church blended elements of Orthodox and Catholic ritual, so that, in effect, it bridged the two ecclesiastical realms.[5] Velikonja notes that Bosnia was initially placed under the jurisdiction of the (Roman Catholic) archbishopric of Bar, then reassigned to the jurisdiction of the archbishopric of Split, and finally, in the second half of the twelfth century, to the archbishopric of Dubrovnik (Ragusa). According to Velikonja, however, Bosnia was only 'nominally Roman Catholic' with considerable differences between the Bosnian Church and both the Western (Catholic) Church and the Eastern (Orthodox) Church. Then, in the thirteenth century, the Bosnian Church became autonomous, being later accused of heresy, dualism, and even ditheism.[6]

Malcolm and Donia/Fine record that the Franciscans set up a mission in Bosnia in the 1340s.[7] Velikonja confirms this, adding, however, that the first Franciscans showed up in Bosnia, in the company of the papal legate, Acontius, in 1222. During the thirteenth century, they worked closely with the local Dominicans, but in the early years of the fourteenth century, they quarrelled over who should be assigned the rights of the inquisitorial office. The Franciscans won the dispute.[8]

Recently, there has been more controversy concerning the conversions to Islam after the Ottoman conquest than about the Bosnian Church. Traditional Croatian historiography claimed that the inhabitants of Bosnia were Croats, that they converted en masse to Islam soon after the conquest of Bosnia in 1463 and Herzegovina in 1481, and that therefore the Bosniaks (Muslims) of Bosnia-Herzegovina are ethnically Croat. All three of these books dispute this approach and affirm that conversion to Islam proceeded much more slowly, and that it makes no sense to think of the Bosniaks as Croats.[9] Malcolm, for example, examined the Ottoman 'defters', or tax records, which categorized people by religion. From these records, Malcolm found that as late as 1548 Muslims accounted for only 40 per cent of the population of Bosnia-Herzegovina[10] – hardly evidence of an immediate mass conversion. The three books offer mutually corroborative accounts. Donia/Fine and Malcolm suggest that the Bosnian Church was already 'largely defunct' (as Malcolm puts it) *before* the Ottoman conquest, deny that the conversions were motivated by the desire to retain property, since Christians were allowed to own property, and affirm the weakness of religious affiliation in the area at the time of the conquest.[11] Velikonja, by contrast, while agreeing that religion in Bosnia, prior to the arrival of the Ottomans, had been 'a very loose, inconsistent, and weak faith . . . and lacked any understanding of the main religious rituals', argues that 'the Bosnian nobility *did* indeed convert to Islam in order to retain their property, privilege, and position . . . [while] others – primarily peasants – converted to Islam in order to avoid the taxes imposed on Christians.'[12] The weakness of religious ties was due to the relative lack of ecclesiastical infrastructure in Bosnia and to the shortage of priests. Donia and Fine argue that the word 'conversion' is inappropriate and that what occurred in Bosnia-Herzegovina was a gradual 'acceptance' of Islam on a syncretic basis, blending Christian and Islamic customs and practices. This picture is corroborated by Malcolm, who notes, for example, that Muslims kissed Christian icons and had Catholic masses said for them when they were ill.[13] Islam and Christianity were therefore not viewed as rivals but as coexistent alternatives which could be mixed. Given the stronger infrastructure which Islam enjoyed, thanks to Ottoman sovereignty and the pre-existing shortage of Christian churches and priests, people living far from Christian churches but close to Islamic mosques tended to convert for reasons of feasibility. This, in turn, provides a partial explanation of the fact that the cities and towns were more quickly Islamicized than the villages. Moreover, as the Ottomans established themselves in Bosnia-Herzegovina, Islam became associated with the upper class and to accept Islam was to associate oneself with the dominant class. The number of Turks who moved to Bosnia was small, according to Malcolm, but, as he points out, migration did play a role in that some Islamicized Slavs arrived in Bosnia in the early years from Serbia, Macedonia, and Bulgaria, with a much larger influx coming at the end of the seventeenth century from Dalmatia, Croatia, Slavonia, and Hungary, as the Ottomans were driven out of those areas.[14]

The Donia/Fine book is less detailed than the works by Malcolm and Velikonja when it comes to the years 1463–1878, but they emphasize that, while confessional identity came to be translated, over time, into ethnic identity (Catholics viewing themselves as Croats, Orthodox viewing themselves as Serbs, and Muslims holding to a primarily confessional identity), ethnic differences did not lead to the establishment of ethnically based political parties or to the development of rival national programmes, with the result that relations among the three dominant groups remained more or less harmonious. They continue by affirming:

Relations among the ethnic groups were marked by mutual tolerance and frequent intermingling in everyday life. Catholics, Orthodox, Muslims, Jews, and others shared the same marketplaces and, particularly in urban areas, were often acquainted with one another and prone to render mutual assistance and cooperation in times of need. They often joined in celebrating one another's holidays . . . [O]ccasional conflicts occurred after 1850 between landlords and the peasants who were expected to give up a portion of their crop, but one cannot reasonably treat such socioeconomic conflicts as continual ethnic strife.

While many outsiders cling to the insupportable generalization that tribal hatreds and ethnic warfare have characterized Bosnia for centuries, those familiar with Bosnian history and culture more typically have the opposite perception. They ask how Bosnians, who lived together in relative tranquility and mutual tolerance for many centuries, can suddenly turn on neighbors and friends and commit the vicious and murderous acts that have become commonplace in the current Bosnian conflict.[15]

Malcolm paints a rather different picture. According to him, the Ottomans introduced Orthodox peasants into Bosnia and favoured the Orthodox Church over the Catholic Church. The influx was necessary to fill up lands depopulated by war or plague.[16] Malcolm places more emphasis than Donia and Fine on the constant wars in which the Ottoman Empire was engaged, with Bosnia close to its northern border. The war with the Habsburg Empire, fought 1683–99, in particular, resulted in the flight of as many as 130,000 refugees to Bosnia.[17] A century later, Joseph II of Austria revived the war against the Ottomans and made overtures to Bosnian Catholics to join the Austrian war effort; in addition, Muslims who surrendered were promised full religious freedom in the event that Austria should prove able to annex Bosnia. This campaign, initiated in 1788, ended in 1791 when Austria agreed to surrender the territorial gains it had temporarily made.[18] A decade and a half later, the uprising in neighbouring Serbia resulted in 'widespread massacres, robberies and forced baptisms of ordinary Slav Muslims as well as Turks'; those who could fled to Bosnia, where they recounted the atrocities they had witnessed in Serbia.[19] Nor was Bosnian society conflict-free. Malcolm draws attention, in particular, to the growing rivalry between the Catholic and Orthodox Churches in Bosnia, whose clergy would spread 'horrible' tales about each other.[20] Velikonja's account is closer in spirit to Malcolm's, as already noted, than to that of the Donia/Fine volume. He describes the Balkans, and Bosnia-Herzegovina in particular, between the fourteenth and early twentieth centuries as 'the battlefield on which Christian and Islamic states and civilizations clashed', implicitly evoking Samuel P. Huntington's famous 'clash of civilizations' thesis. But he also adds that, in spite of occasional tensions between the religious communities, 'Bosnia was able to avoid the kind of religious antagonism and keen conflicts that were characteristic of other European countries. The religious history of Bosnia is therefore a history of religious division as well as religious coexistence.'[21]

That the Ottoman Empire was more tolerant than other states in Europe at the time is well known and not disputed, even though conversions out of Islam were not permitted. As for the well-known proscriptions of horseback riding, bearing of arms, and wearing of green for non-Muslims,[22] Malcolm notes that these proscriptions were not enforced in Bosnia, where 'Christian priests and merchants . . . dressed almost exactly like Muslims, did ride horses and did carry arms.'[23] But by the nineteenth century – the authors of all three volumes agree – religious differences were becoming polarized and religious identity was increasingly being understood as the badge of ethnic identity. Donia and Fine write, in this context, that 'Catholics, Serbian Orthodox, Muslims, and Jews developed differing world views that, over time, became deeply entrenched.'[24] Then, in 1874, the crop failed, but local tax collectors were not inclined to ease the peasants' tax burden and the result was an uprising of (Christian) peasants against (Muslim) landlords. The close coincidence of religion with class enabled the uprising to develop rather quickly into an armed resistance against Ottoman rule per se. Donia and Fine say little about the fighting during the years 1875–8, but the details provided by Malcolm and Velikonja suggest that interethnic bitterness was sown at that time. Ottoman regular and irregular troops – the latter known as *bashi-bazouks* – terrorized the countryside, torching villages and killing at least 5,000 peasants. Between 100,000 and 250,000 (Muslim) refugees fled southeastward.[25] Malcolm writes that, by 1878, the Muslims and Christians of Bosnia-Herzegovina 'detested one another'.[26] As is well known, Austria-Hungary occupied Bosnia-Herzegovina in 1878, but had to bring some 268,000 troops into the province before it was able to put down armed resistance by an odd alliance of Muslims and Orthodox – the latter yearning for union with Serbia. Of course, Malcolm also notes the 'colossal' scale of public investment during the 'Austrian' period in building up the economic infrastructure of Bosnia. The result was the laying of 111 km of broad-gauge railroads and 911 km of narrow-gauge railroads by 1911, more than 1,000 km of major roads, the construction of 121 bridges and also of dams, the establishment of model farms, including a model vineyard and a model fish farm, and so forth.[27]

According to Malcolm, Austro-Hungarian policy was not well attuned to assuring peace and harmony, however. The Austrian announcement in 1881 that all Bosnian males would be subject to conscription into the army sparked a revolt and widespread banditry which continued for more than a decade. Christians were angry that the land reform which they had expected Austro-Hungarian authorities to pass was never introduced. And the policy of encouraging German (not Austrian) colonization in Bosnia – a policy apparently initiated by a German priest – angered locals who demanded that the colonization be halted.[28]

Donia and Fine give the Austro-Hungarian occupation a more positive spin, though they admit that the law passed in 1911, encouraging peasants to purchase the land they tilled on the basis of a cash downpayment to the landlords, made little difference in patterns of land ownership since few peasants could afford to avail themselves of this provision.[29] Donia and Fine note that the Austro-Hungarian authorities subsidized all three major religious organizations in Bosnia-Herzegovina and argue that the Serbian Orthodox Church and school communes 'flourished under Austrian rule'.[30] Although they note the resentments stirred up by Archbishop Josef Stadler's active but largely unsuccessful efforts at proselytization among the Muslims, Donia and Fine report that the statute granted in May 1909, which created the office of reis-ul-ulema as leader of Bosnia's Islamic community and granted the Muslims autonomous control over Islamic charitable foundations, 'met nearly all Muslim demands'.[31] Having won both religious and cultural autonomy by the end of the first decade of the twentieth century, 'the Bosnian Muslim leaders became the most loyal supporters of Bosnia's Austrian regime', they write.[32]

Velikonja agrees with both of the foregoing accounts, including concerning the loyalty of the Muslim elites to the kaiser, but lays stress on the development of rival religio-national mythologies among the separate peoples of Bosnia-Herzegovina as a source of growing problems.[33] He also notes than some 100,000 Bosnian Muslims left Bosnia between 1878 and 1914[34] – a not inconsiderable number. The Austro-Hungarian annexation in 1908, a move with more juridical than practical importance, nonetheless excited widespread criticism in European capitals, resentment in Serbia and Montenegro, and alarm, according to Velikonja, among the Serbs and Muslims of Bosnia-Herzegovina. Rebellions swept over Bosnia, with Serb irredentism inspiring unrest in eastern Herzegovina; and during the great War of 1914–18, Muslims and Croats largely remained loyal to the kaiser, while Bosnian Serbs fought against the empire.[35] The result was the deepening of interethnic antagonisms, which were expressed, at war's end, in widespread anarchy in which Muslims were targeted for attacks, 'especially after the arrival of Serbian and Montenegrin soldiers in early November', as Malcolm points out. But Malcolm adds that the atrocities perpetrated then should not be interpreted 'as evidence of ancient ethnic-religious hatred among

Bosnian Serbs and Muslims. They happened in extreme and unusual circumstances, at the very end of a war in which people had suffered severe privations'.[36]

These three volumes largely agree on what to make of Bosnian experience in the interwar kingdom (1918–41), though Velikonja, given his stated interest in religious separation, devotes more space to the activities of the major religious organizations. None of the three books devotes much space to Milan Stojadinović, the longest-serving prime minister in the interwar kingdom, and only Velikonja has much to say about Croatian Peasant Party leader Stjepan Radić, who was assassinated in 1928. Concerning Radić, Donia and Fine have this to say: 'The leader of the Croatian Peasant Party, Stjepan Radić, spent much of the period obstructing legislative agreement, boycotting Parliament, and seeking support for Croatian separatist positions in London, Moscow, and elsewhere abroad.'[37] Noel Malcolm has the most to say about Mehmed Spaho, leader of the Yugoslav Muslim Organization until his death in June 1939, describing him as "a shrewd politician who had managed to give the Bosnian Muslims a degree of political leverage in the inter-war period out of all proportion to their numerical strength'.[38]

Writing about the Second World War, all of the books under review here carefully avoid any estimate of the number of people killed at the Croatian fascist (Ustaša) concentration camp at Jasenovac, though Donia and Fine note that one Serbian estimate of 1.1 million *Serbian* dead alone (i.e., not counting others who might have died there) at Jasenovac is 'unlikely'.[39] All three accounts portray Chetnik leader Draža Mihailović as dedicated to the restoration of the Yugoslav kingdom (though Malcolm adds that he revised his ideas after the atrocities perpetrated by the Ustaša troops), and all three note the ambivalent response of Bosnian Muslims to the Ustaša regime's efforts to recruit them for the Handžar (Dagger) SS division, while Velikonja points to Muslim suspicions about the NDH's (Independent State of Croatia) endeavours to 'Croatize Islam'.[40] Malcolm observes that evidence of any personal responsibility on Mihailović's part for the atrocities perpetrated against the Bosnian Muslims is lacking.[41]

The differences in treatment of the communist era are sharper. Donia and Fine introduce the new era optimistically, even buoyantly, declaring that 'The new, postwar Yugoslavia gave its citizens the chance to create a forward-looking enterprise, one in which national "brotherhood and unity" was enlisted in the campaign to build a revolutionary new society.'[42] They claim that, after the break with Stalin, Tito 'abandon[ed] earlier policies of control and repression' and embraced 'liberalization',[43] before surveying the economic transformation and insitutional innovations introduced by the Yugoslav communists, noting also the repression of pro-soviet 'Cominformists'. Concerning the Islamic community in Bosnia, they write that the Communist Party of Yugoslavia (CPY) avoided attacking Muslims openly, but cut off subsidies to Islamic cultural institutions. According to Donia and Fine, after the Vakuf Assembly issued a statement of loyalty to the communist regime in August 1946, the communists eased their pressure and allowed the principal Islamic institutions, including the reis-ul-ulema, the Vakuf Commission, and the Vakuf Assembly to function. 'Despite some confiscations and reforms,' they write, 'the vakuf system remained largely intact, and vakufs continued to support major Islamic cultural institutions in Bosnia throughout the socialist period.'[44] On the whole, Donia and Fine devote more space in their chapter on the communist era to sketching out developments affecting Yugoslavia as a whole than does either Malcolm or Velikonja. Passing judgement on Tito, they write in rapture that he 'overcame his own authoritarian instincts' and proved to be 'fearless as a social innovator,' leading the way in fashioning 'an open, prosperous, and progressive society'.[45] They call for forgiveness for his failure to leave behind institutions capable of assuring stability after his death and reject portrayals of Tito as a 'tyrant'. In their eyes, Tito was the 'great arbiter' who has been unfairly blamed by 'nationalist . . . ideologues'.[46]

Noel Malcolm's account of communist-era Yugoslavia strikes a rather different note, starting, as it does, not with a forward glance at eventual liberalization, but by noting that as many as 250,000 people were killed by Tito's Partisans in the eighteen months following the end of the war.[47] Where the Islamic community is concerned, Malcolm stresses the difficulties, noting the suppression of the shariat courts in 1946, the ban on the wearing of the veil in 1950, closure of the mektebs (elementary schools where children learned about the Koran), the closure of all the tekkes (dervish lodges) in 1952, and the ban on the dervish orders. He also notes that the Muslim cultural and educational societies were shut down by the communists, as was the Islamic printing house in Sarajevo.[48] Malcolm notes that the situation for religious believers improved with the passage of a new law governing religious bodies in 1954, but notes that Bosnia had the lowest rate of economic growth of any of the federation's six constituent republics during the years 1952–68.[49] But beginning in the mid-1960s there were sundry nationalist campaigns among the peoples of Yugoslavia, campaigns which had a destructive potential. The Ayatollah Khomeini's portrait could be seen in Bosnian shop windows after the Iranian revolution of 1979. Malcolm provides more details about the 1983 trial of Alija Izetbegović and twelve other defendants on charges of 'hostile and counterrevolutionary acts derived from Muslim nationalism'.[50]

Velikonja's account of the communist era begins with an explanation of the constitutional order, noting the discrediting of religious elites as a result of their wartime collaboration with occupation authorities. Among those sentenced to death was Mufti Ismet Muftić of Zagreb. Velikonja devotes considerable space to the fortunes of the Catholic and Orthodox Churches in the communist system, and even offers a brief sketch of the situation of the Jewish community before turning to the Islamic community. Interestingly, Velikonja writes that, from early in the communist era, 'there was a high level of trust between the Communist authorities and the Muslim community'. But, Velikonja adds immediately, the communists' 'benevolent attitude towards Islam later changed considerably'.[51] The repercussions in Bosnia of the Iranian revolution in 1979 had something to do with this change.

Donia and Fine offer some interesting details on the countdown to the fighting in Bosnia in 1992–5. They note, for example, that at the time when the Yugoslav People's Army (JNA) was making illegal deliveries of arms to Serb militias being organized in Croatia and Bosnia-Herzegovina, some JNA officers opposed the operation.[52] The divisions within the JNA officer corps, which this opposition reflected, were finally resolved only in August 1993, with the forced retirement of forty-three generals, including General Života Panić, the chief-of-staff. The authors blame Serb and Croat nationalists for having promoted hatred among people who had been largely uninfected by its mephitic vapours and blame the international community for failing to respond to the crisis in a responsible way.[53]

All three books make reference to the meeting between Tudjman and Milošević in March 1991, at which a partition of Bosnia was allegedly discussed. All three books report the early preparations by Bosnian Serb militias for an insurgency. Given the way in which the combatants politicized religion after 1992, a 1985 survey cited by Malcolm, setting the proportion of religious believers in Bosnia at about 17 per cent,[54] is particularly striking. Whereas Donia and Fine report the Vance–Owen Peace Plan without enthusiasm,[55] blaming its collapse on its rejection by the Bosnian Serbs, Malcolm quotes himself to the effect that 'a blind man can see that the Vance–Owen plan is never going to be fulfilled', and argues that the use of ethnic labels on the cantons could only prove 'harmful'. Malcolm says that this feature contributed directly to Muslim-Croat fighting and thus to the breakdown of their alliance against the Bosnian Serb forces.[56] Before bringing his history of Bosnia to a close, Malcolm underlines a theme with which Donia and Fine would agree, namely, that the causes of the Bosnian conflict lay outside Bosnia itself.[57]

Given the greater emphasis in Velikonja's book on myths and ideology, it is not surprising that he castigates the Western media and Western diplomats for taking over Serb myths, among which the most common 'was the allegation that all parties involved in the war were equally to blame'.[58] Among those Western diplomats to pick up this refrain were Peter Lord Carrington, Carl Bildt, and Warren Christopher. Insofar as Velikonja's purpose is to come to some assessment of the problem of religious intolerance in Bosnia, and not to provide a history of Bosnia as such, he closes by posing the question whether nationalists manipulated religion for their purpose, or whether religious elites exploited the wave of nationalism for *their* purposes. Velikonja offers the possibly surprising judgement that both of these propositions were true.[59]

All three of these volumes offer insights into Bosnian history, but each frames the story differently. Malcolm's history is, in the most proper sense, a history *of Bosnia*. By contrast, in discussing the years 1918–91, Donia and Fine place Bosnia clearly in a *Yugoslav context*. Finally, Velikonja's volume places Bosnia in the context of *religious diversity*.

II

Croatia

The region which today comprises Croatia was first settled by an ancient tribe called Illyrians, concerning whom there is still controversy today. The Histri (for whom Istria is named) and the Delmatae (for whom Dalmatia is named) were also living in the region in the earliest times. The Celts came to the region in the fourth century BCE, as well as Greek colonists. The Romans conquered the area in the second century BCE, the Avars (a Mongol people) came to Pannonia in the sixth century, and in the seventh century, the Croats, who had been living in the Black Sea steppes between the Caucasus and the Carpathians, arrived in what is today Croatia. Relatively little is known about the Croats until the ninth century, however, when there were large-scale conversions to Christianity. Over the next nearly 300 years, the feudal system developed in Croatia, Benedictine monasteries were built, and fortifications were erected at strategically vital points. The Croatian king, Tomislav (c. 910–c. 928), is remembered today for having defeated armies from both Hungary and Bulgaria. But at the end of the eleventh century, the Croatian Trpimirović dynasty died out, and in 1102, Koloman Arpad,

King of Hungary, was crowned also king of Dalmatia and Croatia. Thus began an 816-year-long association with Hungary, and later the Habsburg Empire, in which, after 1867, Croatia was assigned to the administrative jurisdiction of the Hungarian half of the Dual Monarchy. Between 1918 and 1991, Croatia was part of the Yugoslav state, with the exception of the years 1941–5, when it was set up as a rump satellite of Nazi Germany and fascist Italy, under the ironic name 'Independent State of Croatia' (NDH). Thus, with its declaration of independence in June 1991, Croatia reclaimed an independence it had not enjoyed in 889 years.

The organizational schemes of the books by Ivo Goldstein and Marcus Tanner are strikingly similar. In each of these volumes, the years up to 1526 (the Battle of Mohács) occupy less than 13 per cent of the text, the years 1526–1945 occupy about 45 per cent of the text, with the remainder devoted to the years since 1945. The volume by Ludwig Steindorff, approximately the same length as the Goldstein and Tanner volumes, devotes 27 per cent of its space to the years up to 1526, 51 per cent of its space to the years between 1526 and 1945, and the remainder to the years since 1945. Steindorff's volume is, thus, more detailed on all centuries prior to 1945, offering also a time line, a set of biographical statements, and even a listing of historical towns and sites worth visiting. William Bartlett's *Croatia: Between Europe and the Balkans* – a subtitle which is sure to provoke some controversy – is volume 16 in Routledge's series, 'Postcommunist States and Nations' and follows the general format for that series. That means that the length of the book is half of that of any of the histories, and the years up to 1945 occupy only 16 per cent of the text, with most of the remainder (79 per cent) devoted to the years since 1989. All four volumes are written in a neutral, professional tone, with ample research in each case (though only slight use of Croatian-language materials in the case of the Bartlett volume). Tanner's style is the liveliest of the four, and only Tanner includes reminiscences of the time he spent in Croatia.

Generally speaking, there are few differences concerning the facts at hand, though Bartlett, alone among this set, suggests that the 27 March 1941 coup may have been 'inspired as much by Serbian antagonism to the compromise that Prince Paul had reached with the Croats, and to the creation of the Croatian Banovina' [an autonomous province set, up in 1939] as by opposition to the prince's adherence to the Axis Pact.[60] Still, when it comes to the political activity of Ante Starčević (1823–96), founder of the Croatian Party of Right, there is a considerable consensus, albeit with variations of emphasis. Goldstein and Steindorff point out that Starčević was not interested in union with Serbia and wanted to erect a Croatian state through the unification of the lands of the Kingdom of Croatia with Bosnia-Herzegovina, though Goldstein notes that Starčević admired the medieval Serbian Nemanjić dynasty for its success in state consolidation.[61] Goldstein mentions that, in the 1880s, Starčević's party modified its programmatic goals and began to talk about achieving maximum autonomy for Croatia and Bosnia-Herzegovina *within* the Habsburg Empire. Tanner lavishes the most attention on Starčević, and says that, in his later years, he became more moderate and allowed that Slovenes and Serbs had the right to maintain their own national identities within a Croatian state.[62] And, while Tanner is quite correct in writing that Ante Pavelić's wartime NDH misappropriated and 'grossly misinterpreted' Starčević, he is mistaken in thinking that 'Starčević believed in a united southern Slav state as much as Strossmayer.'[63] Bartlett agrees with Goldstein and Steindorff in arguing that Starčević 'rejected a Yugoslav framework for Croatia'; Bartlett is also correct in noting the importance of some of the liberal ideas associated with the French Revolution for Starčević's thinking.[64] (It is, however, distracting to find that the date given for Starčević's death ranges from 1895 to 1897 among these four books; the correct date is 1896, as given by Goldstein and Steindorff.)

There are differences, too, in reportage of the murder in 1931 of Milan Šufflay, member of the Croatian Party of Right and a prominent historian. Steindorff and Bartlett write that Šufflay, an outspoken critic of the regime, was gunned down by police agents.[65] Goldstein leaves the question of agency to the side and writes simply that Šufflay, who, as he notes, was an accomplished observer of Albanian culture, 'was killed in the street in Zagreb. The killers were never found.'[66]

Where Vladko Maček (1879–1964), leader of the Croatian Peasant Party after the 1928 assassination of Stjepan Radić, is concerned, all four books provide sufficient coverage of his activities in the interwar era to enable the reader to get a good sense of his importance. Tanner provides the richest detail concerning Maček's negotiations with representatives of the Italian government; Maček indicated to Count Galleazzo Ciano, the Italian foreign minister, that given a subvention from Italy he would be prepared to initiate an uprising against Belgrade within six months. Ciano responded enthusiastically. But Maček was leading him on, using the promise of Italian aid to blackmail Belgrade into making concessions.[67] In this way, Maček won wide-ranging autonomy for Croatia within the Banovina set up in 1939.

But more controversial than either Starčević or Maček are Archbishop Alojzije Stepinac (1898–1960), Yugoslav president Josip Broz Tito (1892–1980), and Croatian president Franjo Tudjman (1922–99).

Stepinac, beatified by Pope John Paul II in 1998, has long been considered a genuine Croatian national hero, above all by Croats on the
political right, even while he has been denounced as a war criminal by
people of a variety of political persuasions, including Serb nationalists.
The facts concerning which there is no disagreement are that Stepinac
was named coadjutor to the see of Zagreb in 1934 with the right of
succession, that he succeeded Archbishop Bauer as archbishop of
Zagreb upon the latter's death in 1937, that he initially welcomed the
establishment of the NDH, that he criticized the use of force in achieving
mass conversions of Serbs to Catholicism, that he protected some Jews
from the Croatian fascists during the Second World War, that he was put
on trial by the communists in September 1946 on charges of collaboration with the fascists and sent initially to Lepoglava, and that he was
eventually freed from prison, spending his last years in his native town of
Krašić. Although, after their frustration with politics in the interwar
kingdom, the 'enormous majority' of Croats, including Stepinac, were
spontaneously, if short-sightedly, euphoric at Croatia's separation from
Belgrade's jurisdiction in 1941, Stepinac continues to be criticized for
his decision to pay a call on Slavko Kvaternik, Pavelić's deputy in the
fascistic Ustaša party on 16 April 1941, *a day before the Yugoslav army
surrendered*, and to send around a circular to his clergy twelve days later,
welcoming the establishment of the NDH and, in the excerpt quoted by
Tanner, expressing his confidence 'that the Church in the resurrected
state of Croatia will be able to proclaim in complete freedom the un-
contestable principles of eternal truth and justice'.[68] Was Stepinac so
completely uninformed even about the basics of fascism that he could
have believed this for even a moment? Or was he a 'cunning fool', hoping
to flatter the regime into granting the Church some space to carry out its
mission? Did Stepinac have no clue as to the difficulties the Church had
faced in Germany? Had he never read the 1937 papal encyclical, *Mit
brennender Sorge*? An inspection of the full text of Stepinac's circular
letter, however, conveys a somewhat different impression from that
indicated by Tanner. After confessing the 'national joy and enthusiasm'
which Croats felt at that moment, Stepinac warned that 'the earthly
home is a true mother only when she teaches us to pray and to "give to
God what is God's", and that she is a solicitous mother in our life only
when she directs our steps on the roads which lead to God'[69] This
wording sounds vague and unspecific in the twenty-first century, but
the reference to 'roads which lead to God' would have been clear enough
in the midst of the Second World War. Moreover, Stepinac continues by
declaring, 'We must warn and teach that the holy enthusiasm and noble
zeal in building the foundations of the new Croat state *must* be inspired

by the fear of God and by love of God's law *and His commandments*, for only through God's law and not on false natural principles can the Croat state be solidly established.'[70] Just a fortnight into the life of the new state, Stepinac did not consider it necessary to enumerate the ten commandments, or to explicitly draw attention to the first atrocities which had been committed. Anyone reading the letter at the time would have been quite certain of the archbishop's meaning.

Stepinac was not prepared for the role of thundering critic, however, and hoped to induce the NDH authorities to change their course through quiet diplomacy; this did not work. What is known is that Stepinac was revolted by the atrocities being perpetrated by Pavelić's thugs. Tanner, for example, tells us that, as reports of Ustaša atrocities reached the Church in Croatia, most of the bishops, including Stepinac, turned against the NDH; one of the most outspoken was Bishop Alojzije Mišić.[71] Goldstein, Steindorff, and Tanner all note Stepinac's opposition to the *forced* conversions, while Goldstein draws attention also to Stepinac's opposition to Ustaša atrocities and racial intolerance, which the archbishop initially expressed privately in contacts with NDH officials, later denouncing Ustaša policies in public sermons.[72] Both Tanner and Goldstein note Stepinac's role in saving Jews, including the archdiocese's role in smuggling Jewish children out of the country via Hungary to Palestine.[73] But Stepinac viewed the communist Partisans as a greater threat to the Church than Pavelić's fascists. The four authors report the trial of Stepinac with a minimum of comment, though Steindorff makes it clear that the real reason for his trial had nothing to do with the archbishop's attitude towards the NDH and everything to do with his refusal to toe the communist line.[74]

For reasons which escape me, there is an increasing fashion among historians and political scientists to refer to Tito as 'Broz', thus using the family name he abandoned. In his lifetime he was never 'President Broz' – he was President Tito – and it seems a bit odd, to me, to refer to him in any other way than as 'Tito'. Be that as it may, for Goldstein, Tito used devices 'typical of capable dictators' and 'was completely aware of the serious nature of Yugoslavia's ethnic problems'.[75] Steindorff perhaps comes the closest to capturing something of the majesty which Tito embodied in his lifetime; as Steindorff notes, Tito's grand lifestyle contributed to the sense of majesty.[76]

Today, however, Croats spend more time arguing about Tudjman than about all other historical figures put together. There are problems of substance and style where Tudjman is concerned. Where style is concerned, one may note that Tudjman had a *false* sense of majesty, imagining that he had more charisma and grander authority than was, in fact, the case; his decision to set up palace guards in pseudo-nineteenth-century frock has also been mocked, as has his fixation on resurrecting historical heroes in 1990–1, even at the expense of finding adequate time to make preparations for eventual independence. Where substance is concerned, controversy has ranged from Tudjman's alleged anti-Semitism, to his alleged affinity for the NDH, to his negotiations with Milošević concerning the partition of Bosnia, to his wartime strategy (as already noted in chapters 1 and 5), to his authoritarian style of governance, which often displayed a petty side. Tanner quotes from Tudjman's speech during his campaign for the Croatian presidency in 1990, noting that Tudjman opined at the time that the NDH was 'not only a quisling organisation and a Fascist crime, but was also an expression of the Croatian nation's historic desire for an independent homeland'.[77] In endeavouring to explain this bizarre statement, Tanner speculates that 'The peculiar phraseology, suggesting that the Ustashe was the malevolent manifestation of a benign impulse, high-lighted the delicate balancing act he was trying to perform between the different political factions in his party'.[78] But Tanner is no fool and points to the evident nostalgia for the NDH in Tudjman-era Croatia and pro-Ustaša graffiti as not unrelated to the pervasive authoritarianism of the Tudjman regime.[79]

Goldstein agrees with Tanner, noting that Tudjman's 'authoritarian behaviour and style of governing' made their contribution to the political climate in Croatia in the 1990s.[80] Among the problems noted by Goldstein is the fact that little or no attention was paid to maintaining the separation of powers in the new Croatian state. Goldstein provides some interesting details about Tudjman's life, noting that Tudjman became fascinated with the *banovina* already in the 1960s and began, even then, to question the long-term viability of Bosnia.[81] He also reveals that as late as early spring 1991 Tudjman was prepared to accept a compromise under which Croatia would have remained within the Yugoslav state, on the basis of expanded local autonomy. But, as Goldstein notes, 'as pressure on Croatia increased and armed provocations became more frequent, it was decided to proclaim independence'.[82] It is, of course, well known that Tudjman, who reached the rank of colonel in the Partisan army during the Second World War, lived in Belgrade for some years after the war, reaching the rank of general in 1960, at the young age of thirty-eight. Goldstein describes Tudjman as 'ambitious and hard-working', adding that his historical writings reflected a tendency to bend history to suit his political preferences.[83]

Steindorff notes the various scandals which rocked the Tudjman regime, including concerning corrupt forms of privatization, other forms of corruption, nepotism, and Tudjman's refusal to confirm the legitimate election of the mayor of Zagreb.[84] Tudjman's complicity in wartime atrocities, his subversion of the electoral process, his takeover of key media outlets, his high-handed treatment of moderates among Bosnian Croats, his supercilious contempt for the very notion of a Bosniak ethnic identity, his anti-Semitism, his homophobia, and his readiness to accept the NDH as, in some sense, an expression of Croatian national aspirations all contributed to Tudjman's having a terrible image in the world, and, as Steindorff notes, when he passed away, the only head of state to attend his funeral was Prime Minister Demirel of Turkey – a dramatic contrast with Tito's funeral some two decades earlier.

Bartlett captures some of Tudjman's style, recounting, for example, that, after the successful Croatian reconquest of the Dalmatian hinterland (Krajina) in early August 1995, Tudjman went to Knin, the major town in that region and the erstwhile headquarters of the insurgent Croatian Serbs, and 'in a masterly stroke of propaganda kissed the Croatian flag flying from the battlements of the mediaeval Knin castle, which had been the seat of the mediaeval Croatian King Tomislav'.[85] Bartlett characterizes Tudjman's growing ethnic prejudices, at one point, as 'the ridiculous posturing of an old man living in a fantasy world of distorted nationalist sentiment'.[86] Bartlett readily admits the authoritarian nature of the Tudjman regime, but, at the same time, is concerned to deny that Tudjman's authoritarianism should be 'equated' with that of Serbian president Milošević.[87]

All four of these books are serious, professional pieces of work, characterized by balance and insight. Those by Goldstein and Steindorff are completely reliable for both factual and interpretive aspects, Tanner's is the most readable of this set, and Bartlett's, the shortest by far, is the most focused on the present era, even skipping the years 1974–89 entirely.

III

Slovenia

The five volumes dealing with Slovenia are completely different from each other in purpose and focus. The Benderly/Kraft collaborative volume is perhaps the best introduction to Slovenian history for English-speakers. The Fink-Hafner/Robbins collaborative work is the most thorough English-language analysis of post-1990 politics in Slovenia at this writing. The Gow/Carmichael collaborative volume has a narrower focus than the Benderly/Kraft volume but a somewhat broader one than the Fink-Hafner/Robbins book, incorporating a brief historical overview as well as excellent thematic discussions of culture, economics, politics, and security. The Fink-Hafner/Cox volume provides a useful guide to the economic and political issues surrounding Slovenia's efforts to obtain entry into the European Union, while Erika Harris undertakes, in her volume *Nationalism and Democratisation*, to compare the postcommunist paths taken by Slovenia and Slovakia.

Independent Slovenia, edited by Jill Benderly and Evan Kraft, brings together contributions dealing with political, cultural, and economic history, social movements, punk, gender equality, trade unions, privatization, and foreign policy. Especially masterful are Carole Rogel's sweeping survey of Slovenian history from the seventh century to 1945, Ervin Dolenc's review of the cultural history of the Slovenes from the sixteenth century until 1980, and Gregor Tomc's study of the politics of punk, in which he argues that Slovenian punk made its contribution to the collapse of the socialist system. Tomaž Mastnak, in his contribution on social movements, agrees that democratization, which had been smothered at the end of the 1960s, was revived by the punk movement, but he also underlines that Milošević's 'revolutionary coup and totalitarian mass movement in Serbia determined the broader framework of democratization in Slovenia',[88] thereby providing a rebuff to those writers, such as Woodward and Zimmermann, who take little or no account of the real fears experienced by Slovenes in the years 1989–91. But Mastnak is not entirely sanguine about Slovenia's start down the democratic path, warning that initially the democratic movement enforced a kind of political 'homogenization' which may have been necessary to protect the process, but also impoverished Slovenian democracy – at least in the short run.[89]

Making a New Nation: The Formation of Slovenia, edited by Danica Fink-Hafner and John R. Robbins, brings together some of the leading social scientists of Slovenia, with chapters devoted to transition, Slovenian political culture, defence, state-building, interest groups, development of the party system, the electoral system, local government, labour, social structure, the media, and other subjects. John Robbins sets the stage with a theoretical introduction in which he cites Ralf Dahrendorf's axiom that a democratic constitution might be implemented within half a year, in order to suggest that the establishment of a functioning democracy is, in fact, quite a bit more complex. The development of organizational pluralism is clearly relevant, he notes, adding that democracies-in-the-making are sometimes thought to suffer from a 'democratic deficit'.[90]

That democracies depend upon a political culture favourable to democracy is universally accepted, but which comes first – the system, which then fashions the political culture it requires, or the political culture, which drives system transformation forward? The safe answer is that the process combines elements of both. Danica Fink-Hafner's contribution goes beyond merely safe answers, however, providing concrete data on the basis of which one may make a judgement. She shows that support for the establishment of a multiparty system began to spread among Slovenes already in 1986 – four years before the first multiparty elections – and that by 1989, some 74 per cent of Slovenes favoured the establishment of political pluralism.[91] But, as Bernik, Malnar, and Toš suggest, the support for democratization may have been shallow, even if widespread, so that, in real terms, 'the disintegration of the old political values' may be more clearly marked than the emergence of articulate alternatives, which may take more time; in the meantime, they warn, the political culture may float 'in a state of anomie'.[92] This state of anomie is characterized by Mitja Hafner-Fink, in his contribution on the social structure, as involving the 'co-existence of traditional and modern values', with many Slovenes, for example, being 'closely attached' to their home towns.[93] The contribution of the media to fashioning the political culture is the subject of Sandra Bašić-Hrvatin's chapter, where she points to the apparent paradox that, while the print media played a role in the vanguard of democratization, pushing the transformation forward, the broadcast media, embedded in regulations and bureaucracy, lagged behind.[94]

Into Europe? Perspectives from Britain and Slovenia, edited by Danica Fink-Hafner and Terry Cox, takes up a more specialized, but no less important, theme, looking at British and Slovenian relations with the European Union. British Euro-scepticism contrasts with Slovenian Euro-enthusiasm, with Mirjana Ule warning that Slovenian entry into the EU cannot but figure as a factor contributing to 'a profound psychological transformation' of Slovenian society, which she considers ineluctable.[95] But 'Euro-enthusiasm' is not a simple phenomenon: as Marjan Svetličič notes in his chapter, while nearly 42 per cent of Slovenes in a poll conducted December 1994–January 1995 expressed unqualified support for Slovenian entry into the EU, 19.7 per cent declared that they were against EU membership for Slovenia if negative effects would have to be endured in the short term. On the other hand, as Svetličič adds, some 29.5 per cent declared that they endorsed Slovenian membership in the EU even if there would be short-term costs.[96] As for the long-term costs, there is some fear, as Mirjam Kotar notes, that the high level of full-time female employment in Slovenia (nearly 100 per cent of employed women in Slovenia have been working full-time) may be negatively affected by EU membership.[97]

But joining the EU involves meeting certain criteria, as Irena Brinar points out in her contribution to *Into Europe*. In addition to democratic elections, rule of law, and respect for human rights, countries wishing to enter the EU must also keep the national budget deficit to not more than 3 per cent of the GNP, the inflation rate to no more than 1.5 per cent of the average inflation rate in the EU, and the long-term interest rate to not more than 2 per cent more than the average rate in the EU. At the time of writing, Slovenia met only one of the three fiscal conditions for EU membership.[98]

The economic dimension is further explored in chapters written by Paul Phillips and Bogomil Ferfila in collaboration, and by Mojmir Mrak. Phillips and Ferfila provide a useful account of the costs to Slovenia of the breakup of Yugoslavia, noting that Slovenia lost not just tariff-free markets in the other Yugoslav republics but also almost 3,000 subsidiary branches of economic enterprises, which had been operating in one or another of the other republics.[99] The EU-imposed moratorium on the operationalization of Slovenian independence had the effect of delaying the introduction of a new Slovenian currency until October 1991, at which time Slovenian foreign reserves were sufficient to cover only two weeks' worth of imports. They provide details concerning the disruption of air and road traffic by the war in Croatia and Bosnia, insofar as this affected Slovenia, and concerning the 1993–4 banking dispute with the Bank of Austria and other foreign financial institutions operating in Slovenia. Mrak's chapter complements the Phillips/Ferfila chapter nicely, filling in additional details concerning the 1980s and noting that, with the foreign exchange reserves of socialist Yugoslavia being kept in Belgrade, Slovenia found itself with less than $200 million at the point when it embarked on its independence.[100] In spite of the initial difficulties, however, by February 1993, Slovenia had been admitted to the International Monetary Fund, the World Bank Group, and the European Bank for Reconstruction and Development.

The volume by Gow and Carmichael may be the best-known among these five volumes, at least among non-Slovenes, and reflects research in Slovene-language as well as other materials. The authors note that, prior to independence in 1991, many Slovenian intellectuals suffered from a 'size complex', believing that Slovenia was too small to survive as an independent state, the example of Luxembourg, among others, notwithstanding.[101] Yet Slovenia's success apparently confirms, at least in the minds of the authors, Rousseau's precept that only small states can be truly democratic.[102] The authors trace the growth of Slovene consciousness from the nineteenth century onward, noting the role of the Catholic Church in secular politics and the founding of the nationalist 'Sokol' society in 1862 in this connection. They note that the Slovenian Social Democrats (during the early part of the twentieth century) embraced the Austro-Marxist view of nationalism and national identity, taking the position that all nationalities should be treated as equals. However, the Slovenian Social Democrats were divided as to whether the Slovene nation would be completely absorbed into a nascent Yugoslav nation, or survive as a distinctive collectivity. This question re-emerged after the Second World War, when some Yugoslav communists, such as Aleksandar Ranković, thought that the component national groups which made up Yugoslavia should, over time, fuse into a new, Yugoslav nationality. But Slovenes resisted this idea, which they suspected, not without reason, would entail the disappearance of their language and their distinctive culture.

In the communist era, Slovenia came into its own in the early 1960s, when a group of young Slovene communists launched a new journal, *Perspektive*, in which they subjected the system of socialist self-management to criticism. Stane Kavčič, then a rising star in the Slovenian Communist Party, not only encouraged the *Perspektive* but even entertained the notion that a two-party system could represent an improvement over Yugoslavia's socialist system.[103] Kavčič and his hangers-on were eventually forced to resign in 1972, but just three years later the League of Communists of Slovenia offered to 'rehabilitate' Kavčič provided only that he renounce his earlier activity and views – a demand which Kavčič rejected as unacceptable. During much of the 1970s and 1980s, it was the conservatives, whose loyalty was to the Yugoslav idea, who held power in Slovenia. But by the end of the 1980s, there was a tectonic shift, with the weekly magazine, *Mladina* – at the time the official organ of the League of Slovenian Youth – leading the way with radically bold proposals and penetrating investigative reporting. During 1988, *Mladina* routinely sold out its print run of 50,000 copies, often on the day of release. A pivotal event was the so-called trial of the four, in which three journalists for *Mladina* were put on trial, together with an army sergeant, after they obtained a document detailing an army plan 'to destabilise Slovenia, declare a state of emergency, and replace the liberal Slovene political leadership and [install] more conservative figures'.[104]

The authors retell the story of how Slovenia gravitated towards independence, and recount the story of the fighting during June–July 1991, during which thirteen Slovenes lost their lives but in the course of which Slovenia took a decisive step towards independence. Gow and Carmichael tell the Slovenian story with sympathy, showing that the movement for independence was driven not by Slovenian disregard for their fellow South Slavs, as some observers believe, but by a rejection of

Yugoslav-style communism, a realization that that system was, in any event, no longer functional, a fear of what Milošević was doing to the federation, and a conviction, on the part of many Slovenes, that they were being exploited and milked by the other republics in socialist Yugoslavia.[105] The Gow/Carmichael volume represents a compromise between chronological organization and a thematic organization, a compromise which works well.

Finally, the volume by Erika Harris, *Nationalism and Democratisation: Politics of Slovakia and Slovenia*, involves an ingenious comparison in the quest for an answer to the question: when is nationalism compatible with democratization and when is it not compatible? She enters into this analysis because, as she notes, the postcommunist experience has been that democratization has been inseparable from issues of nation and nationality, and her choice of countries was guided by the notion that Slovenia might provide a more positive example, with Slovakia, at least during periods when Vladimir Mečiar has been prime minister, serving as a negative example of the influence of nationalism in a democratizing state.

Her conclusion is that nationalism was by and large useful in decommunization and that democratization, in turn, contributed to and reinforced nationalist mobilization.[106] But she suspects that nationalism emerges during post communist transitions 'not because democracy has to go hand-in-hand with nationalism, but because the weakness of these states and their democratic institutions allows nationalism to take up a position of the great unifier, mobiliser and legitimiser in all tasks that a newly independent democracy needs to perform'.[107] At the same time, she insists that the association of multiethnicity with problematic democratization, as witnessed in much of the Yugoslav region, is at best a *contingent* association.[108]

Where Slovenia is concerned, Harris argues that it was the Slovenes' commitment to democratic reforms and their realization that such reforms could not be continued within the framework of socialist Yugoslavia which drove them to seek independent statehood.[109] In other words, it was the growing commitment to liberal democracy which engendered the demand for independence which, in turn, engendered a growing sense of collective self. By comparison with Slovakia, Slovenia managed the democratic transition more successfully (where Slovakia is concerned, one might say up to 1998); the reasons for this, Harris suggests, would include Slovenes' greater experience with political participation prior to independence, the wider consensus on independence in Slovenia, and the lesser presence of ethnic minorities by comparison with Slovakia.[110]

These five books are valuable resources for those wishing to acquaint themselves with one of Europe's newest states. But the literature on Slovenia available in English remains thin, and it can only be hoped that this deficit will be filled over time. The need for a comprehensive history of the Slovenes is particularly needed, as well as a thorough review of Slovenia's religious history.

IV

Serbia

The field of Serbian studies is, by contrast with the fields of Bosnian, Croatian, and Slovenian studies – not to mention the marked under-development in the field of Macedonian studies and Montenegrin studies – robust. In addition to those works already published, there are additional works in the pipeline – among them a history of Serbian being written by Thomas Emmert, and a collection of essays on Serbia and Montenegro being edited by Thede Kahl, Walter Lukan, Andrej Mitrović, Miroslav Polzer, Mirjam Polzer-Srienz, Ljubinka Trgovčević, and Dragan Vukčević.

The Serbs: History, Myth and the Destruction of Yugoslavia, written by veteran journalist Tim Judah, is a spirited work, as may be gathered from a sampling of the subheadings used in the book. Among them one may find: 'The Cult of Death', 'Bosnia's Sulphurous Vapours', 'Frankenstein's Monster', 'Bolshevism Is Bad but Nationalism Is Worse', 'On the Highway to Hell', 'Supergrandpa to the Rescue', and – for the section dealing with the flight of Serbian refugees from parts of Croatia and Bosnia – 'House Hunters'. This is history told through the prism of the present: the book begins with a comparison between the seventeenth-century Serbian exodus from Kosovo and the flight of Serbs from the Croatian Krajina in 1995; it begins the story of the fourteenth-century Battle of Kosovo by quoting from Slobodan Milošević's impromptu speech to Kosovar Serbs in April 1987, offers a comment in the context of a retelling of the Serbian uprising of 1804 that a lot of rubbish was written about Russo-Serbian friendship during the war of 1991–5, and, in recounting the territorial aspirations of Ilija Garašanin (1812–74), draws a connection between the nineteenth-century Serb minister's *Načertanije* (which was directed towards con-joining Serb-inhabited areas of the Ottoman Empire to Serbia) and Milošević's campaign for a Greater Serbia which ended in 1995. But Judah does not replicate Cohen's historical determinism (as discussed in Chapter 7). On the contrary, he emphasizes at the outset his conviction that 'The Serbs went to war because they were led into it by their leaders.' But these leaders were able to mobilize Serbs for war, in part, because of their ability to draw 'on the malign threads of their people's history . . . If Serbian history had been different, today's generations could not have been manipulated *in the same way.*'[111] They could, of course, have been manipulated in other ways – but that would have been a different story.

Making use of materials published in Serbian, French, Italian, and English, Judah traces the history of the Serbs from their arrival in the Balkans at the end of the sixth century to the collapse of the Serbian war effort in 1995 and the signing of the Dayton Peace Accords. For Judah, the Serbs' is a tragic history, but one of their own making. 'The Serbs', he writes, 'were misled but they were not sheep. Supremely confident of victory [in the 1990s], too many were happy to be misled.'[112]

As Judah tells it, the era of the Nemanjić dynasty (twelfth to fourteenth centuries) provided the Serbs with a political vision. Judah's history is a history of violence done to and by the Serbs; religious history, economic history, literary history, and social history make small appearances at the most insofar as they relate to the history of this vision and the violence of Serbian history. In a passage which captures much of the spirit of this book, he writes, 'The Balkan Wars [of 1912–13] were to set the precedent in this century for massive waves of ethnic cleansing and the forced migrations of hundreds of thousands of people. All the worst evils that were witnessed in the former Yugoslavia between 1991 and 1995 were present in the Balkan Wars, including large-scale massacres of civilians, the destruction of whole towns and the gross manipulation of the media.'[113] More than half a millennium earlier, a mixed force of Serbs and Albanians met the Ottomans on Kosovo Polje (the field of the blackbirds) on 28 June 1389. But this famous battle, fought seventy years before the Serbian kingdom was snuffed out, had less immediate impact than is sometimes thought, Judah writes, but 'In all of European history it is impossible to find any comparison with the effect of Kosovo on the Serbian national psyche.'[114]

The interwar kingdom, introduced by Judah under the subtitle, 'The Empire Restored', is allocated a meagre seven pages (pp. 106–12). The chapter discusses the passage of the so-called Vidovdan constitution in 1921, the assassination of Stjepan Radić in 1928, the proclamation of the royal dictatorship on 6 January 1929, the assassination of the king in 1934, the rise and fall of Milan Stojadinović, and the Cvetković–Maček Sporazum (understanding) which created the autonomous *banovina* of Croatia. The chapter does not mention the various paramilitary organizations which were operating at that time, such as ORJUNA, SRBAO, and HRNAO, or the activities of the Chetniks, and mentions the establishment of the extremist Ustaša movement by Croat Ante Pavelić only in passing; Serb politicians Dragoljub Jovanović, Ljubomir Davidović, and Jaša Prodanović are also not mentioned.

The four years during which the Yugoslavs found themselves sucked into the maelstrom of the Second World War are allocated twenty-two pages. Judah alludes briefly to Chetnik Kosta Pećanac's collaboration with the Axis[115] but says nothing about other Chetnik collaborators or about the extent of Chetnik collaboration with the Italians and with the quisling government of Milan Nedić in Belgrade. Summing up Chetnik leader Draža Mihailović's career, Judah writes that 'apart from the objective of winning the war Mihailović seems to have had few clear ideas'.[116] But Judah is not convinced that Mihailović was implicated in the plans for creating an ethnically homogeneous Greater Serbia, plans drawn up by his close adviser, Stevan Moljević.

The years 1945–90 are allocated thirty-three pages (pp. 135–67). Judah's emphasis in these pages is on the relations between the diverse nationalities of Yugoslavia, relations which had been strained in the course of the Second World War. Ironically, as Judah points out, when the 'Memorandum of the Serbian Academy of Sciences and Art' first appeared, Milošević denounced its message as an expression of 'nothing else by the darkest nationalism'.[117] Radovan Karadžić, who, as we learn, was at one time best known for having made some suggestions about food labelling, offered the opinion about the same time that 'Bolshevism is bad, but nationalism is even worse.'[118] But their anti-nationalism was superficial, and, when the opportunity presented itself, both Milošević and Karadžić were quite prepared to make nationalist appeals in order to build their power.

Robert Thomas's book, *Serbia under Milošević*,[119] is the most detailed account of the Milošević years and will remain a standard reference work for its subject for years to come. Thomas's objective in this work, as he records, is 'to explain why Serbia failed to make the political leap from totalitarianism to pluralism' and 'to demonstrate that while the inability of democracy to put down firm roots can be attributed in part to weaknesses and fault-lines within Serbian society, the decisions of individuals and personalities have also played a critical role [whether] in the failure to bring about, or in actively seeking to thwart, the processes of democratic consolidation.' This leads him to the conclusion that 'there was no cultural inevitability to the triumph of authoritarianism' in Serbia.[120] At the same time, he emphasizes that the Milošević regime 'was not a dictatorship in the *totalitarian* sense of the word'.[121]

Thomas painstakingly records both the regime's use of a democratic façade to mask its autocratic character and the steadfast resistance by

Zoran Djindjić, Vesna Pešić, and Serbian Orthodox patriarch Pavle, as well as the on-again, off-again opposition-cum-collaboration on the part of the charismatic Vuk Drašković and the apparently lunatic Vojislav Šešelj. What is striking, as Thomas notes, is that all of these opposition figures, except for Pešić, were nationalists – though Djindjić later broke with his earlier nationalism. Thus, even 'civic' parties tended – indeed, according to Thomas, were induced by the situation – to place their demands for democratic reform within a 'national' context. Thus, 'The perception that the primary political imperative was to provide an answer to the conundrum of the Serbian national question meant that for many such politicians it appeared "natural" or "rational" if the borders of such a national state should correspond to the boundaries of the national group'.[122]

Thomas has no doubts about Milošević's primary role both in planning the war and in orchestrating Serb military strategy. Milošević's control extended even to the attack on Srebrenica in July 1995, which, in Thomas's view, would not have taken place without Milošević's having specifically sanctioned it.[123] Interestingly, given the background of Milošević's difficulties with Karadžić, summer 1995 found Milošević asking General Mladić to carry out a coup against the Bosnian Serb leader, according to Thomas, who says that Mladić refused to grant Milošević's wish.[124] Thomas also captures very well the flamboyance and 'romantic' nationalism of opposition leader Vuk Drašković who issued a leaflet in late September 1991, warning that 'The strategy of total and fatal war, which Serbia does not want, will leave it without prosperity, without allies and friends.'[125] At the same time, even after Slovenia and Croatia had been granted international recognition and membership in the UN, Drašković continued to hope that those two republics would find it attractive to reassociate with Serbia, Montenegro, and the rest, in a loose economic union,[126] which he seems to have confused, in spite of himself, with a Greater Serbia.[127] Finally, in bringing his monumental work to a close, Thomas takes note of those forces and factors for democratization which existed in Serbia by the close of the Milošević era.

In Norman Cigar's view, nationalism remains a problem in Serbia. It is a problem for two reasons, he argues: first, because Yugoslav president (now prime minister of Serbia) Vojislav Koštunica, who took office in October 2000, embraces a nationalist programme; and, second, because his nationalism is expressly irredentist. The portrait Cigar paints of Koštunica is anything but pretty. He notes, for example, that it was Koštunica's opposition to the adoption of the 1974 constitution's provisions for greater autonomy for Kosovo and Vojvodina (provisions which went a distance, in Kosovo's case, towards satisfying some long-standing demands among the province's Albanians) that cost Koštunica his university post. When Milošević abolished the autonomy of the two provinces in 1989 – a completely unconstitutional and illegal manoeuvre – using police intimidation to pressure the Albanian deputies into rubber-stamping this act, Koštunica enthusiastically applauded this development, his reputation for legal propriety notwithstanding. Koštunica subsequently criticized Serbia's 1990 constitution for defining Serbia as a state of all its citizens, rather than as the Serbian national state; or, to put it more simply, he objected to the constitution's (albeit hypocritical) declaration of the principle of equality.

During the Bosnian war (1992–5), Cigar's account reveals, Koštunica claimed that Izetbegović's people were laying siege to Sarajevo from within, even as Karadžić's forces did so from the hills, and suggested later that the mass murder of 8,000 Muslim men and boys ('more than 7,500' according to the report issued by the Netherlands Institute for War Documentation in April 2002)[128] at Srebrenica in July 1995 was 'perhaps' a 'defensive action' by the Serbian side, dismissing reports of concentration camps in Bosnia-Herzegovina as 'lies'.[129] When Bosnian Serb leader Radovan Karadžić quarrelled with then Serbian president Milošević over Western peace proposals, Koštunica supported Karadžić's rejectionist stance, hoping, as Karadžić did, that Serbia could end up with a larger share of Bosnia-Herzegovina than was on offer. According to Cigar, Koštunica also supported the Bosnian Serbs' programme of ethnic cleansing as a necessary means to create an ethnically homogeneous Greater Serbian state.[130]

The record of Koštunica's statements over the years is troubling, because they appear to fit a consistent pattern. In 1995, for example, Koštunica went on record as characterizing Croats – all Croats – as 'genocidal';[131] in 1996, he made a public statement praising Serb fascist leader Dimitrije Ljotić; and even after the Dayton Peace Accords of 1995, Koštunica, who as a trained constitutional lawyer should know something about the contractual nature of peace accords and constitutional charters alike, continued to demand that the Bosnian Serbs' Republika Srpska (RS) be separated as much as possible from the Bosnian federation as a prerequisite for eventual unification with Serbia.[132]

Cigar argues that Koštunica as president remained committed to the goal of eventually absorbing the RS into Serbia, in spite of the Yugoslav president's joint declaration with Croatian president Stipe Mesić in June 2001, in which the two declared their recognition of the sovereignty and territorial integrity of Bosnia-Herzegovina within its internationally recognized borders.[133] But the problems with Koštunica do not end there, according to Cigar, who notes Koštunica's efforts to block, derail, or delay extraditions to The Hague of Serbs wanted on charges of war crimes, his endeavours to absolve the Yugoslav Army of any blame for the blood-letting in Kosovo during 1998–9, his opposition during 1998 to proposals to restore Kosovo's autonomy, and his denial, even after becoming president of the country, 'that systematic war crimes and genocide often accompanied the implementation of Serb nationalist policy'.[134]

In a word, Cigar views Koštunica as dishonest when it comes to confronting Serbia's recent bloody past, and cunningly calculating. He rejects the standard image of Koštunica as honest and legalistically minded, which he says was constructed by the Serb establishment in order to market Koštunica in the West.

Now if opinion polls had found the more liberal-minded Zoran Djindjić, prime minister of Serbia, to be more popular than Koštunica, there might have been somewhat less reason for concern. But, as Cigar notes, Koštunica remained, even until the eve of his failure to be elected president of Serbia (because of low voter turnout) in late 2002, by far the most popular politician among Serbs. His nationalism, with its contempt for the Kosovar Albanians and for the Dayton Peace Accords alike, is mainstream in Serbia. And even if it may be true, as Cigar suggests, that Serbs are too fed up with war to be likely to return to the battlefield anytime soon, the prevalence of nationalist rhetoric in Serbia and the continued refusal by Koštunica and others (such as Serbian Radical leader Vojislav Šešelj, whom Cigar portrays as ideologically akin to Koštunica) to abandon the Greater Serbian project can only hinder real progress towards stable liberal democracy. Cigar is a meticulous scholar and his documentation is thorough. He presses his argument with such relentless logic that it is hard to escape sharing his cautious pessimism.

During the period from October 2000 until the end of 2002, Koštunica and Djindjić dominated the Serbian political scene.[135] But at the end of 2002, Koštunica failed to be elected president of Serbia, and soon after his term as president of Yugoslavia expired when the third Yugoslavia itself expired, being replaced by a new state union called 'Serbia and Montenegro'. Djindjić, meanwhile, had sworn to rein in organized crime, which was trafficking in heroin and cocaine and which was intermeshed with the JSO,[136] a military unit commanded by 'Frenki' Simatović and tied to organized crime, known colloquially as the Red Berets, whose ultimately unsuccessful revolt in November 2001 had been supported by Koštunica.[137] But, on 12 March 2003, Djindjić was gunned down by Zvezdan Jovanović, deputy commander of the Red

Berets. The government swore in Zoran Živković, Djindjić's erstwhile deputy, as the new prime minister and declared a state of emergency. Within two weeks, the Red Berets were dissolved.[138] By 4 April, more than 7,000 people had been taken into custody both in connection with the assassination and as part of a new and more resolute campaign to uproot organized crime.[139] At the end of the month, Rade Bulatović, Koštunica's former security adviser, and Lieut. Gen. Aco Tomić, former head of the Yugoslav Army's counterintelligence service, who had also been close to Koštunica, were under arrest, because of meetings they had had in December 2002 with key underworld figures and paramilitary leaders charged with complicity in the assassination of Djindjić.[140]

More than a half a million people turned out for Djindjić's funeral, in an outpouring of grief not seen in Belgrade since the death of Tito nearly a quarter of a century earlier. The assassination had a sobering effect on Serbs, and some observers speculated that it might contribute to effecting a turning point for Serbs in their effort to come to terms with the Milošević legacy – a legacy, among other things, of the proliferation of organized crime and corruption. Instead, there has been a recrudescence of Chetnik-style nationalism, symbolized, for example, in the passage of a law equating the (collaborationist) Chetniks with the anti-fascist Partisans, and manifested most clearly in the parliamentary elections held in December 2003. In those elections, the Serbian Radical Party, now headed by Tomislav Nikolić, emerged with the largest bloc of votes, capturing 27.7 per cent of the vote and winning eighty-two seats in the 250-seat Assembly. Koštunica's DSS (Democratic Part of Serbia) came in second place (18 per cent of the vote, fifty-three seats), while the DS (Djindjić's Democratic Party; headed, after the assassination of Djindjić, by Boris Tadić) came in third (12.6 per cent of the vote, thirty-seven seats).[141] Given the refusal of other political parties to work together with Nikolić's party, Koštunica was given the mandate to form a government. One of Koštunica's first public statements as prime minister was to declare (in February 2004) that the extradition of people indicted for war crimes would not occupy a high priority for him – although he would later modify that stance after the American government froze $25 million in aid.[142]

Chauvinistic nationalism doesn't just happen. There are almost always players who deliberately foment nationalism in one or another society. In Serbia, one must mention not only the Serbian Socialist Party and the most important opposition political parties in the Milošević era, but also the Serbian Writers' Association, the Serbian Academy of Sciences and Art, and the Serbian Orthodox Church, which specifically encouraged the victim psychology which is apt to imbue the 'victim' with a sense that violence against the 'perpetrator' is justified. On this point, it is deeply disturbing to find that the main theme in Serbian Orthodox Church pronouncements and publications during 1990–1, as tensions between Serbia and Croatia were rising, was not the need for reconciliation and dialogue, but the genocide committed against Serbs by Croatian fascists during the Second World War.[143] In August 1991, as the Yugoslav People's Army and Serb paramilitaries were expelling local Croat civilians from Banija and Baranja, and laying siege to Vukovar and Dubrovnik, and as the Milošević regime escalated the persecution of Albanians in Kosovo, and as Karadžić and Milošević prepared to bring the war to Bosnia by arming Serb civilians in that republic, the Serbian Church's organ *Glasnik* offered an inverted picture, alleging that

Once again the Serbian nation is on the cross in Kosovo-Metohija and in Dalmatia and in the Krajina and in Slavonia and in Banija, Lika, Kordun, Srem, Bosnia and Herzegovina. This is a nation which has gotten accustomed to carrying a cross, because we are condemned to carry this cross. In this hour we ask God to give us the strength to carry our cross with dignity, as we have carried it in the past. And in order to say other than what the wise Jewess [Golda Meir] said to the malicious and aggressive Muslims: 'Forgive us for killing you, but we cannot forgive you if you force us to kill you.'[144]

But the Church's nationalist rhetoric was not just the by-product of absent-mindedness, according to Milorad Tomanić, who suggests that the Serbian Orthodox Church nurtured territorial pretensions vis-à-vis Croatia which 'were almost identical with the demands of certain Serbian political figures such as, for example, Vojislav Šešelj and Vuk Drašković'.[145]

The nationalist neurosis is still alive and well in Serbia and is manifested in such things as expressions of outrage in the parliament that Serbian state television had shown (on 11 July 2001) a BBC documentary concerning the Srebrenica massacre, or the introduction of new history textbooks in the elementary schools in autumn 2001 in which Draža Mihailović, the Second World War-era Serbian collaborator with the Italian fascists, is whitewashed and in which there is no mention of Milošević and no hint that any Serbs might have had any responsibility for any of the misfortunes of the past decade.[146] Or again, in summer 2001, the Serbian government announced that catechism instruction would be introduced into primary and secondary schools in the autumn. While it is possible that part of the motivation for this might be moral education, the rhetoric accompanying and following this announcement suggested that the main interest in this was to promote Serbian national ideology.[147] Nor is the Church without its more reactionary fringe. On 6 December 2001, for example, the Philosophical Faculty of the University of Belgrade made its facilities available for a meeting of 'Orthodox-national Serbian youth' organized by a group of Serbian Orthodox Church associations.[148] The participants in this meeting still dream of a Serbian state that would unite all Serbs 'wherever they might be' and adopted a ten-point proclamation which spoke fondly of 'a new world order [which] will be more totalitarian than all [previous] totalitarian-isms put together'.[149] Those in attendance also expressed their hostility to gender equality, gay and lesbian marriages, and any suggestion of atonement for past wrongs, demanding 'retraditionalization' as the 'answer to the social crisis and crisis of values' in Serbia.[150] In other words, for the participants in this meeting, the answer to the social and moral crisis in Serbia is not less nationalism, but more.

Nationalism-as-neurosis, however, is hostile to notions of individual rights, respect for the harm principle, equality, tolerance, and neutrality of the state in the religious sphere – key classical liberal values – demanding that collective rights take priority over individual rights, denying the equality of peoples implicitly if not explicitly, and justifying violence against those considered undeserving of tolerance. Extreme nationalism, thus, is not merely delusion; it is dangerous delusion having clear authoritarian overtones. And authoritarian culture, as is well known, is not conducive to a flourishing of liberal-democratic politics.

But the supreme irony is that quite a number of policy-makers in the West, operating on the assumption that the replacement of Milošević by Koštunica and the extradition of Milošević to The Hague signify that Serbia is on the road to political health, have underestimated the importance of religious and cultural factors in the nationalist dynamic, ignoring such fundamentally important issues as the nature of the text-books used in the country's schools. Or, to put it another way, they want to change Serbian politics, while ignoring Serbian culture. And, in this way, they may be failing to provide constructive input in areas which, in the long run at least, may make the difference between stable liberal democracy and a reversion to authoritarian politics, or, at another level, between peace and renewed warfare.

In early April 2002, after the United States froze some $40 million in aid pending a resumption of co-operation with the extradition of war crimes suspects, Belgrade adopted a law mandating co-operation with the International War Crimes Tribunal in The Hague and issued arrest warrants for four of Milošević's closest aides: Dragoljub Ojdanić, a former army commander and former defence minister; Milan Milutinović, the sitting president of Serbia; Nikola Šainović, a former deputy prime minister; and Vlajko Stojiljković, a former Serbian interior minister, who had directly supervised the destructive activities of special police forces against Albanian villages in Kosovo in 1998. Ojdanić and Šainović quickly turned themselves in, while Stojiljković committed suicide, leaving a fifteen-page handwritten suicide note in which he called on 'patriotic citizens' to avenge his death, blaming Djindjić and also Koštunica for his suicide.[151]

Even as the law was being passed, Deputy Prime Minister Miroljub Labus, a highly popular political figure, declared, 'I agree completely that the law being adopted today is an insult to our nation's dignity. But it's not the end of history or the end of the Serbian spirit.'[152] His reaction was probably typical, reflecting not only some lingering resistance to co-operation but also – and this is where I would place the stress – a grudging acceptance that such co-operation is ineluctable given Serbia's economic morass and the impossibility of returning to its earlier status as an international pariah. But grudgingly or not, the Serbian authorities are co-operating, and as indicted war crimes suspects come to trial the chances are better than not that Serbian attitudes about the recent past will be affected. It would be foolish to expect a full recovery from nationalism overnight, but such recovery can come over time. Individuals and even generations may be stuck in habits which feed into nationalist syndromes, but societies, in the long run, are not.

NOTES

1 Robert J. Donia and John V. A. Fine, Jnr, *Bosnia and Hercegovina: A Tradition Betrayed* (London: C. Hurst & Co., 1994), p. 10.
2 *Ibid.*
3 *Ibid.*
4 *Ibid.*, p. 19.
5 Noel Malcolm, *Bosnia: A Short History* (Washington Square, NY: New York University Press, 1994), pp. 28, 36.
6 Mitja Velikonja, *Religious Separation and Political Intolerance in Bosnia-Herzegovina*, trans. from Slovenian by Rang'ichi Ng'inja (College Station, TX: Texas A&M University Press, 2003), pp. 23, 25.
7 Malcolm, *Bosnia*, pp. 14, 17; Donia and Fine, *Bosnia and Hercegovina*, p. 20.
8 Velikonja, *Religious Separation*, p. 35.
9 Malcolm, *Bosnia*, pp. 51–69; Donia and Fine, *Bosnia and Hercegovina*, pp. 35–6; Velikonja, *Religious Separation*, pp. 56–7.
10 Malcolm, *Bosnia*, p. 53.
11 Donia and Fine, *Bosnia and Hercegovina*, pp. 41–4; Malcolm, *Bosnia*, pp. 56–8, 63–5.
12 Velikonja, *Religious Separation*, pp. 64, 65, my emphasis.

13 Donia and Fine, *Bosnia and Hercegovina*, p. 44; Malcolm, *Bosnia*, pp. 58–9.

14 Malcolm, *Bosnia*, p. 68.

15 Donia and Fine, *Bosnia and Hercegovina*, p. 84.

16 Malcolm, *Bosnia*, pp. 55, 71–2.

17 *Ibid.*, p. 83.

18 *Ibid.*, p. 87.

19 *Ibid.*, p. 89.

20 *Ibid.*, p. 100.

21 Velikonja, *Religious Separation*, p. 15.

22 Recorded, for example, in Wayne S. Vucinich, *The Ottoman Empire: Its Record and Legacy* (Princeton, NJ: Van Nostrand, 1965); and Dimitri Gondicass and Charles Issawi (eds.), *Ottoman Greeks in the Age of Nationalism: Politics, Economy, and Society in the Nineteenth Century* (Princeton, NJ: Darwin Press, 1999).

23 Malcolm, *Bosnia*, p. 66.

24 Donia and Fine, *Bosnia and Hercegovina*, p. 80.

25 Malcolm, *Bosnia*, p. 132; Velikonja, *Religious Separation*, p. 118.

26 Malcolm, *Bosnia*, p. 133.

27 *Ibid.*, pp. 141–2.

28 *Ibid.*, pp. 138–43.

29 Donia and Fine, *Bosnia and Hercegovina*, p. 96.

30 *Ibid.*, p. 101.

31 *Ibid.*, p. 107.

32 *Ibid.*, p. 109.

33 Velikonja, *Religious Separation*, pp. 91–115, 122.

34 *Ibid.*, p. 127.

35 *Ibid.*, pp. 140–1.

36 Malcolm, *Bosnia*, pp. 162–3.

37 Donia and Fine, *Bosnia*, p. 128.

38 Malcolm, *Bosnia*, p. 172.

39 Donia and Fine, *Bosnia and Hercegovina*, p. 141.

40 Velikonja, *Religious Separation*, p. 180.

41 Malcolm, *Bosnia*, p. 179.

42 Donia and Fine, *Bosnia and Hercegovina*, p. 156.

43 *Ibid.*, p. 158.

44 *Ibid.*, pp. 163–4.

45 *Ibid.*, p. 192.

46 *Ibid.*, pp. 192–3.

47 Malcolm, *Bosnia*, p. 193.

48 *Ibid.*, p. 195.

49 *Ibid.*, pp. 196, 201.

50 *Ibid.*, p. 208.

51 Velikonja, *Religious Separation*, p. 219.

52 Donia and Fine, *Bosnia and Hercegovina*, p. 216.

53 *Ibid.*, p. 245.

54 Malcolm, *Bosnia*, p. 222.

55 They say it was 'forced' on the parties to the conflict. See Donia and Fine, *Bosnia and Hercegovina*, p. 260.

56 Malcolm, *Bosnia*, pp. 249, 248.

57 *Ibid.*, p. 251.

58 Velikonja, *Religious Separation*, p. 256.

59 *Ibid.*, p. 287.

60 William Bartlett, *Croatia: Between Europe and the Balkans* (London and New York: Routledge, 2003), pp. 19–20.

61 Ivo Goldstein, *Croatia: A History*, trans. from Croatian by Nikolina Jovanović (London: C. Hurst & Co., 1999), pp. 94, 98; and Ludwig Steindorff, *Kroatien: Vom Mittelalter bis zur Gegenwart* (Regensburg and Munich: Verlag Friedrich Pustet and Südosteuropa-Gesellschaft, 2001), p. 246.

62 Marcus Tanner, *Croatia: A Nation Forged in War* (New Haven, CT, and London: Yale University Press, 1997), pp. 105–6.

63 *Ibid.*, pp. 106–7.

64 Bartlett, *Croatia*, p. 75.

65 Steindorff, *Kroatien*, p. 166; Bartlett, *Croatia*, p. 17.

66 Goldstein, *Croatia*, p. 111.

67 Tanner, *Croatia*, p. 136.

68 Quoted *ibid.*, p. 145.

69 'Circular Letter to the Venerable Clergy of Zagreb Archdiocese', in *Katolički list* (Zagreb), 29 April 1941, trans. as Document VII in Richard Pattee, *The Case of Cardinal Aloysius Stepinac* (Milwaukee, WI: Bruce Publishing Co., 1953), p. 259.

70 *Ibid.*, pp. 259–60.

71 Tanner, *Croatia*, p. 155.

72 Goldstein, *Croatia*, pp. 138–9. For further discussion of Stepinac's attitude towards the NDH, see: Stella Alexander, *The Triple Myth: A Life of Archbishop Alojzije Stepinac* (Boulder, CO: East European Monographs, 1987); Ivan Mužić, *Katolička crkva, Stepinac i Pavelić*, 2nd edn (Zagreb: Dominović, 1997); Pattee, *The Case*; Marina Stambuk-Skalić, Josip Kolanović, and Stjepan Razum (eds.), *Process Alojziju Stepincu: Dokumenti* (Zagreb: Kršćanska sadašnjost, 1997); and Sabrina P. Ramet, *The Three Yugoslavias: State-Building and Legitimation, 1918–2004* (Bloomington, IN, and Washington, DC: Indiana University Press and Wilson Center Press, forthcoming), chaps. 4–5.

73 Tanner, *Croatia*, p. 156; Goldstein, *Croatia*, p. 139.

74 Steindorff, *Kroatien*, p. 195.

75 Goldstein, *Croatia*, pp. 170, 198.

76 Steindorff, *Kroatien*, p. 205.

77 Quoted in Tanner, *Croatia*, p. 223.
78 *Ibid.*
79 *Ibid.*, pp. 302–3.
80 Goldstein, *Croatia*, p. 211.
81 *Ibid.*, p. 206.
82 *Ibid.*, p. 226.
83 *Ibid.*, p. 205.
84 Steindorff, *Kroatien*, pp. 228–9.
85 Bartlett, *Croatia*, p. 47.
86 *Ibid.*, p. 50.
87 *Ibid.*, p. 49.
88 Tomaž Mastnak, 'From Social Movements to National Sovereignty', in Jill Benderly and Evan Kraft (eds.), *Independent Slovenia: Origins, Movements, Prospects* (New York: St Martin's Press, 1994), p. 104.
89 *Ibid.*, p. 107.
90 John R. Robbins, 'Setting the Scene: Problems of Transition', in Danica Fink-Hafner and John R. Robbins (eds.), *Making a New Nation: The Formation of Slovenia* (Aldershot: Dartmouth, 1997), pp. 4, 11, 15.
91 Danica Fink-Hafner, 'Development of a Party System', in Fink-Hafner and Robbins , *Making a New Nation*, p. 137.
92 Ivan Bernik, Brina Malnar, and Niko Toš, 'Slovenian Political Culture: Paradoxes of Democratization', in Fink-Hafner and Robbins, *Making a New Nation*, p. 58.
93 Mitja Hafner-Fink, 'Social Structure and Cleavages: Changing Patterns', in Fink-Hafner and Robbins, *Making a New Nation*, p. 265.
94 Sandra Bašić-Hrvatin, 'The Role of the Media in the Transition', in Fink-Hafner and Robbins, *Making a New Nation*, pp. 272–6.
95 Mirjana Ule, 'Re-creating the Slovenian Identity', in Danica Fink-Hafner and Terry Cox (eds.), *Into Europe? Perspectives from Britain and Slovenia* (Ljubljana: Faculty of Social Sciences, 1996), p. 167.
96 Marjan Svetličič, 'A Small Country Going into Europe: Economic Pragmatism and Nationhood', in Fink-Hafner and Cox (eds.), *Into Europe*, p. 200.
97 Kotar notes that, in Great Britain, only 56.2 per cent of working women have full-time employment with figures of 69.4 per cent in Germany, 76.2 per cent in France, 89.1 per cent in Italy, and 38.3 per cent in the Netherlands, as of 1990–1. See Mirjam Kotar, 'Women's Employment in Great Britain and Slovenia', in Fink-Hafner and Cox, *Into Europe*, pp. 364, 381.
98 Irena Brinar, 'The Enlargement of the EU and Slovenia', in Fink-Hafner and Cox, *Into Europe*, pp. 26–7, 41.
99 Paul Phillips and Bogomil Ferfila, 'Slovenia and Europe: Economic Aspects', in Fink-Hafner and Cox , *Into Europe*, p. 226.
100 Mojmir Mrak, 'Becoming a "Normal" Country in the International Financial Community', in Fink-Hafner and Cox, *Into Europe*, pp. 252–3.
101 James Gow and Cathie Carmichael, *Slovenia and the Slovenes: A Small State and the New Europe* (Bloomington, IN: Indiana University Press, 2000), p. 20.

102 *Ibid.*, p. 12.
103 *Ibid.*, p. 56.
104 *Ibid.*, p. 153.
105 *Ibid.*, p. 212.
106 Erika Harris, *Nationalism and Democratisation: Politics of Slovakia and Slovenia* (Aldershot: Ashgate, 2002), pp. 2, 8.
107 *Ibid.*, pp. 8–9.
108 *Ibid.*, p. 14.
109 *Ibid.*, p. 169.
110 *Ibid.*, p. 166.
111 Tim Judah, *The Serbs: History, Myth and the Destruction of Yugoslavia* (New Haven, CT: Yale University Press, 1997), pp. xi–xii.
112 *Ibid.*, p. xiii.
113 *Ibid.*, p. 84.
114 *Ibid.*, p. 30.
115 *Ibid.*, p. 117.
116 *Ibid.*, p. 121.
117 Slobodan Milošević, as quoted *ibid.*, p. 160.
118 Radovan Karadžić, as quoted *ibid.*, p. 166.
119 Robert Thomas, *Serbia under Milosevic: Politics in the 1990s* (London: C. Hurst & Co., 1999).
120 *Ibid.*, p. 4, emphases removed.
121 *Ibid.*, p. 424, emphasis in original.
122 *Ibid.*, p. 429.
123 *Ibid.*, p. 238.
124 *Ibid.*, p. 240.
125 Quoted *ibid.*, p. 107.
126 *Ibid.*, p. 109.
127 See his comments, as quoted *ibid.*, p. 179.
128 *The Guardian* (London), 11 April 2002, at www.guardian.co.uk.
129 Norman Cigar, *Vojislav Koštunica and Serbia's Future* (London: Saqi Books, in association with the Bosnian Institute, 2001), p. 32.
130 *Ibid.*, p. 40.
131 *Ibid.*, p. 105, n. 150.
132 *Ibid.*, pp. 41–2.
133 *Jutarnji list* (Zagreb), 10 June 2001, p. 2.
134 Cigar, *Vojislav Koštunica*, p. 72.
135 See Sabrina P. Ramet and Philip W. Lyon, 'Discord, Denial, Dysfunction: The Serbia-Montenegro-Kosovo Triangle', *Problems of Post-Communism*, 49, 5 (September–October 2002), pp. 3–19.
136 Jedinica za Specijalne Operacije, or Unit for Special Operations.
137 Davor Pašalić, 'Ratko Mladić živi u ulici Blagoja Parovica u Beogradu', *Nacional*, 316 (4 December 2001), p. 36.
138 Details in *Adresseavisen* (Trondheim), 27 March 2003, p. 6.
139 *Glas javnosti* (Belgrade), 18 March 2003, at www.glas-javnosti.co.yu; and 'Serbian Police have taken in 7,000 during state of emergency', on the web site of the Serbian Government (4 April 2003), at www.serbia.sr.gov.yu.

278   Thinking about Yugoslavia

140 *Guardian*, 10 April 2003, p. 6; *Boston Globe*, 10 April 2003, at www.boston. com/dailyglobe.
141 *Glas javnosti*, 29 December 2003, at www.glas-javnosti.co.yu.
142 The US government froze the aid on grounds of 'insufficient' co-operation with the International Criminal Tribunal on the former Yugoslavia on the part of Belgrade.
143 Milorad Tomanić, *Srpska crkva u ratu i ratovi u njoj* (Belgrade: Medijska knjižara krug, 2001), pp. 58–9.
144 Quoted *ibid.*, p. 56.
145 *Ibid.*, p. 73.
146 'Učenici u Srbiji iz udžbenika povijesti ne znaju za Miloševića', *Vjesnik* (Zagreb), 17 September 2001, at www.vjesnik.hr.
147 See the discussion in Mirko Djordjević, 'Veronauka kao politika – i obrnuto', *Republika* (Belgrade), 13, 270–1 (1–30 October 2001), at www.yurope. com/zines/ republika/arhiva.
148 Specifically, the St Justin the Philosopher Association of Students, the Council of the journal *Dveri Srpske*, and the Church Choir of the Shrine of St Alexander Nevsky.
149 Marijana Milosavljević, 'Pravoslavni protiv Madone', *NIN* (Belgrade), 2659 (13 December 2001), at www.nin.co.yu/2001/12/13/21071.html.
150 *Ibid.*
151 *International Herald Tribune* (Paris), 1 April 2002, p. 3; *The Times* (London), 2 April 2002, at www.thetimes.co.uk; *Večernji* list (Zagreb), 4 April 2002, at www.vecernji-list.hr; *The Guardian*, 12 April 2002, at www.guardian.co.uk; and *Glas javnosti* (Belgrade), 27 April 2002 and 29 April 2002 – both at www.glas-javnosti.co.yu.
152 Quoted in *Washington Post*, 12 April 2002, p. A20, at www.washingtonpost. com.

REFERENCES

Bosnia-Herzegovina

Donia, Robert J. and John V. A., Fine, Jnr, *Bosnia and Hercegovina: A Tradition Betrayed* (London: C. Hurst & Co., 1994), p. 318.
Malcolm, Noel, *Bosnia: A Short History* (Washington Square, NY: New York University Press, 1994), p. 340.
Velikonja, Mitja, *Religious Separation and Political Intolerance in Bosnia-Herzegovina*, trans. from Slovenian by Rang'ichi Ng'inja (College Station, TX: Texas A&M University Press, 2003), p. 365.

Croatia

Bartlett, William, *Croatia: Between Europe and the Balkans* (London and New York: Routledge, 2003), p. 176.
Goldstein, Ivo, *Croatia: A History*, trans. from Croatian by Nikolina Jovanović (London: C. Hurst & Co., 1999), p. 281.

Steindorff, Ludwig, *Kroatien: Vom Mittelalter bis zur Gegenwart* (Regensburg and Munich: Verlag Friedrich Pustet and Südosteuropa-Gesellschaft, 2001), p. 272.

Tanner, Marcus, *Croatia: A Nation Forged in War* (New Haven, CT, and London: Yale University Press, 1997), p. 338.

Serbia

Cigar, Norman, *Vojislav Koštunica and Serbia's Future* (London: Saqi Books, in association with the Bosnian Institute, 2001), p. 120.

Judah, Tim, *The Serbs: History, Myth and the Destruction of Yugoslavia* (New Haven, CT: Yale University Press, 1997), p. 350.

Thomas, Robert, *Serbia under Milošević: Politics in the 1990s* (London: C. Hurst & Co., 1999), p. 443.

Slovenia

Benderly, Jill and Evan Kraft (eds.), *Independent Slovenia: Origins, Movements, Prospects* (New York: St. Martin's Press, 1994), p. 262.

Fink-Hafner, Danica and Terry Cox (eds.), *Into Europe? Perspectives from Britain and Slovenia* (Ljubljana: Faculty of Social Sciences, 1996), p. 433.

Fink-Hafner, Danica and John R. Robbins (eds.), *Making a New Nation: The Formation of Slovenia* (Aldershot: Dartmouth, 1997), p. 330.

Gow, James and Cathie Carmichael, *Slovenia and the Slovenes: A Small State and the New Europe* (Bloomington, IN: Indiana University Press, 2000), p. 234.

Harris, Erika, *Nationalism and Democratisation: The Politics of Slovakia and Slovenia* (Aldershot: Ashgate, 2002), p. 237.

12 Southern republics: Macedonia and Montenegro in contemporary history

There are certain nationalities in Europe that remain the subject of controversy even today. Chief among these are the Ruthenes (said by many, but not by all, to be really Ukrainians), the Silesians (whose purportedly distinct ethnicity has found little acknowledgement), the Vlachs (variously alleged to be a distinct national group or merely Romanians living in Serbia or perhaps even Romanianized Serbs),[1] the Montenegrins (said by many, including many but not all Montenegrins, to be really Serbs), and the Macedonians (described variously as 'South Serbs', as 'Slavophone Greeks', as western Bulgarians, and, of course, as a distinct nationality). And where the Macedonians are concerned, disputes about their identity are connected with the state interests of Macedonia's neighbours.

Hugh Poulton derives the title of his *Who Are the Macedonians?* from precisely this still-unresolved controversy. As Poulton notes, there are (at least) three rival ways of identifying 'Macedonians': the first refers to all the inhabitants of what is often called 'geographic Macedonia', comprising not only the Republic of Macedonia but also part of northern Greece, a portion of southwest Bulgaria, and a sliver of Albania; the second refers to all citizens of the Republic of Macedonia; and the third refers to the Slav population living within either of the former two areas, i.e., to ethnic Macedonians. As he notes, the Slavs arrived in the Balkans only in the sixth century CE and, in 864, the 'Proto-Bulgarians' (including the ancestors of present-day Macedonians) converted en masse to Christianity. By the late thirteenth century, Serbian King Milutin had taken Skopje from the Byzantine empire, only to lose the area to the Ottomans within the next century and a half. A distinct sense of Macedonian national identity began to develop only in the course of the nineteenth century, during the period of national awakening in Central and Eastern Europe.

In spite of his title, Poulton's primary objective in his short volume is to provide a survey history of the Macedonian people from the early Neolithic period (c. 6200 BCE) to Macedonian independence after 1991. He notes in brief the careers of Philip of Macedon and Alexander the Great, before turning to the various migrations which brought not only Slavs into the region but also Vlachs, Roma (Gypsies), and Jews. Subsequent chapters are devoted to the Ottoman Empire, destabilization in the nineteenth century and Macedonia's partition in the course of the Balkan wars of 1912–13, the interwar years (1918–41), the Second World War, the communist years, Macedonians as minorities in neighbouring countries, and the years since 1989. The author records how 'Vardar Macedonia' – the portion of geographic Macedonia which had come under Belgrade's rule – was seen in the interwar years as 'ripe for Serb settlement and colonisation,' with plans being developed for some 50,000 Serbian families to be settled in Macedonia.[2] Classes were held in Serbian, and Macedonians were routinely and officially described as 'South Serbs'. The Internal Macedonian Revolutionary Organization (VMRO) resisted Belgrade's policies and mounted some 467 armed attacks on regime targets in the years 1919–34, killing some 185 Yugoslav officials and wounding an additional 235.[3] After twenty years of forced Serbianization, Macedonia was 're-Bulgarianized' in the course of the Bulgarian occupation during the Second World War. Thoroughly alienated from the Serbian national programme, the Macedonians initially welcomed the Bulgarian troops and administrators as liberators, and were gratified when the Bulgarian occupation authorities opened more than 800 new schools and even established a university in Skopje. But the Bulgarians failed to recruit local Macedonians into the administrative bureaucracy and, in general, behaved arrogantly towards the locals, so that by the end of the war the Macedonians had become quite disenchanted with the Bulgarian national programme as well. Thus, as Poulton tells it, Macedonian national consciousness was only in germination in the years up to 1945, but, as a result of Serbian and Bulgarian excesses, was ripe for development when, at the end of the Second World War, Tito decided to establish Macedonia as a constituent republic in the Federated People's Republic of Yugoslavia and to encourage the consolidation of Macedonian national identity.

There was still some 'residual pro-Bulgarian feeling among the population',[4] which was, however, overcome with time. The newly established communist authorities chose the spoken dialect of northern Macedonia as the basis for a written language, accepting an official alphabet for Macedonian on 3 May 1945 and approving an orthography for the language on 7 June 1945. The haste with which these moves were made may be taken as an indication of the priority which Macedonia held for the Yugoslav communists. By 1952, a grammar book for the Macedonian literary language had also appeared. But there were challenges ahead, chiefly coming from the Albanians who, already by 1971, comprised some 17 per cent of the population of Macedonia.[5] Since Macedonia's Albanians were, for the most part, concentrated along the western border (with Kosovo), when, in November 1968, Kosovo's Albanians revived the call for granting Kosovo status as a constituent republic, Albanians in Macedonia added the demand that their areas be attached to this new republic. Of course, neither the authorities in Belgrade nor those in Skopje wanted to have anything to do with creating a seventh republic, and in July 1981, in the wake of a second rash of demonstrations in Kosovo, Macedonian authorities authorized a revision to the syllabi and textbooks in use in Macedonian schools, increasing the number of hours devoted to teaching Macedonian in schools using Albanian as the language of instruction. But the general tendency during the 1980s was in the direction of ethnic polarization, with illegal Albanian groups appearing, irredentist leaflets in circulation, accusations being hurled back and forth, and criminal prosecutions being mounted mostly against Albanians in the municipalities of Gostivar, Tetovo, Skopje, Struga, Kičevo, Titov Veles, and Kumanovo. Then, in 1988, in a signal demonstration of their discontent, young Albanians in Kumanovo (in August) and Gostivar (in October) took to the streets, demanding that their rights under the 1974 constitution be honoured. Thus, when, in 1989, the Macedonian authorities amended the constitution to define their republic as 'the national state of the Macedonian people', it was not difficult to anticipate an Albanian reaction. Tellingly, when a referendum on independence was held on 8 September 1991, Macedonia's Albanians boycotted the vote, in order to protest 'what they saw as the government's non-compliance with their demands – e.g., for the reopening of Albanian secondary schools which had recently been closed'.[6] Subsequently, as Poulton notes, when a referendum on Albanian autonomy in Macedonia was conducted in January 1992, 99 per cent of the Albanians who voted (as 90 per cent of Albanians did) favoured autonomy.[7]

Independence brought an exacerbation of the internal dispute with the Albanians and an intensification of the quarrel between the Macedonian Orthodox Church (which had declared its autocephaly in 1967 with the full backing of the Tito regime and which now enjoyed the Macedonian government's support) and the Serbian Orthodox patriarchate in Belgrade. Independence inflamed a hitherto largely latent quarrel with neighbouring Greece, which owed its territorial extent to its annexation in 1912–13 of land inhabited by Macedonians and which had expelled local Macedonians after the First World War (as part of the population exchanges orchestrated via the Treaty of Lausanne) and after the Greek Civil War (in which many local Macedonians had fought on the side of the losing communists).

In fact, it is Loring Danforth who, in his volume, *The Macedonian Conflict: Ethnic Nationalism in a Transnational World*, discusses the question of Macedonian national identity at greater length. His purpose in the book is to disentangle the sundry threads of the argument about just who are the Macedonians, and to discuss the nature of identity formation not only in historical terms, but in terms of individuals as well. He begins by outlining the Greek nationalist and Macedonian nationalist narratives, in which the history of the region is viewed through nationally tinted glasses. According to the Greek narrative, Alexander the Great and the ancient Macedonians were Greeks, 'linked in an unbroken line of racial and cultural continuity',[8] Macedonians called themselves 'Bulgarians' until 1944, there is no such thing as a Macedonian nation anyway, and the language spoken in the Republic of Macedonia cannot be called Macedonian but should be known as 'the linguistic idiom of Skopje'.[9] Moreover, not only are there no Macedonians in Greece, but there are also no Turks in Greece; there are, however, 'Slavophone Greeks' and 'Muslim Greeks' – but these groups are ethnically Greek, since 'the only Slavs in Greece are tourists', as a sign held up by a rally of Greek émigrés in Melbourne maintained.[10] According to the Greek narrative, the ancient heritage to which Macedonians look back as part of the history of their region belongs exclusively to the Greek nation. As for the Macedonians who were driven out of Greece in 1949 and who nurture deep resentments even today, these people should be seen, according to the Greek narrative, as 'Slavophones who had been reared as Greeks and felt themselves to be Greeks . . . . [They] were neither Bulgarians nor "Macedonians" of the Yugoslav type; they were merely a group of resentful Slav-speaking inhabitants from a remote part of Greece who . . . turned first towards the Bulgarians and later towards the Yugoslavs.'[11]

Macedonians generally object to the Greek use of terms such as 'Greek–Macedonian' and 'Slav–Macedonian', noting that no one speaks of 'Slav–Russians' or 'Slav–Poles.'[12] Macedonian sources claimed that there are some 50,000 Macedonians in Albania, another 200,000 in 'Pirin Macedonia' (in Bulgaria), and at least 200,000 Macedonians in 'Aegean Macedonia' (in northern Greece). More nationalist Macedonians sometimes claim that modern Macedonians are not Slavs at all, but are direct descendants of the ancient Macedonians who were not Greeks either. More moderate Macedonians do not deny the Slavic identity of Macedonians, though some of them consider it likely that the Slavs who migrated into Macedonia in the sixth century intermarried with the indigenous 'ancient' Macedonians.[13] Some Macedonians even reply in kind to the Greek declaration that there is no Macedonian nation and, citing the work of the discredited scholar Jakob Fallmerayer, allege that there is no 'Greek race' as such, and that the contemporary Greek community owes its ethnogenesis to the intermarriage of Slavs and Albanians in the Middle Ages. The Macedonian narrative, as Danforth tells it, points to the second half of the nineteenth century as a time of 'Macedonian national renaissance' and highlights the work of Georgi Pulevski, Grigor Prlichev, Konstantin and Dimitar Miladinov, and Krste Misirkov, but Macedonians also recall the 'violent campaign of assimilation and denationalization' launched by the Greek government after it had annexed southern Macedonia in 1913.[14] The repression of Macedonians continued under the Metaxas dictatorship (1936–40) and, in the course of the civil war in the late 1940s, thousands more were killed or imprisoned or driven from their land.

Although Danforth's sympathies lie more with the Macedonians than with the Greeks, he develops an alternative narrative, rejecting both the extreme Macedonian claim that their ethnogenesis can be traced to ancient times and the Greek nationalist claim that Macedonian national identity was the invention of Tito and cannot be dated earlier than 1944. Although a number of nineteenth-century observers identified Macedonians as 'Bulgarians', Danforth argues (in agreement with Poulton) that it was precisely in the nineteenth century that a Macedonian national identity began to emerge. Among the bits of evidence he cites is the fact that, in 1892, the parish school council in Kostur (Kastoria) adopted a proposal 'to eliminate both Bulgarian and Greek [in the school] and introduce Macedonian as the language of instruction in the town school'.[15] Yet it was, indeed, the Yugoslav communists' decision to support Macedonian separateness which allowed, indeed encouraged, Macedonian culture to come into its own.

Danforth recounts the repressive measures taken by Greek governments against their Macedonians since 1913, noting, for example, the Hellenization of the names of hundreds of villages and towns between 1913 and 1928 and a ban, issued in 1927, on the conduct of church services in any Slavic language.[16] Similar measures, inspired by the same spirit, continue even today in 'democratic' Greece.

Danforth also recounts the Greek government's pressure on Macedonia, in the 1990s, to change its name, to change its constitution, and to change its national symbols, suggesting that the Macedonians could call themselves 'Skopjans', even if some of them were not from Skopje! Moreover, it was not until 1988 that Athens used the name 'Macedonia' to designate an administrative district – and this came as a response to perceived competition from Skopje.[17]

The remainder of Danforth's book is devoted to discussing the Macedonian human rights movement and to tracing the interactions of émigré Macedonians and émigré Greeks in municipalities in Australia. One of his conclusions is that it is not enough to think of national identity simply in terms of belonging to one or another community; he urges that it must also be understood as a form of political consciousness. Moreover, rather than seeing national identity as innate, Danforth provides examples of specific individuals who changed their consciousness (from Greek to Macedonian), by way of leading to the conclusion that 'it is ultimately the individual who chooses what national identity to adopt, or in some cases whether to adopt any national identity at all', although he immediately qualifies this by urging that 'identity formation is not entirely a matter of self-ascription; it is a matter of ascription by others as well'.[18]

II

The volumes by Abrahams, Kolbow and Quaden, and Oschlies shift the focus to Macedonia's 'Albanian question'. To be sure, Abrahams's short volume also encompasses a discussion of the Turkish, Roma, Serb, Macedonian–Muslim, and Vlach minorities in Macedonia, but the focus is above all on the Albanians, whose discontent seemed to Abrahams, already in 1996, to open up the question of the short-term stability of the country. As he notes, Macedonia's Albanians enjoyed both a higher status and more extensive language rights in the years 1974–89 than they did after the adoption of constitutional amendments by Skopje in 1989. Moreover, where they had enjoyed easy access to the University of Priština, where Albanian had been the language of instruction, there was, as of the declaration of Macedonian independence, no institution of higher education with Albanian as the language of instruction in their new country. The discontent generated by these considerations was reinforced by Albanian underrepresentation in the army office corps, in the police, and among the staff of the Ministry of Internal Affairs, among other institutions.[19] Albanian students are also underrepresented among high school and university students. Specifically, while the 1994 census reported that Albanians comprised 22.9 per cent of the population of the republic, as of 1995 only 12.4 per cent of high schools and a mere 6.5 per cent of university students were Albanians.[20]

Albanians claimed that part of the problem was that there were not enough primary and secondary schools in their communities. Moreover, even where there were Albanian-language schools operating, officials at the Ministry of Education admitted that the Albanian schools were, in general, not as good as the Macedonian-language schools.[21] Add to that the controversy which developed after Macedonian authorities ordered the bulldozing of the University of Tetovo, which Albanians set up on their own initiative, in early 1995, the arrest and trial of ten Albanians on charges of anti-state paramilitary activity (they were eventually released from custody), and the closure of some eighty-eight private radio and television stations, some of them broadcasting in Albanian, and one could conclude, as Abrahams did in 1996, that Macedonia's Albanians were on a collision course with the Skopje government.

But, as Abrahams notes, there were also problems with due process under the law and abuse by law enforcement officials, as well as allegations that the state-run media offered slanted coverage during the parliamentary elections in 1991 and 1994.[22] The international community became aware that Macedonia's stability was at risk and therefore took a number of measures designed to head off catastrophe, whether through formal institutions or behind the scenes. But, Abrahams charged, the international community also downplayed violations of human rights in Macedonia and muted its criticism of the Macedonian government. He cites an unnamed European diplomat as saying that there was no real democracy in Macedonia and that Macedonians were excluding non-Macedonians from their fair share in politics. Commenting on the OSCE's apparent readiness to keep quiet about Macedonian violations of human rights, Abrahams writes, 'Certainly, long-term stability is a noble goal. However, human rights violations should not be tolerated in order to achieve it. A lasting peace can only take root when there is the institutionalization of democratic norms that guarantee full respect for human rights.'[23]

In the five years that passed between the publication of Abrahams's study of human rights violations and the Kolbow/Quaden volume, Macedonia was admitted to the UN, there was a reconciliation of sorts between Macedonia and Greece, and strides were made in terms of Albanian representation in the rungs of administration, the police, and the officer corps of the Macedonian Army. There was even movement towards the creation of a new university in Tetovo (to be known officially as the Southeast European University of Tetova), with classes to be held in Albanian, English, and Macedonian; the university was the brainchild of OSCE high commissioner Max van der Stoel, who called for foreign donors to fund the institution in its initial stages.[24] Macedonian president Boris Trajkovski, who owed his election in 1999 to support from Macedonia's Albanian community, began to talk of Macedonia as offering a model of toleration and ethnic harmony. It was during this 'halcyon' phase that Walter Kolbow, a parliamentary state secretary of the German Ministry of Defence, and Heinrich Quaden, deputy commissioner for education with the General Inspector of the German Bundeswehr, put together their volume. Almost a third of the book is devoted to chapters dealing with Macedonia's internal and external relations; another third is devoted to the effects of the Kosovo war of 1999 and German assistance to Macedonia; the remaining third is given over to a survey of Macedonia's co-operation within various international settings, efforts at stabilization, and the economic interests at stake. The 'halcyon' phase notwithstanding, the contributors to this volume are duly cautious, recognizing the sensitivity of the Albanian question and the vulnerability of the Macedonian state to destabilization.

Perhaps the most striking contribution to the Kolbow/Quaden volume is provided by Arben Xhaferi, then chairman of the Democratic Party of Albanians. He begins by recalling how Albanians had joined Macedonians in the Kruševo uprising of 1903 and portrays the goal of that uprising as the creation of a 'Balkan Switzerland' in which the sundry peoples of Macedonia could live together in mutual respect and harmony. He blames Serbian expansionism (i.e., the establishment of the Kingdom of Serbs, Croats, and Slovenes) for the railroading of local aspirations in this direction. Later, Xhaferi recalls, in the course of the National Liberation Struggle (1941–5), Macedonian communists wooed Albanians to the Partisan cause with promises of an autonomous region for Macedonia's Albanians, but, after the war was won, they reneged on their promise, claiming that the Albanians were 'potential collaborators with the foreign enemy'.[25] Even so, the Macedonian constitution promised Albanians education in their native language at the elementary and secondary schools, as well as in institutions of higher education, the use of their national symbols, the use of their language, including in the parliament, and the right to establish their own institutions, including radio stations, theatres, and newspapers. Xhaferi adds, however, that some of these rights existed only in theory.

After the aforementioned unrest in Kosovo in 1981, Macedonian communists started to bring Macedonian schoolchildren to Albanian schools, thereby establishing ethnically mixed classes; having turned strictly Albanian schools into ethnically mixed schools, the authorities used this *fait accompli* to justify replacing Albanian as the language of instruction with Macedonian.[26] In 1989, altogether twenty-five amendments were passed to the Macedonian constitution, which, in Xhaferi's view, betrayed the spirit of the earlier common aspiration to build a 'Balkan Switzerland'. After that, and in particular after the declaration of independence, the toughest and 'saddest' challenge for Macedonia, according to Xhaferi, was not the conflict with Greece, nor the question of the republic's territorial integrity, but the 'incompatibility of the ethnocentric concept of the state with the multiethnic reality of the country'.[27]

Klaus Schrameyer strikes a somewhat different chord, however, emphasizing that, in his view, the Macedonian government has behaved 'rationally' since independence, while the office-holders in Macedonia have proven to be 'rationally thinking patriots, who know the limits and their responsibility'.[28] At the same time, he urges that the West do whatever it can to promote Macedonian co-operation with its neighbours, especially in the economic sphere.

A certain portion of the Kolbow/Quaden volume is given over to a celebration of the contributions of the primary editor, Walter Kolbow, who headed an office in Skopje after April 1999, channelling German aid to the troubled republic. Kolbow's contributions are noted in many places in the book, with one chapter given over entirely to describing his work.[29] And there are detailed discussions of Daimler-Chrysler's investments in Macedonia, the German economic initiative 'Southeast Europe', the work of Germany's political foundations in Macedonia, and the role of the German–American Exchange Service (DAAD) and the Tempus Project in Macedonia. All in all, this volume makes a useful contribution to appreciating the interest of the international community, and especially Germany, in Macedonia.

The other German monograph on Macedonia discussed in this chapter is the work of the veteran Balkanist, Wolf Oschlies, who has made important contributions to the study of not only Yugoslavia and its successor states, but also Bulgaria, and issues related to young people in Eastern Europe as a whole. Oschlies is quite open about his sympathies, announcing at the outset that Macedonia lies close to his heart. After a short eulogy for the late Macedonian president, Boris Trajkovski, who was killed in a helicopter accident in late February 2004, and a brief retrospective, Oschlies focuses his attention on the years 2001–4. He dismisses the claims made by some Macedonian Albanians that they constitute some 40 per cent of the republic's population, together with the 'compromise' offered in some German newspapers that they comprise about a third of the population of Macedonia, urging that the census of 1994 should be considered reliable. According to that census, there were (at the time) about 420,000 Albanians in Macedonia, making up about 22 per cent of the population.[30] Indeed, the results of the census held in 2002, in which the Albanian political parties co-operated, urging Albanians to take part, showed that Albanians constituted 25.17 per cent of the population at the time (up from 22.4 per cent in 1994), while the Macedonians constituted 64.18 per cent (down from 67.0 per cent in 1994).[31]

As Oschlies notes, Ljupčo Georgievski, founder (in June 1990) and president of the revived VRMO (now cast as a nationalist political party) and prime minister of Macedonia 1998–2002, has played an ambivalent role in Macedonian politics. Georgievski began a career as a lyricist, writing an erotic verse novel, *The City*, which, upon publication in 1991, captured public attention. In the years prior to 1998, he played the role of amateur opposition leader, weaving a tapestry of nationalistic and pro-labour notions possibly reminiscent of the American politicians George Wallace and Pat Buchanan. Then, as prime minister, he brought the Albanians into the governing coalition, only to adopt a stridently nationalist (i.e., Albanophobic) posture during and after the Albanian insurrection of 2001. Still later, in April 2003, Georgievski contributed an article to a local daily newspaper, in which he proposed the partition of Macedonia along ethnic lines in order to create an ethnically homogeneous Macedonian state, warning that, if the country were not partitioned, Macedonians would soon become a minority in their own country. Claiming that all Albanians 'carry a destructive energy in themselves',[32] Georgievski also criticized the international community for seeking to create a 'sovereign Greater Kosovo'. The official website of his VMRO–DPMNE also complained that 'The economic growth of our country bothers the international community, and therefore we had to keep our successes secret.'[33] In fact, Oschlies suggests, the international community still hopes to avoid seeing Kosovo independent, even though the Albanian population of Kosovo has made clear its commitment to achieving that goal.

Oschlies disputes Xhaferi's notion that Macedonians and Albanians were ever allies. He writes that 'The relationship between Macedonians and Albanians in Macedonia was never good, but also never as bad' as they became in 2001.[34] But he seems disinclined to take Albanian complaints about discrimination at face value, alleging that the Albanians never provided any evidence to back up their complaints.[35] In fact, internal circumstances are not sufficient to explain the Albanian insurrection of 2001, according to Oschlies. On the contrary, the insurrection should not be interpreted as a purely internal phenomenon; it was, rather, an 'export' from the international protectorate of Kosovo, which also involved mercenaries from certain Islamic countries.[36] But, that said, he does not let local Albanians off the hook, criticizing them for a decade of enmity towards Macedonia.

He returns to Albanian disputation of the census results several times, noting among other things Shkëlzen Maliqi's claim, in the course of an interview with the Croatian weekly magazine, *Feral Tribune*, that Albanians would constitute a majority of the population of Macedonia within a decade. Oschlies dismisses this as wishful thinking, noting that the birthrate among the Albanians of Macedonia is markedly lower than that among their compatriots in Kosovo, that the life expectancy of Albanians is lower than that of Macedonians, that the growing assimilation of Serbs and Vlachs into the Macedonian community will enter into the equation, that there has continued to be some emigration of Albanians to Western Europe and the United States, and that, if Kosovo becomes prosperous, additional numbers of Macedonian Albanians may choose to move there.[37] Indeed, unemployment in Macedonia was recorded at 37 per cent in 2003, which could, in itself, constitute an inducement to emigrate.

Oschlies also includes brief discussion of tensions between Macedonia and Greece, which he traces back to 1986, when the government in Athens passed a law under which Greece would no longer recognize academic degrees from the Cyril and Methodius University of Skopje, on the pretext that instruction in Skopje was conducted 'in an internationally unrecognized language'.[38] Until then, members of Greece's Macedonian minority had been able to attend the University of Skopje and then return to Greece to work; the law ended that possibility. But as of this writing, Greece is one of Macedonia's five largest trading partners and also the source of considerable investment. That storm, at least, seems to have passed.

III

The edited collections assembled by James Pettifer[39] and Jane Cowan[40] present a study in contrasts. Pettifer's collection includes contributions from historians, political scientists, jurists, and one journalist, as well as an interview with Kiro Gligorov, who was president of the Republic of Macedonia at the time the book was prepared. Cowan's collection, by contrast, is largely the work of anthropologists (with one historian represented in the collection). The purposes of the two works also differ. Where Pettifer's volume is driven by the ambition to present a contemporary survey of Macedonian history, politics, ethnic makeup, and diplomatic wrangling, Cowan's study is inspired by the more modest desire to shed light on the multiplicity of meanings associated with Macedonia, the interconnections between peoples who share a common

'Balkan mentality', and the existence of alternative interpretations of remote or ambiguous historical events and personalities.[41]

Pettifer's *New Macedonian Question* is divided into four sections, with part I devoted to the national question past and present, part II devoted to ethnic minorities (focusing on Albanians, non-Albanian Muslim minorities, Vlachs, and an overview of the status of national minorities in Macedonia), part III devoted to historical perspectives, and part IV devoted to international relations of Macedonia since 1990 (with two of this part's five chapters focusing on relations with Russia, and one focusing on relations with Greece). The best chapters in this eighteen-chapter collection, in my view, are those contributed by Stefan Troebst, Hugh Poulton, Reginald Hibbert, and Evangelos Kofos, and it is to these chapters that I shall now turn.

Troebst's chapter reviews the state of Macedonian historiography, highlighting the work of Ivan Katardžiev and Blaže Ristovski. He notes that, in the 1950s, Macedonian historiography traced Macedonian statehood back to Tsar Samuel in the late tenth century and associated the birth of the Macedonian people with the arrival of the Slavs in the peninsula in the sixth and seventh centuries CE. But in the early 1990s, this approach was revised, with Macedonian national history now being traced back to the fourth century BCE, with Philip II of Macedon and his son, 'Alexander the Macedonian'.[42] While commending the insights offered in the course of historical research into Macedonian history carried out in Athens, Belgrade, Skopje, Sofia, and Thessaloniki, he warns that 'the fact that these interpretations are all in tune with programmes of Macedonian, Greek, Bulgarian and Serbian nationalisms arouses the suspicion that the professional ethics of expert historians are being made – either voluntarily or otherwise – to fit the ups and downs of current politics'.[43] He also notes that, under the impact of diplomatic and economic pressure emanating from Greece, present-day amateur historians and archaeologists in Macedonia have been toying with the problematic thesis that contemporary Macedonians should trace their ethnogenesis to an ancient people related to the Etruscans and Basques being, thus, much more ancient than the Greek people. It is 1991 which marks the boundary not only between an autonomous Macedonia and an independent Macedonia but also between historiographic battles which could have their effect on perceptions of culture and minority rights and scholarly battles which reflected a more vital struggle over the identity and perhaps even the survival of the newborn Macedonian state. And, in this context, the Macedonian hit song of summer 1992 ('Play for me, Gypsy', by Rosana Sarik-Todorovska) captured the uncertainty of the moment with its line, 'Today we are happy and healthy, tomorrow we may not be so.'[44]

Hugh Poulton is, of course, the author of the fine study, *Who Are the Macedonians?*, already discussed in this chapter. Poulton's chapter reviews the status of the Torbeši (Macedonian Muslims), Turks, Roma, and 'Egyptians' living in Macedonia; Albanians and Vlachs are excluded from his survey because they are the subjects of separate chapters (written by James Pettifer and Tom Winnifrith respectively). Poulton begins with a brief overview of the millet system in Ottoman times and also discusses policies adopted in Greek and Bulgarian Macedonia between 1913 and 1993, before turning to the situation in the Republic of Macedonia. He notes the establishment by Torbeši of a cultural association in 1970 and its apparent success in attracting a receptive membership with the authorities' blessings. But Poulton suggests that the Torbeši have been susceptible to assimilation to the local Albanian community.

He outlines the difficulties experienced by local Turks in the early postwar period, when some seventeen Macedonian Turks were put on trial in January 1948 on charges of terrorism and espionage. The trial frightened many of the country's Turks, some of whom took the precaution of declaring themselves 'Albanians' in the census later that same year. But, as Poulton notes, after Tito's split with Stalin in June 1948 and the fallout in Yugoslav–Albanian relations, it became safer to be a Turk than an Albanian and, in the 1953 census, some 27,086 people who gave Albanian as their native language nonetheless declared that they were 'Turks.'[45] There were, already in the 1960s and 1970s, controversies about the ethnic status of Muslims who spoke Serbo-Croatian.[46] But, as Poulton notes, the controversies were revived in a new form in the 1990s when locals proved indisposed to accept Bosniak refugees from the war in Bosnia-Herzegovina. Indeed, authorities in Skopje were unwilling to recognize the existence of a Bosniak people and even obstructed efforts by Izetbegović's Party of Democratic Action (SDA) to set up a local branch in Macedonia.[47]

The Roma enjoyed equal legal standing with other national minorities in socialist Yugoslavia after 1981, though this formal equality was not always adequately translated into practice. With Macedonian independence, many Roma have declared themselves to be either Macedonians or Turks, although there have also been claims that local Roma were being subjected to pressures to assimilate to the Albanian community. In the census of April 1991, Poulton notes, there were some 55,575 Roma registered in Macedonia.[48] By contrast, there were reportedly between 20,000 and 30,000 citizens of Macedonia who claimed to be 'Egyptians' as of 1990, some of them claiming to be the descendants of Egyptian infantry troops and horsemen who allegedly came to Macedonia between 306 and 337 CE.[49]

Sir Reginald Hibbert is the author of an excellent study of wartime Albania.[50] He is also a veteran of the Special Operations Executive (SOE) who joined that agency in 1943 and was subsequently parachuted into Albania, where he spent a year as British liaison officer attached to the Partisans during 1943–4. He draws upon his rich experience in his incomparably fine recollections of those years on site.[51] He brings to life the complicated situation in which local Albanian leaders found themselves, having to choose between collaboration with Axis Powers prepared to give them the 'Greater Albania' of which they had been dreaming, albeit under Axis auspices, and collaboration with the Yugoslav Partisans, who were ill disposed to allow the Albanians to enjoy self-determination. Hibbert pays especial attention to the situation in Dibra, held for a while by Italian forces, and notes how the local Ndreu family provided officers for all four sides in the Albanian conflict: the Albanian Partisans, the Balli Kombëtar, the Zogists, and the collaborationists.[52] There are plenty of glimpses into the real world of warfare, including arduous hikes in pouring rain, relief at the prospect of warm meals, 'fine views of Struga and Lake Ochrid', and how he learned that Albanian communist Mehmet Shehu had been given command of a joint Albanian and Macedonian Partisan force.[53]

The chapter by Evangelos Kofos is by far the longest chapter in Pettifer's volume.[54] Kofos, a senior adviser on Balkan Affairs at the Hellenic Foundation for European and Foreign Policy of Athens and author of several books, including *Nationalism and Communism in Macedonia*,[55] is among the best-known specialists on Macedonian affairs. His chapter represents an endeavour to make the Greek position on recognition of Macedonia intelligible to a non-Greek audience and goes a long way towards accomplishing this goal. At a minimum, the reader will appreciate how intelligent Greeks viewed the issue and how some Greeks, at least, worried about the destabilization caused by the breakup of Yugoslavia and about the potential long-term effects of the establishment of an independent Macedonian state where Greek interests were concerned. One catches a glimpse of Kofos's view of the Balkan Wars of 1912–13 not as a period when the youthful Greek state was greedily annexing land populated by Macedonians (as per traditional Macedonian historiography) but as a time when the Greeks saw 'large parts of their northern regions of Macedonia and Thrace occupied by the armies of a neighbouring country (Bulgaria)'.[56] Where more contemporary events are concerned, Kofos implicitly criticizes Greek nationalists for going overboard, chastising them for misleading propaganda which left ordinary Greeks with the false impression that there was only one Macedonia – and that that was in northern Greece.[57] Kofos clearly feels that the tendency among some Greeks to refer to the new country as 'Skopje' and to its residents as 'Skopjans' made as much sense as it would have to have referred to Greece as 'Athens' and to its residents as 'Athenians'. But Kofos is not interested in criticizing his fellow Greeks, but, as already indicated, in making their response intelligible. And in this connection the public demonstrations in Skopje as early as October 1989, at which Macedonians shouted slogans such as 'reunification of Macedonia' and 'Solun [Thessaloniki] is ours' were surely not irrelevant. Moreover, the founding of a nationalist party under the provocative name, Internal Macedonian Revolutionary Organization–Democratic Party of Macedonian National Unity (VMRO–DPMNE), in January 1990 was disquieting, especially given that this openly irredentist organization won the largest number of votes in Macedonia's first free elections.[58]

In spite of these and other troubling signals emanating from Macedonia, the Greek government headed by Prime Minister Konstantin Mitsotakis continued the traditional line on Macedonia, at least for a while. But in October 1993, Andreas Papandreou, a former professor at Occidental College in Los Angeles, became prime minister of Greece and took Athens's diplomacy in a more hardline direction, demanding that Macedonian president Gligorov agree to surrender the name of his republic and imposing a total embargo on the Republic of Macedonia, except for food and pharmaceuticals. But, as Kofos notes, the embargo failed to accomplish its goal (to force Macedonians to agree to call themselves "Skopjans") and succeeded only in 'rais[ing] a world outcry against Greece' and in 'plac[ing] the country in the unenviable position of a social pariah in Europe'.[59] Yet it is possible, Kofos seems to be saying, that the principal objective of the embargo was domestic, namely, to mobilize Greek public opinion behind Papandreou's PASOK party. But even here the policy was at least partially unsuccessful in that some influential circles in Greece began to criticize the Greek government's policy vis-à-vis Macedonia in public.

Space does not permit a full discussion of all of the chapters in Pettifer's collection. But I hope that, in highlighting the four chapters in which I personally found the most profit, I have excited in some readers an interest in picking up this interesting volume.

I have already noted that the volume edited by Cowan provides a stark contrast to the Pettifer book. Indeed, among the tomes being reviewed in this chapter, Cowan's collection bears the closest comparison to the

book produced by Loring Danforth, who is, for that matter, the contributor of a useful chapter to Cowan's collection.[60] In this chapter,
following lines already laid down in his earlier study, Danforth highlights
the fact that national identity may be a matter of choice and that, in
ethnically mixed environments, individuals may adopt a language,
change their names, and choose an ethnic Church as a byproduct and
mark of a choice already made.[61] He also cites work by Mary Waters
showing that an individual may change his or her identity over time,
while the ethnic identity of a family may evolve over generations.

In a related chapter, Riki van Boeschoten asks why, in conditions of
interethnic interaction in the last two decades of the twentieth century,
with increasing rates of ethnic intermarriage, ethnic distinctions still
matter. He answers his own question by connecting ethnicity to class,
arguing that, without reducing ethnicity to class or vice versa, it is
important to factor in class differences as marking a boundary between
groups.[62]

Georgios Agelopoulos, in a fascinating study of Salonika, argues that
the dominant version of multiculturalism accepts an essentialist view of
ethnicity in which ethnicity is seen as fixed, unchanging, and inherited
automatically. He suggests, in particular, that historiographical depic-
tions of Ottoman-era Salonika as 'multicultural' presuppose modern
understandings of cultural communities – understandings which, in the
context of considering Ottoman society, are misunderstandings. In the
process, Agelopoulos warns, culture comes to be interpreted 'not . . . as
an outcome of social relations but as a definite and essential form of
demarcation of the self'.[63] In this essentializing and homogenizing
discourse, communities are concatenated on the basis of language (or
sometimes other criteria), whether for political purposes or out of ignorance; and there can be political effects, regardless of the motivation.
Cowan and Brown, for example, in their introduction to the volume,
note the tendency among many observers to view Albanians in Albania
as 'the same' as Albanians in Macedonia or Kosovo, in terms of
culture.[64] One need only recall the fate of Kosovar Croats who, during
the years they lived in Kosovo, always viewed themselves as Croats pure
and simple, only to find, upon their move to Croatia in the 1990s, that
their 'fellow Croats' in Croatia viewed them not in fact as 'fellow Croats'
but as culturally Albanian, as foreign, as 'southern'. Ethnicity, like
beauty, may be in the eye of the beholder as much as it is in one's own
self-perception.

Cowan's volume includes chapters by Iakovos Michailidis on alternative histories among defeated peoples, by Keith Brown on symbolic
politics in Macedonia 1994–9, by Piero Vereni on memory and national

identity in western Greek Macedonia, and by Jonathan M. Schwartz on questions of identity in diaspora and in the homeland. As a contribution to de-essentializing national identity, this anthropological study is valuable and will help readers to understand that national identity can be fluid even when the name endures (think just of the meanings attached over the centuries to the words 'Roman', 'Egyptian', 'Turk', or, for that matter, 'Greek' and 'Macedonian') and that national identity is ultimately subjective, both at the individual level and at the level of the collective.

IV

Finally, there are the two volumes devoted to contemporary Montenegrin history and politics, both published in 2003. Florian Bieber's collection brings together seven essays, two of them of a historical nature, three dealing with current developments, one with economics, and one with national minorities. The two historical chapters, written by Šerbo Rastoder and Srdja Pavlović, are especially valuable. Rastoder's chapter,[65] placed fifth in the volume, is a brilliant short introduction to the history of this neglected republic. In the space of thirty pages, Rastoder traces Montenegro's history over a thousand years, from its first mention in a papal epistle dated 9 November 1053 to the present. He suggests that Montenegro (then known as Zeta), unlike Serbia, shared in the Renaissance, provides a short but lucid account of tribal organization and traditional law in fifteenth- to seventeenth-century Montenegro, and summarizes the remarkable career of Šćepan Mali (Stephen the Small), who turned up in Montenegro in 1766, introducing himself as the dethroned Russian tsar, Peter III, and who, having united the country behind himself, created the first executive organs in the country. The role of Petar II Petrović Njegoš (reigned 1830–51) is also discussed in this chapter. Best known for his works of epic poetry (*The Mountain Wreath*, *The Ray of the Microcosm*, and *The False Tsar, Stephen the Small*), Njegoš established the first primary school in Montenegro and built up the organs of central administration.

But it is in discussing the end of Montenegrin independence that Rastoder makes a particular contribution. In histories of Yugoslavia, one may typically read that it was the Grand National Assembly, meeting in Podgorica (the present capital of Montenegro) which deposed King Nikola (who had reigned as prince since 1860 and as king since 1910) and proclaimed the unification of Montenegro with Serbia in the emerging Kingdom of Serbs, Croats, and Slovenes. What is not always noted but what is stressed in Rastoder's account is that the 'Grand

National Assembly' was an ad hoc body created by the so-called Central Executive Committee for the Unification of Serbia and Montenegro, which had been called into existence after the arrival of Serbian troops in Montenegro. In other words, the so-called 'Grand National Assembly' was not the legitimately elected parliament of Montenegro (which had its seat in the then-capital, Cetinje) and indeed met in defiance of the king, the parliament, and the constitution of Montenegro. The entire proceedings of the 'Grand National Assembly' were, thus, 'illegitimate and illegal' – as Rastoder puts it.[66] This, in turn, explains the ferocious resistance to unification mounted by Montenegrins loyal to the king – a resistance which continued even after the king's death, in exile, in March 1921 and which petered out only after the death of Queen Milena two years later.[67]

During the Second World War, there were three fighting forces active in Montenegro – Chetniks, whom Rastoder holds responsible for slaughtering Muslim civilians living in Montenegro; communist-led Partisans, 36 per cent of whose generals were Montenegrins; and a grouping of Montenegrin nationalists led by Krsto Popović, one of the loyalists after the shotgun marriage of 1918.[68] Rastoder's treatment of the communist era is brief, but he does mention that, during the socialist era, 'Montenegro experienced the greatest economic regeneration in its entire history.'[69]

Pavlović's chapter,[70] which precedes Rastoder's contribution, complements it nicely. Focusing on the identity, culture, and civic society of Montenegrins and addressing the age-old question of whether Montenegrins are 'really' Serbs, Pavlović starts by stressing that 'it is possible to make a distinction between Montenegrins and Serbs in terms of their independent political histories, as well as their tradition, customs, moral codes and the elements that best define the social cultures of their respective societies'.[71] In his view, then, the identification which Montenegrins felt with Serbs was 'of a general, non-nation-specific nature' and had more to do with shared religion than shared national traditions, national myths, or national identity.[72] Indeed, Pavlović emphasizes, prior to the closing decades of the nineteenth century, national consciousness was essentially irrelevant in the Balkan peninsula so that such conflicts as did take place had nothing to do with ethnic or national animosities. But once Montenegro had been conjoined with Serbia as part of the interwar kingdom, Serbian politicians sought to appropriate Montenegro (and, for that matter, Macedonia too) as authentically Serbian. Much as the Ustaše would describe the Muslims of Bosnia as the purest branch of the Croatian nation, Serb nationalists sought to represent Montenegrins as 'racially pure or even the purest of Serbs'.[73] More particularly, to appropriate Montenegro meant also to appropriate its poetry, its myths, its history as somehow Serbian; this project of appropriating Montenegro served, among other things, to provide a discourse in which 'Serbs' could be 'recollected' to have resisted Ottoman domination for centuries[74] – no matter that it was the Montenegrins who were resisting. And if Montenegrins are just Serbs, then any assertion of Montenegrin distinctiveness is at best self-delusion, at worst the perpetuation of a great lie – as Dobrica Ćosić suggested in 2000, in claiming that Montenegrin identity was an 'invention' of Stalinism.[75]

The remaining chapters in Bieber's collection focus on more contemporary politics, with Bieber noting, in his introductory chapter, how the pyramid schemes set up with the implicit consent of Belgrade authorities during the time of hyperinflation served to generate a new class of super-rich who were tied to the ruling party and to organized crime.[76] Tracking Serb–Montenegrin relations through the 1990s up to December 2002, Bieber concludes that Montenegro has differed from other post-Yugoslav successor states insofar as the ethnic element has been less salient in political discourse, with members of national minorities preferring to vote for one or another of the leading Montenegrin parties rather than for their respective ethnic parties.[77] It may even be the case, as Bieber suggests, that Montenegrin nationalism is characterized by tolerance and a tendency towards interethnic co-operation, with national myths which stress tolerance towards minorities.[78]

The last book to be discussed in this chapter is Jens Becker and Achim Engelberg's *Montenegro im Umbruch*.[79] More contemporary in focus than Bieber's volume, the Becker/Engelberg volume nonetheless includes, among its twelve chapters, German versions of three of the chapters published in Bieber's *Montenegro in Transition*, namely, chapters by Bieber himself (on Montenegrin politics during the 1990s), by Wim van Meurs (on the Belgrade agreement of March 2002), and by František Šistek and Bohdana Dimitrovová (on Montenegro's national minorities). Among the other chapters included in this volume are an extremely useful survey of Montenegro's economic development, written by Dragan Djurić, an analysis of the Montenegrin mafia written by the renowned expert Norbert Mappes-Niediek (see the review of his book, *Balkan-Mafia*, in chapter 10), and a fine discussion of the situation of Croats living in Montenegro, written by Carl Bethke. From the last mentioned chapter, the reader will learn that alongside Orthodox Serbs and Montenegrins, and Muslim and Catholic Albanians, one has also been able to find Catholic Serbs, Catholic and Muslim Montenegrins, and Catholic Yugoslavs living in Montenegro.[80] But the War of Yugoslav Succession changed the ethnic composition of Montenegro, with many

Croats fleeing, their places being taken by Serbian refugees from the Krajina and from Bosnia-Herzegovina. The same point is made, more generally, by Šistek and Dimitrovová, who also provide some details of the ways in which that war impinged directly on Muslim civilians living in Montenegro; in February 1993, to take just one example, Muslims living in the vicinity of Bukovica, north of Pljevlja, were attacked by Serb paramilitaries, and were variously murdered, kidnapped, or driven out of their houses.[81] And yet the war did not result in ethnic polarization in Montenegro, at least not along simple lines: while anti-Serb feelings were shared by many non-Serbs in the republic, some two-thirds of local Albanians voted for the Montenegrin DPS–SDP coalition in April 2001, leaving the three Albanian parties to divide the remaining one-third of Albanian votes. Šistek and Dimitrovová also confirm Bieber's judgement cited above that Montenegrin nationalism is characterized by a tendency towards inclusiveness, citing the friendly relationship maintained towards local Muslims (Bosniaks), Albanians, Croats, and members of other national minorities.[82]

The dramatic signing of the Belgrade agreement on 14 March 2002 marked a watershed in recent Montenegrin history, as Wim van Meurs notes,[83] but it is by no means the end of the story where Montenegrin independence is concerned. But for the EU, which has wanted to post-pone Kosovar independence for as long as possible, a central aspect of the entire question of Montenegrin independence is what impact it would have on the Kosovo question. It was precisely in this connection, as van Meurs records, that the EU specified that, in the event that Montenegro were to pull out of the union with Serbia, Serbia would be treated as the successor to the Federal Republic of Yugoslavia, with all the rights and prerogatives guaranteed under UN Resolution 1244, the resolution guaranteeing Yugoslav sovereignty over Kosovo.[84]

But the Montenegrin story would not be complete without some consideration of its economic development – which is where the chapters by Djurić, Mappes-Niediek, and Fetscher enter the picture. As Djurić tells it, the Montenegrin economy took a nosedive during the war, so that by 1994 its real GDP stood at only 44 per cent of what it had been just four years earlier; even in 1999, Montenegro's GDP had managed only a partial recovery, standing at 58 per cent of the 1990 level.[85] As the economy plunged, the number of impoverished rose, with some 28.9 per cent of Montenegrin citizens living below the official poverty line as of 1996.[86] A 'grey economy' has inevitably grown in such circumstances, employing some 35.3 per cent of women, though only 4.2 per cent of men.[87] Some of the regime's steps to address its economic difficulties – for example, the declaration in 1996 of an international off-shore free trade zone in Montenegro and the subsequent adoption first of the DM and later of the euro as the republic's official currency – have provoked conflicts with Belgrade. During 1999–2000, as Djurić records,[88] Montenegro received the second-highest (after Israel) amount of financial support, on a per capita basis, from the United States.[89] But this ended with the fall of Milošević in October 2000. Again, the activity of local smuggling, recorded by Mappes-Niediek,[90] is part of the story, but is conditioned by various factors, including regional politics and economics, the UN-imposed embargo, the decisions taken by certain elites, and the role of personal networks (in this case, in Montenegro). Whether the long-range project to turn Montenegro into a major tourist destination – a project described in some detail by Caroline Fetscher[91] – will succeed remains, at this writing, an open question.

V

The disintegration of socialist Yugoslavia began in the 1980s. Where the southern republics are concerned, one may note that, as early as the mid-1980s, Macedonians began to rebel against the decades-long celebrations of the Balkan Wars, which the Serbs viewed as a liberation of Macedonia but which Macedonians remembered as the replacement of Turkish rule by Serbian rule.[92] Macedonia and Montenegro were, at the time, the two poorest republics in the Yugoslav federation and, in the 1980s, the economy took a turn for the worse. Montenegro even declared bankruptcy in 1987, with some 6,000 workers losing their jobs in the final years of that decade.[93] Montenegro was rocked by workers' protests and, subsequently, by nationalist protests organized on Milošević's behalf by the Committee for the Protection of Kosovo Serbs and Montenegrins. Montenegro, which at first stood against Milošević, was eventually taken over by Milošević loyalists in 1989, while Macedonia, which at first took Milošević's side against Slovenia, eventually became concerned at the implications of Milošević's programme and drew back.

The Socialist Federated Republic of Yugoslavia was, for many, an attractive country, which, at least in Tito's time, combined socialist egalitarianism with charismatic monarchy. It is not for nothing that Tito has been dubbed 'the last Habsburg', even if he made his capital in Belgrade rather than in Vienna. But the fragmentation of Yugoslavia has not yet reached its endpoint, with continuing pressures from the Bosnian Serbs, the Bosnian Croats, and the Kosovar Albanians to be allowed to secede from the jurisdictions to which they have been assigned, and voices being raised in the Sandžak and in Vojvodina, demanding more autonomy, with occasional half-whispered hints that even secession might be an option. Meanwhile, Serbia is once more being warmed by a Chetnik sun, as already noted in the previous chapter. This embrace of xenophobic nationalism suggests that Serbia itself has not yet come to terms with the meaning of its own past or with the requirements of liberal democracy, and, as such, may contribute to a political atmosphere in which distrust, secessionist projects, and grand designs for reform will continue to emerge and re-emerge.

NOTES

1 *Human Rights in the Shadow of Nationalism: Serbia 2002* (Belgrade: Helsinki Committee for Human Rights in Serbia, 2003), pp. 240–1.
2 Hugh Poulton, *Who Are the Macedonians?* (Bloomington, IN: Indiana University Press, 1995), p. 91.
3 *Ibid.*, pp. 92–3.
4 *Ibid.*, p. 118.
5 *Ibid.*, p. 125.
6 *Ibid.*, p. 177.
7 *Ibid.*, p. 136.
8 Loring M. Danforth, *The Macedonian Conflict: Ethnic Nationalism in a Transnational World* (Princeton, NJ: Princeton University Press, 1995), p. 32.
9 *Ibid.*, p. 33.
10 *Ibid.*, p. 34.
11 Evangelos Kofos, *Nationalism and Communism in Macedonia* (Thessaloniki: Institute for Balkan Studies, 1964), p. 131, as quoted in Danforth, *The Macedonian Conflict*, p. 42.
12 Danforth, *The Macedonian Conflict*, p. 43.
13 *Ibid.*, pp. 45–6.
14 *Ibid.*, p. 53.
15 Hristo Andonovski, 'Makedonističkoto dviženje vo Kostursko' (1985), as quoted *ibid.*, p. 62.
16 Danforth, *The Macedonian Conflict*, p. 69.
17 *ibid.*, pp. 157–8.
18 *Ibid.*, pp. 198, 199.
19 Fred Abrahams, *A Threat to 'Stability': Human Rights Violations in Macedonia* (New York: Human Rights Watch/Helsinki, 1996), pp. 28–9.
20 *Ibid.*, pp. 32–3.
21 *Ibid.*, pp. 34, 37.
22 *Ibid.*, pp. 98–9.
23 *Ibid.*, p. 104.
24 For details, see Sabrina P. Ramet, *The Three Yugoslavias: State-building and Legitimation 1918–2005* (Bloomington, IN, and Washington, DC: Indiana University Press and Wilson Center Press, forthcoming), chap. 19.
25 Arben Xhaferi, 'Makedonien zwischen Ethnozentrismus und Multiethnie', in Walter Kolbow and Heinrich Quaden (eds.), *Krieg und Friede auf dem Balkan*

– *Makedonien am Scheideweg?* (Baden-Baden: Nomos Verlagsgesellschaft, 2001), p. 40.
26 *Ibid.*
27 *Ibid.*, p. 42.
28 Klaus Schrameyer, 'Makedonien – Hintergründe und Perspektiven', in Kolbow and Quaden, *Krieg und Friede auf dem Balkan*, p. 77.
29 Volker Barth, 'Das Büro Kolbow – Beitrag zur Stabilisierung eines bedrohten Landes', in Kolbow and Quaden, *Krieg und Friede auf dem Balkan*, pp. 105–17. But see also Delfina Baftiri, 'Radusha – Das vergessene Flücht-lingslager', Malte Bardt, 'Evakuierung von Flüchtlingen aus Makedonien', Hans-Peter Grünebach, 'Der "Runde Tisch" – Ein Modell?', Peter Braun-stein, 'Die Zusammenarbeit der Bundeswehr mit den Hilfsorganisationen – Grundsätze und Konzepte der zivil-militärischen Zusammenarbeit (CIMIC)', and Gerhard Behrendt, 'Der schwierige Beginn – Erfahrungen beim Aufbau der Zusammenarbeit mit der Universität "Ss. Kiril i Methodij" in Skopje' – all in the same volume.
30 Wolf Oschlies, *Makedonien 2001–2004: Kriegstagebuch aus einem friedlichen Land* (Berlin: Xenomos, 2004), pp. 32, 57–8, 66.
31 *Ibid.*, p. 76.
32 As quoted *ibid.*, p. 223.
33 As quoted *ibid.*, p. 222.
34 *Ibid.*, p. 61.
35 *Ibid.*
36 According to Oschlies, fighters from Islamic countries were paid 5,000–8,000 DM per month, while fighters from Kosovo were paid 3,000–5,000 DM per month. He adds that locals (fighters recruited in Macedonia) were paid 1,000–3,000 DM per month *ibid.*, p. 59.
37 *Ibid.*, pp. 68–9.
38 *Ibid.*, p. 52.
39 James Pettifer (ed.), *The New Macedonian Question* (Houndmills, Basingstoke: Macmillan, 1999).
40 Jane K. Cowan (ed.), *Macedonia: The Politics of Identity and Difference* (London and Sterling, VA: Pluto Press, 2000).
41 Jane K. Cowan and K. S. Brown, 'Introduction: Macedonian Inflections', *ibid.*, pp. 1–27.
42 Stefan Troebst, 'IMRO + 100 = FYROM? The Politics of Macedonian Historiography', in Pettifer, *New Macedonian Question*, p. 63.
43 *Ibid.*, p. 64.
44 Quoted *ibid.*, p. 71.
45 Hugh Poulton, 'Non-Albanian Muslim minorities in Macedonia', in Pettifer, *New Macedonian Question*, pp. 117–18.
46 For details, see Sabrina P. Ramet, *Nationalism and Federalism in Yugoslavia, 1962–1991*, 2nd edn (Bloomington, IN: Indiana University Press, 1992).
47 Poulton, 'Non-Albanian Muslim', p. 116.
48 *Ibid.*, p. 120.
49 *Ibid.*, p. 121.
50 Reginald Hibbert, *Albania's National Liberation Struggle: The Bitter Victory* (London: Pinter, 1991).

51 Reginald Hibbert, 'Albania, Macedonia and the British Military Missions, 1943 and 1944', in Pettifer, *New Macedonian Question*, pp. 184–98.
52 *Ibid.*, p. 189.
53 *Ibid.*, pp. 192–3.
54 Evangelos Kofos, 'Greek Policy Considerations over FYROM Independence and Recognition', in Pettifer, *New Macedonian Question*, pp. 226–62.
55 Evangelos Kofos, *Nationalism and Communism in Macedonia* (Thessaloniki: IBS, 1964; reissued by Caratzas Publisher of New Rochelle, NY, in 1993).
56 Kofos, 'Greek Policy Considerations', p. 229.
57 *Ibid.*, p. 235.
58 *Ibid.*, p. 236.
59 *Ibid.*, p. 245.
60 Loring M. Danforth, '"How Can a Woman Give Birth to One Greek and One Macedonian?" The Construction of National Identity among Immigrants to Australia from Northern Greece', in Cowan, *Macedonia: The Politics of Identity*, pp. 85–103.
61 *Ibid.*, p. 86.
62 Riki van Boeschoten, 'When Difference Matters: Sociopolitical Dimensions of Ethnicity in the District of Florina', in Cowan, *Macedonia: The Politics of Identity*, pp. 28–30.
63 Georgios Agelopoulos, 'Political Practices and Multiculturalism: The Case of Salonika', in Cowan, *Macedonia: The Politics of Identity*, p. 150.
64 Cowan and Brown, 'Introduction', p. 13.
65 Šerbo Rastoder, 'A Short Review of the History of Montenegro', in Florian Bieber (ed.), *Montenegro in Transition: Problems of Identity and Statehood* (Baden-Baden: Nomos Verlagsgesellschaft, 2003), pp. 107–37.
66 *Ibid.*, p. 129.
67 *Ibid.*, pp. 130–3.
68 *Ibid.*, pp. 135–6.
69 *Ibid.*, p. 137.
70 Srdja Pavlović, 'Who are Montenegrins? Statehood, Identity, and Civic Society', in Bieber, *Montenegro in Transition*, pp. 83–106.
71 *Ibid.*, p. 84.
72 *Ibid.*
73 *Ibid.*, p. 96.
74 *Ibid.*, p. 100.
75 Dobrica Ćosić, in conversation with Timothy Garton Ash (2000), as cited *ibid.*, p. 101.
76 Florian Bieber, 'Montenegrin Politics since the Disintegration of Yugoslavia', in Bieber, *Montenegro in Transition*, p. 25.
77 *Ibid.*, p. 42.
78 *Ibid.* See also František Šistek and Bohdana Dimitrovová, 'National Minorities in Montenegro after the Break-up of Yugoslavia', in Bieber, *Montenegro in Transition*, p. 178.
79 Jens Becker and Achim Engelberg (eds.), *Montenegro im Umbruch: Reportagen und Essays* (Münster: Verlag Westfälisches Dampfboot, 2003).
80 Carl Bethke, 'Die Kroaten in Tivat, Kotor und Montenegro', in Becker and Engelberg, *Montenegro im Umbruch*, p. 118.

81 František Šistek and Bohdana Dimitrovová, 'Nationale Minderheiten in Montenegro', in Becker and Engelberg, *Montenegro im Umbruch*, p. 102.
82 *Ibid.*, p. 111.
83 Wim van Meurs, 'Das Belgrader Abkommen und die EU als Mediator', in Becker and Engelberg, *Montenegro im Umbruch*, pp. 63–74.
84 *Ibid.*, p. 71.
85 Dragan Djurić, 'Die wirtschaftliche Entwicklung Montenegros – eine vorläufige Bilanz', in Becker and Engelberg, *Montenegro im Umbruch*, p. 75.
86 *Ibid.*, p. 78.
87 *Ibid.*, p. 79.
88 *Ibid.*, p. 84.
89 *Ibid.*
90 Norbert Mappes-Niediek, 'Mafia in Montenegro', in Becker and Engelberg, *Montenegro im Umbruch*, pp. 89–97.
91 Caroline Fetscher, 'Montenegro – ein wiederentdecktes Reiseziel', in Becker and Engelberg, *Montenegro im Umbruch*, pp. 127–42.
92 Nina Dobrković, 'Yugoslavia and Macedonia in the Years 1991–96: From Brotherhood to Neighbourhood', in Pettifer, *New Macedonian Question*, p. 86.
93 Bieber, 'Montenegrin Politics since the Disintegration of Yugoslavia', p. 13.

REFERENCES

Macedonia

Abrahams, Fred, *A Threat to 'Stability': Human Rights Violations in Macedonia* (New York: Human Rights Watch/Helsinki, 1996), p. 114.
Cowan, Jane K. (ed.), *Macedonia: The Politics of Identity and Difference* (London and Sterling, VA: Pluto Press, 2000), p. 166.
Danforth, Loring M., *The Macedonian Conflict: Ethnic Nationalism in a Transnational World* (Princeton, NJ: Princeton University Press, 1995), p. 273.
Kolbow, Walter and Heinrich Quaden (eds.), *Krieg und Frieden auf dem Balkan – Makedonien am Scheideweg?* (Baden-Baden: Nomos Verlagsgesellschaft, 2001), p. 290.
Oschlies, Wolf, *Makedonien 2001–2004: Kriegstagebuch aus einem friedlichen Land* (Berlin: Xenomos, 2004), p. 321.
Pettifer, James (ed.), *The New Macedonian Question* (Houndmills, Basingstoke: Macmillan, 1999), p. 311.
Poulton, Hugh, *Who Are the Macedonians?* (Bloomington, IN: Indiana University Press, 1995), p. 218.

Montenegro

Becker, Jens and Achim Engelberg (eds.), *Montenegro im Umbruch: Reportagen und Essays* (Münster: Verlag Westfälisches Dampfboot, 2003), p. 156.
Bieber, Florian (ed.), *Montenegro in Transition: Problems of Identity and Statehood* (Baden-Baden: Nomos Verlagsgesellschaft, 2003), p. 194.

Conclusion: controversies, methodological disputes, and suggested reading

I

It is my hope that the foregoing chapters have provided some clarification of the nature of the debates within the field of Yugoslav and post-Yugoslav studies as well as concerning the differences in point of view among the various authors discussed. I have tried, to the extent of my knowledge and ability, to discuss those works which have had the greatest impact in the field and/or are the most deserving of attention. I have left to the side books which are best left to the side, though I hasten to point out that no survey of literature in a given field can ever hope to be complete and that no special meaning should be read into the exclusion of one or another book from discussion in the foregoing pages. What an alert reader will note at once is that scholars in the field of Yugoslav studies (and, of course, principals engaged in writing their memoirs) have some serious disagreements with each other and that these involve both substantive questions and questions related to research methodology.

Where substantive controversies are concerned, there are differences of opinion concerning when the conflict 'really' started – did it start, for example, somewhere between 1986 and 1991 as most scholars think, with 1991 being the 'common sense' view, or should one trace the conflict back in time? And if one traces the roots of the conflict, let us say, to the interwar kingdom, which was founded in December 1918, then how does that change our view of the role played by Milošević and all the others? Closely related to this is the question: who is to blame? Veljko Kadijević tells us that it was the United States and Germany that orchestrated the fighting in Slovenia, Croatia, and Bosnia-Herzegovina to serve their own imperialist ends, with Germany even dreaming of establishing some form of dominion over the Yugoslav area. Brendan Simms blames not the United States and Germany, but Britain in the first place, although in Simms's account Britain is culpable not for planning the war, only for failing to take steps to stop the conflict and for preventing others from doing so. Most scholars agree with James Gow, Reneo Lukić, Viktor Meier, and James J. Sadkovich in attributing primary culpability to the Serbian side in the conflict,[1] which, in practice, means first of all Milošević, Borisav Jović, Karadžić, and, as supporting players, Ćosić, Šešelj, and Šolević. Other scholars, such as Susan Woodward and Paul Mojzes, are inclined to agree with Warren Zimmermann that the Slovenes must somehow be held partially accountable for the bloodshed which came after they withdrew from the Yugoslav federation. But while Mojzes spreads the blame widely, including in his list of suspects even the religious leaderships of the Catholic and Orthodox Churches, he repeatedly returns to the theme that the principal reason for the outbreak of fighting in 1991 was 'the inability of this multi-national country to solve the national question',[2] an interpretation specifically repudiated by Woodward. Mojzes provides no examples of Catholic bishops or clergy stoking the flames of nationalism, but Pejanović describes how the Catholic Church provided concrete assistance to members of all the major faiths, without regard to nationality or religious affiliation, and argues that, far from stoking the flames of nationalism, the Catholic Church worked for tolerance and interethnic harmony.[3] Lenard Cohen, by contrast, while noting the role of Milošević and his associates in stirring up trouble, ties their activity to a theory of historical determinism in which, as he puts it, the operative factor is a 'collectivist nationalism . . . rooted in the mythic lore passed from one generation to another',[4] and in which the present-day collective 'Serbian political psyche' was formed in the course of 'the long period of Turkish domination, and the nineteenth and twentieth century struggles with Austria-Hungary's and Germany's intervention in the Balkans'.[5] For those who are inclined to think that one can indeed discuss collective mental states, the alternative (to postulating historically determined collective mental states) is to connect such states to more recent events; C. G. Schoenfeld, who takes this approach, suggests, thus, that the Serbs are a classic case of a people with damaged self-esteem, who are therefore more vulnerable to certain kinds of appeal.[6]

Not entirely unrelated to Mojzes's approach is the 'civilizational' approach taken by Harvard professor Samuel P. Huntington in his national bestseller, *The Clash of Civilizations*. But for Huntington, unlike Mojzes, the cultural fault lines are so serious that it may be beside the point to worry about agency at all. The starting point for Huntington is what he calls 'civilizational fault lines', which divide peoples by religion in the first place. It is because of these fault lines and because, as he tells us, that 'it is human to hate',[7] that 'people who share ethnicity and language but differ in religion may slaughter each other, as happened in Lebanon, the former Yugoslavia, and the [Indian] Subcontinent'.[8] In Huntington's view, the danger of fault lines became 'most notable' in postcommunist states where, he tells us, 'culture replaced ideology as the magnet of attraction and repulsion'.[9] In his earlier *Political Order in Changing Societies*, Huntington had expressed his view that 'Leninist' systems, as he called communist systems, had solved the problem of political institutionalization and therefore were, in consequence, likely to prove to be stable over the long run, in spite of their obvious failure to solve the problem of legitimation (the importance of which Huntington downplayed).[10] But if the question of system legitimacy is not a factor worth considering in accounting for system decay, then where should one look for an answer? In 1968, Huntington thought the answer was inadequate institutionalization relative to political participation; nearly twenty years later, turning his attention to the global world order, Huntington looked to differences in religion and culture to explain why at least some conflicts had broken out. In a pessimistic spirit, he writes that 'Fault line wars are intermittent; fault line conflicts are interminable.'[11] In *Clash* he portrays the 'fault line' between Muslims and non-Muslims as running especially deep, so that he concludes that 'Fault line conflicts are particularly prevalent between Muslims and non-Muslims.'[12] And hence, in his view, the War of Yugoslav Succession, in which Bosnian Muslims fought Christian Serbs and Croats, should be seen as an 'intercivilizational' war.[13] Huntington does not say, of course, that Muslims and non-Muslims have hated each other since 'ancient' times; what he says rather is that their civilizations have evolved in such different directions, since long ago, that conflict (or hatred, if one likes) is far more natural between them than understanding.

Scholars also disagree about just how many wars were fought in the period 1991–9. James Gow stakes out the boldest position, arguing that the fighting in Slovenia, Croatia, Bosnia-Herzegovina, and Kosovo should also be seen as theatres in a single war planned by Belgrade and having the objective of securing the borders of an ethnically homogeneous state. At the other extreme, Paul Mojzes, writing in 1994, argues that 'the Yugoslav conflict is really not a single war but, rather, a series of different wars intermingled within a larger context'.[14] Most scholars adopt the convention of describing the fighting during 1991–5 as the War of Yugoslav Succession, while identifying the conflict in Kosovo during 1998–9 as a distinct war, albeit linked with the war of 1991–5.[15] Ultimately, the question of how many wars there were may not be as important as it might seem at first glance, since, for example, we routinely write of 'the Napoleonic Wars', without making any particular distinction among them, indeed without even thinking of them as 'them'.

Those who are concerned with the nature of the war typically ask whether it should be seen as having been an 'ethnic' war and whether it should be seen as having had a genocidal dimension. The dispute about the term 'ethnic' often turns out to hinge on different uses of the word. Those who feel that the word may be used to refer to the way in which Belgrade and Zagreb mobilized the hatred of entire groups of people are inclined to think that calling the War of Yugoslav Succession an 'ethnic war' serves to identify the primary pole of mobilization and to distinguish it, let us say, from a 'class war' or a 'religious war'. Those who fear that the word conjures up images of historical determinism and of hatreds 'rooted in the mythic lore passed from one generation to another', typically avoid using the word.

The question of genocide is, however, a more fundamental one, though again one concerning which there is no agreement. James Gow and Norman Cigar have been among those scholars who have unambiguously identified processes of genocide in the Yugoslav war, while Steven Burg and Paul Shoup, even granting their internal disagreement, have been more reluctant to use the word 'genocide' in referring to the war. Taking a different approach, Robert Hayden, in an article for *Slavic Review*, outlined a logic under which genocide would be hard to demonstrate in *any* context, because 'genocide must be a collective act', while no collectivity lacks innocent people.[16] In fact, Serbian nationalists used the term 'genocide' themselves in the late 1980s and early 1990s – to recall the murders of Serbs and other Yugoslavs at the Jasenovac concentration camp during the Second World War[17] or to mount allegations against the Albanians of Kosovo.

The dispute about genocide fed directly into a debate about humanitarian intervention, with those who identified processes of genocide typically demanding international intervention to stop it (as required under the Genocide Convention) and those who thought that the extent of the killing did not rise to the level of genocide being opposed to intervention. One of the most systematic studies of the debate surrounding humanitarian intervention is Rasmus Tenbergen's volume, discussed in chapter 10, which argues that 'humanitarian interventions are legitimate when they protect more human rights than they damage'.[18] Andreas Hasenclever's *Die Macht der Moral in der internationalen Politik*, discussed in the same chapter, outlines three schools of thought – the 'realists', who typically want to prioritize strategic or economic interests, the 'rational liberals', who shift the focus to competing interests within a given state, and advocates of the 'moral-sociological approach', such as

Hasenclever himself, who believe that moral concerns have a natural role to play in foreign policy decision-making.

Tenbergen agrees with Hasenclever that morality has a legitimate role in policy-making, but at least one scholar has argued that concern with morality threatens to obstruct one's understanding of real political processes and events,[19] from which it would seem that one should conclude that judgements about morality have no place in politics and that no state should ever come to the rescue of another state or its people – a conclusion which strikes me as rather odd. But while I believe I am correct in suggesting that the vast majority of observers of the War of Yugoslav Succession and the War for Kosovo have felt that intervention by external powers could play a role in ending the suffering of locals, few observers of the Yugoslav scene have been prepared to go as far as Zimmermann and Mojzes in characterizing the war as a struggle between good and evil. Indeed, Mojzes, who identifies the struggle between good and evil not with the warring sides but with a moral struggle taking place 'within each community and even within each person', looks to religion for a solution, expressing the conviction that the overcoming of the hatreds which he sees as lying behind the problems in the Yugoslav region 'will require that the good of God prevail in the soul of each person'.[20]

II

Alongside these substantive controversies there have also been a number of methodological controversies. In using the term 'methodological', I have in mind questions about what constitutes relevant evidence, which dialogues should be seen as relevant to the questions being examined: how is agency discussed, what are the timeline and sequence of events (what is included or excluded), and are 'they' like 'us'? On the last of these, for example, Misha Glenny's work would allow a reader to conclude that the people of Yugoslavia were (and are) somehow wilder and less civilized than 'we' are, whoever that 'we' might be. Susan Woodward's emphasis on the economic factor, in her *Socialist Unemployment*, leads in the opposite direction, that is, to an emphasis on the common vulnerability of any society, under specified conditions, to dissolution, fragmentation, and war. Where timeline and sequence are concerned, I can suggest a warning against works which purport to explain how Yugoslavia ended up in war but do not include any discussion of Milošević's instrumentalization of Serb resentments in connection with Kosovo and encouragement of an escalation of such resentments. By the same token, treatments of the Bosnian political scene at the dawn of the 1990s in which Serbian political views are presented, while Croatian and Bosniak views are ignored, cannot be considered complete.

There is the question of how one identifies agency. The use of the passive voice, for example, serves to conceal agency, though the concealment should not be assumed to be deliberate. Other formulations, such as 'the Serbs', 'Milošević', 'Belgrade', 'the Serbian side', 'Milošević and his cronies' (or, in polemical literature, 'the Bolshevik–Chetnik bandits'), or 'the Croats', 'Tudjman', 'Zagreb', 'the Croatian side', 'Tudjman and his cronies' (or, in polemical literature, 'the Ustaše'), are, with the exception of the polemical examples, interchangeable up to a point, but carry implications. For example, if only 'Tudjman and his cronies' are responsible for the Croatian involvement in Bosnia-Herzegovina (perhaps understanding by 'cronies' the Herzegovinian lobby), does that mean that Croats at large are innocent? Or, if one writes 'the Serbs' or 'the Croats', is one in danger of implying collective guilt? Most scholars sensibly reject the concept of collective guilt as it is usually understood, namely, as signifying that each and every member of a given nation somehow shares in the guilt for atrocities perpetrated by forces controlled by that nation's government. But common sense also suggests that, when people vote for political parties and candidates who have been identified with well-known atrocities, those who vote for those parties and candidates are also identifying themselves with those atrocities; while they may not have perpetrated the atrocities themselves, there is at least a question as to whether they have, by their votes, given their endorsement to those atrocities after the fact. In writing these lines, I am thinking specifically of the groundswell of support for the Serbian Radical Party at the Serbian parliamentary elections in December 2003.

III

Given the sheer number of books discussed herein, it may be helpful, at least for students, if I identify at least some of those books which are the most useful, in my view, for someone wishing to acquaint him- or herself with Yugoslav and post-Yugoslav history, including with the histories of Slovenia, Croatia, Bosnia-Herzegovina, Serbia, Macedonia, and Kosovo. This list is offered as a list of my own personal favourites, in the hope that it may be of some interest or use at least to those who are new to the field.

There are a number of general histories of Yugoslavia written by other scholars, but I have decided against any discussion or rating of them. Nor shall I rate, in this chapter, works published in languages other than English (with one exception). Readers able to read German may, however, turn with confidence to the works of Klaus Buchenau,[21] Marie-Janine Calic, Konrad Clewing, Srećko M. Džaja,[22] Daniel Eisermann, Andreas Hasenclever, Joachim Hösler, Karl Kaser,[23] Walter Manoschek,[24] Viktor Meier, Dunja Melčić,[25] Ludwig Steindorff, Holm Sundhaussen,[26] Christine von Kohl, and Wolfgang Libal.[27] (Those authors whose works have already been discussed herein are not foot-noted.) Francophone readers should consult the works of Reneo Lukić[28] and Paul Garde.[29] Italophone readers should consult the works of Stefano Bianchini[30] and Jože Pirjevec.[31] Norwegophones should consult the works of Svein Mønnesland.[32] Swedophones may turn to the works of Christian Palme[33] and Bo Pellnäs.[34] Spanish speakers may turn with confidence to the works of Xabier Agirre Aranburu.[35] People able to read Slovenian may turn to the works of Marjan Brezovšek, Danica Fink-Hafner,[36] Aleš Gabrič,[37] Mitja Hafner-Fink,[38] Alenka Krasovec,[39] Samo Kropivnik, Igor Lukšić,[40] Janko Prunk,[41] Božo Repe,[42] Rudi Rizman,[43] and Drago Zajc.[44] Those able to read Serbian/Croatian/Bosnian may turn to the works of Ljubo Boban,[45] Tihomir Cipek,[46] Ivan Čolović, Vladimir Ćorović,[47] Ferdo Čulinović,[48] Branislav Gligorijević,[49] Mustafa Imamović,[50] Dušan Janjić, Fikreta Jelić-Butić,[51] Nada Kisić Kolanić,[52] Hrvoje Matković,[53] Olivera Milosavljević,[54] Miloš Mišović,[55] Dušan Pavlović, Branko Petranović,[56] Drago Roksandić,[57] Nedim Šarac,[58] Ferdo Šišić,[59] Ivo Žanić,[60] and Siniša Zrinščak.[61]

My list of personal favourites does not offer a rank-ordering of books (though those I consider to be the 'top ten' in English are identified with two asterisks). Rather, I have chosen to organize the list thematically. Thus, to my mind, the best single book in English on interwar Yugoslavia remains: **Ivo Banac, *The National Question in Yugoslavia: Origins, History, Politics* (Ithaca: Cornell University Press,1984)★★**. Although focused on the early years of the kingdom, Banac's treatment of the interwar kingdom is witty, comprehensive, and insightful. For an understanding of the Second World War, one might highlight: **Walter Roberts**, *Tito, Mihailović, and the Allies* **(New Brunswick, NJ: Rutgers University Press, 1973; reissued by Duke University Press),★★** and **Jožo Tomašević**, *War and Revolution in Yugoslavia, 1941–1945: Occupation and Collaboration* **(Stanford, CA: Stanford University Press, 2001)**. Tomašević has also written a distinguished account of the Chetniks, but I prefer Roberts's treatment because it is more compact and more focused on the question of the relationship of the Chetniks to the Allied war effort. Tomašević's posthumous volume on 'Occupation and Collaboration' is, at this writing, the most serious analysis in English of the occupation zones and wartime quislings in the Yugoslav area during the Second World War.

For the communist era, two of my favourite books are: **Ivo Banac, With Stalin, Against Tito: Cominformist Splits in Yugoslav Communism (Ithaca, NY: Cornell University Press, 1988)**; and **Dennison I. Rusinow, The Yugoslav Experiment, 1948–1974 (Berkeley and Los Angeles: University of California Press, 1977)★★**. Banac's discussion of the Tito–Stalin split moves beyond the description of the relations between Belgrade and Moscow and their various policy instruments and looks at the impact of the rift in Yugoslavia itself. Rusinow's *Yugoslav Experiment* starts where Banac's account leaves off and is the classic account of the Tito years, ending with the passage of the 1974 constitution.

There is a growing literature dealing with Serbia, Croatia, Slovenia, Bosnia-Herzegovina, and Kosovo/a separately. There is a small literature on Macedonia. Montenegro and Vojvodina have been largely ignored in English-language books and have not fared much better even in Serbian/ Croatian/Bosnian. There are, of course, a number of distinguished books focusing on Serbia. My own favourites, among those dealing with recent years, are: **Robert Thomas, *Serbia under Milošević: Politics in the 1990s* (London: C. Hurst & Co., 1999)★★**; and **Louis Sell, *Slobodan Milošević and the Destruction of Yugoslavia* (Durham, NC: Duke University Press, 2002)★★**. Given the paucity of work on Montenegro, I am pleased that Florian Bieber has produced such an excellent book on Montenegro, which offers new insights into the history of that state. This book, **Florian Bieber (ed.), *Montenegro in Transition: Problems of Identity and Statehood* (Baden-Baden: Nomos Verlagsgesellschaft, 2003)**, was discussed in the previous chapter.

For the history of Kosovo, the two leading contenders are Miranda Vickers and Noel Malcolm, each having strengths. Although Miranda Vickers provides more extensive coverage of the Tito and post-Tito eras, Noel Malcolm's is the better book, by far, for the ancient and medieval periods, reflecting extensive research into sources which have been neglected by other scholars. The care with which Malcolm reviewed the various primary sources, contrasting their accounts, will impress any impartial reader, and therefore, after due reflection, I find that my favourite book on Kosovo is **Noel Malcolm, *Kosovo: A Short History* (London: Macmillan, 1998)**.

For Slovenia, there is a very good history and overview, published a decade ago: **Jill Benderly and Evan Kraft (eds.), *Independent Slovenia: Origins, Movements, Prospects* (New York: St Martin's Press, 1994)**. It does not have the strength of the

Fink-Hafner/Robbins collection when it comes to post-1990 politics, but the merit of the Benderly/Kraft volume is its historical sweep.

On Croatia, the most reliable account in English is **Ivo Goldstein, *Croatia: A History*, capably translated from Croatian by Nikolina Jovanović (London: C. Hurst & Co., 1999)**, though Tanner's competing volume is written with unusual grace and style and continues to impress me favourably. My own favourite history of Bosnia-Herzegovina, in spite of an inaccurate representation of Borisav Jović, is: **Noel Malcolm, *Bosnia: A Short History* (Washington Square, NY: New York University Press, 1994)**. Malcolm's scrupulously comprehensive research is matched by his balance and good judgement. For Macedonia, the obvious place to start is: **Hugh Poulton, *Who Are the Macedonians?* (Bloomington, IN: Indiana University Press, 1995)**.

The years 1986–91 may be considered the prelude to dissolution, and for these years there are three truly splendid books from which to choose: **Viktor Meier, *Yugoslavia: A History of Its Demise* (London and New York: Routledge, 1999)★★**; Jasna Dragović-Soso, *'Saviours of the Nation': Serbia's Intellectual Opposition and the Revival of Nationalism* (London: C. Hurst & Co., 2002); and **Nebojša Popov (ed.), *The Road to War in Serbia: Trauma and Catharsis* (Budapest: Central European University Press, 2000)**. Meier discusses developments throughout the country, casting the blame firmly on the Serbian elite led by Milošević but also holding Lazar Mojsov, Stane Dolanc, and Stipe Šuvar responsible for the political crash. Popov's volume looks at the way in which Serbian society became politicized and gripped by nationalism, surveying many aspects of society, including religious currents, the university, and sports. Dragović-Soso focuses on the role of the Serbian intellectual elite in fanning the flames of nationalist hatred. My own ***Balkan Babel: The Disintegration of Yugoslavia from the Death of Tito to the Fall of Milošević*, 4th edn (Boulder, CO: Westview, 2002)★★** covers a somewhat broader terrain, beginning with the death of Tito in 1980 and bringing the story up through July/August 2001, with specific treatment also of post-1991 Slovenia and Macedonia.

For the war of 1991–5 itself, in spite of a certain tendency to pay more attention to Serbian than to Croatian and Bosniak points of view, the classic treatment remains: **Laura Silber and Allan Little, *The Death of Yugoslavia* (London: Penguin Books and BBC Books, 1995; rev. ed., 1996)★★**. Other works which should certainly be read by anyone interested in the causes, dynamics, and consequences of the war include: **Norman Cigar, *Genocide in Bosnia: The Policy of 'Ethnic Cleansing'* (College Station, TX: Texas A&M University Press, 1995); James Gow, *The Triumph of the Lack of Will: International Diplomacy and the Yugoslav War* (New York: Columbia University Press, 1997)★★; James Gow, *The Serbian Project and Its Adversaries: A Strategy of War Crimes* (London: C. Hurst & Co., 2003); Carole Hodge, *The Serb Lobby in the United Kingdom*, 2nd edn, Donald W. Treadgold Papers in Russian, East European, and Central Asian Studies No. 22 (Seattle: Henry M. Jackson School of International Studies of the University of Washington, July 2003); CIA, *Balkan Battlegrounds: A Military History of the Yugoslav Conflict, 1990–1995*, 2 vols. (Washington, DC: Central Intelligence Agency, Office of Russian and European Analysis, May 2002); James J. Sadkovich, *The US Media and Yugoslavia, 1991–1995* (Westport, CT: Praeger, 1998); Mark Thompson, *Forging War: The Media in Serbia, Croatia, Bosnia and Herzegovina*, completely revised and expanded edn (Luton: University of Luton Press, 1999); and Branka Magaš and Ivo Žanić (eds.), *The War in Croatia and Bosnia-Herzegovina 1991–1995* (London and Portland, OR: Frank Cass, 2001). To this list I would add Daniele Conversi's *German-Bashing and the Breakup of Yugoslavia*, Donald W. Treadgold Papers in Russian, East European, and Central Asian Studies No. 16 (Seattle: Henry M. Jackson School of International Studies at the University of Washington, March 1998),** which provides a serious argument that Germany has been unfairly blamed for the Yugoslav meltdown. All of these have been discussed in the present volume except *Balkan Battlegrounds* and Mark Thompson's *Forging War*. *Balkan Battlegrounds* is the single most detailed account of the military campaigns of the war of 1991–5, providing accounts of troop movements, strategies, and battles, as well as of shifting alliances. *Forging War*, considerably expanded in its revised edition, offers a glimpse into the workings of the local press, showing how they distorted events, shifted points of view according to political expediency, and, in some instances, wielded enormous influence over local public opinion.

Finally, for a thematic history of Yugoslavia from its founding, I refer the reader to my forthcoming book, **The Three Yugoslavias: State-building and Legitimation, 1918–2005 (Bloomington, IN, and Washington, DC: Indiana University Press and Wilson Center Press, forthcoming)★★.** Based on archival research at the Croatian State Archives and at the National Archives II outside Washington, DC, as well as on interviews with many of the principals in the Yugoslav drama, *The Three Yugoslavias* provides the most comprehensive account available in English of the Yugoslav theatre in the Second World War and of early postwar Yugoslavia, offers insights into the paramilitary activities associated with the interwar kingdom and the Croatian opposition not readily available elsewhere, and provides a detailed account of Yugoslavia's descent into savagery and of the efforts by the Yugoslav successor states to chart a course to democratic life.

To the foregoing list of personal favourites I would add my vote for the best memoirs yet published concerning the war: **Raif Dizdarević, *Od smrti Tita do smrti Jugoslavije: Svjedočenja* (Sarajevo: Svjedok, 1999)**; an English translation exists, and has been accepted for publication by Purdue University Press. As I have noted in chapter 5, Dizdarević provides an insider's account of the turmoil and growing crisis in the 1980s, writing with deep insight and judicious balance. Finally, I indicated above that I would make one exception to my English-only rule for this chapter: that exception is **Marie-Janine Calic, *Krieg und Frieden in Bosnien-Hercegovina*, revised and expanded edn (Frankfurt-am-Main: Suhrkamp, 1996)**, which I consider the finest short treatment of the Bosnian war with which I am familiar. It is my hope that this book can be translated into English in the near future.

NOTES

1 See, for example, Reneo Lukić, *The Wars of South Slavic Succession: Yugoslavia 1991–1993*, PSIS Occasional Paper No. 2/93 (Geneva, Switz.: Graduate Institute of International Studies, Programme for Strategic and International Security Studies, 1993), p. 8.
2 Paul Mojzes, *Yugoslavian Inferno: Ethnoreligious Warfare in the Balkans* (New York: Continuum, 1994), p. 71.
3 Mirko Pejanović, *Through Bosnian Eyes: The Political Memoirs of a Bosnian Serb*, trans. from Serbo-Croatian by Marina Bowder (Sarajevo: TDK Šahinpašić, 2002), *passim*.
4 Lenard J. Cohen, *Serpent in the Bosom: The Rise and Fall of Slobodan Milošević* (Boulder, CO: Westview Press, 2001), p. 398.
5 *Ibid.*, p. 81.
6 C. G. Schoenfeld, 'Psychoanalytic Dimensions of the West's Involvement in the Third Balkan War', in Stjepan G. Meštrović (ed.), *Genocide after Emotion: The Postemotional Balkan War* (London and New York: Routledge, 1996), p. 160.
7 Samuel P. Huntington, *The Clash of Civilizations and the Remaking of World Order* (New York: Simon & Schuster, 1996), p. 130.
8 *Ibid.*, p. 42.
9 *Ibid.*, p. 138.
10 Samuel P. Huntington, *Political Order in Changing Societies* (New Haven, CT: Yale University Press, 1968). In a review of Huntington's book, Richard

Sklar traced Huntington's belief that communism was permanent to his 'realist' assumptions. See review in *American Sociological Review*, 34, 4 (August 1969), p. 573.

11 Huntington, *The Clash of Civilizations*, p. 291.

12 *Ibid.*, p. 208.

13 *Ibid.*, p. 260.

14 Mojzes, *Yugoslavian Inferno*, p. 94.

15 See, for example, Norman Cigar, 'The Serb Guerrilla Option and the Yugoslav Wars: Assessing the Threat and Crafting Foreign Policy', *Journal of Slavic Military Studies*, 17, 3 (2004), pp. 485–562.

16 Robert M. Hayden, 'Schindler's Fate: Genocide, Ethnic Cleansing, and Population Transfers', *Slavic Review*, 55, 4 (Winter 1996), pp. 734–6, 742–3.

17 For example, in Srdjan Bogosavljević, 'The Unresolved Genocide', in Nebojša Popov (ed.), *The Road to War in Serbia: Trauma and Catharsis*, English version by Drinka Gojković (Budapest and New York: Central European University Press, 2000), pp. 146–59.

18 Rasmus Tenbergen, *Der Kosovo-Krieg und das Völkerrecht* (Frankfurt-am-Main: Suhrkamp, 2000), p. 14.

19 Hayden, 'Schindler's Fate', p. 731.

20 Mojzes, *Yugoslavian Inferno*, p. 227.

21 See, in particular, Klaus Buchenau, *Orthodoxie und Katholizismus in Jugoslawien 1945–1991* (Wiesbaden: Harrassowitz Verlag, 2004).

22 See, in particular, Srećko M. Džaja, *Die politische Realität des Jugoslawismus (1918–1991): Mit besonderer Berücksichtigung Bosnien-Herzegowinas* (Munich: R. Oldenbourg Verlag, 2002).

23 See, in particular: Karl Kaser, *Südosteuropäische Geschichte und Geschichtswissenschaft: Eine Einführung* (Vienna: Böhlau, 1990); and Karl Kaser, Wolfgang Petritsch, and Robert Pichler, *Kosovo, Kosova: Mythen, Daten, Fakten* (Klagenfurt: Wieser, 1999).

24 See, in particular, Walter Manoschek, *'Serbien ist judenfrei': Militärische Besatzungspolitik und Judenvernichtung in Serbien 1941/42* (Munich: R. Oldenbourg Verlag, 1995).

25 See, in particular, Dunja Melčić (ed.), *Der Jugoslawien-Krieg: Handbuch zu Vorgeschichte, Verlauf und Konsequenzen* (Opladen/Wiesbaden: Westdeutscher Verlag, 1999).

26 See, for example, Holm Sundhaussen, 'Der Ustascha-Staat: Anatomie eines Herrschaftssystems', *Österreichische Osthefte*, 37, 2 (1995).

27 See, in particular, Christine von Kohl and Wolfgang Libal, *Kosovo: Gordischer Knoten des Balkan* (Vienna and Zürich: Europaverlag, 1992).

28 See, in particular, Renéo Lukić, *L'Agonie Yougoslave (1986–2003): Les États-Unis et l'Europe face aux guerres balkaniques* (Saint-Nicolas, Quebec: Les Presses de l'Université Laval, 2003).

29 See, in particular, Paul Garde, *Vie et mort de la Yougoslavie* (Paris: Fayard, 1996), available in Croatian translation, *Život i smrt Jugoslavije*, trans. by Živan Filippi (Zagreb: Ceres, 1996).

30 See, for example, Stefano Bianchini, *Sarajevo: Le radici dell'odio* (Roma: Terzo Edizione Marzo, 2003).

31 See, in particular, Jože Pirjevec, *Le guerre jugoslave 1991–1999* (Turin: Giulio Einaudi editore, 2001).

32 See, in particular, Svein Mønnesland, *Før Jugoslavia og etter*, 4th edn (Oslo: Sypress, 1999).

33 See, in particular, Christian Palme, *Om ondskan i vår tid: Sökandet efter rättvisa på Balkan* (Stockholm: Bokförl, 2002).

34 See, in particular, Bo Pellnäs, *Utan slut? Kriget på Balkan: Bilder från ett FN-uppdrag* (Stockholm: Bonnier, 1995).

35 See, in particular, Xabier Agirre Aranburu, *Yugoslavia y los ejércitos: la legitimad militar en tiempos de genocido* (Madrid: Los Libros de la Catarata, 1997).

36 See, for example, Danica Fink-Hafner, *Politične stranke* (Ljubljana: Fakultet za družbene vede, 2001).

37 See, in particular, Aleš Gabrič, *Socialistina kulturna revolucija: Slovenska kulturna politika 1953–1962* (Ljubljana: Cankarjeva založba, 1995).

38 See, in particular, Mitja Hafner-Fink, *Sociološka razsežja razpada Jugoslavije* (Znanstvena knjižnica, 1994).

39 See, for example, Alenka Krasovec, *Moč v političnih strankah: Odnosi med parlamentarnimi in centralnimi deli političnih strank* (Ljubljana: Fakultet za družbene vede, 2000).

40 See, in particular, Igor Lukšič, *Politični sistem republike Slovenije: Ocrt* (Ljubljana: Znanstveno in publicistično središče, 2001).

41 See, for example, Janko Prunk, *Nova slovenska samozavest: Pogovori s slovenskimi političnimi prvaki* (Ljubljana: Lumi/Panatal, [1990]).

42 See, in particular, Božo Repe, *'Liberalizem' v Sloveniji* (Ljubljana: Borec, 1992).

43 See, for example, Rudi Rizman, *Izzivi odprte družbe* (Ljubljana: LDS, 1997).

44 See, for example, Drago Zajc, *Parlamentarno odločanje. (Re)parlamentaricacija v Sredni in Vzhodni Evropi – funkcija novih parlamentov* (Ljubljana: Fakultet za družbene vede, 2000). See also Drago Zajc and Tomaž Boh, 'Slovenia', in Sten Berglund, Joakim Ekman, and Frank H. Aarebrot (eds.), *The Handbook of Political Change in Eastern Europe*, 2nd edn (Cheltenham: Edward Elgar, 2004), pp. 255–88.

45 See, in particular, Ljubo Boban, *Maček i politika Hrvatske seljačke stranke 1928–1941* (Zagreb: Liber, 1974), 2 vol., vol. I.

46 See, in particular, Tihomir Cipek, *Ideja hrvatske države u političkoj misli Stjepana Radića* (Zagreb: Alinea, 2001).

47 See, in particular, Vladimir Ćorović, *Istorija Srba* (Belgrade: Logos-art, 2004).

48 See, in particular, Ferdo Čulinović, *Jugoslavija izmedju dva rata* (Zagreb: Jugoslavenska akademija znanosti i umjetnosti, 1961), 2 vols.; and Ferdo Čulinović, *Okupatorska podjela Jugoslavije* (Belgrade: Vojnoizdavački zavod, 1970).

49 See, in particular, Branislav Gligorijević, *Parlament i političke stranke u Jugoslaviji 1919–1929* (Belgrade: Narodna knjiga, 1979).

50 See, in particular, Mustafa Imamović, *Historija Bošnjaka*, 2nd edn (Sarajevo: Bošnjacka zajednica kulture, 1998).

51 See, in particular, Fikreta Jelić-Butić, *Ustaše I NDH/Ustaše i Nezavisna Država Hrvatska 1941–1945* (Zagreb: S. N. Liber and Školska knjiga, 1977); and Fikreta Jelić-Butić, *Četnici u Hrvatskoj 1941–1945* (Zagreb: Globus, 1986).

52 See, for example, Nada Kisić Kolanović, *NDH i Italija: Političke veze i diplomatiski odnosi* (Zagreb: Naklada Ljevak, 2001).

53 See, for example, Hrvoje Matković, *Povijest Hrvatske seljačke stranke* (Zagreb: Naklada PIP Pavičić, 1999); and Hrvoje Matković, *Povijest Nezavisne Države Hrvatske*, 2nd, expanded edn (Zagreb: Naklada PIP Pavičić, 2002).

54 See, in particular, Olivera Milosavljević, *U tradiciji nacionalizma, ili stereotipi srpskih intelektualaca XX veka o 'nama' i 'drugima'* (Belgrade: Helsinški odbor za ljudska prava, 2002).

55 See, for example, Miloš Mišović, *Ko je tražio republiku: Kosovo 1945–1985* (Belgrade: Narodna knjiga, 1987).

56 See, in particular, Branko Petranović, *Istorija Jugoslavije 1918–1988*, (Belgrade: Nolit, 1988), 3 vols.

57 See, in particular, Drago Roksandić, *Srbi u Hrvatskoj od 15. stoljeća do naših dana* (Zagreb: Vjesnik, 1991).

58 See, in particular, Nedim Šarac, *Uspostavljanje šestojanuarskog režima 1929. godine, sa posebnim osvrtom na Bosnu i Hercegovinu* (Sarajevo: Svjetlost, 1975).

59 See, in particular, Ferdo Šišić, *Pregled povijesti Hrvatskoga naroda* (Zagreb: Nakladni Zavod MH, 1975).

60 See, for example, Ivo Žanić, *Prevarena povijest* (Zagreb: Durieux, 1998).

61 See, in particular, Ivan Grubišić and Siniša Zrinščak (eds.), *Religija i integracija* (Zagreb: Institut društvenih znanosti, 1999). See also: Siniša Zrinščak, 'Religion and Society in Tension in Croatia: Social and Legal Status of Religious Communities', in James T. Richardson (ed.), *Regulating Religion: Case Studies from Around the Globe* (New York and Dordrecht: Kluwer Academic/Plenum Publishers, 2002), pp. 299–318; and Dinka Marinović Jerolimov, Siniša Zrinščak, and Irena Borowik (eds.), *Religion and Patterns of Social Transformation* (Zagreb: Institute for Social Research, 2004).

Index

Lightning Source UK Ltd.
Milton Keynes UK
UKHW020009030519

342040UK00017B/297/P

9 780521 616904